Autodesk® Maya® and Autodesk® 3ds Max® Side-by-Side

Les Pardew and Mike Tidwell

THOMSON

COURSE TECHNOLOGY

Professional ■ Technical ■ Reference

Publisher and General Manager, Thomson Course Technology PTR: Stacy L. Hiquet

Associate Director of Marketing: Sarah O'Donnell

Manager of Editorial Services: Heather Talbot

Marketing Manager: Heather Hurley

Acquisitions Editor: Megan Belanger

Marketing Assistant: Adena Flitt

Project Editor: Cathleen D. Snyder

Technical Reviewer: Dan Whittington

PTR Editorial Services Coordinator: Erin Johnson

Copy Editor: Laura R. Gabler

Interior Layout Tech: Jill Flores

Cover Designer: Mike Tanamachi

CD-ROM Producer: Brandon Penticuff

Indexer: Sharon Shock

Proofreader: Kim V. Benbow

ISBN-10: 1-59863-242-6

ISBN-13: 978-1-59863-242-2

Library of Congress Catalog Card Number: 2006923275

Printed in the United States of America

07 08 09 10 11 PH 10 9 8 7 6 5 4 3 2 1

Thomson Course Technology PTR,
a division of Thomson Learning Inc.
25 Thomson Place
Boston, MA 02210
http://www.courseptr.com

Acknowledgments

I want to acknowledge and thank all of the many people who have helped me to create this book. Big thanks to Mike Tidwell, who has been a great co-author and a big support to the whole project. My deepest thanks go to my family and especially to my wife, who has put up with living with an artist and all of the ups and downs that brings. I also want to thank the many mentors who have taught me about art. They may never know how much they have influenced my life. I also want to thank my editors, Cathleen Snyder, Megan Belanger, Laura R. Gabler, Dan Whittington, Kim Benbow, Jill Flores, and Stacy Hiquet, without whose help this book would be impossible.

—Les Pardew

Writing this book with Les has been a wonderful opportunity and a learning experience, to say the least. I have enjoyed the chance to work with Les again and would like to thank him for the opportunity and for thinking of me as a competent associate in this endeavor. I would also like to thank our friends at Thomson and beyond for having patience and understanding with me as a first-time author. Megan Belanger, Cathleen Snyder, Laura Gabler, Dan Whittington, Kim Benbow, and Jill Flores are among the people who deserve a huge amount of thanks!

—Mike Tidwell

About the Authors

LES PARDEW is a video game and entertainment industry veteran with more than 22 years of experience. His work in the industry includes more than 120 video game titles, 11 books, and numerous illustrations in magazines, books, and film. He began his career in film animation and later moved to video games, where he has found a permanent home. He currently serves as president of Alpine Studios, a game development firm specializing in handheld and cell-phone games.

Les is a prolific artist who loves to work on the computer and with traditional media. On the computer he is an accomplished 3D artist, creating and animating characters for many video games. In traditional media his first love is drawing, followed closely by oil painting. His favorite subject is people. He can often be seen drawing a portrait in his sketchbook or designing a character for a game.

Les loves to share himself with others, teaching business and art classes at the university level and authoring several books and curriculum on art, animation, and game design.

MIKE TIDWELL has been enthralled with 3D since before it was available on consumer machines. Some of his first real experiences with 3D were in 1994, when he helped to develop the use of 3D at a company called Saffire. It was for a Super Nintendo video game called *Wayne Gretzky and the NHLPA All-Stars*. He built some of the first 3D characters used in the games industry in a program called Playmation (which later became Animation Master). Shortly thereafter, he stumbled upon a much more complicated and intriguing application called 3D Studio for DOS.

Saffire continued to use Animation Master for several years before making the switch to 3D Studio Max 2.0. Mike was very skilled at Max, having used it on a hobbyist basis during those years, so it was easy to help the company make the transition.

Mike has been working as a project manager for many years and has many video game titles under his belt, as well as two 3D software packages. He continues to be an active hobbyist in the 3D art field.

Contents

Introduction

For anyone who has struggled to transfer from one 3D program to another, this book needs no introduction. The process of switching programs is frustrating at best. It's kind of like trying to find your way home with all of the streets changed. You know where you want to go, but the process of getting there is different.

This book is designed to help both beginners and advanced 3D artists to see how the same project is created in two different software programs. It starts out with very basic tutorials, so that someone who is completely unfamiliar with 3D can learn the basics. All of the projects are the same; the only difference is that each project is created twice—once using Maya and once using 3ds Max.

If you are familiar with one of the programs, you will be able to see how we created a project in it, and then go to the other program and see how the same project was created in that one.

We have included trial versions of both programs on the CD that comes with the book, so you will be able to test them out for free if you already don't have one or the other. Other helpful software from Corel is also included on the CD, making this book completely self-contained. You won't need anything else except a computer to complete all of the tutorials in the book.

Rather than doing a feature-by-feature comparison of the two programs, we felt the book would be more useful if we put things into context by building actual models. Unfortunately, this process required us to leave out some features, but we felt as if it was a better way for someone to get familiar with both programs. Besides, a feature-by-feature comparison would take several volumes, rather than the one we have here. As it is, we had to cut a lot of material just to fit everything into this one volume.

We hope you enjoy this book and that it helps you in your 3D adventures. 3D art is a fascinating process. Good luck, and enjoy the book.

Chapter 1

Whys and Hows

3D modeling and animation programs by nature are very complex. Building any object in 3D and getting it to look real is a sophisticated process. The artist not only has to create the object as a 3D model but also has to apply surface textures, lighting, and sometimes animation for the object. Any one of these aspects of creating the object is complex and often requires hundreds of individual steps.

Learning how to use one of these programs can be a very daunting task, so once someone becomes proficient with a program, it becomes difficult to have to switch and learn a new program. However, many 3D artists find that one program is not enough in the constantly changing market for 3D artwork. Often an artist will have to learn two or three programs to keep pace with clients.

This book is intended to help those artists who have already learned how to use one program quickly understand how to use another. For this book, we have two of the most popular 3D modeling and animation programs—Maya and 3D Studio Max—laid out in each chapter. The idea is that an artist familiar with a method of modeling in one program needs only to flip to the section covering the other program later in the same chapter to see how the same task is accomplished in the other program.

Where Did This Book Come From?

Back when I started my game development studio, I had to make a decision on a 3D software program. At the time, there were many competing programs on the market, but our budget was such that we could only really support one. This type of decision was common back then because these programs were a lot more expensive than they are today, so studios often couldn't afford to purchase multiple sets of different software. At the time, I chose to go with Maya as the studio's primary 3D modeling program. Maya seemed to have a good all-around package for game development, and many of the top publishers in the industry were using it.

At first, our choice was difficult for some of the artists who didn't have any training on our chosen software. Some of the artists were unable to make the transition and had to leave the company. Others did learn the program after several weeks of struggle. I learned from this experience that it is not an easy task for an artist to learn a new 3D program, even if they have experience with a different program.

The problem seems to be that these programs are all very different in the way they approach modeling and animation. Functions and processes have different names. Tools are in different places. The workflow is often very different. All of these factors require artists to learn new ways of doing things while they try to retain the old ways so they don't abandon the knowledge of their original program.

In many ways, learning a new 3D software program is like learning a second language. Artists have to learn new terms and methodologies for each new program even though they are already familiar with the original program. It becomes doubly hard when an artist has to use both programs at the same time.

At one point a few years ago, I had to learn 3D Studio Max because one of our clients used only that program, and we had to be compatible with them in order to complete the project. I couldn't stop using Maya because of other projects that were already under way, but I had to learn 3D Studio Max and use it at the same time. During this experience, I often said to myself, "I wish there was something that would tell me how to do in 3D Studio Max what I already know how to do in Maya."

Because I couldn't find a book that dealt well with both Maya and 3D Studio Max on a function-by-function level, the idea of creating that type of book became obvious. I knew that I could handle the Maya side of the book, but I wanted someone well-versed in 3D Studio Max to do that side, so I contacted some friends of mine, and was happy when Mike Tidwell agreed to co-author the book. I have known Mike for many years, and he is quite knowledgeable in all aspects of 3D Studio Max.

A New Way to Learn

As Mike and I, along with our editors Megan Belanger and Cathleen Snyder, discussed the possibilities of the book, it soon became apparent to us that the best way to do the book was to take two beginning books and make them into one book. In other words, I would write a beginning Maya book and Mike would write a beginning 3D Studio Max book, resulting in half of each chapter being about Maya and the other half being about Max. So what you are really getting here is two books in one.

We didn't just want to take the two programs and show them feature by feature. Instead, we wanted to put the entire process of 3D development in context. Therefore, we made the decision to make the book a project-oriented book. By creating the projects in the book, the reader is able to learn not only what the tools and functions are but also how to use them.

In order to keep the books in sync with each other, I would first write a chapter using Maya, and when I finished, Mike would then take the chapter and match the production step by step in 3D Studio Max. The result is that after reading about how to create a project in Maya, for example, the reader can simply flip to the Max section in the same chapter and follow the same general procedure to create the same project in Max.

We are all very excited about this new way of learning a software program. It gives all of those who know one program a way to quickly learn the other. It also gives anyone who is new to 3D a way to become familiar with both programs at the same time. Our hope is that this new and unique system of matching the two programs step by step will be a great innovation in helping the beginner and professional alike to understand both of these great 3D software programs.

How to Use This Book

There are many ways to use this book. It can be used as a reference for comparing functions of the two programs. It can also be used as a tutorial because the projects detail step-by-step processes for building, texturing, and animating 3D models.

The book is laid out in a logical manner, with an explanation of basic tools and functions in the beginning and then progressively taking the reader through the process of building, texturing, and animating 3D objects. The projects in the book proceed from simple to complex, for the most part. In the projects, functions and tools are explained as they are used to give them context in the building process.

Not all functions for the two programs are covered in this book. These two software programs have so many features and uses that for one book to contain everything would be impossible. Instead, the book takes the approach of teaching how to use the programs by having the reader create projects that use many of the common features and tools. Once the reader becomes comfortable with a program, the use of online help available in both programs can help with learning those aspects that were not covered in the book.

For Beginners

For the beginning 3D artist, the best way to learn the programs will probably be to start at the beginning, choose one program, and do all of the exercises for that program. Then go back through the book again with the other program.

Some people may want to have both programs running at the same time and work on them simultaneously; however, that approach may cause problems if you are working on a single computer. Both of these 3D programs require a lot of system resources.

For Those Who Already Know One Program

If you already are familiar with one program and want to learn the other program, you should complete the exercises in order for the other program, using the one you are familiar with as a guide to help you understand the process. For those who only need to know one aspect of the new program, such as texturing or animation, you can skip to that part of the book; however, because each chapter builds on those that precede it, you may need to refer to earlier chapters, if there is a function or tool that is not completely explained in the later chapters.

Good Luck!

Mike and I, as well as all of the people at Thomson, hope that this book will be a very useful addition to your training in 3D graphics. 3D graphics are a major aspect of art today. Any artist who can master both Maya and 3D Studio Max will have a huge advantage in the marketplace. Leaving out one or the other can effectively cut the artist's marketing in half, particularly in the fast-growing video game market.

We hope that you use this book and wear it out to help you gain mastery of these two very important software programs.

Chapter 2

Where Did I Put That?

3D applications such as Maya and 3ds Max are very complex programs with what seems like an endless number of functions and features. Learning how to use Maya or 3ds Max is kind of like moving to a new city. When you first arrive, you don't have any idea where anything is. You don't know where to go to buy groceries or where to get your dry cleaning done. You might know a few roads to and from your new home, but you know little else. As you begin your stay in the new city, you first find the businesses and services that are essential for your existence, such as the phone company and the utility company. You also locate places to buy food and other necessities. After a while, you start to become more accustomed to your surroundings and find better stores and services that fit your needs more closely. Given time, you start to feel comfortable with your surroundings and confident in your ability to navigate the streets in an ever-expanding area.

Even if you lived in a city before, it will take you some time to find all of the services you need in the new one. The same is true for a 3D application such as Maya and 3ds Max. In this chapter, we will be looking at the screen interfaces and features of Maya and 3ds Max side by side. Just as cities may have many things in common, such as streets, banks, grocery stores, malls, churches, and so on, 3ds Max and Maya have many similarities. We will try to point out similar features and tools in each program.

The Maya Screen

The first look at the Maya interface can be a little overwhelming. The sheer number of menus and icons seems endless, and it would take volumes of books to explain every feature in Maya. Don't worry right now about learning every feature. The step-by-step instructions in this book are designed to help you understand the features of the program that are needed to create each project. As you work with Maya, you will become accustomed to the features.

Like moving to a new city, the first thing that you need to know about Maya is how the program is set up and where the essential tools are located. From there, you can move forward in creating 3D digital art. The more you use Maya, the more accustomed you will become to the tools.

Figure 2.1 shows the Maya interface screen as it comes up for the first time.

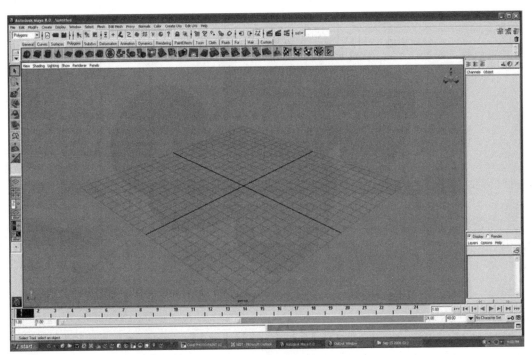

Figure 2.1 The Maya interface screen has many features and options.

The interface screen can be broken down into several component parts to help give clarity to how the program works. To help you better understand the different elements of the screen, we will go over each in detail.

The Workspace

The Workspace is where most of your work will take place. It is where you will build the model, animate your characters, apply textures, and do almost everything else. Notice that it has its own menu in the upper-left corner. This menu is called the *Panels menu*. Figure 2.2 shows the area of the screen called the Workspace.

There are a few important elements of the Workspace that you should know about. The Panels menu is used to control functions and features specific to the Workspace.

Within the Workspace is a grid with two intersecting dark lines. The point at which these two lines intersect is called the *origin*. The origin is the zero point of the X, Y, and Z axes.

In the upper-right and lower-left of the screen, there are two helpful little indicators. These are the Axis Direction Indicators.

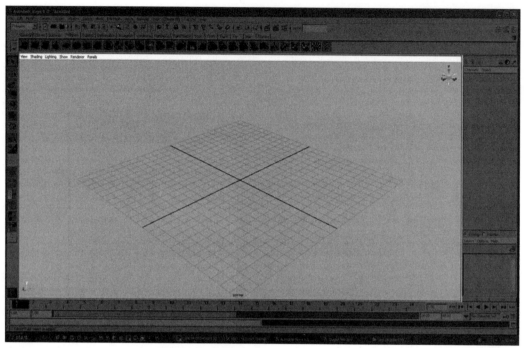

Figure 2.2 The Workspace is the work area of the interface.

In the bottom-center of the Workspace is the name of the camera. In Maya, you view a scene through a camera. It isn't a real camera; rather, it is a virtual camera. Imagine a director shooting a movie with multiple cameras looking at the scene from several different angles. The scene will look different from one camera to another, even though they may all be pointed at the same scene. Maya also has several cameras, which are called *camera views*, or just *views* for short.

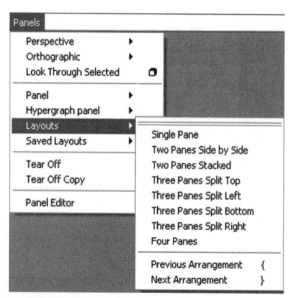

Currently the Workspace has only one view. You can lay out the Workspace to have a single view or many views. Go to Layouts in the Panels menu, as shown in Figure 2.3.

Choose the layout titled Two Panes Side by Side. Notice that the Workspace now has two views, or, as they are called in Maya, *panes* (as in window panes). Experiment with some of the different layouts to see what they look like. When you are finished, go back to the Single Pane view.

Figure 2.3 There are several preset panel layouts in Maya.

Next we'll take a look at what can go in a pane. Take a look at the Panels menu, as shown in Figure 2.4. Notice that the first two menu items are Perspective and Orthographic. Each menu item has a submenu. Go to Orthographic, Front. Orthographic views are like drafting views. They show the model straight on with no perspective. The Perspective views, on the other hand, show objects as if you were looking at them in real life, with perspective.

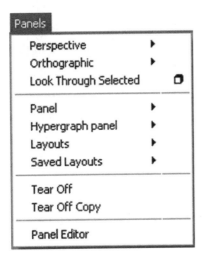

Figure 2.4 Perspective and Orthographic are the two types of views at the top of the menu.

Let's create an object so you can better see how these views work. Go to the main menu (it is the one at the very top of the screen) and bring up the Create menu by clicking on it. Under Polygon Primitive, select Torus. Now change the layout to four panes, as shown in Figure 2.5.

Note

When you change the Workspace to four panes, whatever view you started from will be in the upper-left pane. Because you started from the Front view, you currently have two Front views. You can change any pane to a new view from the Panels menu. There is a Panels menu for each pane.

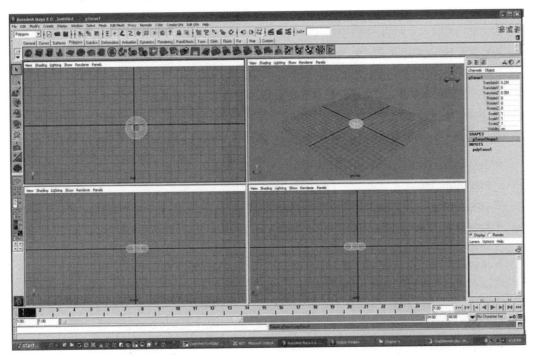

Figure 2.5 Change the Workspace to four panes.

Now that you know how to change views and layouts, let's take a look at navigating within the Workspace. Go back to the single-pane Perspective view.

Maya uses the Alt key for navigation. Press the Alt key, and then hold down the left mouse button. You will see the cursor change to two arrows, making a circle. Move the mouse around a little. Notice how easy it is to look at the torus from almost any angle. In Maya, this action is called *tumbling*.

Now press on the Alt key and hold down the center mouse button or, if you have a wheel mouse, press and hold down the wheel. The cursor will change to a circle with four arrows extending from it. Move the mouse around. Notice that the view is now panning. In Maya, this is called *tracking*.

In addition to tumbling and tracking in the Workspace, you can also dolly. *Dolly* is an old cinematic term from when cameras were mounted on tripods with wheels so that the camera could be moved in and out of a scene. Press the Alt key and the right mouse button. Moving the mouse down or to the right will move the view into the scene, and moving the mouse up or to the left will pull back from the scene.

The Toolbox and Quick Layout Buttons

Figure 2.6 highlights the area to the far left of the screen. This area houses the Toolbox and the Quick Layout buttons. The Toolbox is in the upper section of the area, and it contains model manipulation tools. An icon represents each tool. The lower part of the area has icons that are used to change the view layout of the Workspace.

There are 10 tools in the Toolbox; each is used to either select or modify an object or part of an object. The tools going from top to bottom are as follows:

- **Selection tool.** Use this tool to create a selection by clicking or by drawing a bounding box.
- **Lasso tool.** Use this tool to create a selection by drawing a defined area.
- **Paint Selection tool.** Use this tool to select parts of an object by painting on the object.
- **Move tool.** Use this tool to move or translate a selected object or component in the scene. In Maya, the word "translate" is used to describe the movement of an object from one location to another.
- **Rotate tool.** Use this tool to rotate a selected object or component in a scene.
- **Scale tool.** Use this tool to scale up or down in size a selected object or component.

Selection tool

Lasso tool

Paint Selection tool

Move tool

Rotate tool

Scale tool

Universal Manipulator tool

Soft Modification tool

Show Manipulator tool

Last tool

- **Universal Manipulator tool.** This tool combines the Move, Rotate, and Scale tools into a single tool.

- **Soft Modification tool.** This tool is used to soft-modify an object. Soft modification adjusts vertices in an object similar to how a sculptor modifies a lump of clay.

- **Show Manipulator tool.** Some elements, such as lights, have their own manipulators. Clicking this tool activates the manipulator for an element.

- **Last tool.** The last tool in the Toolbox is not really a tool; rather, it holds the last tool or function used. This becomes very handy when you have a repeating function.

Below the Toolbox are the Quick Layout buttons. You can change the Workspace layout to a few widely used configurations by simply clicking on one of these buttons.

Figure 2.6 This area contains the Toolbox and the Quick Layout buttons.

Main Menu

Figure 2.7 shows the main menu. This is where many of Maya's features are located. Almost every function or tool can be found in the main menu or one of its submenus. There are several configurations of the main menu, depending on the type of work being performed. We will go over how to change the menu configuration in the next section. The first menu items are common to all menu configurations and do not change. The remaining menu items change.

File Edit Modify Create Display Window Select Mesh Edit Mesh Proxy Normals Color Create UVs Edit UVs Help

Figure 2.7 Many of Maya's features are located in the main menu.

Status Line

Figure 2.8 shows the status line, which contains many buttons. On the far left side of the status line is a drop-down list that you can use to configure the main menu. The available configurations are as follows:

- **Animation.** This brings up the Animation submenu.
- **Polygons.** This brings up the Polygons submenu.
- **Surfaces.** This brings up the Surfaces submenu.
- **Dynamics.** This brings up the Dynamics submenu.
- **Rendering.** This brings up the Rendering submenu.
- **Cloth.** This brings up the Cloth submenu.
- **Customize.** This allows the user to customize the menus.

Figure 2.8 The status line is directly below the main menu.

The status line also contains many common functions. If you hover the cursor over any icon on the status line, a window will appear, identifying the icon. These functions are split into groups, as follows, from left to right:

- **Scene buttons.** These are used to bring up new scenes or to save and load scenes.
- **Selection Mask drop-down list.** This is used to change the selection mask so that it is easier to select a specific element in the scene.
- **Selection Mask buttons.** These are used to help with selections by masking objects of components.
- **Snap Mode buttons.** These are used for selecting different modes of snapping.
- **History buttons.** These are used to enable, disable, and access the construction history.
- **Render buttons.** These are used to render the scene and set rendering parameters.
- **Set Field Entry Mode buttons.** These are used to change the field entry.
- **Show/Hide Editors buttons.** These are used to show or hide editors and tools used to modify or manipulate objects or parts of objects. These editors appear in what is called the *sidebar*, which is the area directly to the right of the Workspace.

Shelves

The area shown in Figure 2.9 directly below the status line is called the *shelves*. The shelves contain icons and tabs. Each tab has different icons, and each icon has a different function in Maya. The tabs are used to group functions for specific tasks.

Figure 2.9 The shelves contain icons that call up specific functions.

The current tab shown in Figure 2.9 is the Polygon tab. Click on a few other tabs to see how they look. You can build your own shelf if you want to. On the far left of the screen is a black down arrow. This arrow brings up several editing functions for the shelves, including the Shelf Editor.

Sidebar

Figure 2.10 The Channel box and Layer Editor are part of the sidebar.

Figure 2.10 shows the area of the screen called the sidebar. This area contains several editor elements and consists of two parts. The top part is the Channel box, which is used to edit object attributes. The bottom part is the Layer Editor, which is used to edit display and render layers.

The Channel box is used often in modeling and animating 3D models. It contains entries for a number of attributes for a selected object. These attributes can be modified numerically in the Channel box. This is very helpful when you need an attribute to be a specific number. Below the attribute list in the Channel box is a history. The history contains a list of all modifications made to the object.

The Layer Editor is used to organize scene elements. It is very useful in complex scenes. For example, a city scene might be organized into roads, buildings, foliage, and vehicles. Each type of scene element is put on a different layer so the artist can make them visible or invisible by turning on or off the layer.

The Channel box and Layer Editor are not the only sidebar configurations. As stated earlier, on the right side of the status line are three icons. These three icons control the sidebar configuration. The Channel box is the icon on the right. The middle icon shows and hides the tool options, and the icon on the left shows and hides the Attribute Editor.

Animation Tools

Figure 2.11 highlights the lower part of the Maya screen. This is where Maya's animation tools are located. It includes the Time slider on the upper portion of the highlighted area and the Range slider on the lower portion of the highlighted area. The right side of the highlighted area contains several tools for playing and viewing animations.

Figure 2.11 Maya's animation tools are located in the lower part of the screen.

Command and Message Boxes

At the bottom of the screen shown in Figure 2.12 are three text windows. The one on the upper-left side of the highlighted area is the command line. This is where special scripts can be entered. The text window directly to the left of the command line is the area that shows the results of each command. Below the command line is the help line. This window is used for help messages. On the far right is an icon that brings up the Script Editor.

Figure 2.12 The command and help lines are located at the bottom of the screen.

See, that wasn't so bad. Now that you know the basic parts of the Maya screen, it's time to put some of that knowledge to work. Click on the New Scene icon on the status line to reset the scene.

Having a Ball

This section is very basic, so if you have experience with 3D programs, you may want to skip it. If, however, you are new to Maya, this section will help you get started. In this section, you will learn to create a simple 3D ball.

1. Create a polygonal sphere, as shown in Figure 2.13. To do so, open the Create menu, choose Polygon Primitive, and click the box next to the Sphere command.

Note

The box next to the Sphere menu entry indicates that there is a dialog box associated with the function. Dialog boxes are used to change attributes or settings for the function.

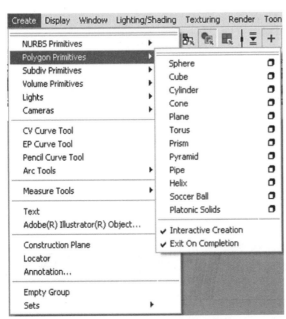

2. The Polygon Sphere Options dialog panel will open. Change the Radius setting to 10.

3. Change the Subdivisions Around Axis and Subdivisions Along Height settings to 20.

4. Change the Axis setting to Y.

5. Change the Texture setting to Sawtooth at Poles. The dialog box should match the one in Figure 2.14.

Figure 2.13 Select the box next to the Sphere option.

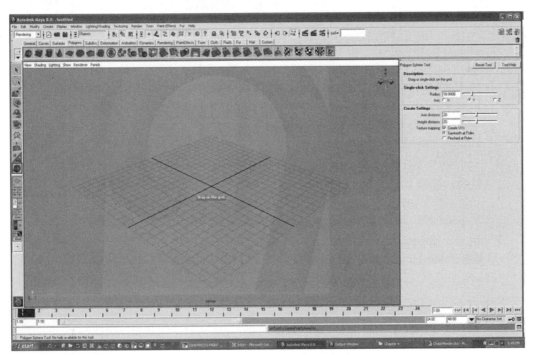

Figure 2.14 Use this dialog box to set the options for creating a polygonal sphere.

6. Click the Create button to create the sphere; the results are shown in Figure 2.15.

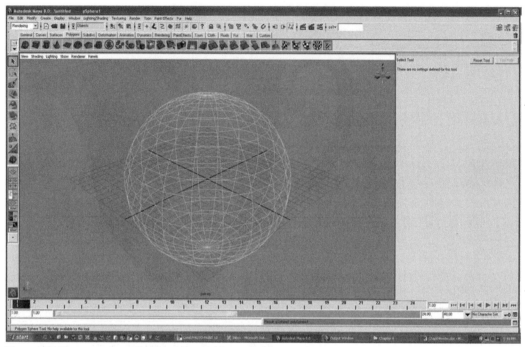

Figure 2.15 The new polygonal object is now in the work area.

7. The 4, 5, and 6 keys on the keyboard control the view modes in Maya. The 4 key changes the view mode to Wire Frame; the 5 key changes the view mode to Flat Shaded; and the 6 key changes the view mode to Smooth Shaded. (The view modes can also be controlled using the View option in the Panels menu.) Press the 6 key on the keyboard to change to Smooth Shaded view; Figure 2.16 shows the result.

8. The next step is to change the surface of the sphere. Maya has a tool called Hypershade that is used to change the surfaces of objects. To access this tool, open the Window menu, choose Rendering Editors, and select Hypershade, as shown in Figure 2.17.

9. In the Hypershade window, open the Create menu, choose Materials, and select Blinn, as shown in Figure 2.18.

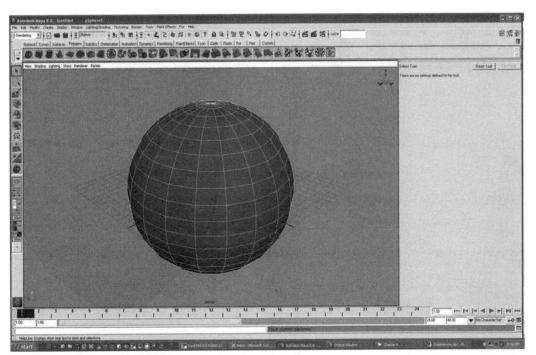

Figure 2.16 Change the view mode to Smooth Shaded.

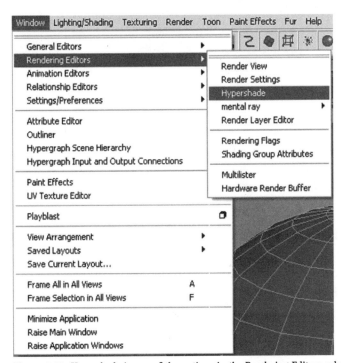

Figure 2.17 Hypershade is one of the options in the Rendering Editors submenu.

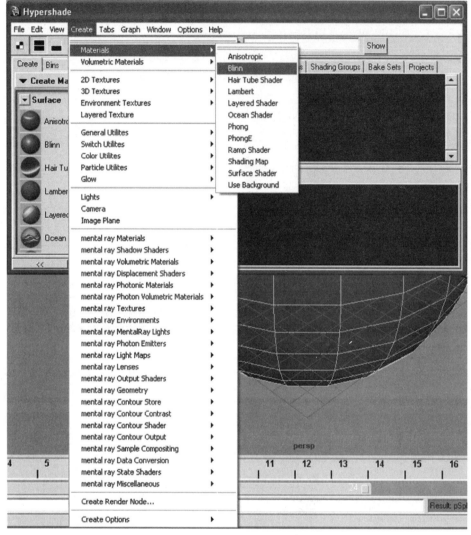

Figure 2.18 Create a Blinn material.

10. Blinn materials have a number of attributes that can be adjusted to create sophisticated surfaces on 3D objects. To do so, you use the Attribute Editor. To launch the Attribute Editor, click the Attribute Editor button in the status line (it's the third button from the end). The Attribute Editor will open in the sidebar, as shown in Figure 2.19.

11. Click the checkered button to the right of the Color setting in the Attribute Editor to open the Create Render Node window, as shown in Figure 2.20.

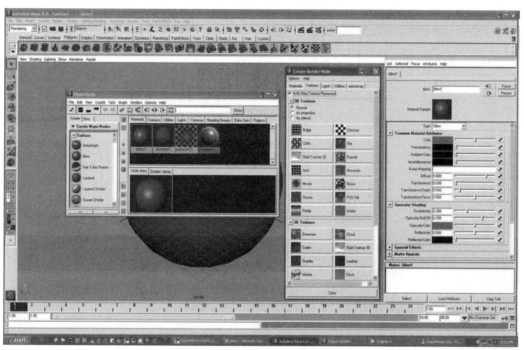

Figure 2.19 Open the material's Attribute Editor.

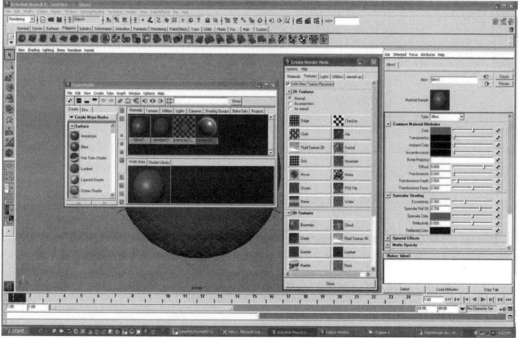

Figure 2.20 Launch the Create Render Node window.

12. The Create Render Node window features many choices for changing the color and texture of a material; click the Checker button. The material in the Hypershade window will assume a checkered pattern.

13. Apply the material to the sphere. To do so, select the sphere in the Workspace, right-click the new material in Hypershade to open the marking menu, and choose Apply Material to Object. The sphere now has a checkered pattern, as shown in Figure 2.21.

Figure 2.21 Apply a new material to the sphere.

Note

Marking menus are floating menus in Maya that are used for quick access to common functions. You access marking menus by selecting an item and then right-clicking it. When the marking menu appears, simply drag the cursor over the desired menu item and release the mouse button.

14. Click the X button in the upper-right corner of the Hypershade window to close it.

15 Before you progress to the next section, you need to clear the scene. To do so, click the New Scene button in the status line.

There you have it; you have created and textured your first model in Maya. That wasn't so hard, was it?

Menus

Although there are many buttons on the Maya interface, really understanding how to use the program will require an understanding of the layout of Maya's menus. This section shows how Maya's menus are arranged and how to use them. It also shows their main purposes. Because covering all the menu items in detail would be excessively boring, not all of them are covered here. Instead, you'll learn how to use Maya's menus by using them in animation projects throughout the book. In the meantime, take a moment to explore Maya's menus to get a sense of where everything is.

Note

If you are new to Maya, you might feel a little lost as you explore the menus because they contain many terms that may be unfamiliar. Don't worry too much about not knowing everything right now. Just use this section as a reference. You will learn most of the terms associated with the menus through the projects in the book.

Menu Layout

Grouping menu items helps to define related functions. For this reason, each menu in Maya contains groups of commands separated by lines. In the File menu (see Figure 2.22), the first group contains two menu items: New Scene and Open Scene. Both are used to start a session in Maya, one by starting a new scene and the other by loading a saved scene.

Note

Notice the double line at the top of the File menu. This double line indicates that the menu is detachable. If you click this line, Maya copies the functions to a separate menu that you can place anywhere on the screen for easy access.

New Scene	Ctrl+n	
Open Scene...	Ctrl+o	
Save Scene	Ctrl+s	
Save Scene As...		
Save Preferences		
Optimize Scene Size		
Import...		
Export All...		
Export Selection...		
View Image...		
View Sequence...		
Create Reference...	Ctrl+r	
Reference Editor		
Project	▶	
Recent Files	▶	
Recent Increments	▶	
Recent Projects	▶	
Exit	Ctrl+q	

Figure 2.22 The File menu is the first menu in the main menu.

Menus in Maya have four columns:

- The first column, starting from the left, is the name of the menu item.
- The second column gives a keyboard shortcut for the menu item. The keyboard shortcut, or *hotkey*, enables you to access the function through the keyboard. You can see from the File menu that Ctrl+N is the keyboard shortcut for the New Scene command. This means that instead of clicking the New Scene button or selecting New Scene from the File menu, you can simply press Ctrl+N to create a new scene.
- The third column contains arrows. These indicate that if you select the menu item, a submenu will appear. For example, selecting the Project menu item from the File menu reveals a submenu. You can then slide your cursor over the submenu and select one of the items it contains.
- The fourth column indicates whether the menu item has a dialog box associated with it. If a box icon is present in this column, it means that selecting the box will launch a dialog box or panel, which you use to adjust settings for the menu function. For example, click the box icon next to the New Scene menu item, and the dialog box shown in Figure 2.23 will appear. As shown, the settings in this dialog box relate to setting up new scenes.

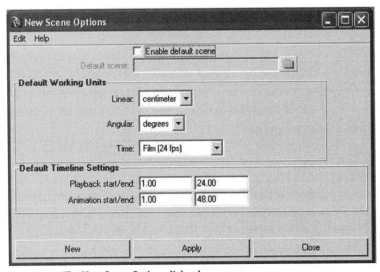

Figure 2.23 The New Scene Options dialog box.

Many dialog boxes, including the New Scene Options dialog box, are divided into sections. For example, the first section of the New Scene Options dialog box is for setting up custom new scenes. This is useful if you want to start every new scene with specific settings, such as a particular background or specialized geometry. The second section of the New Scene Options dialog box lets you customize your default working units. By default, centimeters are used, which is fine for small objects but becomes a problem if you are building, say, a diesel truck. Angles can be set to degrees or radian. The Time setting relates to animation and has a long list of options depending on the end target for your scene. Currently Time is set for film animation. The third section of the New Scene Options dialog box lets you customize the length of the playback and the total number of frames in the animation. At the bottom of most dialog boxes, including the New Scene Options dialog box, are three buttons: Now, Apply, and Close. Clicking the Now button activates the function with the current settings and closes the dialog box. Clicking the Apply button activates the function with the current settings, but leaves the dialog box open, which is useful if you need to apply the function multiple times. The Close button closes the dialog box without activating the function. For now, close the New Scene Options dialog box, and let's continue our tour of the menus.

Note

Dialog boxes are available via the menu, but not via hotkeys or onscreen buttons. Hotkeys and buttons are useful if you want to perform a function, but you don't need to change any settings first.

Common Main Menu Options

As shown in Figure 2.24, there are seven common menus in the main menu, plus a series of menus that vary depending on which option is selected in the drop-down list on the status line.

Note

Some menu items that follow may not appear on the Maya PLE version that came with this book. This is because these menu items are only in the Maya Unlimited version of the software. They are included here to give you an idea of the full capabilities of the software.

Figure 2.24 The common menus in the main menu.

From left to right, these common menus are as follows:

- **File.** The File menu contains functions dealing with files, projects, importing, and exporting.
- **Edit.** The Edit menu contains functions dealing with basic editing, selecting, grouping, and parenting operations.
- **Modify.** The Modify menu contains functions dealing with modifying geometry or other scene elements.
- **Create.** The Create menu contains functions dealing with the creation of scene elements, such as geometry, lights, curves, and text.
- **Display.** The Display menu contains functions dealing with onscreen display elements, including objects, components, and interfaces.

- **Window.** The Window menu contains functions dealing with the many editors and tools in Maya.
- **Help.** The Help menu contains functions dealing with online help, tutorials, references, and product information.

The Animation Menu Options

When Animation is selected from the drop-down list on the status line, the main menu features six Animation menu items (see Figure 2.25).

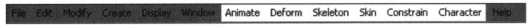

File Edit Modify Create Display Window | Animate Deform Skeleton Skin Constrain Character | Help

Figure 2.25 The Animation menu set includes six menu items.

From left to right, they are as follows:

- **Animate.** The Animate menu contains functions dealing with keys, clips, and paths.
- **Deform.** The Deform menu contains functions dealing with high-level tools used to manipulate low-level components.
- **Skeleton.** The Skeleton menu contains functions dealing with the creation and editing of joints, as well as animation helpers.
- **Skin.** The Skin menu contains functions dealing with attaching geometry to skeletal systems.
- **Constrain.** The Constrain menu contains functions dealing with setting limits or constraints on animated objects.
- **Character.** The Character menu contains functions dealing with the creation and editing of characters.

The Polygon Menu Options

When Polygons is selected from the drop-down list on the status line, the main menu features eight Polygons menu items (see Figure 2.26).

File Edit Modify Create Display Window Select Mesh Edit Mesh Proxy Normals Color Create UVs Edit UVs Help

Figure 2.26 The Polygons menu set includes eight menu items.

From left to right, they are as follows:

- **Select.** The Select menu deals with selection options for polygon objects and components.
- **Mesh.** The Mesh menu deals with modifying polygon objects.

- **Edit Mesh.** The Edit Mesh menu deals with editing polygon object components.
- **Proxy.** The Proxy menu is for creating and editing a polygon proxy for sub-division surface models.
- **Normals.** The Normals menu is used for editing polygon normals.
- **Color.** The Color menu is used to edit vertex color on polygon objects.
- **Create UVs.** The Create UVs menu contains functions for applying and editing UVs on polygon objects.
- **Edit UVs.** The Edit UVs menu contains functions for editing UVs once they have been placed on an object.

The Surfaces Menu Options

Surfaces menu options control the building of objects using NURBS and subdivision surfaces. There are four main menu items in the Surfaces submenu, as shown in Figure 2.27.

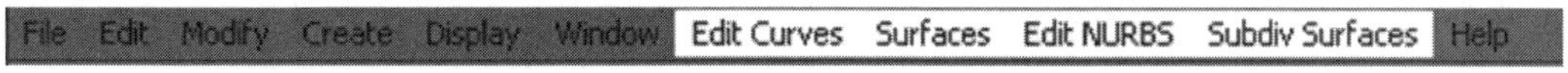

File   Edit   Modify   Create   Display   Window   Edit Curves   Surfaces   Edit NURBS   Subdiv Surfaces   Help

Figure 2.27 The Surfaces menu set includes seven menu items.

From left to right, they are as follows:

- **Edit Curves.** The Edit Curves menu contains functions dealing with editing and modifying curves.
- **Surfaces.** The Surfaces menu contains functions dealing with creating and editing surfaces.
- **Edit NURBS.** The Edit NURBS menu contains functions dealing with NURBS modeling and NURBS editing.
- **Subdiv Surfaces.** The Subdiv Surfaces menu deals with building and editing subdivision surfaces.

The Dynamics Menu Options

When Dynamics is selected from the drop-down list on the status line, the main menu features seven Dynamics menu items (see Figure 2.28).

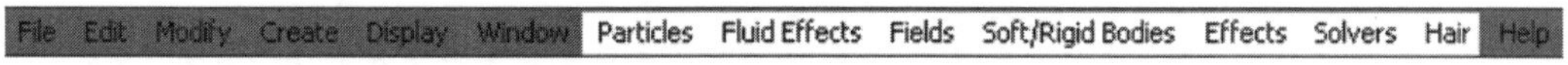

File   Edit   Modify   Create   Display   Window   Particles   Fluid Effects   Fields   Soft/Rigid Bodies   Effects   Solvers   Hair   Help

Figure 2.28 The Dynamics menu set includes seven menu items.

From left to right, they are as follows:

- **Particles.** The Particles menu contains functions dealing with the creation and editing of particles.
- **Fluid Effects.** The Fluid Effects menu contains functions for creating and editing fluid effects.
- **Fields.** The Fields menu contains functions dealing with the creation of fields.
- **Soft/Rigid Bodies.** The Soft/Rigid Bodies menu contains functions dealing with the creation and editing of soft and rigid body objects.
- **Effects.** The Effects menu contains functions dealing with the creation of specialized effects, such as fire or lightning.
- **Solvers.** The Solvers menu contains functions dealing with a collection of specialized solutions for dynamics animation.
- **Hair.** The Hair menu contains functions for creating and editing hair effects.

The Rendering Menu Options

When Rendering is selected from the drop-down list on the status line, the main menu features six Rendering menu items (see Figure 2.29). From left to right, they are as follows:

File   Edit   Modify   Create   Display   Window   Lighting/Shading   Texturing   Render   Toon   Paint Effects   Fur   Help

Figure 2.29 The Rendering menu set includes six menu items.

- **Lighting/Shading.** The Lighting/Shading menu contains functions dealing with editing materials and lights.
- **Texturing.** The Texturing menu contains functions dealing with 3D paint, PSD, texture referencing, and NURBS texture application.
- **Render.** The Render menu contains functions dealing with the rendering of scenes.
- **Toon.** The Toon menu contains functions dealing with Maya's Toon Shader.
- **Paint Effects.** The Paint Effects menu contains functions dealing with creating paint effects.
- **Fur.** The Fur menu contains functions for creating and editing fur.

The Cloth Menu Options

The Cloth menu set, as shown in Figure 2.30, is used for controlling cloth effects in Maya. Cloth is an advanced feature only available in Maya Unlimited.

| File | Edit | Modify | Create | Display | Window | Cloth | Constraints | Simulation | Help |

Figure 2.30 The Cloth menu set includes three menu items.

The Cloth menu contains three menu items, listed from left to right as follows:

- **Cloth.** The Cloth menu contains functions for creating and defining cloth objects.
- **Constraints.** The Constraints menu contains menu items used to constrain the movement and reaction of cloth objects.
- **Simulation.** The Simulation menu contains solvers and other tools for simulating the effects of cloth objects.

Summary

You have just finished a tour of the interfaces and menus in Maya. You should have at least a beginning knowledge of some of the tools and features of the program. As you continue to go through the next few chapters, you will gain an even broader knowledge of this program, as well as 3ds Max. Don't be afraid to experiment and try a few models on your own.

This chapter was an introduction to Maya's user interface. Some of the subjects covered include

- An overview of the Maya interface
- A breakdown of the features and tools for Maya
- A discussion of how to build and texture a ball
- A look at the menu system in Maya
- A quick explanation of the menu items in Maya

Chapter 2

Where Did I Put That?

Here we are...the first real look at Max versus Maya in a corresponding step-by-step guide to each program. We have tried hard to match feature for feature, so if you are familiar with one of these great applications, you will have little trouble understanding the opposing program, at least on a feature-by-feature basis. Both of these programs are extremely complex entities and quite challenging in their own right; however, if you do have working knowledge of Max or Maya, we hope that through this book you will find some common ground and have an easier transition to the program with which you're less familiar.

The Max Screen

When opening Max for the first time, you will see far fewer initial icons and menus to choose from compared to Maya, but fear not—many of the same features you are used to in Maya are here, just put away in an attempt to ease workflow. Max has a rather powerful interface customization options panel that I encourage you to explore once you have the basics down and feel comfortable with the interface. There are many options to make the interface fit your working style.

Have a look around and try things like right-clicking on various parts of the screen, clicking and holding buttons with a small triangle in the bottom-right corner of the icon, or grabbing and dragging menu tabs. You will soon start to get a feel for the basics of how the Max interface works.

Figure 2.1 shows the Max interface screen as it comes up for the first time.

In the following sections I will go over the basics of the Max interface to help get you up to speed quickly and feel more comfortable working in Max.

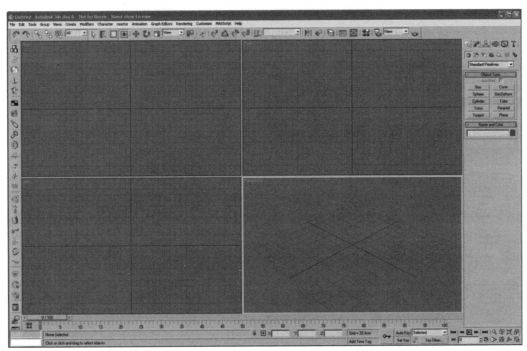

Figure 2.1 The default Max screen.

The Workspace

Eighty-five percent of the work you do in Max will happen in the 3D viewport (see Figure 2.2). Here you will manipulate your newly created world. The other 15 percent will happen in various pop-up windows and menus. There are four basic ways to change the viewport(s) to suit your working style and/or to match Maya.

- Right-click on the viewport labels (Top, Right, Left, Perspective) and choose Configure, and then choose the Layout tab.
- Right-click on the Maximize Viewport Toggle button at the bottom-right corner of the screen, and then choose the Layout tab.
- Use the basic viewport-manipulation tools common to most 3D applications.
- Click and hold the center bars between the viewports and slide the bar around to suit your preference.

You will also notice the Grid and the World Space Tripod in the viewport. (The World Space Tripod is the small axis indicator in the corner of each viewport.)

The Grid is adjustable to suit your needs and is used as a reference in 3D space. The dark black lines in the grid represent the X, Y, and Z world origin points. The small icon in the lower-left of each viewport is called the World Space Tripod. It's used as a reference to help you navigate 3D via the 2D interface (the screen).

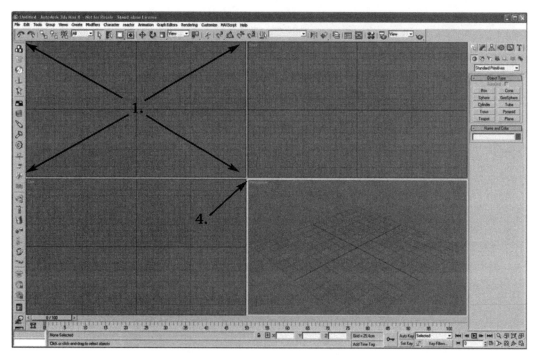

Figure 2.2 The viewport is the main work area of the interface.

You will also notice that one of the viewports is always highlighted in yellow. This is considered your active viewport. You can make any viewport active just by clicking on it.

Max defaults to four standard views—Top, Right, Left, and Perspective. You will notice the viewport labels in the upper-left corner of each viewport. You can also change each of these viewports by right-clicking on the viewport label and choosing View.

You will need to add a camera if you want to see a view through a real camera instead of seeing the standard orthogonal views. For starters and basic work, you can use the Perspective viewport because it demonstrates many of the same features of a real camera view. However, once you get familiar with the viewports, you will want to switch to a real camera for greater control and functionality.

Figure 2.3 shows the dialog box for changing the basic viewport layout I just mentioned.

You can choose from many different layouts to suit your taste or needs, and you can configure each one by clicking on the larger layout representative and choosing which view you want in each viewport.

Max doesn't split the views into Orthogonal or Perspective; rather, it groups all the views (including any cameras/lights that you have set up in your scene) into one view menu. In Figure 2.4, I have added a camera and a spot light to the scene so you can see where they show up in the menu when present.

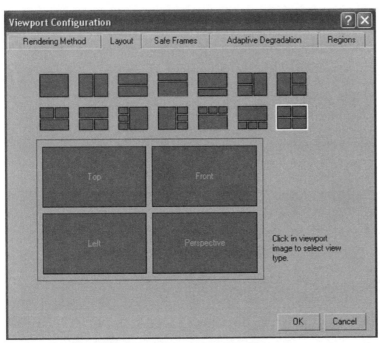

Figure 2.3 There are several preset viewport layouts in Max.

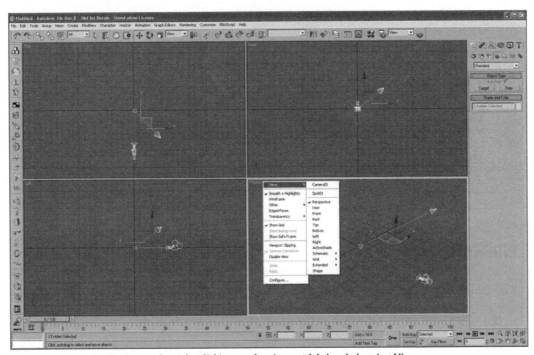

Figure 2.4 Access the View menu by right-clicking on the viewport label and choosing View.

As in the Maya example, let's create a torus in Max.

Note

By holding your mouse pointer over a button or icon briefly, you will see a small pop-up showing the name or function of the button or icon.

Although many of the same functions are available in the main menu, the majority of Max's object creation and manipulation is done in the Command Panel, which is the long box running down the right side of your screen, as shown in Figure 2.5.

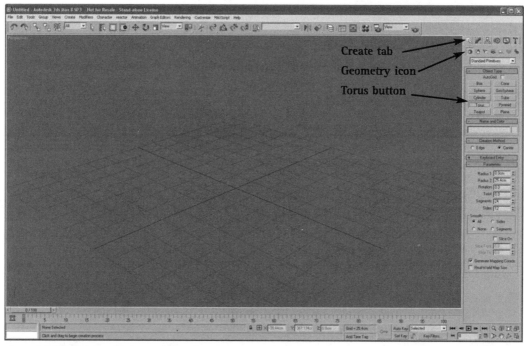

Figure 2.5 Highlighting the Command Panel

Note

At times the Command Panel gets a little long, so you can adjust its width for ease of workflow by holding your mouse over the leftmost edge until the cursor changes to a double-headed arrow, at which point you can drag the box to be wider or narrower. You can also undock the Command Panel by grabbing near the tabs at the top. This is a nice feature that can give you tons more workspace if you have multiple monitors.

Now let's create that torus.

1. Click on the Create icon (the top-left tab on the Command Panel).
2. Click on the Geometry icon right below the Create icon.
3. Click the Torus button and click and drag a torus in the Top viewport. You will need to click twice to create the torus—once to set its diameter and the second time to set its thickness. Many of the primitives in Max work this way. Try out a few of them. Once you get the hang of it, it's easy to make and place primitives.

Now that you know how to change views and layouts, take a look at navigating within the viewport. Although the following commands work in all views, you might want to switch to the full viewport for clarity by pressing Alt+W or clicking the Maximize Viewport toggle icon in the lower-right corner of the interface. Make sure you have the Perspective viewport selected first.

To speed up workflow, Max uses several keyboard shortcuts to help you quickly manipulate the viewports. The basic set includes the mouse wheel, middle mouse button, Control key, and Alt key.

To zoom the viewport in or out, simply use the scroll wheel on your mouse. To pan the view, use the middle mouse button by clicking and holding down the scroll wheel. To rotate the view in any direction, hold down the Alt key and the middle mouse button while moving the mouse around. Finally, to dolly the viewport or camera, use the Control key with the Alt key and the middle mouse button.

To help manipulate the viewport even more quickly, you can add the Control key to the mix. Using the Control key with zooming (scroll wheel) or panning (middle mouse button) will magnify the action, meaning a greater panning distance or faster zooming.

If your mouse does not have a wheel or a middle button, you will find all of these commands for manipulating the viewports and camera views in the eight icons located in the lower-right corner of the Max interface, right below the Command Panel.

The Toolbar

The Maya Toolbox contains items for manipulating objects in the 3D viewport. You will find many of the same tools (as well as many others) along the top toolbar in Max (see Figure 2.6).

Figure 2.6 The default toolbars.

The top toolbar contains the following tools from left to right.

- **Undo/Undo drop-down.** This is the standard Undo command; right-clicking will bring up the drop-down menu. You can set the number of undo steps in the Customize/Preference menu.
- **Redo/Undo drop-down.** This is the standard Redo command; right-clicking will bring up the drop-down menu.
- **Link.** This option is used to link objects together.
- **Unlink.** This option is used to break the link between objects.
- **Bind to Space Warp.** This option allows you to link a Space Warp to an object.
- **Selection Filter drop-down.** This option is used to set types of objects that can be selected.
- **Select.** This option allows you to select objects without affecting them by moving, rotating, or scaling, for example.
- **Select by Name pop-up.** This option brings up a dialog box for selecting objects in your scene.
- **Rectangular Selection/Selection Shapes drop-down.** This option allows you to set the type of Selection Marquee.
- **Window/Crossing Selection toggle.** This option toggles between requiring the object to be fully enclosed by the Selection Marquee to select it, or only requiring the Marquee to be touching the thing you want to select.
- **Move.** This option allows you to move objects (Transform tool).
- **Rotate.** This option allows you to rotate objects (Transform tool).

- **Scale/Scale Types drop-down.** This option allows you to choose and set the scale method and to scale objects (Transform tool).
- **Reference Coordinate drop-down.** This option allows you to choose and set which coordinate systems you want to use for the Transform tools.
- **Use Pivot Center/Select Pivot Choice drop-down.** This option allows you to choose and set which pivot you want to use for the Transform tools.
- **Manipulate toggle.** This option allows you to manipulate parameters.
- **Snaps toggle/Snap Types drop-down.** This option allows you to choose and set the snap mode you want to use.
- **Angle Snap toggle.** This option allows you to set the rotation snap to use certain angles. You set the angle by right-clicking on this icon.
- **Percent Snap toggle.** This option allows you to set the scaling to snap to predefined settings. You set the percent setting by right-clicking on this icon.
- **Spinner Snap toggle.** This option allows you to set the spinners to snap to preset increments. You set this number or fraction by right-clicking on this icon.
- **Edit Named Selection Sets pop-up.** This option opens a pop-up for managing named selection sets.
- **Named Selection Sets drop-down.** This option allows you to name and/or select previously named sets.
- **Mirror Selection pop-up.** This option allows you to flip and duplicate objects.
- **Align/Align Types drop-down/pop-up.** This option allows you to select the alignment type and to align objects using the drop-down menu. (This option brings up the Align dialog box as well as a drop-down menu with tools related to the Align tool.)
- **Layer Manager pop-up.** This option allows you to manage layers.
- **Curve Editor pop-up.** This option opens the Track view - Curve Editor.
- **Schematic View pop-up.** This option opens the Schematic view.
- **Material Editor pop-up.** This option opens the Material Editor.
- **Render Scene pop-up.** This option opens the Rendering Options dialog box.
- **Render Types drop-down.** This option allows you to set various areas or objects to be rendered.
- **Quick Render/Quick Render drop-down.** This option renders the selected viewport with the last render settings.

You will also notice the Reactor toolbar down the left side of the screen. This toolbar holds icons for controlling the reactor plug-in. Reactor is Max's soft- and hard-body dynamics engine.

Main Menu

As in Maya, you will find links to most of the tools and functions in Max on the main menu bar (see Figure 2.7). Max's menu bar is highly configurable, and you can save different main menu sets and recall them for different tasks and working styles. You will find the configuration options for the menu bar on the Menu tab under Customize, Customize User Interface.

| File Edit Tools Group Views Create Modifiers Character reactor Animation Graph Editors Rendering Customize MAXScript Help |

Figure 2.7 Most of Max's features are located in the main menu.

Status Bar

The status bar in Max has nothing in common with the status line in Maya. Many of the status line items in Maya can be found on the Max toolbar and in the main menu.

The status bar can be divided neatly into four sections. From left to right you will find the info box, two icons, the XYZ Transform boxes, and the Grid Info window (see Figure 2.8).

| File Edit Modify Create Display Window | Particles Fluid Effects Fields Soft/Rigid Bodies Effects Solvers Hair Help |

Figure 2.8 The status bar is located near the bottom of the screen.

The status bar section shows useful information, such as the number of objects selected. The two icons are the Selection Lock toggle, which locks the selection to the selected object until the lock is toggled off, and the Absolute Mode Transform type-in, which toggles between typing absolute and relative values into the three boxes to the right of the toggle (the XYZ Transform boxes).

The X, Y, and Z Transform boxes are used to show information about the selected object in the scene and to quickly type in new values for the selected object.

The Absolute Mode Transform type-in and the XYZ Transform boxes are transform-dependent, meaning if you are in Scale mode, then you will be typing in scale values, for example.

Last, you will see a small box denoting the current Grid designation. You can change the Grid units via the Customize, Units Setup menu option.

Note

To change the grid properties, you need to go to the Home Grid tab under Customize, Grid, Snap Settings.

Shelves

Max does not contain an equivalent to the shelves you find in Maya. Older versions of Max had a tabbed toolbar, but that feature has been removed.

You can modify many of the icons on the main toolbar as well as create new toolbars for existing functions, tools, and macros. You can save these toolbar modifications and recall them at will.

Max Script Mini Listener

Figure 2.9 The Max Script Mini Listener is next to the status bar.

The Max Script Mini Listener is the quick or command-line version of the Max Script Editor (see Figure 2.9). You can enter Max Script commands into the pink box, and they will be executed immediately. You can also right-click on the box and bring up the full Max Script Listener.

Command Panel

Figure 2.10 The default Command Panel dominates the right side of the screen.

The Command Panel is one of the most used sections of the interface and second only to the viewports in the time spent in Max. Most of Max's settings, as well as editing and tweaking of your 3D scenes, will happen in the various tabs of the Command Panel (see Figure 2.10). Because so much of the work done in 3D is tweaking and perfecting your scenes, you will find that most of your time spent in the Command Panel will be spent on the Modify tab.

The Command Panel is divided into six tabs, with each tab having many submenus and options. The tabs are named appropriately, and if you need to work on a particular aspect of your scene, you will likely find the tools you need under the appropriate tabs. The tabs are as follows.

- **Create.** You will find primitives, lights, cameras, and helpers galore on this tab.
- **Modify.** Here you can adjust and change your object, light, and camera properties.
- **Hierarchy.** Much of the 3D world is based on hierarchies, and you can work with those here.
- **Motion.** Animation is a key part of 3D, and many of the necessary tools are here.

- **Display.** 3D scenes can get very complex, and there are tools here to help simplify your scenes and workflow.
- **Utilities.** This tab contains various tools to help your workflow in 3D.

Don't worry about this complex section of Max. With so much of your time spent in this panel, you will quickly get the hang of it.

Animation Tools

This section of the screen contains the navigation interface between you and the animation (see Figure 2.11). Here you are able to move between frames, play animations, set basic key frames, and change some of Max's animation properties.

Figure 2.11 Max's fundamental animation tools are located in the lower part of the screen.

Prompt Line

The prompt line will let you know what Max expects you to do with the currently selected tool (see Figure 2.12). It will also report things such as render times.

Click or click-and-drag to select objects	Add Time Tag

Figure 2.12 The prompt line is located at the bottom of the screen.

There is a small box with the text Add Time Tag. Clicking on this box will give you the option to Add Tag or Edit Tag. The time tag is a way to label a point in time (a key frame in your animation). After you have some time tags set up, you can easily click on this box and quickly jump to a labeled time in your animation.

Now that I have very briefly run through the Max interface, you should have a rough idea of how Max relates to Maya in most interface areas. Both programs are extremely deep, and I have only scratched the surface in this quick comparison. Let's move on and start getting a little deeper into the fun!

Having a Ball

This next part is very basic, so if you have experience with 3D programs you might want to skip this section. If, however, you are new to Max or you have not used it before, this section will help you get started. In this section, you will create a simple textured 3D ball.

First you will examine how to create a sphere. As with the torus you created earlier in the chapter, you will be using the Command Panel (see Figure 2.13).

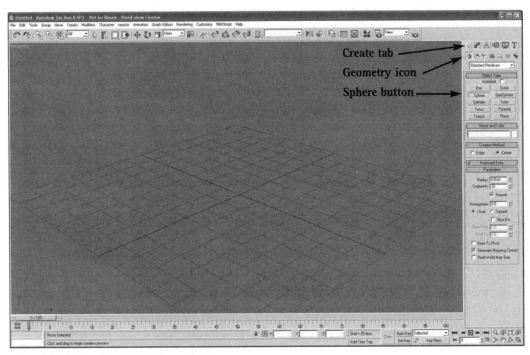

Figure 2.13 The location of the Sphere primitive.

1. Click on the Create tab.
2. Click on the Geometry icon.
3. Click on the Sphere button.
4. Click on the plus sign to open the Keyboard Entry rollout (see Figure 2.14). This rollout is common to most of the primitives. Here you can enter a location and radius for the sphere and create spheres automatically; however, I encourage you to go to the next step and create a sphere interactively.
5. At this point you can click in any viewport and drag out a sphere of any size in the location you desire (see Figure 2.15).

Note

When you are finished, the Sphere button will remain active, and you can place any number of spheres desired. To deactivate the button and move on, you simply need to right-click in any of the viewports.

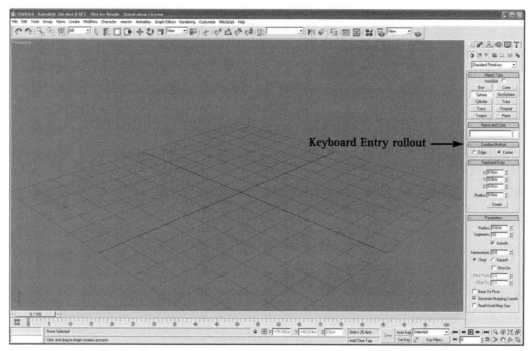

Keyboard Entry rollout ⟶

Figure 2.14 Click on the plus sign to expand the rollout box for setting the size and placement of primitives manually.

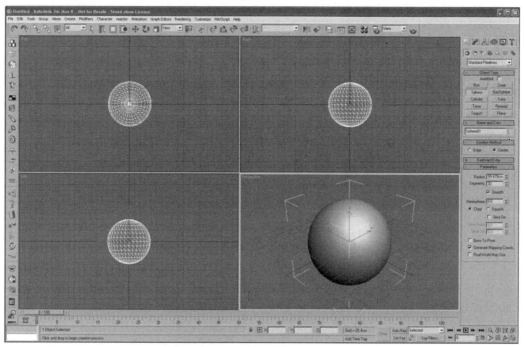

Figure 2.15 The new polygonal object is now in the work area.

6. By default the Max view is Shaded. However, should you want to change it to another shading mode or perhaps Wireframe mode, right-click on any of the viewport labels to bring up the menu shown in Figure 2.16, and choose the desired shading mode.

7. Press M or click on the highlighted button shown in Figure 2.17 to call up Max's Material Editor. The Material Editor dialog is very complex and deep; however, for this example you will just be skimming the surface to get familiar with the Material Editor.

Figure 2.16 Change the view mode.

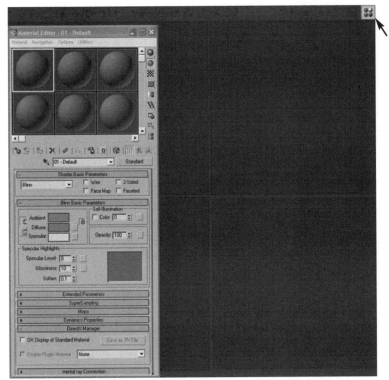

Material Editor button

Figure 2.17 The Material Editor is Max's equivalent to Maya's Hypershade.

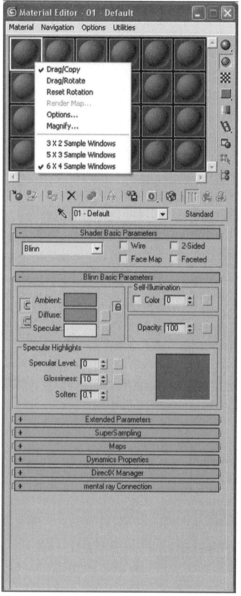

Figure 2.18 Setting up a new material is easy.

Max has a set of default or blank material shaders set up and ready to go (see Figure 2.18). All you need to do is assign some basic attributes, such as colors or texture maps, and you are ready to assign the material to your object and render. You don't create new shaders per se; rather, you edit and change attributes for the existing shaders.

Don't worry about only seeing six sample windows or a limited number of options because this Editor is extremely deep, and you will not run out of sample windows or things to tweak once you get the basics down and start to feel comfortable with the Editor.

8. You can also experiment with this Editor, but for now, right-click on the sample windows and set the number of visible samples to 6×4 or open up some of the rollouts to start getting familiar with the Editor.

You will find that the Max Material Editor contains the equivalent of Hypershade and the Attribute Editor all in the same editor, making it really easy to create complex and highly realistic textures and effects.

There are four basic areas of the Material Editor to get you started (see Figure 2.19).

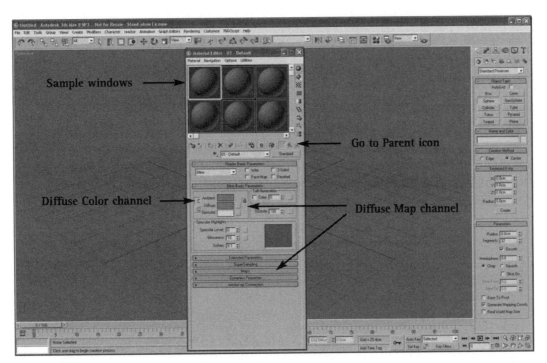

Figure 2.19 There are four basic areas to get you started.

- **Sample windows.** The shader balls are called sample windows; they give you a rough idea of how the material will look on your model.
- **Diffuse Color channel.** This is where you set the color of the material.
- **Diffuse Map channel.** This is where you load bitmaps that will display as texture on your models. (You can also access the Map channels via the Map rollout.)
- **Go to Parent icon.** Max's materials and settings are organized in a hierarchy, so you need this button to move back up the hierarchy.

9. To follow the Maya example and create a textured material you can apply to your sphere, click on the Diffuse Map button shown in Figure 2.20. This will bring up a second dialog box in which you can choose the type of material you want to apply to the Diffuse Map channel.

10. Choose the Checker material, as shown in Figure 2.20, and click on OK. This will do two things: First, it will apply the procedural Checker map to the Diffuse Map channel, and second, it will automatically open the Checker map settings. You will notice in the sample window that there is a checkered pattern applied to the shader sphere (see Figure 2.21). Try adjusting the numbers in the Tiling U and V input boxes. You can also try adjusting the colors if you want.

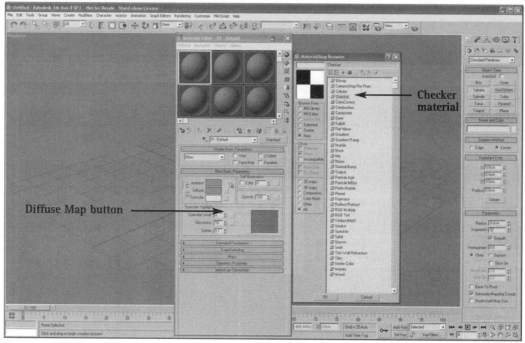

Figure 2.20 Creating the basic look of the material is only a few clicks away.

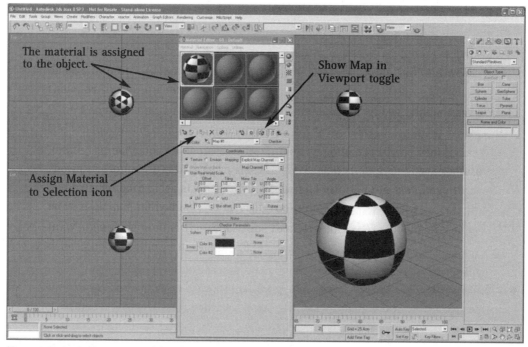

Figure 2.21 Apply the new material to the sphere.

There are three important things to note in reference to assigning materials to the object.

- The Show Map in Viewport toggle will display the material in the viewport if you are in a shaded mode. It's off by default for speed, so you will want to click on it to enable it.
- Once you assign a material to an object, you will see four small white corners in the sample window. These indicate that the material is assigned to an object in the scene. The four corners are bright white when the object that the material ball is assigned to is selected or dark gray when the object is not selected but the material is assigned.
- The Assign Material to Selection icon is for assigning the selected material to the selected object.

Note

You can use the button to assign the selected material to the selected object, but I find it much easier to click on the sample window and drag the material to the object to which I want to assign it.

Now you should see the results of your material editing in the viewport and on your model. At this point I would encourage you to adjust the U and V Tiling in the Material Editor and watch the results in the viewport.

11. When you are happy with the results, click on the Go to Parent icon, as shown in Figure 2.19. This will take you back to the top level of this material. Alternatively, you can just close the Material Editor because we are done with this tutorial.

12. If you want to see a rendering of your new creation, you can click on the Quick Render button at the very end of the toolbar. The button looks like a teal teapot.

Menus

By default, Max does not contain the task-specific main menu items listed in the corresponding section on the Maya side of the book. Most of the tools you need are on the main menu by default; however, if you feel that key tools that match your workflow are missing, there are a few options you can choose that will help ease the transition if you are used to those context-specific menu entries.

First, you will find most of the corresponding functions and tools from the context-specific Maya menus in the Command Panel, under the Create and Modify tabs. To ease your transition into Max, I recommend getting familiar with where your favorite tools and functions reside in the Max Command Panel.

Until you are familiar with where to find those tools, you could set up some new main menu items that match what you're used to in Maya via Customize, Customize User Interface. The feature is quite powerful and useful for that sort of thing.

Last, you can set up additional toolbars or modify the existing toolbar via the same customization menu. If you have multiple monitors, this is a nice way to go.

In light of this difference between the two programs, I will highlight the specific menus from the main menu for the items listed in the following sections.

Menu Layout

Figure 2.22 File is the first menu on the main menu bar.

The File menu contains many standard Windows commands, such as Save, Load, Import, and Export (see Figure 2.22). You will also find other options for dealing with scene files.

First let's talk about menu layouts in Maya. Each menu in Maya has groups separated by lines. Grouping menu items helps to define related functions. In the File menu, the first group contains four menu items: New, Reset, Open, and Open Recent. The ellipsis (...) after a menu item indicates that clicking on the item will open a dialog box (see Figure 2.23).

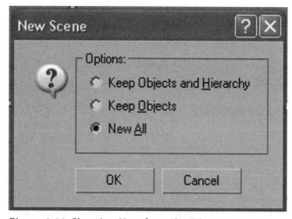

Figure 2.23 Choosing New from the File menu brings up a simple dialog box.

Menus in Max have three columns. Starting from the left, the first column is the name of the menu item. The second column gives a keyboard equivalent of the menu item. The keyboard equivalent is a keyboard shortcut that accesses the function through the keyboard. You can see from the File menu that Ctrl+N is the keyboard equivalent of the New option. This means that instead of clicking on the New icon or selecting New from the File menu, you can simply press Ctrl+N to get a new scene.

The third column has arrows that indicate submenus for those menu items that have multiple functions. In the File menu, Open Recent has a submenu. If you slide the cursor down to Open Recent and leave it there for a second, the submenu will appear by the black arrow. You can then slide the cursor over the submenu items and select one of them.

When creating a new scene, Max will use the default settings. If you want to override these settings and have a custom scene open when you choose New or when you open Max, you can save a file named Maxstart.max in the Scenes folder. Max will use this file to set up the new scene with the defaults saved in that file.

An example of when this is useful is when you like your default Max file to start with 1,000 frames instead of 100 and you don't like the Grids turned on. Just open or reset Max, turn off the Grids by pressing G, edit the frame count and set it to 1,000 by right-clicking on the Play arrow on the bottom-right side of the screen, and adjust the animation length. Now just save this scene as Maxstart.max in the Scenes folder, and the next time you start Max you will have these new settings.

The Max Menus

Unlike Maya, this menu will not change based on your context (see Figure 2.24). You can add to or delete things off this menu by choosing the Customize, Customize User Interface menu options.

File   Edit   Tools   Group   Views   Create   Modifiers   Character   reactor   Animation   Graph Editors   Rendering   Customize   MAXScript   Help

Figure 2.24 Max has a constant main menu that does not change.

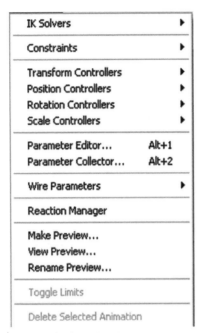

Figure 2.25 The Animation menu contains powerful tools.

You will find a powerful set of tools under the Animation menu (see Figure 2.25). Because animation is complex, there are three other main menu items that also contain tools to help with animation. Those are Reactor (the Dynamics menu), Character (which contains tools for working with Character Studio), and Graph Editors (which contains tools for editing animations via curves).

The Create menu has many options for creating geometry and helpers (see Figure 2.26). This is a big menu class, and I recommend using the Command Panel for creating geometry because it's much easier to navigate.

Reactor is Max's tool for adding dynamics simulation to your 3D world (see Figure 2.27). There is also a toolbar running vertically along the left side of the screen that contains many of the Reactor options and tools.

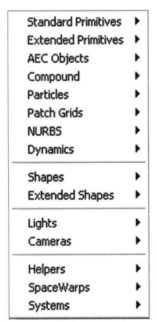

Figure 2.26 The Create menu includes many options with submenus.

Figure 2.27 The Reactor menu includes many dynamics-related tools.

The Rendering menu contains options and tools related to the final output of your scene. In addition to rendering options, you will find effects tools, environmental tools, and lighting tools (see Figure 2.28).

```
Render...                          F10
Environment...                     8
Effects...
Advanced Lighting                   ▶
Render To Texture...               0
Batch Render...

Raytracer Settings...
Raytrace Global Include/Exclude...

mental ray Message Window...

ActiveShade Floater...
ActiveShade Viewport

Material Editor...                  M
Material/Map Browser...

Video Post...

Show Last Rendering

Panorama Exporter...
Print Size Wizard...
RAM Player...
```

Figure 2.28 The Rendering menu deals with all things rendering.

Summary

Well, there you have it. Your first foray into changing over to the dark side! Whether you are a Max or Maya user, you have just taken the first step to switching over and gaining some valuable experience in the "other side."

This chapter has taken a very brief glance at the interface of Max, and I have skimmed over many details to keep you from feeling overwhelmed. The following chapters will explore these two fine programs in greater detail in a step-by-step, program-by-program format, so I encourage you to continue getting to know Max. It's a great program!

Chapter 3

Building Simple 3D Models

Building 3D models is the process of creating a virtual 3D representation of a character, an object, or a setting. In this chapter, we will be looking at creating simple objects using *primitives*, which are basic geometric shapes like cubes, spheres, and cones. Modeling using primitives is very common because even complex models have their roots in basic shapes.

Maya has a number of basic primitive shapes that can be used to create models. In this chapter, you will learn about how to create primitive shapes, and then modify them to create more complex models using many of the tools in Maya. Although Maya is often thought of as a NURBS modeling program, it does have a number of very powerful modeling tools for polygons as well.

Polygon Modeling Tools

In simple terms, building 3D game characters is the process of creating a virtual 3D representation of a character on the computer that can later be exported into a game engine. This section looks at creating simple objects using primitives. *Primitives* are basic polygon objects—that is, geometric shapes like cubes, spheres, cones, and so on.

Maya has many tools that are useful for building models with polygons. Understanding these tools will help you to master the techniques of building models with them. Some of these tools were used in Chapter 2 to create the ball. Now is a good time to explain them in greater detail. First, take a look at creating polygon primitives; then you will examine how these primitive objects can be modified.

Creating Polygon Primitives

You can find the Polygon Primitives creation tools on the Create menu, as shown in Figure 3.1.

At the bottom of the Polygon Primitives submenu are two check-marked options. These options were added in Maya 8 to support the interactive creation of objects in the Workspace. Interactive creation works best for objects that are not a specific size and are not in a specific location. If you want to create objects that are defined exactly in size and location, you should turn these options off. If you want to sculpt your objects in a more freehand visual way, you should leave these menu items checked.

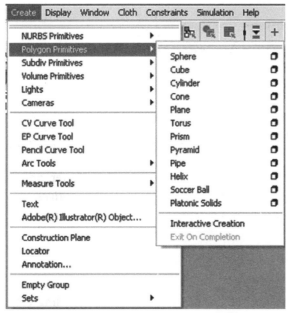

Figure 3.1 The Polygon Primitives command is located in the Create menu.

The Freehand modeling technique is a more advanced procedure for modelers who are already familiar with 3D modeling and use a more organic approach to constructing models. For the purposes of this book, we will leave these features unchecked to help the beginner with the creation of models that are scaled and placed appropriately in the scene. If you are a more advanced modeler, you can use the freehand tools in creating the projects in the book. Just be aware that you may need to move and scale the objects after creation to get the right size and placement.

The twelve polygon primitives supported by Maya and available from the Create menu are as follows. Each option offers a dialog box for setting the creation options such as the size, shape, and number of polygons in the object.

- **Sphere.** Figure 3.2 shows the Polygon Sphere Options dialog box. The first option, Radius, defines the size of the sphere; you can set the number in the box by using the slider or by typing it directly in the box. The next two options, which also use sliders, set the number of polygons in the sphere. The Axis option buttons establish the orientation of the sphere. The Texture Mapping options control how the UVs are placed on an object. UVs are points that control the placement of textures. If the Create UVs check box is checked, UVs will be placed on an object. If it is not, the object will not have any UV information. Without UVs, textures can't be placed on an object. The radio buttons below the UV check box are options for the placement of the UVs at the poles of the sphere.

Note

Maya remembers the options for dialog boxes. If you want to make several primitives with the same options, you don't need to go back into the primitive's dialog box. Just selecting the primitive on the menu or on the shelf will create a new primitive with the same options as the last one created. This feature in Maya is called *persistence.*

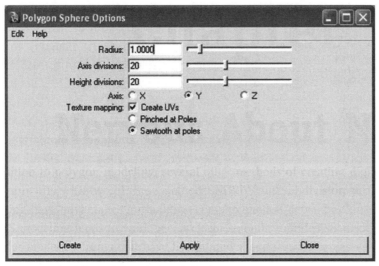

Figure 3.2 The Polygon Sphere Options dialog box.

- **Cube.** The Polygon Cube Options dialog box is shown in Figure 3.3. The first three fields in this dialog box control the width, height, and depth of the cube, and the next three fields control the number of polygons in each. The Axis option buttons control the axis of the cube.

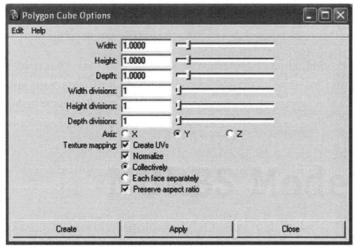

Figure 3.3 The Polygon Cube Options dialog box.

Each polygon primitive will have UV options. These options affect how UVs are organized on the object. The following are common options for polygon primitives.

- **Create UVs.** If this box is checked, UVs will be created with the object.
- **Normalize.** If this box is checked, it forces the UVs to all be inside the 0 to 1 texture area. This is the optimum texture area for objects and should be left on in most instances.

- **Collective.** Collective maps the texture over the entire surface of the object, as shown in Figure 3.4.

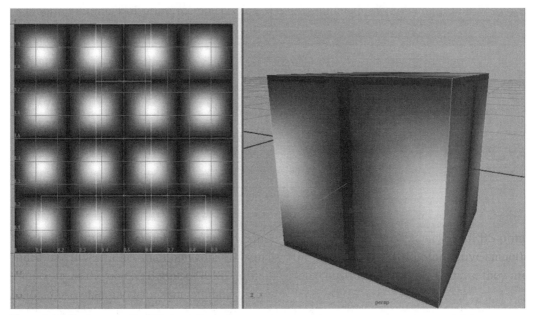

Figure 3.4 Collective maps the UVs across the texture.

- **Each Face Separately.** This option maps the texture to each plane, as shown in Figure 3.5.

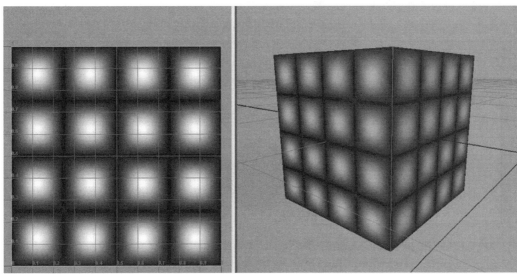

Figure 3.5 Each Face Separately maps the texture to each UV.

- **Preserve Aspect Ratio.** This option does not distort the UVs when placed on the texture plane. When this option is turned off, the UVs are stretched to fit the texture area.

- **Cylinder.** Figure 3.6 shows the Polygon Cylinder Options dialog box. Like the sphere, the cylinder has a radius, but it also has a height—hence the first two fields in the dialog box, which control the cylinder's radius and height. The next three fields control the number of polygons around the axis, height, and cap of the cylinder, and the Axis option buttons control the axis. Like the cube, the Polygon Cylinder Options dialog box also has options for applying the UVs.

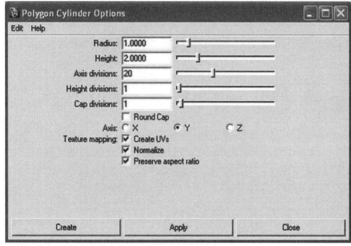

Figure 3.6 The Polygon Cylinder Options dialog box.

- **Cone.** Figure 3.7 shows the Polygon Cone Options dialog box. The options for the cone are very similar to the options for the cylinder.

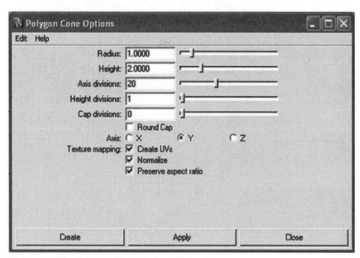

Figure 3.7 The Polygon Cone Options dialog box.

- **Plane.** Figure 3.8 shows the Polygon Plane Options dialog box. A *plane* is a flat polygonal object. It has only two directions for size and two directions for polygons, but has an axis like other objects. The default texture mode for a plane is Preserve Aspect Ratio. Figure 3.9 shows two planes. The one on the right has Preserve Aspect Ratio selected and the one on the left does not. For most objects it is better to not have Preserve Aspect Ratio checked.

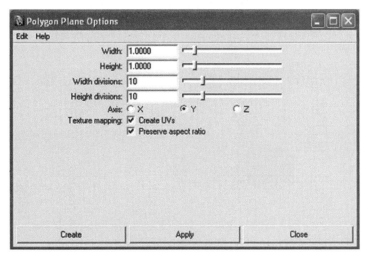

Figure 3.8 The Polygon Plane Options dialog box.

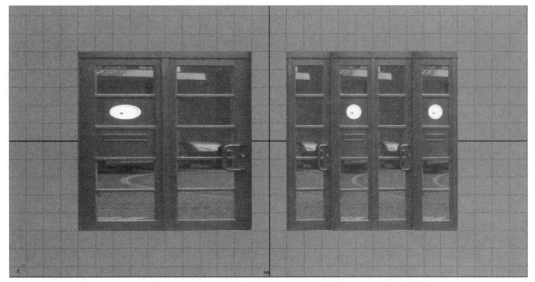

Figure 3.9 In most cases, it is preferable to turn Preserve Aspect Ratio off when creating polygon planes.

- **Torus.** Figure 3.10 shows the Polygon Torus Options dialog box. This dialog box is similar to the other polygon dialog boxes. The first three fields deal with the size of the object, the next two fields deal with the number of polygons in the object, the option buttons deal with the object's axis, and the other option relates to texture.

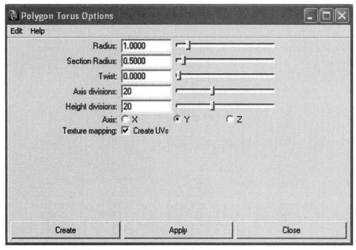

Figure 3.10 The Polygon Torus Options dialog box.

- **Prism.** Figure 3.11 shows the Polygon Prism Options dialog box. This dialog box follows the same pattern as the others; indeed, it has the exact same settings as the Polygon Cylinder Options dialog box. The difference is that edges on a prism are sharp rather than soft, as on a cylinder.

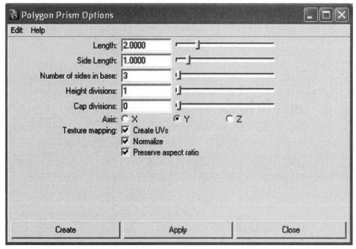

Figure 3.11 The Polygon Prism Options dialog box.

- **Pyramid.** Figure 3.12 shows the Polygon Pyramid Options dialog box. This dialog box is a little different from the others; it has only one size field because all the sides are the same length. The pyramid can have a three-, four- or five-sided base, which you select using the dialog box's option buttons. The Divisions, Axis, and Texture options are like similarly named options in other dialog boxes.

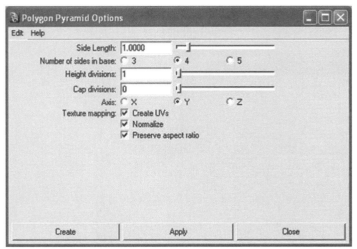

Figure 3.12 The Polygon Pyramid Options dialog box.

- **Pipe.** Figure 3.13 shows the Polygon Pipe Options dialog box. This dialog box is similar to the Polygon Cylinder Options dialog box with one major exception: The Polygon Pipe Options dialog box contains a Thickness field, which specifies the distance from the inner cylinder to the outer cylinder.

Figure 3.13 The Polygon Pipe Options dialog box.

- **Helix.** Figure 3.14 shows the Polygon Helix Options dialog box. A helix, which looks like the coil of a spring, is more complex than other polygon primitives. Hence, the Polygon Helix Options box contains a few extra settings. The first field, Coils, specifies the number of coils in the helix. The next two fields set the height and width of the coils. The last size-related fields establishes the radius of the coil. As with the other option boxes, the size settings are followed by Division options. There are three of them—Axis Divisions, Coil Divisions, and Cap Divisions. The next setting is for the spiral direction and can be either counterclockwise or clockwise. The Axis and Texture options are similar to the ones in other polygon primitive dialog boxes.

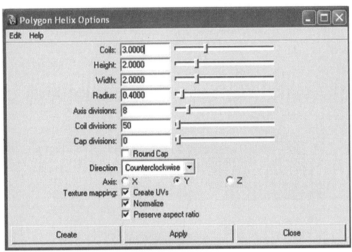

Figure 3.14 The Polygon Helix Options dialog box.

- **Soccer ball.** Figure 3.15 shows the Polygon Misc Options dialog box, used to set the options for the Soccer Ball primitive. The first thing you might notice about this dialog box is that there are no division options; that's because the object already has a predefined division. If you try to change the size options, you will notice that the two are tied together. If you increase or decrease one, the other one will automatically change to match. The Axis and Texture options are similar to those options in other dialog boxes.

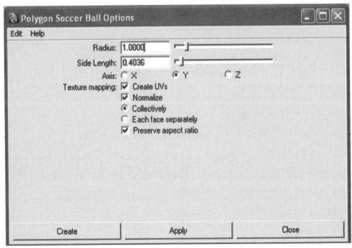

Figure 3.15 The Polygon Misc Options dialog box.

■ **Platonic solids.** Figure 3.16 shows the Platonic Solid Options dialog box. Platonic solids are geometric objects whose edges, angles, and faces are all the same. There are only five platonic solids: tetrahedron, hexahedron (cube), octahedron, dodecahedron, and icosahedron, all of which are shown in Figure 3.17. The Polygon Platonic Solid Options dialog box is similar to the Polygon Misc Options dialog box, except that the dialog box for platonic solids features a drop-down list below the size fields that enables you to choose which platonic solid to create. (Note that cube is not included because it is already one of the polygon primitives in Maya.)

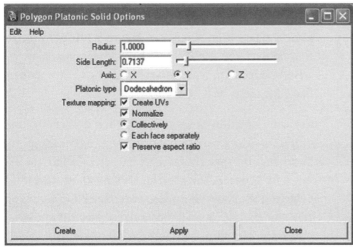

Figure 3.16 The Polygon Platonic Solid Options dialog box.

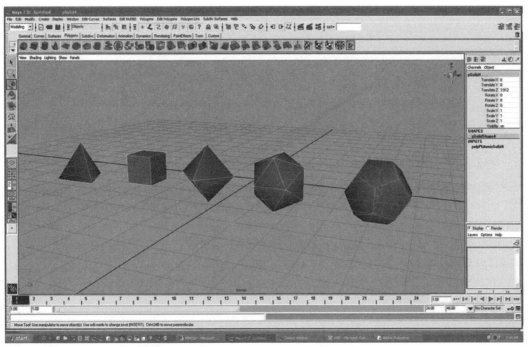

Figure 3.17 There are only five platonic solids.

Menus

Maya has a separate menu set for modeling polygons. as discussed previously. Change the menu set to Polygons. You don't need to know every function in these menus for now, but there are several that are very important to understand.

Using the Select Menu

Figure 3.18 The Select menu.

The Select menu reveals several options for selecting component types of an object (see Figure 3.18). With the selection options you can change the type of component you wish to select. You can also select groups of components, like edge loops or border edges.

Convert Selection is very useful when a selection does not correspond to a function. For example, UVs often need to be rotated on specific faces. It is easy to select the faces but hard to select the specific UVs for those faces. Selecting the faces and then using Selection to change the selection to UVs is a simple way to select only the UVs you want to rotate.

Using the Mesh Menu

The Mesh menu, shown in Figure 3.19, includes several functions for modeling a polygon primitive:

- **Combine.** Combine is a commonly used function that combines all selected objects into one object. Say, for example, that you are creating a tree, whose leaves are made up of many small polygons. You can combine all the leaves into one object by using the Combine function.

- **Separate.** Separate is used to separate unmerged polygons from each other. The Separate function could be used to separate the original objects from the combined object. This is useful if modifications are needed in the original objects that comprise the combined object.

- **Extract.** The Extract function detaches a selected set of polygons from a model, creating a separate object. It is used for separating model parts such as a door on a car or a window in a building.

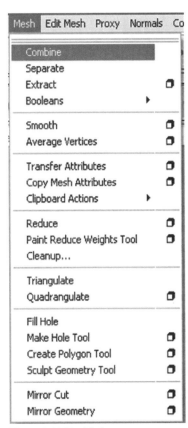

Figure 3.19 The Mesh menu.

- **Smooth.** The Smooth function adds polygons to an object to reduce the sharp edges of a model. The function averages the angles of the polygons to make the surface of a model more rounded. Modelers often use Smooth because making a simple object is faster than a making a complex one. After the basic object is created using just a few polygons, the artist can then use the Smooth function to round the rough-faceted surface.

- **Average Vertices.** The Average Vertices function smoothes an object or selection by moving the vertices rather than creating new geometry. This function is useful when the model needs to retain a set number of polygons but needs to be less irregular. The down side of the Arrange Vertices function is that because the vertices move, modeling problems may result.

- **Cleanup.** Cleanup is used to find and correct problems in a polygonal model. It has a number of options that let the artist define the parameters of a search to detect specific problems. It is similar to a spelling and grammar check in a word processor.

- **Sculpt Geometry Tool.** This function has many uses, but its main use is to interactively move polygons, similar to sculpting clay.

- **Mirror Geometry.** A commonly used function in Maya is Mirror Geometry. This function mirrors an object across a plane. It is frequently used for symmetrical models, enabling the modeler to focus on building only half the model and then mirror the model to complete it. A good example of when using the Mirror Geometry function would be useful is when modeling a car. The modeler needs to build only half of the car. Then, using the Mirror Geometry function, the other half can be added at the end of the modeling process.

Using the Edit Mesh Menu

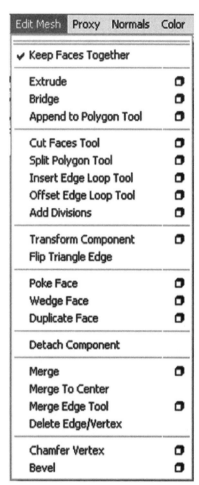

Figure 3.20 The Edit Mesh menu has many useful tools and functions.

The Edit Mesh menu, shown in Figure 3.20, has many useful tools and functions for modifying elements of a polygon object. The functions in the Edit Mesh menu differ from those in the Mesh menu in that Mesh menu items are used on polygon objects, where Edit Mesh menu items are for modifying *components* of an object. When using functions in the Edit Mesh menu, the selected item should generally be a component of a polygon rather than an object.

- **Extrude.** Extrude is a commonly used tool. It allows the artist to select a number of individual components and extrude them. Extrude is commonly used to add features to primitive models—for example, adding arms and legs to a character or building walls from a floor plan of a room. The Extrude feature works with faces, edges, and vertices.

- **Split Polygon Tool.** The Split Polygon function is used to divide individual polygons when specific geometry is needed to complete a model. The tool lets the artist draw in edges on a polygon.

- **Insert Edge Loop Tool.** Edge loops are used to add a single plane edge to an object. Say for example, you want to add some polygons to an arm so you can increase the detail. You can use Insert Edge Loop to insert an edge loop dividing the polygons, as shown in Figure 3.21.

- **Offset Edge Loop Tool.** The Offset Edge Loop Tool places a new edge on either side of an existing edge along the entire length of that edge, as shown in Figure 3.22.

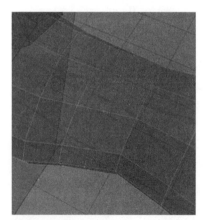

Figure 3.21 Use edge loops to divide polygons along a plane.

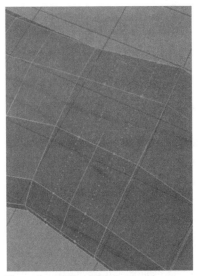

Figure 3.22 Offset Edge Loop adds new edges along both sides of an existing edge.

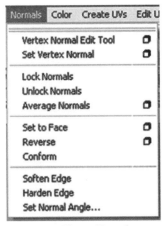

Figure 3.23 Choose Normals to see your options for adjusting the direction of a normal on a polygon.

- **Add Divisions.** The Add Divisions function is used to increase the density of the polygon mesh in selected areas of a model. Subdivide splits selected faces evenly and is used when a denser mesh is needed in specific locations on a model.

- **Duplicate Face.** The Duplicate Face function makes a copy of a selected set of polygon faces. It is often used to create copies of repetitive polygons—for example, when building a fence or creating wheels for a car.

- **Merge.** The Merge functions are used to combine two or more components into a single one. Merge is often used to join two parts of an object or to reduce the number of polygons in an area.

A polygon normal indicates which direction a polygon surface is facing. When a texture is applied to a polygon, the texture will appear correctly if the polygon normal is facing the viewer. If the polygon normal is facing away form the viewer, the texture will be reversed. Choosing the Normals menu reveals a menu of functions for adjusting the direction of the normal on a polygon (see Figure 3.23).

Figure 3.24 The Channel box and Layer Editor are part of the sidebar.

Sidebar Tools and Editors

Figure 3.24 shows the sidebar. This area contains several editor elements and consists of two parts:

- **The Channel box.** The Channel box, located in the top portion of the sidebar and often used in modeling and animating in 3D, is used to edit object attributes such as the object's position, rotation, scale, and so on. Using the Channel box is the way to go when you need an attribute to be assigned a specific numeric value. Below the attribute list in the Channel box is a history, which contains a list of all modifications made to the object. Figure 3.25 shows the Channel box for a polygon object.

- **The Layer Editor.** Found in the bottom portion of the sidebar, the Layer Editor is used to define objects in the Workspace as layers so that those objects can be isolated in groups from the rest of the scene. The Layer Editor is used to organize scene elements, and is particularly useful in complex scenes. For example, a city scene might be organized into roads, buildings, foliage, and vehicles. Each type of scene element is put on a different layer, enabling the artist to hide or reveal each type of element simply by turning its layer on or off.

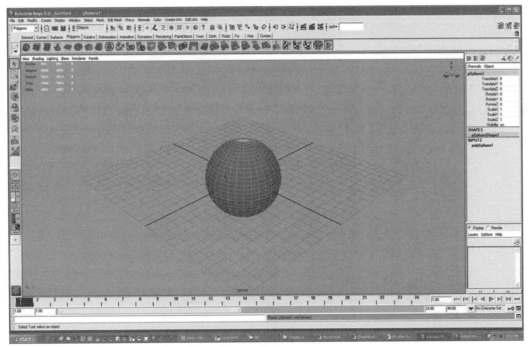

Figure 3.25 The Channel box is used to change object attributes.

The Channel box and Layer Editor are displayed in the sidebar by default, but you can display other tools in this area if you prefer. To do so, use the three buttons on the far right side of the status line. Clicking the button on the right shows or hides the Channel box. Clicking the middle button shows or hides the Tool Options pane. (The Tool Options pane contains specific options for many of Maya's tools. Figure 3.26 shows the 3D Paint tool, one of a number of tools that contain multiple options. Using the Tool Options pane, the artist can set and change options for the tool.) Clicking the button on the left shows or hides the Attribute Editor. (The Attribute Editor is used to edit attributes of a single node. A *node* holds specific information about a construct in Maya. Figure 3.27 shows a Lambert material; all editable aspects of the Lambert material are contained in the Attribute Editor.)

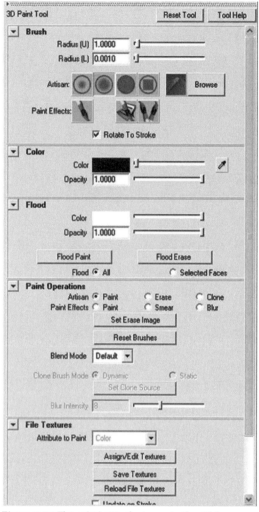

Figure 3.26 The painting tools appear in the sidebar.

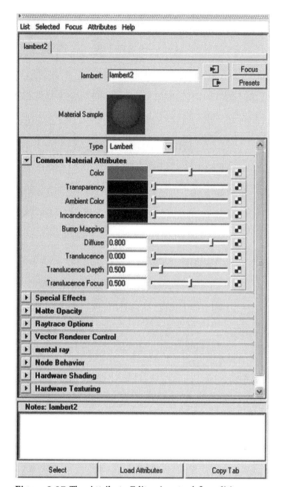

Figure 3.27 The Attribute Editor is a tool for editing attributes of a single node.

Summary

Creating objects with polygon primitives is an easy way to quickly get your models started. In this chapter, you learned about a number of features in the menus in Maya. You also learned how to create a simple polygon object from polygon primitives.

The polygon primitives in Maya are as follows:

- Sphere
- Cube
- Cylinder
- Cone
- Plane
- Torus
- Prism
- Pyramid
- Pipe
- Helix
- Soccer Ball
- Platonic Solid

Polygon modeling uses five menus from the Polygon main menu, namely Select, Mesh, Edit Mesh, Normals, and Create UVs. Only the first four were covered in this chapter. Create UVs, which deals mainly with textures, will be covered later. The sidebar and its common uses were also covered in this chapter.

In the next chapter, you will learn how to model a more complex polygon object.

Chapter 3

Building Simple 3D Models

Building 3D models is the process of creating a virtual 3D representation of a character, an object, or a setting. In this chapter, we will be looking at creating simple objects using *primitives*, which are basic geometric shapes like cubes, spheres, and cones. Modeling using primitives is very common because even complex models have their roots in basic shapes.

Over the years, Max has added several new types of primitives to give users a wider array of starting points. Once you feel comfortable with the various primitives, you will be able to choose the ones most suitable to your task or model.

Polygon Modeling Tools

Max has many default shapes that are useful for building models with polygons. Learning how to make these shapes, or primitives, will help you to master the techniques of building models with them. You should be familiar with some of the tools because they were used in Chapter 2 to create the ball. Now is a good time to explain them in greater detail. First, let's take a look at creating polygon primitives, and then we will take a look at how these primitive objects can be modified.

The following section on the various primitives will differ from the Maya side of the book due to Max's extended primitives set. They are listed as you will find them in Max.

Note

Remember, you can always choose the Keyboard Entry rollout for these primitives if you would like to enter precise numbers, but I would encourage you to choose the primitive and then click and drag your mouse in the viewport to "draw" the primitive. This is easy to do and a simple way of getting your object created.

Note

It will take two or three clicks in the viewport to finalize most of the primitives. For example, with the torus, you will click and drag to set the radius and then let go of the button and move the mouse to set the thickness of the torus. This takes a bit of getting used to, but once you get the hang of it, you will be able to quickly populate your scenes and speed up your workflow.

Creating Polygon Primitives

Although you can find all the basic and extended primitives in the main menu under Create, I would encourage you to use the Command Panel on the right, as in Chapter 2. That is the preferred way to work in Max.

There are some differing primitives between Max and Maya. Primitives unique to Max are Teapot, GeoSphere, Hedra, ChamferBox, OilTank, Spindle, Gengon, RingWave, Torus Knot, ChamferCyl, Capsule, L-Ext, C-Ext, and Hose. And only Maya has Helix, Soccer Ball, and Platonic Solid. In Max you will find something similar to Soccer Ball in GeoSphere, and Maya's Platonic Solid is most easily matched with Max's Hedra. There are a few examples of naming syntax that you may find useful. Max refers to Maya's Cube primitive as a Box. Maya's Pipe primitive can be found as the Tube in Max.

Several common rollouts exist for most of the primitives. You will notice that the Keyboard Entry and Creation Method are in nearly all the primitive options. The Keyboard Entry rollout is exactly what it states and allows you to create a primitive to an exact size. The Creation Method rollout allows you to choose if you want to create the primitive from the center or the edge. As most items in 3D get lots of tweaking, the choice between creating from the center or creating from the edge probably doesn't matter, but there are occasions when this is a nice feature and can save some time.

Max uses various colored primitives, choosing the colors randomly for clarification; however, you can easily choose your own default color by selecting the object and clicking on the small colored box located in the Command Panel. This will bring up a dialog box where you can set the color of the object.

Starting with the Box primitive, you will find Max's primitives listed next in order of how they appear in Max. The first 10 are in the Standard Primitives rollout, and the remaining 13 are in the Extended Primitives rollout.

Figure 3.1 shows the default Max screen with the Create tab selected on the Command Panel.

On the default Command Panel, the Standard Primitives are open. The Extended Primitives list can be found by clicking on the drop-down menu directly above the Standard Primitive buttons. You will find other menu items related to primitives in this drop-down, but the key items for this chapter are the Standard Primitives and Extended Primitives. Between these two menus you will find 23 basic shapes. Once you choose a primitive to create, various options for the selected primitive will show up in the empty gray area immediately under the primitive selection area.

Most of the primitives have common rollouts. Those are Keyboard Entry and Creation Method. The Keyboard Entry rollout allows you to type in exact sizes and locations for the primitive, and the Creation Method rollout lets you create primitives from the center or the edge when you are creating primitives interactively.

Many of the primitives have similar fields—for example, height, width, length, segments, and radiuses. For the following primitive examples, I will highlight unique entry fields where appropriate.

Chapter 3
Max

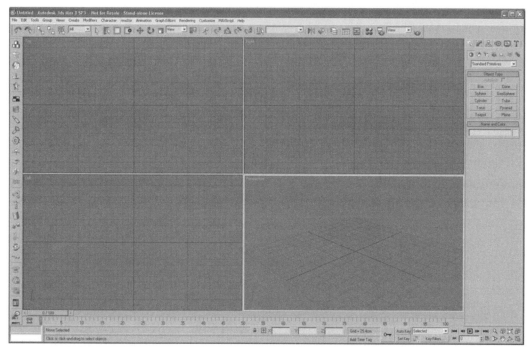

Figure 3.1 The default Max screen layout.

Box

Figure 3.2 shows the Box primitive displaying the standard options.

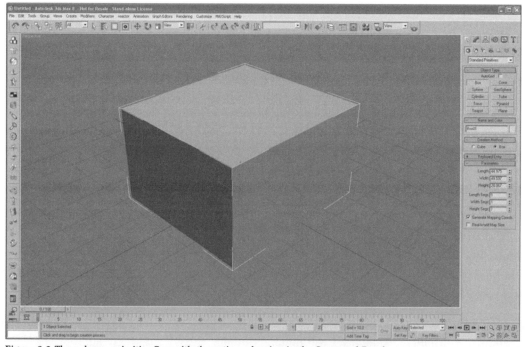

Figure 3.2 The polygon primitive Box with the options showing in the Command Panel.

The Hemisphere option allows you to create partial spheres (for example, from the South Pole to the North Pole). The Slice option lets you create partial spheres in the opposite direction of the hemisphere.

Sphere

Figure 3.3 shows the Sphere primitive displaying the standard options.

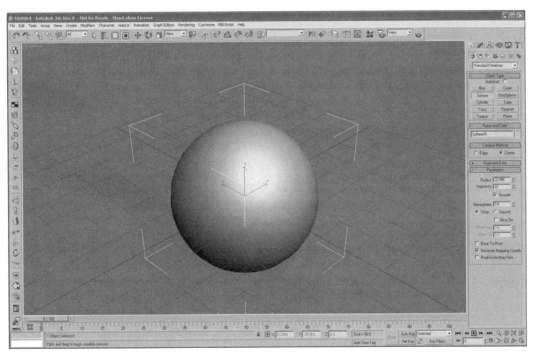

Figure 3.3 The polygon primitive Sphere with the options showing in the Command Panel.

Cylinder

Figure 3.4 displays the Cylinder primitive showing the standard options.

Torus

Figure 3.5 displays the Torus primitive showing the standard options.

Teapot

The Teapot (see Figure 3.6) is sort of the mascot for Max. Many 3D programs have a defining primitive.

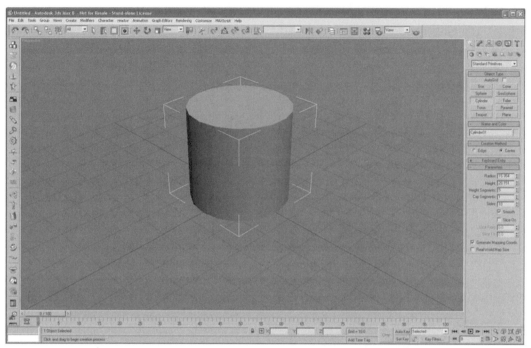

Figure 3.4 The polygon primitive Cylinder with the options showing in the Command Panel.

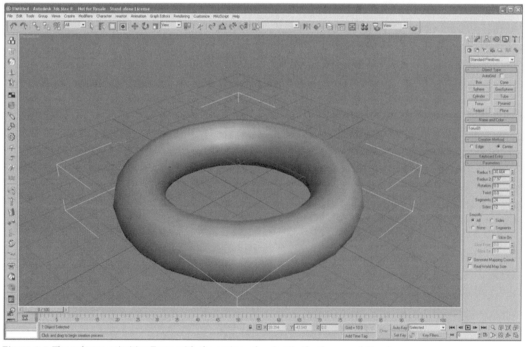

Figure 3.5 The polygon primitive Torus with the options showing in the Command Panel.

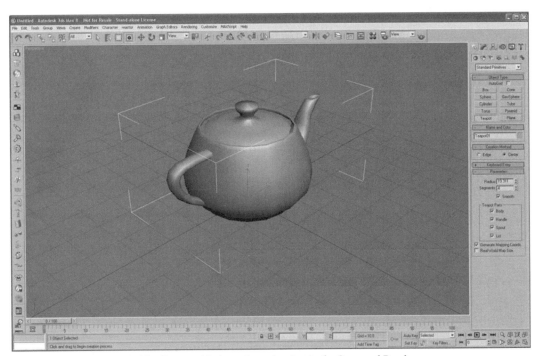

Figure 3.6 The polygon primitive Teapot with the options showing in the Command Panel.

Cone

Figure 3.7 displays the Cone primitive showing the standard options.

GeoSphere

Figure 3.8 shows the GeoSphere, which comes in three types, Tetra, Octa, and Icosa.

Tube

Figure 3.9 shows the Tube primitive displaying the standard options.

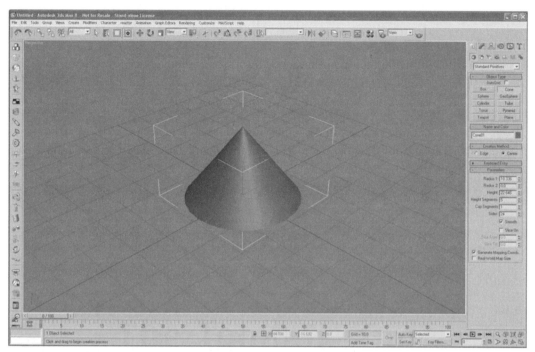

Figure 3.7 The polygon primitive Cone with the options showing in the Command Panel.

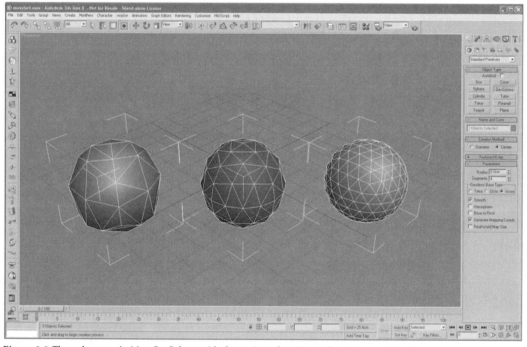

Figure 3.8 The polygon primitive GeoSphere with the options showing in the Command Panel.

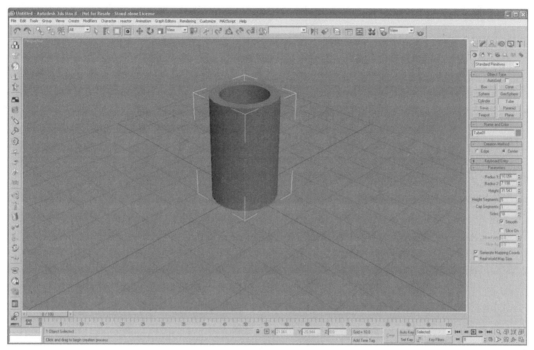

Figure 3.9 The polygon primitive Tube with the options showing in the Command Panel.

Pyramid

Figure 3.10 displays the Pyramid primitive showing the standard options.

Plane

The Plane primitive (see Figure 3.11) has a unique option for multiplying geometry at render time. This is a useful feature for complex render techniques, such as displacement.

Hedra

The Hedra menu (see Figure 3.12) is one of the most unique of the primitives. There are many types of polyhedrons, and the options here will give you good control over that creation. There are Tetra, Cube, Octa, Dodec, Icos, and Star polyhedra shapes. You have even more control over these shapes with the Family Parameters section.

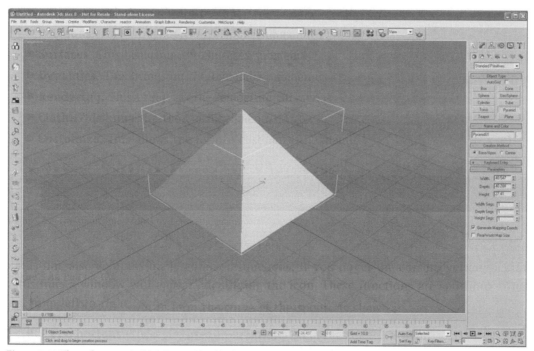

Figure 3.10 The polygon primitive Pyramid with the options showing in the Command Panel.

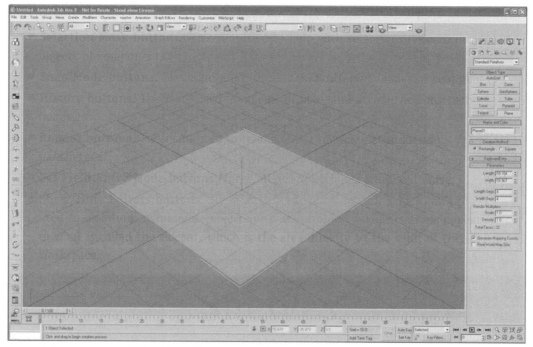

Figure 3.11 The polygon primitive Plane with the options showing in the Command Panel.

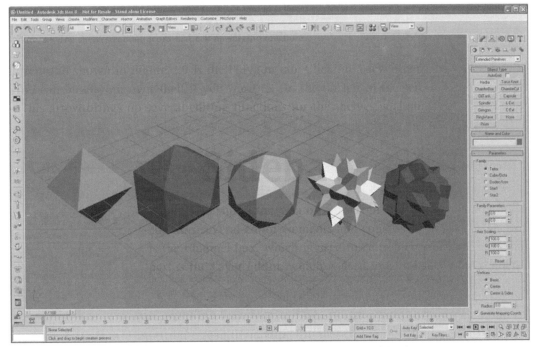

Figure 3.12 The polygon primitive Hedra with the options showing in the Command Panel.

ChamferBox

The ChamferBox primitive (see Figure 3.13) will allow you to create boxes with nicely rounded edges and corners.

OilTank

The OilTank primitive (see Figure 3.14) creates something reminiscent of an oil tank or a silo.

Spindle

Spindles (see Figure 3.15) are similar to OilTanks; however, they have a pointed top.

Figure 3.13 The polygon primitive ChamferBox with the options showing in the Command Panel.

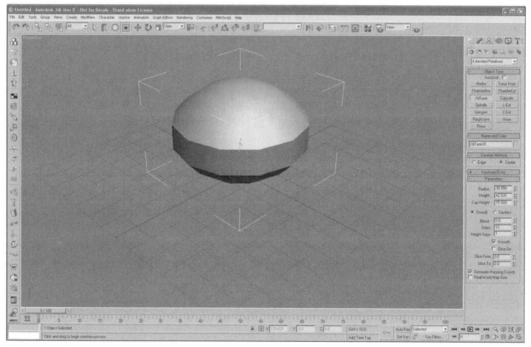

Figure 3.14 The polygon primitive OilTank with the options showing in the Command Panel.

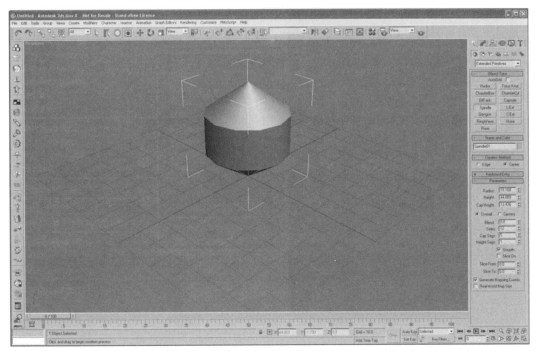

Figure 3.15 The polygon primitive Spindle with the options showing in the Command Panel.

Gengon

Gengons (see Figure 3.16) are tube-like primitives with non-rounded sides. However, you can chamfer the corners to take the edge off.

RingWave

RingWave primitives (see Figure 3.17) are almost exclusively used for quickly creating explosion shockwaves. They have some great options and animation controls for creating the shockwave from an explosion.

Prism

Figure 3.18 displays the Prism primitive showing the standard options.

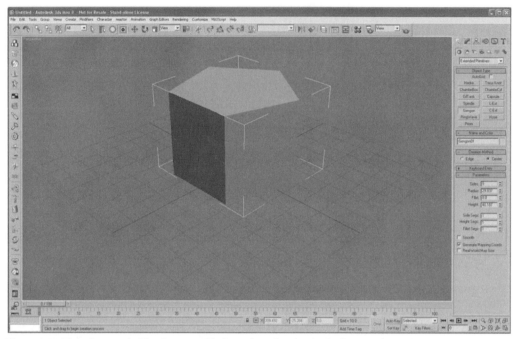

Figure 3.16 The polygon primitive Gengon with the options showing in the Command Panel.

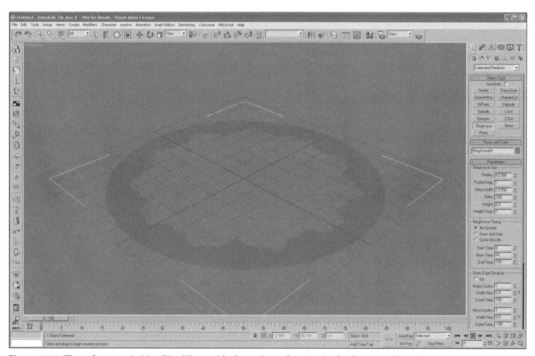

Figure 3.17 The polygon primitive RingWave with the options showing in the Command Panel.

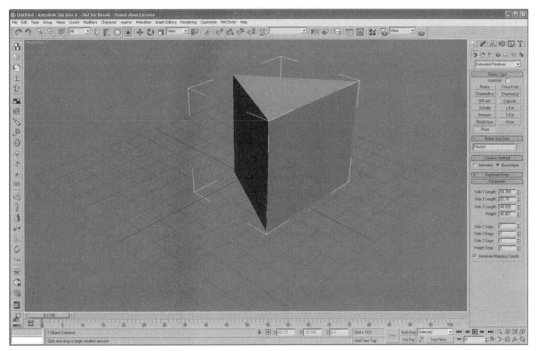

Figure 3.18 The polygon primitive Prism with the options showing in the Command Panel.

Torus Knot

The Torus Knot (see Figure 3.19) is a unique primitive, and it has some great options that can produce some very fun and useful shapes.

ChamferCyl

The ChamferCyl (see Figure 3.20) is the same as the Cylinder with the option to chamfer the top and bottom edges.

Capsule

The Capsule (see Figure 3.21) makes a convincing pill or a solid rocket booster.

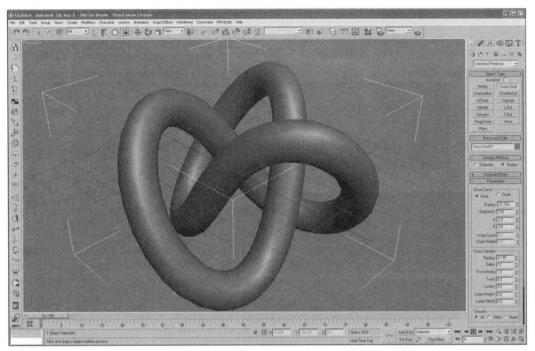

Figure 3.19 The polygon primitive Torus Knot with the options showing in the Command Panel.

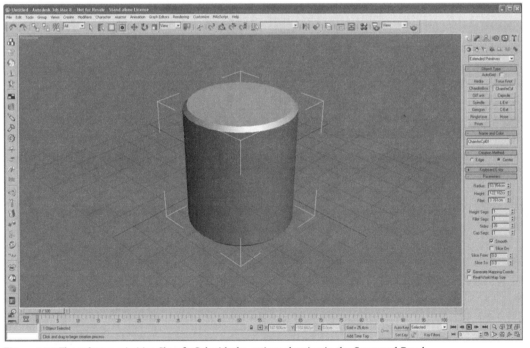

Figure 3.20 The polygon primitive ChamferCyl with the options showing in the Command Panel.

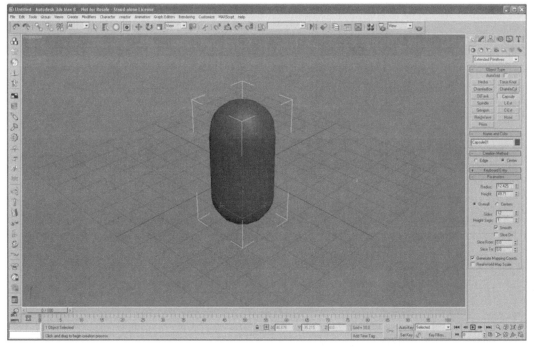

Figure 3.21 The polygon primitive Capsule with the options showing in the Command Panel.

L-Ext

The L-Ext primitive (see Figure 3.22) is best used for architectural elements, such as walls.

C-Ext

The C-Ext primitive (see Figure 3.23) is similar to the L-Ext and is best used for architectural elements.

Hose

The Hose primitive (see Figure 3.24) is one of the most complex primitives and even has options for animation. This is best used in mechanical models.

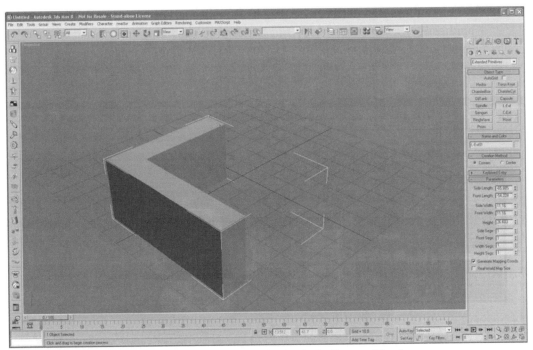

Figure 3.22 The polygon primitive L-Ext with the options showing in the Command Panel.

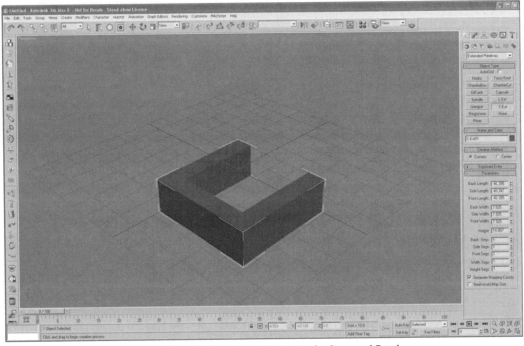

Figure 3.23 The polygon primitive C-Ext with the options showing in the Command Panel.

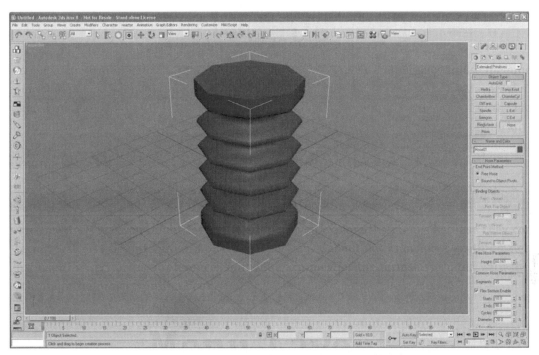

Figure 3.24 The polygon primitive Hose with the options showing in the Command Panel.

Menus

Now we are getting to the fun part! Max differs quite a bit from Maya in its paradigm for modeling and the modification of objects. This will take some getting used to, but it's easy and it fits well with the way you work in Max as a rule.

Max keeps a "stack" of the various high-level modifications that you do to your objects. While this can take some getting used to, there are some neat things you can do with this. For example, you have created a box and you are starting to edit it, but you realize you need some more subdivisions in your model. Simply move back in the stack and add the needed subdivisions to your model, and then move back up the stack and continue editing your model. There are some things to watch out for and I will point them out as we go, but for now they are not important.

As with Maya, Max is a very deep program, and we will only scratch the surface in these pages. But once we get through a few examples, you will start to get the feel of where you can find the tools that you need. Both programs are laid out fairly logically, so if you are looking for a tool or function, you will probably find it grouped with like tools or functions. I would encourage you to get one of the fine reference and or tutorial books available for Max. Having a complete guide you can refer to is priceless and will save you much frustration. Max's complete User Reference and Tutorials guides, which are searchable, are available from the Help menu.

Max's main modeling interface is on the Modify tab. The second tab from the left in the Command Panel, the Modify tab looks like a box with a bent cylinder in it. All of the functions that are in Maya's Modeling menu are found here. You can also find the same functions in the main menu under the Modifiers, Character, and Reactor menus.

Note

From here on out you may want to click on the viewport label and choose Edged Faces so that you can see the geometry you are working with. If you have an older video card, you can choose Wireframe so that your system doesn't bog down while you are working with your models.

Note

It's important to note that some of the Command Panel rollouts get very long. You can click and scroll the rollouts by moving the cursor over near the edge of the screen on a blank section of the rollout. The cursor will change to a hand icon, and you can then click and move the rollouts up or down. By holding the Control key and clicking, you can scroll the rollouts even faster.

If you don't mind a smaller viewport, you can also click and drag the edge of the Command Panel so that it is double or triple wide. This is very useful when you have a complex set of rollouts or you have multiple monitors.

Modify Tab (Polygons Menu)

Note

In this section and the next several sections and subsections, the terms in parentheses in the headings refer to menu names and terms in Maya, to help you see where to find similar menus and functions in that program.

For the next few command/tool explanations, let's create two box primitives next to each other in the viewport. Click on the Create tab in the Command Panel. Click on Box, and then click and drag out a box. Once you let go of the mouse button, you can move your mouse up to give the box depth.

Once you have both boxes ready to go, click on the Modify tab in the Command Panel. Select one of the boxes and notice that the word *Box* appears in the small window near the top of the Command Panel. This is your modifier stack window. Also notice that down below that window there are some options related to the box primitive. Those are the numbers and such used to create the selected object. You're welcome to modify them and see the results on the selected object.

Let's set Length Segs, Width Segs, and Height Segs to 4 for both boxes on the screen. Remember to turn on Edged Faces in the viewport label so you can see the results as you adjust the numbers. Using Edged Faces allows you to see the wireframe overlaying the shaded model. Once you have set the numbers to 4, just select the other box and repeat the process.

We have one more step before these primitives can really be useful. We need to set the primitives to be editable. To do this, simply click on the drop-down labeled Modifier List, directly above the stack window, and choose Edit Poly approximately nine spots down the list of modifiers. This will allow you to access individual vertices and polygons on the boxes and make the tools listed in the following figures available. Do this for both boxes.

Now let's move on to some common commands.

Attach (Combine)

You should see something that resembles Figure 3.25 at this point, with two boxes set to Edit Poly in the stack. Notice that the box on the left has been highlighted. Click on the Attach button, and then select the other (unhighlighted) box. This will combine both boxes into one object.

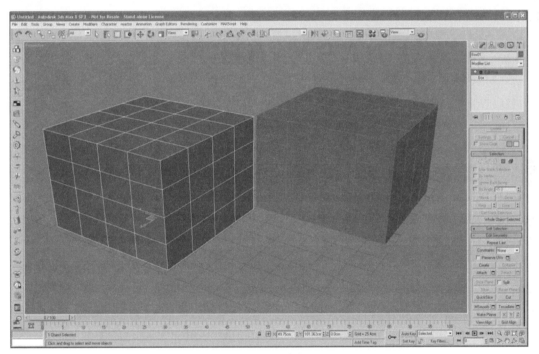

Figure 3.25 Combine both boxes into one object with the Attach button.

Note

You can also use the Group tool for grouping objects together. This is most useful for making one object out of many parts that are typically edited separately. A car would be a good example of grouping. You would edit the wheels separately from the body, but they need to stay together as a whole for moving around your scene or animating. You can also ungroup objects at any time.

Detach (Separate)

Because you just used Attach and not Group, you will need to do one step before Detach becomes active. You will see five red icons starting with three points and ending with a box in the Selection rollout. Click on the box, which stands for "select element," meaning the entire set of connected polygons are selected (see Figure 3.26).

Once the Element icon is highlighted, click on one of the boxes; it should turn red, meaning all the connected polygons are selected. At this point the Detach button will become active. Just a quick click, and you now have two separate objects again.

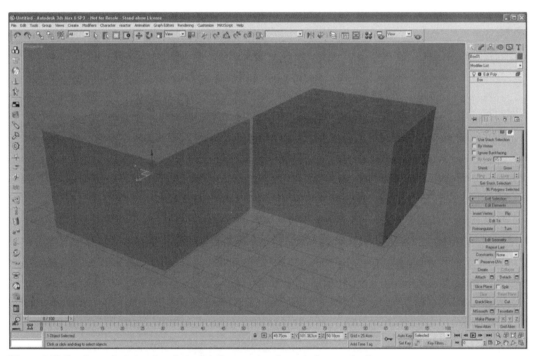

Figure 3.26 One box selected and ready to detach separates elements from each other.

Note

It's a good time to introduce a key term in Max: *Sub Object mode*. This is the mode you must be in to edit vertices, edges, and polygons. We automatically entered Element Sub Object mode when we clicked on the Element icon. To exit this mode and get back to the Object level, simply click on the highlighted Element icon or the highlighted Edit Poly stack modifier near the top of the Command Panel.

Note

Let's clean up the scene and get ready for the next set of commands/tools. Make sure you are not in Sub Object mode. Delete one of the boxes by selecting it and pressing the Delete key. Select the remaining box and move it to the center of your screen by pressing W (to enter Select and Move mode) and then sliding it around via the red, green, and blue Move Transform Gizmo icon on the object until it's roughly in the center of your viewport.

Mirror (Mirror Geometry)

Mirror (see Figure 3.27), which works on the Object level, has several options. No Clone means mirror this object only. Copy means duplicate and mirror accordingly. Instance means make a copy and mirror. And Reference means make a copy and mirror. There are subtle differences between Instance and Reference, but to go into them would be beyond the scope of this book.

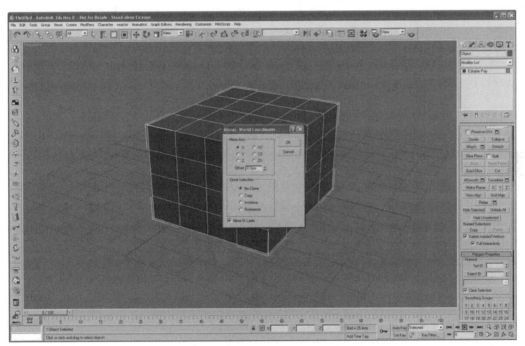

Figure 3.27 Mirror duplicates an object across a plane.

Instance and Reference are unique in that the copy made is tied to the original and edits you make to the original also happen on the Instance or Reference object. You can break this link by applying the Make Unique modifier to the stack.

MSmooth (Smooth)

Make sure the box is selected, and click the MSmooth button on the Command Panel. This will subdivide the polygons once and relax the results (see Figure 3.28).

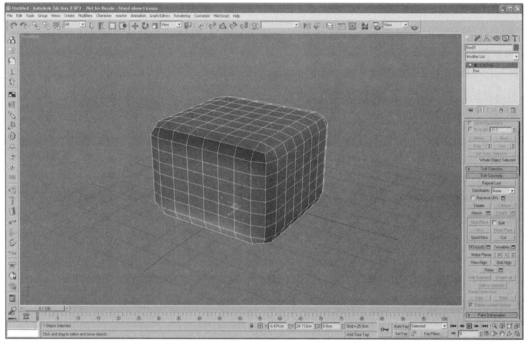

Figure 3.28 MSmooth adds polygons and smoothes the surface of an object.

NURMS (Smooth Proxy)

NURMS is a fun tool and the start of subdivision modeling (see Figure 3.29).

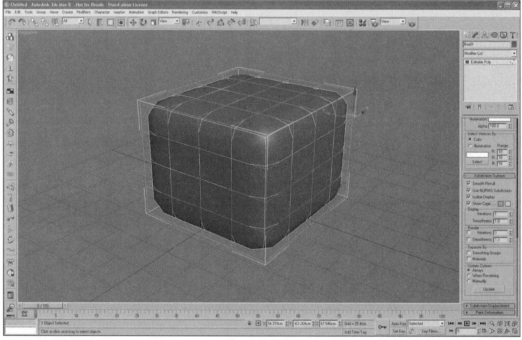

Figure 3.29 NURMS creates a smoothed version of a mesh tied to the original.

Note

At times you will want to collapse the stack. Collapsing the stack takes all of your changes and modifiers that are on the stack and collapses them to a basic mesh. This has the added benefit of freeing up memory and speeding up Max.

Using NURMS is one of those times when you will need to collapse the stack. Simply right-click in the modifier stack window and choose Collapse All. This will turn your object into an editable poly mesh.

Once the stack is collapsed, click on the Edit Vertex icon (the one with three red dots), and scroll down the Command Panel. You will see that a new rollout (Subdivision Surface) has appeared. Check the box Use NURMS Subdivision. This will smooth the object (without adding geometry) and create a "cage" around your box. You are now ready to model using subdivision surfaces.

Click and pull a point or two on the cage and watch the results. If you're extra daring, choose Face mode (the red square) in the Command Panel and extrude a face or two.

Relax (Average Vertices)

When you click on the Relax button a few times in Sub Object mode, the box starts to become a sphere (see Figure 3.30). This also works with selected vertices in Sub Object mode.

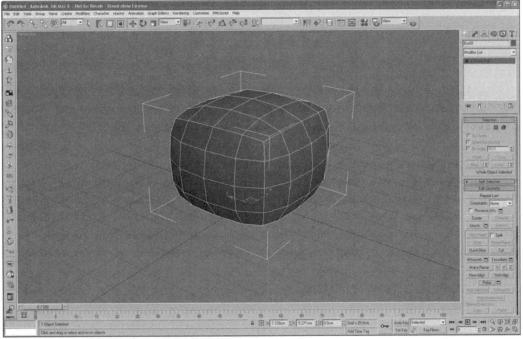

Figure 3.30 Relax smoothes without creating new geometry.

(Cleanup)

There is no equivalent to Maya's Cleanup tool in Max. You can use tools like Remove Unused Vertex and Weld to clean up most problems that arise.

Collapsing the stack in Max is also similar to the Cleanup menu in Maya. It collapses the stack or modifiers in the Commands menu and reduces the file size, and so on.

Edit Polygons

We have started to touch on editing polygons, so now let's look a bit deeper. For the next several commands/tools, we will need to be in one of the Sub Object modes; just click on the appropriate icon: 3 Dots for Vertex, Empty Triangle for Edge, and filled Red Square for Polygon.

Note

This is a good time to show you a shortcut. When you right-click on the box in the viewport, Max will bring up a context-sensitive menu that lists the Sub Object modes—making them quickly and easily accessible.

Tessellate (Subdivide)

To use the Tessellate command, enter Polygon Sub Object mode and select several polygons by clicking on them while holding down the Control key. Once you are happy with the selection, use the Tessellate button on the Command Panel. This will neatly subdivide the selection.

Note

You can change the look of the selection in the viewport by pressing the F2 key. This will toggle the selection "look" from solid red-filled polygons to red-outlined polygons. In Figure 3.31, I have toggled the selection to outline.

Cut (Split Polygon Tool)

To use the Cut command (see Figure 3.32), enter Polygon Sub Object mode, and select the Cut tool. Simply click from edge to edge to divide the faces any way you like. You will see a dashed line indicating the cut. You can also cross more than one polygon at a time in a single cut. Right-click to disable the Cut tool.

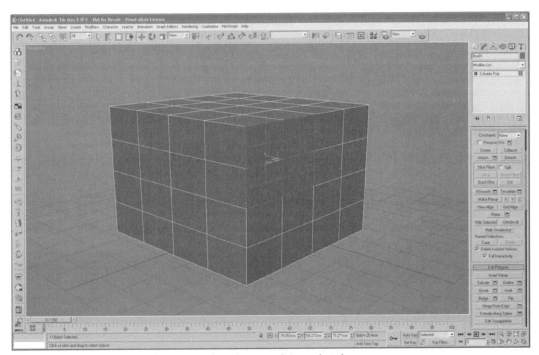

Figure 3.31 Tessellate increases the density of a polygon mesh in a selected area.

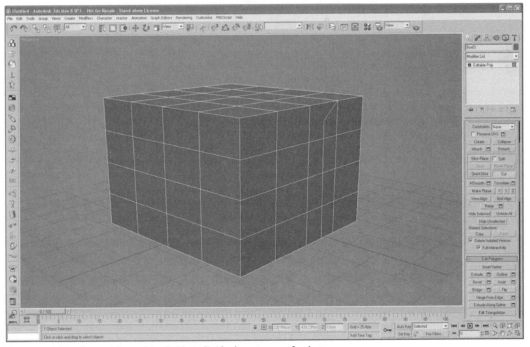

Figure 3.32 The Cut tool is used to divide individual or groups of polygons.

Extrude (Extrude Face)

You can use Extrude (see Figure 3.33) in two ways. First, in Sub Object mode, you can click on the tool and select individual or groups of polygons and extrude them interactively. The second method involves selecting polygons that you want to extrude and clicking on the small box next to the Extrude tool. This will bring up a dialog box with various options and a spinner for setting the extrusion length or depth more precisely.

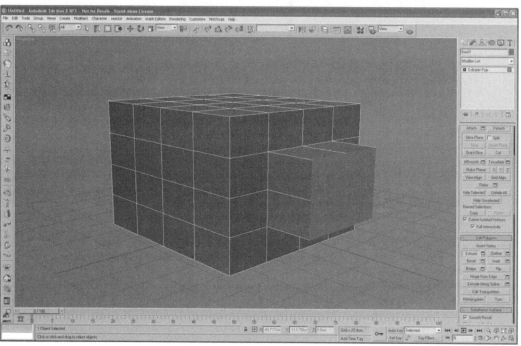

Figure 3.33 Extrude is commonly used to add features to primitive models.

Note

The small number boxes with up and down arrows on the right side are called *spinners*. Spinners are easy to manipulate. Simply click on one of the spinner arrows, and hold the mouse button down while dragging the mouse up and down.

Extrude (Extrude Edge)

The Extrude Edge tool (see Figure 3.34) works much like the Extrude Polygon tool, with one added function, chamfer. In Edge Sub Object mode click on the Extrude button and click on any edge or series of edges. While holding the mouse button down, move the mouse up and down to extrude and/or right and left to chamfer the base of the extrude.

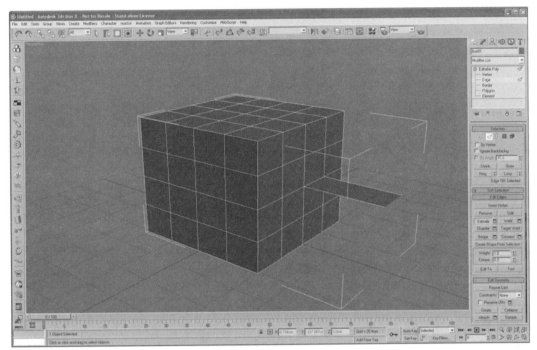

Figure 3.34 Extrude extends a plane from selected edges.

This Extrude tool also has a small box next to the button that will bring up a dialog box, where you can make more precise adjustments.

Collapse (Merge Vertices)

To access the Collapse tool (see Figure 3.35), you will need to be in Vertex Sub Object mode. Once there, select the vertices you wish to collapse into one vertex and click the Collapse button. All selected vertices will collapse to the center of the selection area and become one vertex.

As you can do with Extrude, you can also use the Collapse tool on edges and polygons.

Duplicating Polygons (Duplicate Face)

To make a copy of an individual polygon or a group of polygons (see Figure 3.36), simply select the Move command by pressing the W key, select the polygon(s) you wish to duplicate, hold the Shift key, and click and drag the polygon axis. This will "pull" off a copy of the selected polygon(s) and pop up a dialog box with the options to create a new object or create an element of the selected polygons.

A good real-life example of an element (as a part of an object) in Max would be a jawbone. It's a part of you and moves with you, but it's also a physically individual element that is a part of a whole (you, in this case).

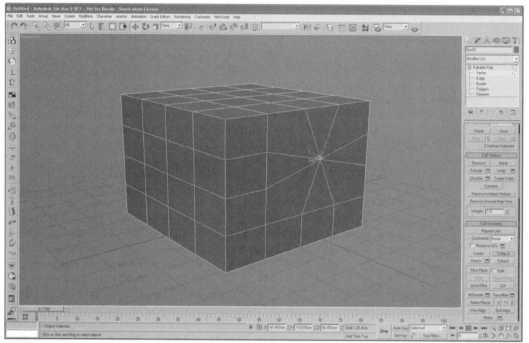

Figure 3.35 Collapse merges two or more vertices into a single vertex.

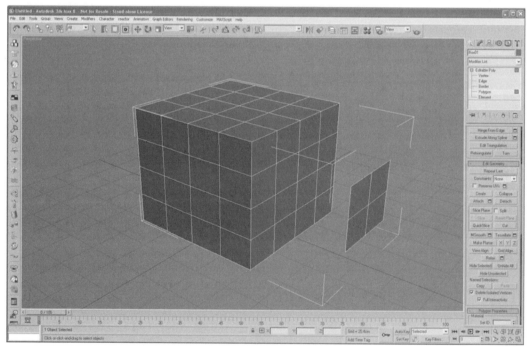

Figure 3.36 A copy of four polygons created as an element.

Detach (Extract)

Clicking on the Detach button makes the selected polygons a new object, as happened in Figure 3.26. In Figure 3.37, I have moved them out for clarity.

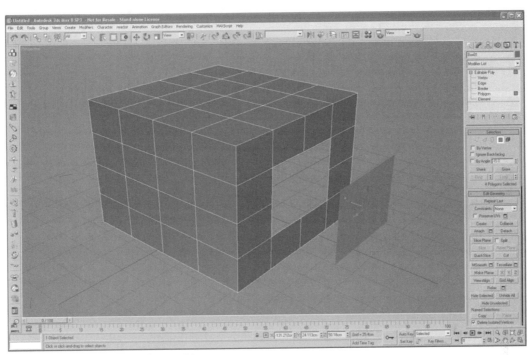

Figure 3.37 Polygons detached from a object.

With the resulting dialog box, you have the options to "cut" the faces from the object and create an element rather than a completely new object.

Push/Pull (Sculpt Geometry Tool)

For this example, I have turned off Edged Faces in the viewport label and significantly increased the number of polygons in the model to give the Push/Pull tool a lot more geometry to work with (see Figure 3.38).

Click on the Push/Pull button and paint away! You may want to change some of the settings so the effect is more subtle. Tools like this do better with more polygons than fewer. Once you are done, don't forget to press the Commit button at the bottom of the rollout.

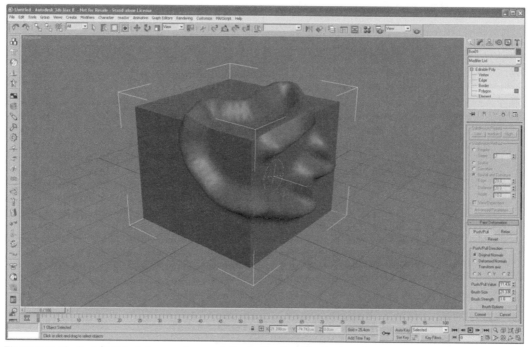

Figure 3.38 The Push/Pull tool shapes polygons similar to the way that clay is sculpted.

Selection

There are several tools that you can choose from to make selecting items easier (see Figure 3.39). The Soft Selection rollout gives you additional power over your selection. Enter Vertex Sub Object mode and enable the soft selection. Now pick any vertex and notice the selection "fall off." If you move that vertex, you will see the other vertices in the soft selection move at varying amounts depending on the strength of or proximity to the selected vertex.

Normals

To work with polygon normals (see Figure 3.40), you will need to add the Edit Normals modifier. It's about halfway down the screen under the Mesh Editing header. Unless you take special measures, all polygons in Max are single sided. If you reverse the normals, the polygon will "disappear." It isn't really gone—it's only flipped so you are seeing through the back side of the polygon.

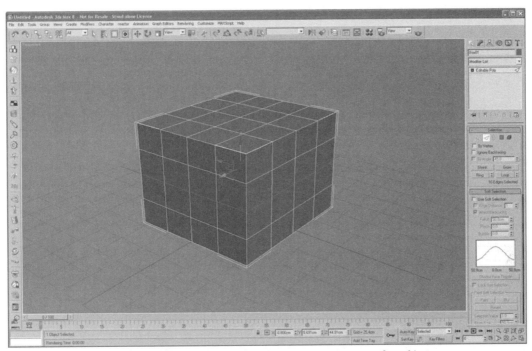

Figure 3.39 Selection gives the artist several options for selecting component types of an object.

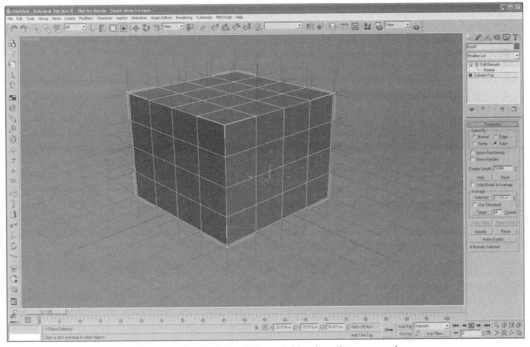

Figure 3.40 The direction a polygon surface is facing is indicated by the polygon normal.

Sidebar Tools and Editors

In Max you will find the Maya Sidebar tools and editors in the Command Panel on the right side.

Modify Tab (Channel Box/Layer Editor)

As in Maya, the object properties are adjustable if you have not collapsed the stack. By collapsing the stack, you change the primitive you started with to real geometry that you can work with beyond what is possible with simple primitives. Because primitives are merely a starting point, you will want to make some educated guesses about size and number of subdivisions needed for your project. After that it's best to collapse the stack to the Editable Poly and start your project there.

For precisely changing position, rotation, and scale, you can right-click one of the transform icons (see Figure 3.41). This will bring up a small dialog box where you can enter numbers for greater control over your 3D world.

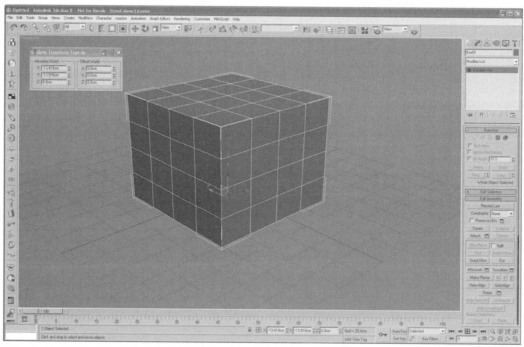

Figure 3.41 Access the Move Transform type-in by right-clicking the Move icon.

(Attribute Editor)

Max does not have one place where you will find an attribute editor. You would look in the Material Editor for material attributes and the Object Properties dialog box (see Figure 3.42) for things related to the selected object. (To get to the dialog box, right-click on the selected object and choose Properties.) You will find related attributes for tools and such in the Command Panel when working with those tools.

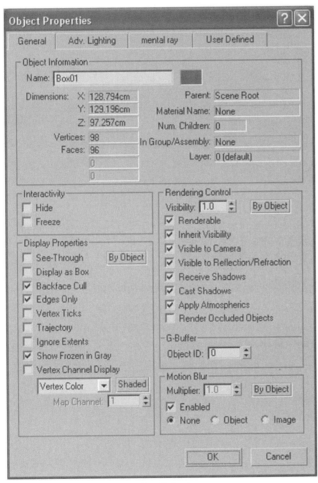

Figure 3.42 The Object Properties dialog box.

Command Panel (Tool Settings)

You will find most tool settings in Max in the Command Panel. Occasionally, more complex tools— like UV Unwrap, for example—will have additional pop-up dialog boxes. Other tools, such as those for hiding or displaying objects, can be found on the Command Panel under the Display tab (see Figure 3.43).

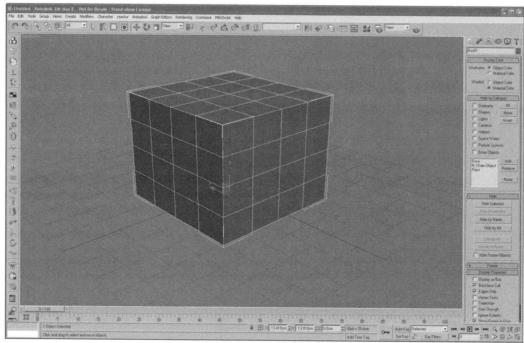

Figure 3.43 The Command Panel Display tab.

Summary

Creating objects with polygon primitives is an easy way to quickly get your models started. In this chapter, you learned about primitives and converting them to editable geometry, as well as about the stack and many tools in the Command Panel. You also learned the basics about viewports and manipulating your views to make working in 3D easier.

The polygon primitives in Max are as follows:

- Box
- Sphere
- Cylinder
- Torus
- Teapot
- Cone
- GeoSphere
- Tube
- Pyramid
- Plane
- Hedra

- ChamferBox
- OilTank
- Spindle
- Gengon
- RingWave
- Prism
- Torus Knot
- ChamferCyl
- Capsule
- L-Ext
- C-Ext
- Hose

As you can see, it's easy to create everyday objects using primitives as a starting point. Let's move on to the next chapter, where we'll explore more advanced modeling.

Chapter 3
Max

Chapter 4

Polygons Anyone?

Polygons are the foundation of most 3D modeling. While there are many ways to build a 3D model, such as NURBS, patches, and subdivision surfaces, most of them output to polygons in the final steps. Polygon rendering is common with most if not all rendering engines for games and other real-time applications. For these reasons, Maya has a robust modeling system for polygon modeling.

In Chapter 3, we discussed polygon modeling. In this chapter, those polygon-modeling concepts will be expanded upon and more tools will be introduced. Hopefully by the end of this chapter you will begin to be comfortable with polygon modeling in Maya.

Polygon Modeling

Creating a good polygon model is a process. Understanding the process and having a clear vision of the final goal are important to completing a good model. The first step is to plan your model-building process. I find it very helpful to go through the process in my mind first before I approach building it on the computer. For example, the project in this chapter will be to build a toy wagon. One of the challenges will be to build the wagon's bed. The bed has a lip along the top that curls out and over the edge. It also has rounded corners along the bottom. The obvious solution is to create the bed from a cube, but how do you create a cube that is rounded on one side and flat on the other?

In order to find a solution to the wagon bed problem, I thought about each of the tools that could be used to modify a cube in the way I needed it for the end result. If I was unfamiliar with a particular tool, I did some experimenting to see what that tool could do. I also tried changing some of the tool settings to get the right result. I decided that the Smooth tool would work best for rounding the edges, but the Smooth tool rounded too much from a simple single-sided polygon cube. I found that to get the rounded edges I wanted, I had to have a cube that was subdivided in just the right way.

To get the flat top of the bed, I decided to delete the top of the cube down to where it wasn't rounded. That meant I had to build the cube high enough to compensate for the part that I would cut off. Planning and experimenting helped me find a workable solution to the wagon bed.

Building the Wagon Bed

The bed of the wagon is basically a rectangular cube shape. You'll begin the modeling process by creating a cube. Make the cube four units wide and four units deep to start. This will help when you create the lip along the top of the bed. Later, the cube will be expanded to the rectangular shape of the bed.

1. Create a polygon cube that is two units high and four units wide and deep. Subdivide the cube in width and depth by 8 and in height by 4, as shown in Figure 4.1.

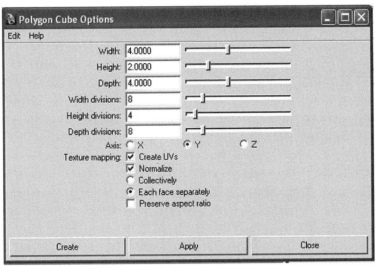

Figure 4.1 Create a polygon cube for the wagon bed.

2. Go to the Front view and change the selection mode to Edge.

3. Use the bounding box to select the edges in the middle of the cube, as shown in Figure 4.2.

Note

A good rule of thumb when creating polygon models is to keep the model as simple as possible so you don't create too many polygons. The more polygons in a model, the longer it will take to render. In this example, the middle of the cube does not need the tight subdivision but the corners do. Deleting the middle subdivisions will make the model more manageable in the future.

4. Now go back, and with the Shift key held down, deselect the edges of the very center as well as the horizontal edges of the model, leaving just the four vertical edges selected, as shown in Figure 4.3.

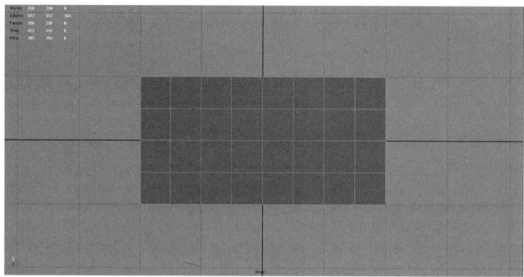

Figure 4.2 Select the edges in the middle of the cube.

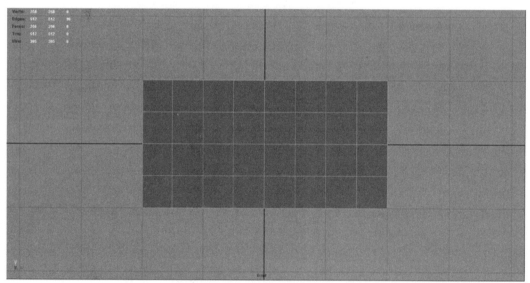

Figure 4.3 Deselect the center and horizontal edges.

5. Delete these edges by pressing the Delete key.
6. Change the selection mode to Vertex, and select the vertices of the deleted edges, as shown in Figure 4.4.
7. Delete the selected vertices.

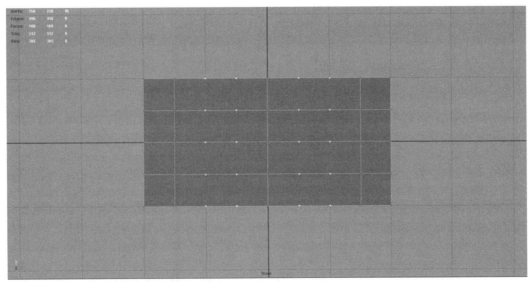

Figure 4.4 Select the vertices of the deleted edges.

8. Now change the view to the Side view, and delete the unneeded edges and vertices in the same way that you did from the Front view. The resulting model should now look similar to Figure 4.5.

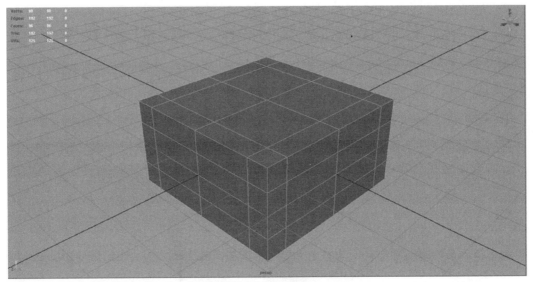

Figure 4.5 Delete the edges and vertices from the side of the model.

9. Bring up the Smooth Options box from the Mesh menu.

10. Set Division Levels to 2 and apply smoothing to the cube, as shown in Figure 4.6.

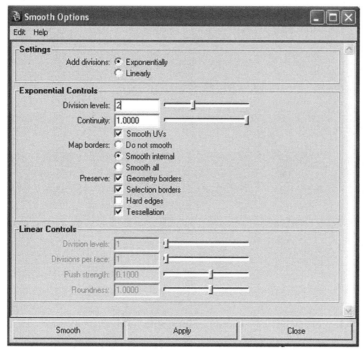

Figure 4.6 Apply smoothing to the polygon cube.

11. Go back to the Front view and change the selection mode to Faces.

12. Select the faces of the rounded top of the cube, as shown in Figure 4.7.

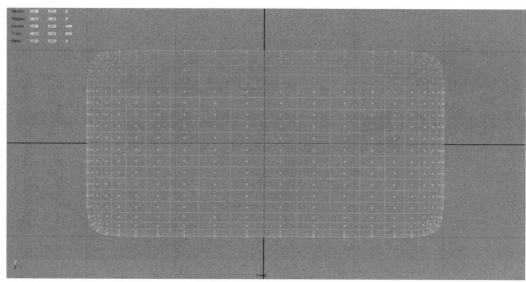

Figure 4.7 Select the faces of the top of the cube.

13. Delete the faces so the top of the model is now flat.

14. The wagon will have a decorative indentation along its sides. Select five rows of faces below the top two rows.

15. Use the Scale manipulator to scale in the selected faces to create the decorative indentation, as shown in Figure 4.8.

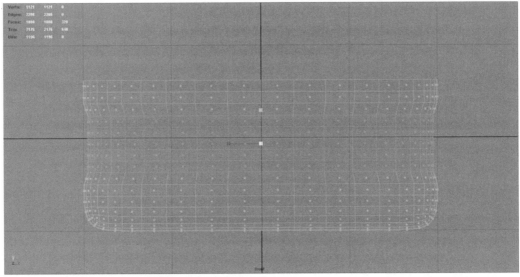

Figure 4.8 Scale the faces in along the sides of the wagon bed.

16. By default, polygons in Maya are one-sided and face a specific direction. On a cube, all of the polygons are facing outward. To see how this works, you need to turn on Backface Culling. Having Backface Culling turned on will make the polygons visible only from the side they are facing. Backface Culling is located in the Shading menu of the Panel menu, as shown in Figure 4.9. It only works if you are viewing a flat-shaded or smooth-shaded object.

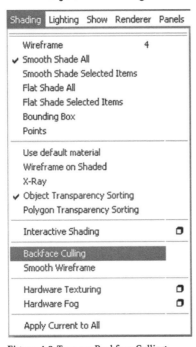

Figure 4.9 Turn on Backface Culling.

17. As you can see, only the outside of the bed is viewable. You could make the polygons double-sided, but that would give the metal of the wagon bed no thickness because polygons are flat planes with no thickness. Instead, change the selection mode to Object and duplicate the wagon bed.

18. Go to Normals, Reverse to flip the normals from facing out to facing in toward the center of the duplicated cube, as shown in Figure 4.10. A face normal refers to the direction the face is facing.

19. To create the thickness of the metal for the wagon, scale the duplicate cube using the Channel box. Type in 0.995 in the Scale X, Scale Y, and Scale Z boxes, as shown in Figure 4.11.

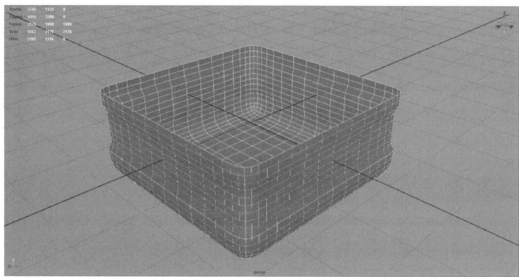

Figure 4.10 Reverse the normals of the duplicated cube.

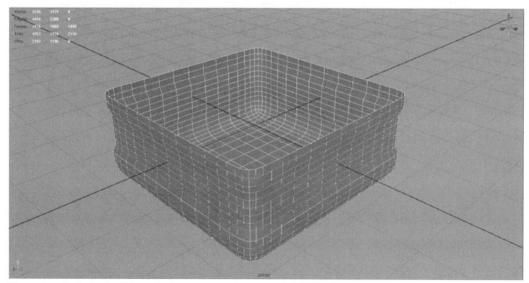

Figure 4.11 Scale the duplicate cube in.

20. Go to the Front view, and move the duplicate cube up slightly to match the top lip of the original cube, as shown in Figure 4.12. Now the wagon bed has both an inside and an outside.

Figure 4.12 Line up the duplicate cube with the top of the original.

21. The next process is to create an overhanging lip around the top of the wagon. You will use Extrude from the Edit Mesh menu to do this. First, however, you will need to select the top edges around the inner cube. An easy way to select those edges is to use a tool called Select Using Constraints, which is found under the Select menu. Change the view to Perspective and the selection mode to Edge, and choose Select Using Constraints.

22. In the Polygon Selection Constraint on Edges box, click OnBorder under Properties and then All and Next under Constrain. The top edges of the inner cube should now be selected, as shown in Figure 4.13.

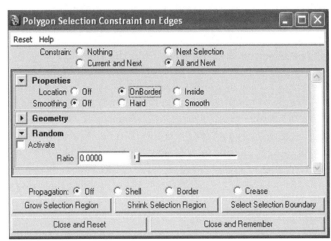

Figure 4.13 Use Select Using Constraints to select the top edges of the inner cube.

Note

For the next several steps, you will be extruding the edge of the cube and then modifying the extrusion by using the Channel box.

23. First, extrude the selected edges.

24. In the Channel box, change Translate Y to 0.02, Scale X to 1.02, and Scale Z to 1.02, as shown in Figure 4.14.

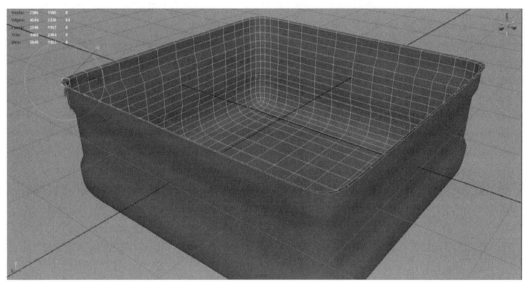

Figure 4.14 Extrude the lip up and outward.

Note

Maya remembers the last function performed with its settings. When you have to repeat a function, you just need to press the G key to do so.

25. Extrude the edge again by either selecting Extrude Edge from the Edit Polygons menu or pressing the G key.

26. Modify the extrusion by changing Translate Y to −0.02, Scale X to 1.02, and Scale Z to 1.02, as shown in Figure 4.15.

27. Extrude the edge again, and this time change Translate Y to −0.04, Scale X to 1.01, and Scale Z to 1.01. The model should look similar to Figure 4.16.

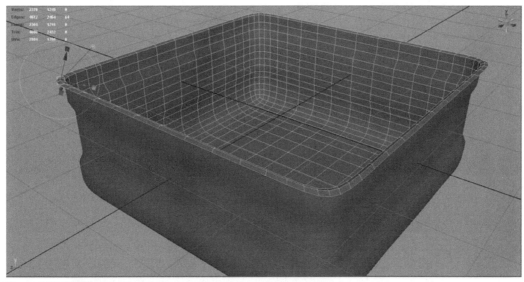

Figure 4.15 Modify the extruded edges down and out from the wagon bed.

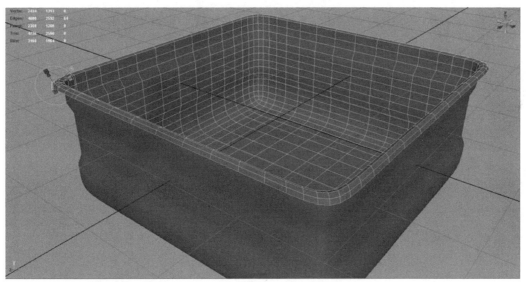

Figure 4.16 Extrude the lip of the wagon down to start forming the curl of the edge.

28. Extrude once again, and change Translate Y to −0.04, Scale X to 0.99, and Scale Z to 0.99 to start curling the lip back toward the wagon, as shown in Figure 4.17.

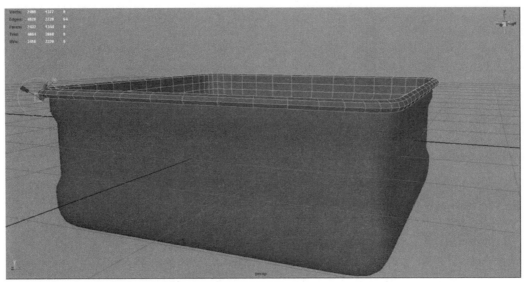

Figure 4.17 Curl the lip back toward the wagon bed.

29. Now the extrusions are starting to look like the lip of a wagon. Extrude once more, and change Translate Y to −0.02, Scale X to 0.98, and Scale Z to 0.98 (see Figure 4.18).

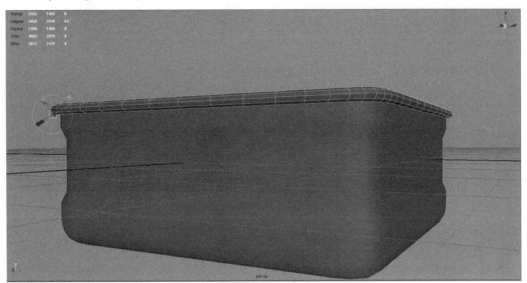

Figure 4.18 Continue the curl of the lip toward the wagon bed.

30. The inside and outside portions of the wagon bed need to be joined together for some of the future modifications. First, extrude the edge again and change Translate Y to 0.1. Figure 4.19 shows the result after I have zoomed into the lip in the Perspective view.

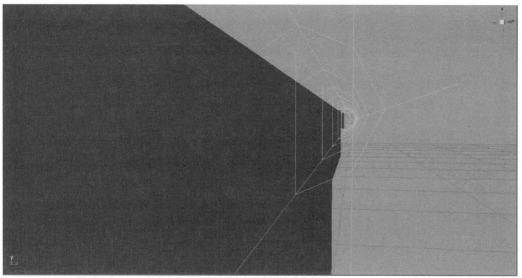

Figure 4.19 Extrude the edge upward.

31. Now, extrude the edge one more time, and change Scale X to 0.986 and Scale Z to 0.986 to line it up closely with the edge of the outward-facing polygon part of the wagon bed, as shown in Figure 4.20.

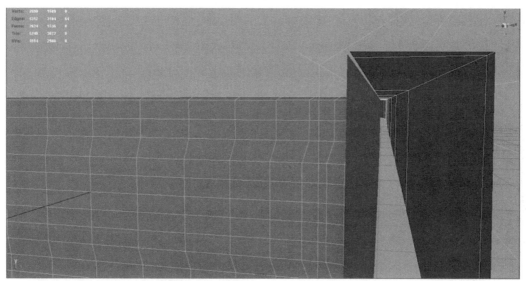

Figure 4.20 Extrude the edge in toward the wagon bed.

32. To join the inner and outer portions of the wagon bed, you first have to combine the two models into a single object. Change the selection mode to Object and select both objects by dragging a selection bounding box over part of both objects. Use the Combine command, as shown in Figure 4.21.

Figure 4.21 Combine the two meshes into a single mesh.

33. Change the selection mode to Vertex.

34. Use Select Using Constraints to find the border vertices similar to finding the border edges in Step 21, as shown in Figure 4.22. Press Close and Reset.

35. Bring up the Merge Vertex Options dialog box found in the Edit Polygons menu. Set Distance to 0.03 or 0.035 and press Apply to merge the vertices between the inner and outer mesh, forming one continuous mesh (see Figure 4.23). Check to make sure all the vertices along the edge are merged.

36. The wagon bed is now ready to elongate into a rectangular shape. Go to the Side view and change the selection mode to Faces.

37. Select the faces on the left side of the wagon, excluding the row next to the center of the model.

38. Extrude the faces and change Translate Z in the Channel box to 0.5, as shown in Figure 4.24.

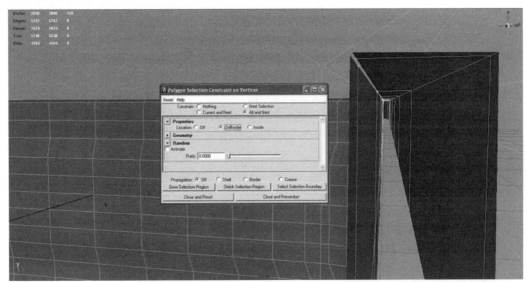

Figure 4.22 Select the vertices along the edge of both meshes.

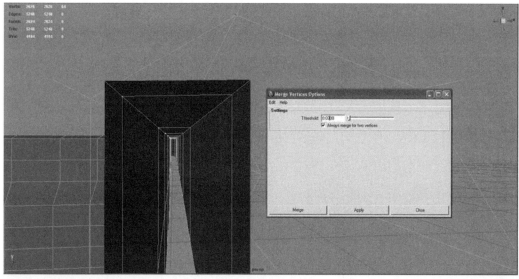

Figure 4.23 Merge the vertices of the inner and outer meshes.

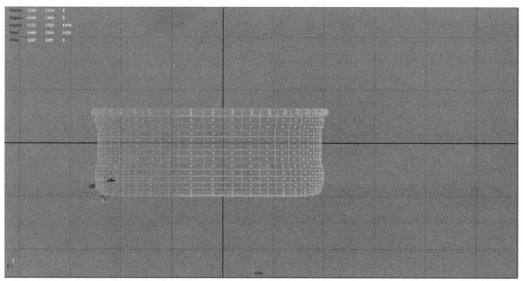

Figure 4.24 Extrude the faces of the wagon bed toward the left of the screen.

39. Extrude and translate Z 0.5 three more times.

40. Select the faces on the right side of the model, excluding the row next to the center.

41. Extrude the faces and change Translate Z to −0.5.

42. Repeat step 41 three more times, until your model looks similar to Figure 4.25.

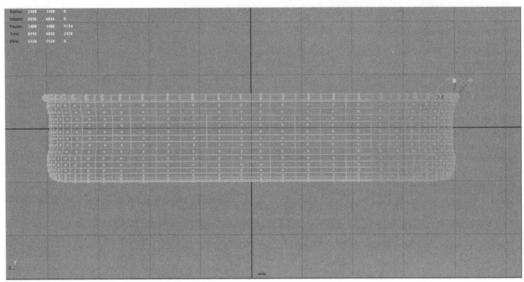

Figure 4.25 Extrude the edge in toward the wagon bed.

Note

You may have noticed that although the main body of the wagon looks smooth, the lip seems faceted. This is because the smoothing process smoothed the edges of the body, but the lip was extruded after the smoothing process. You can adjust the appearance of a polygon model by changing the properties of its edges. Hard edges make polygon models look faceted. Soft edges make polygon models take on a more rounded appearance.

43. Bring up the Set Normal Angle options from the Normals menu.

44. Change the selection mode to Edge and select all of the edges of the wagon bed.

45. Set Angle to 180 and click OK, as shown in Figure 4.26.

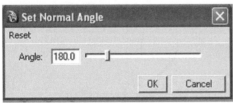

Figure 4.26 Soften the edges of the model.

46. Not all of the edges need to be softened. The edges along the top and bottom of the indentation on the wagon bed's sides should be hard. Select those edges, then change Angle to 0 and click OK, as shown in Figure 4.27.

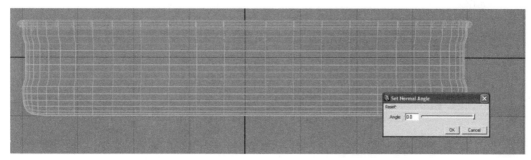

Figure 4.27 Make the upper and lower indentation edges hard.

The wagon bed is now complete. Thinking ahead saved a lot of time with building the model. Using the Channel box for the extrusion modifications enabled accurate changes. Creating the wagon bed as a square instead of a rectangle helped to keep the smoothed corners symmetrical. Joining the inner and outer meshes kept the extrusions of the bed from creating unwanted polygons along the edges of the two meshes.

Creating the Wagon Wheels

Now that you have a wagon bed, you can start creating some of the other parts of the wagon. Next will be the wagon wheels.

1. Create a polygon cylinder for the wheel. Set Radius to 1 and Height to .5. Set Axis Divisions to 32, Height Divisions to 15, and Cap Divisions to 5 (see Figure 4.28).

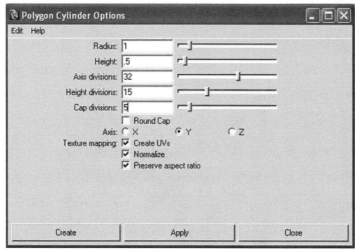

Figure 4.28 Create a new polygon cylinder object for the wheels.

2. It will be a lot easier to work on the wheel if the wagon bed is not hanging around. A simple and easy way to focus on a single object is to make it the only object visible. With the wheel selected, go to Show, Isolate Select, View Selected, as shown in Figure 4.29.

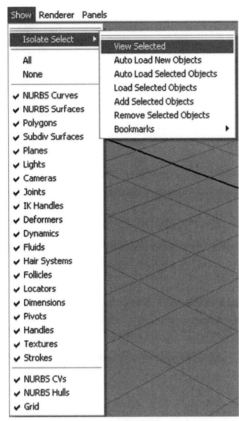

Figure 4.29 View Selected isolates the selected object.

3. Change the selection mode to Faces and go to the Front view.

4. Select every other row of faces starting one in from the side, as shown in Figure 4.30.

5. To form the tread on the tires, change Scale Y to 0.97 and Scale Z to 0.97 in the Channel box, as shown in Figure 4.31.

6. Maya has a helpful feature that allows you to expand or shrink a selection. You press the > key for expanding and the < key for shrinking. In this case, you want to expand your selection. Press the > key twice so that all of the tire tread is selected.

7. Use the Scale manipulator to scale the selected faces inward in the X axis, as shown in Figure 4.32.

8. Press the > key again to expand your selection to the first ring of faces on the sidewall of the tire.

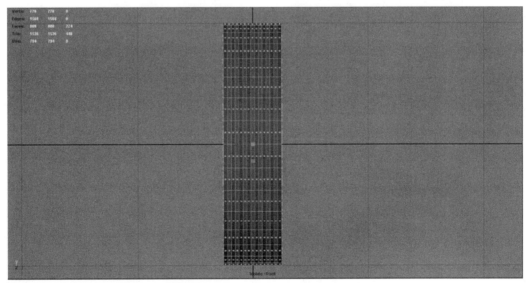

Figure 4.30 Select every other row of faces.

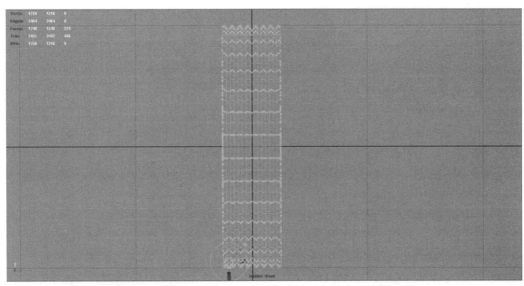

Figure 4.31 Create the tread on the tires.

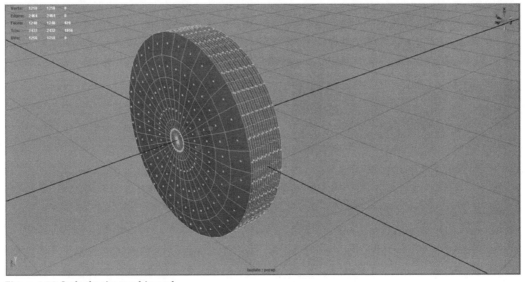

Figure 4.32 Scale the tire tread inward.

9. Scale the new selection outward in the X axis, as shown in Figure 4.33, to give the tire's sidewall an inflated bulge.

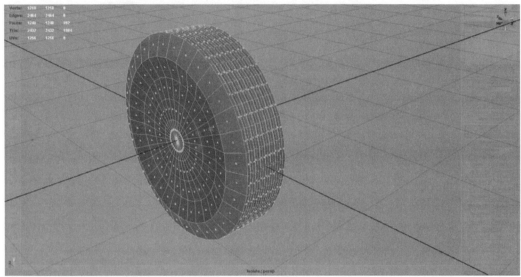

Figure 4.33 Scale the tire outward in the X axis.

10. Expand the selection again and scale the tire again in the X axis to continue the taper of the tire inward to the rims (see Figure 4.34).

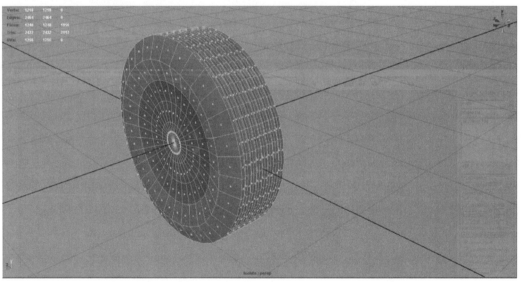

Figure 4.34 Continue the taper of the tire to the rims.

11. Expand the selection again.

12. Extrude faces to create a lip for the rim of the tire and scale inward in the X axis, as shown in Figure 4.35.

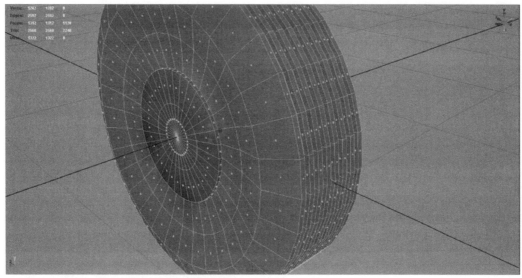

Figure 4.35 Create a ridge around the rim of the tire.

13. Expand the selection again and scale outward in the X axis to create a deep swell for the rim of the tire, as shown in Figure 4.36.

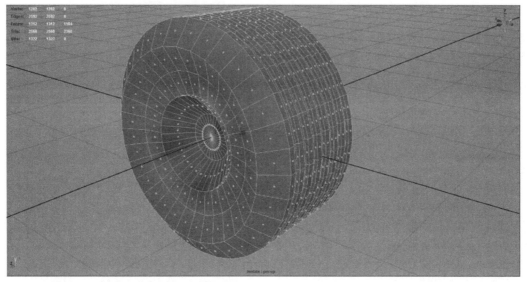

Figure 4.36 Create a deep swell for the rim of the tire.

14. Expand the selection one more time, and then scale the tire inward in the X axis to the desired thickness of the tire. The finished tire should look similar to that shown in Figure 4.37.

15. If you look around the rim of the tire, you may notice some odd shading issues. These were caused by the extrusion process; they need to be fixed. The problem is in a variableness of the edges around the extrusion. Change the selection mode to Vertices and select all of the vertices of the extruded rim.

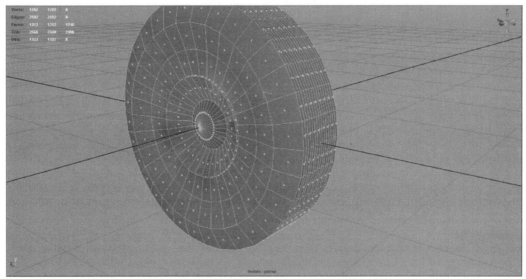

Figure 4.37 Scale the tire inward to finish shaping it.

16. Go to Select, Convert Selection, To Contained Edges, as shown in Figure 4.38, to convert the selection to edges. Often it is easier to select one component and convert it to another. This is particularly true for selecting edges.

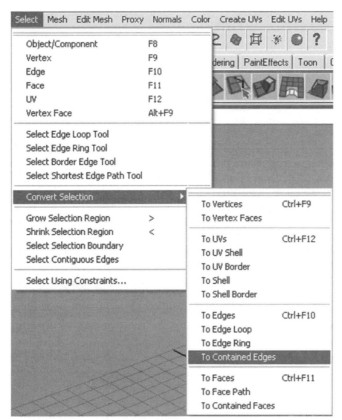

Figure 4.38 Convert the selected vertices to edges.

17. Make all of the edges hard, as shown in Figure 4.39. This should fix the abnormal shading issues around the rim.

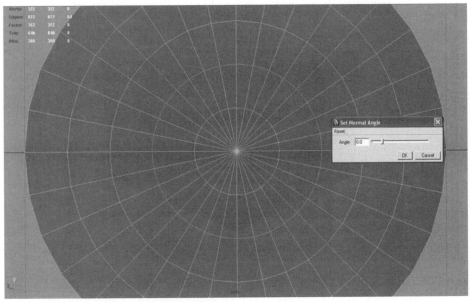

Figure 4.39 Make the edges around the rim hard.

18. Bring the wagon bed back into the view by selecting View, Isolate Selected, View Selected.

19. Move the tire to where it should be located below the wagon bed by changing Translate X to 1.5, Translate Y to −2.1, and Translate Z to 3 in the Channel box, as shown in Figure 4.40.

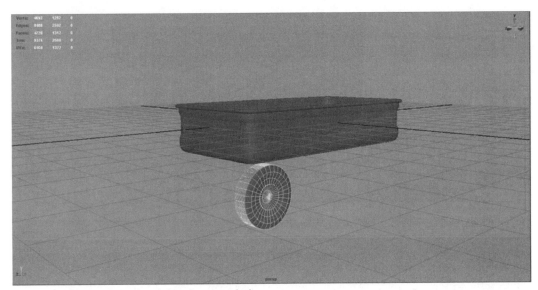

Figure 4.40 Put the tire in place below the wagon bed.

20. Duplicate the wheel by pressing Ctrl+D on the keyboard. Ctrl+D is a hot key for duplicating objects. To work, the selection must be in Object mode. It creates an exact duplicate of the object right over the top of the existing object. Make sure when you use the Duplicate command that you only press the key one time, otherwise you may make multiple copies of the object without realizing it.

21. Move the new duplicate wheel to the other side of the wagon bed by changing Translate X to −1.5.

22. Duplicate the original wheel again and move this duplicate to the back of the wagon bed by changing Translate Z to −3.

23. Duplicate the wheel one more time and this time change Translate X to −1.5 and Translate Z to −3. The wheels should now be positioned beneath each corner of the wagon bed, as shown in Figure 4.41.

Figure 4.41 Place the wheels below the corners of the wagon bed.

The wagon is starting to take shape. You have the wagon bed and wheels modeled. All you need to do to finish is to connect the wheels to the wagon and build the tongue out to the handle. In the next section, you will connect the wheels and the wagon together.

Connecting the Wheels to the Bed

To connect the wheels to the wagon bed, you will require many individual pieces. The wheels will need to be connected with axles, and the axles will need to be attached to the wagon. The front axle will need to have a swivel attachment so the front wheels can be turned, while the rear axle can be attached directly to the bed because the rear wheels don't turn.

1. Start by creating an axle. Create a polygon cylinder in the X axis with a radius of 0.025 and a height of 3. Set Axis Divisions to 16, Height Divisions to 4, and Cap Divisions to 1, as shown in Figure 4.42.

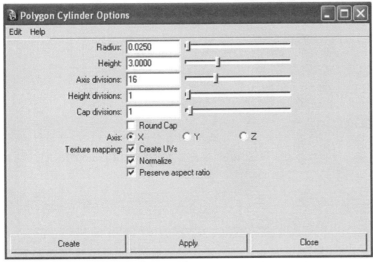

Figure 4.42 Create an axle for the wagon.

2. Move the axle to fit between the two front tires by changing Translate Y to −2.1 and Translate Z to 3 in the Channel box, as shown in Figure 4.43.

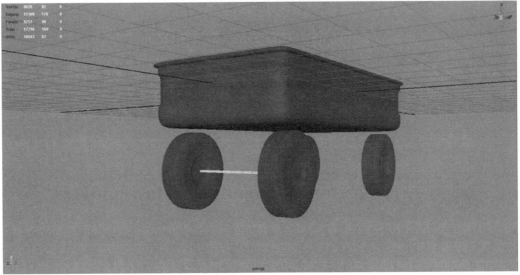

Figure 4.43 Place the axle between the two front tires.

3. Duplicate the axle and move the duplicate to the back wheels by changing Translate Z to −3 in the Channel box, as shown in Figure 4.44.

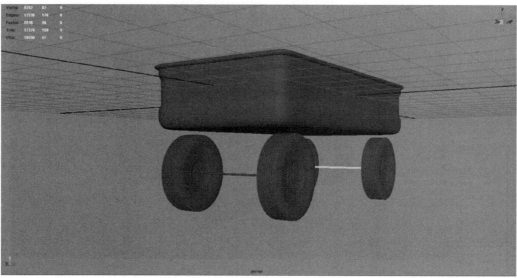

Figure 4.44 Move a duplicate of the front axle to the back.

4. Create a polygon prism with a length of .5 and a side length of 1.5, as shown in Figure 4.45. Set Number of Sides to 3, Height Divisions to 1, and Cap Divisions to 0. Create it in the X axis.

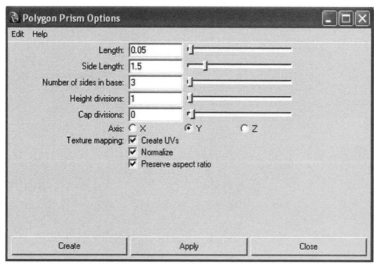

Figure 4.45 Create a polygon prism.

5. Next, bevel the edges of the prism, using Bevel from the Edit Mesh menu, as shown in Figure 4.46. The Bevel function is used to give objects a beveled edge appearance. When used on an object, it will bevel all of the object's

edges based on the options in the Bevel Options dialog box. The tool can also be used to bevel selected components of an object.

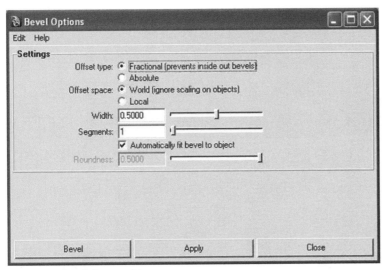

Figure 4.46 Bevel the new object.

6. Move the prism object to the front axle by changing Translate X to 1, Translate Y to −1.5, and Translate Z to 3, as shown in Figure 4.47.

Figure 4.47 Place the new object to connect with the front axle.

7. The corner of the triangle at the bottom of the new object is too sharp. Change the selection mode to Faces, and select the faces at the bottom of the triangle.

8. Scale the selected faces in the Z axis to flatten the corner (see Figure 4.48).

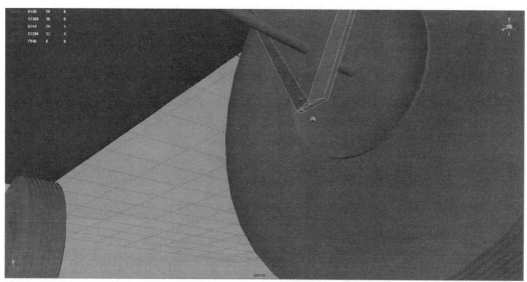

Figure 4.48 Flatten the bottom of the triangle.

9. Next, use the Move tool to move the selected faces up closer to the axle, as shown in Figure 4.49.

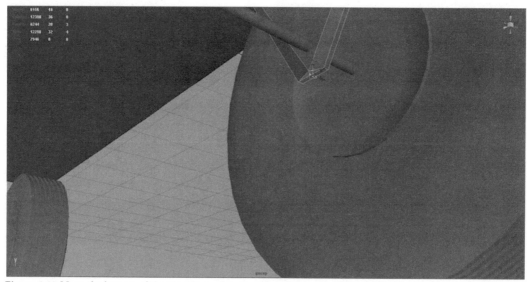

Figure 4.49 Move the bottom of the triangle up closer to the axle.

10. Duplicate the triangle and move it next to the other wheel by changing Translate X to −1 in the Channel box.

11. Duplicate the triangle again and move it to the back axle by changing Translate Z to −3.

12. Duplicate the triangle one more time and move it to the remaining wheel by changing Translate X to −1 and Translate Z to −3. The result should look similar to Figure 4.50.

Figure 4.50 Place a triangle by each wheel.

13. Go to the back-right triangle and change its selection mode to Faces.

14. Rotate the selected faces to about a 45-degree angle, as shown in Figure 4.51.

Figure 4.51 Rotate the top of the triangle.

15. Use the Move tool to pull the top of the triangle up until it touches the bottom of the wagon bed, as shown in Figure 4.52.

Figure 4.52 Move the top of the triangle up to the bottom of the wagon bed.

16. Extrude the selected faces and change Translate X to −1 in the Channel box, as shown in Figure 4.53.

Figure 4.53 Extrude the selected faces to the center of the wagon.

17. Now select the top faces of the left-hand triangle and rotate them to the right 45 degrees.

18. Extrude the faces and change Translate X to 1 in the Channel box. The back wheels are now attached to the wagon bed, as shown in Figure 4.54.

Figure 4.54 Attach the left triangle to the wagon bed.

19. Repeat the process of rotating and extruding the front triangles similar to the way you did the back triangles, except do not move them up to the wagon bed. You need to build a swivel for the front tires and wagon tongue. The wagon should now look similar to that shown in Figure 4.55.

Figure 4.55 Connect the triangles in the front of the wagon.

20. Create a new polygon cylinder in the Y axis with the following options: Radius 1.5, Height 0.0250, Axis Divisions 8, Height Divisions 1, and Cap Divisions 2, as shown in Figure 4.56.

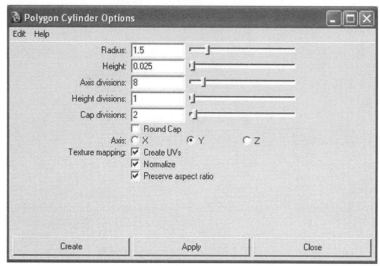

Figure 4.56 Create a new cylinder object.

21. Change Scale Z in the Channel box to 0.5.

Change Translate Y to −1.01 and Translate Z to 3, as shown in Figure 4.57. This plate will form the top of the swivel.

Figure 4.57 Place the top of the swivel next to the bottom of the bed.

22. Create a new polygon cylinder in the Y axis with the following options: Radius .25, Height .1, Axis Divisions 16, Height Divisions 1, and Cap Divisions 1, as shown in Figure 4.58.

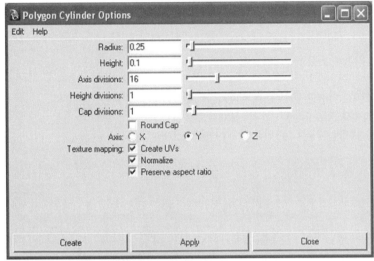

Figure 4.58 Create the middle of the swivel.

23. Move the middle of the swivel into position by changing Translate Y to 1.05 and Translate Z to 3, as shown in Figure 4.59.

Figure 4.59 Place the middle of the swivel centered under the plate.

The main body of the wagon is now finished. All that remains is to build and attach the tongue. By now you should be starting to get the hang of creating polygon objects and placing them in a model using the Channel box. You should also be getting familiar with several of the tools used to modify and extend polygon objects.

Building the Tongue

The tongue is attached to the wagon at the front swivel with a hinge, which enables the tongue to move up and down and turn the wagon left and right. You will start by creating the hinge and then building the tongue and handle.

1. To start building the hinge, you will need an object similar to the triangles used to connect the wagon with the axles. Rather than creating a new object when there is an existing object that is already the approximate shape needed for the hinge, use the existing object. First, select the two wheel mounts and combine them into a single object, as shown in Figure 4.60.

Figure 4.60 Combine the two front wheel mounts into a single object.

2. Duplicate the wheel mounts.

3. Center the pivot of the new object by selecting Modify, Center Pivot, as shown in Figure 4.61. You need to center the pivot because when the object was combined, the pivot was set at the origin instead of the center of the object.

Figure 4.61 Center the pivot of the new object.

4. In the Channel box, change Scale X to 0.5, Scale Y to 0.25, and Scale Z to 0.5 to shrink the new object to the correct size for the hinge mount (see Figure 4.62).

5. Move the new object up to connect with the wheel mounts, as shown in Figure 4.63.

6. The hinge needs an axle. Duplicate the front wheel axle.

7. Scale the new axle in the X axis to 0.4, and translate it up to the hinge by changing Translate Y to −1.3, as shown in Figure 4.64.

8. Now for the tongue. Create a new polygon cylinder in the Z axis with the following options: Radius 0.2000, Height 6.0000, Axis Divisions 16, Height Divisions 3, and Cap Divisions 1, as shown in Figure 4.65.

Figure 4.62 Scale the new object to the correct size for the hinge.

Chapter 4
Maya

Figure 4.63 Connect the hinge with the swivel.

Figure 4.64 Create an axle for the hinge.

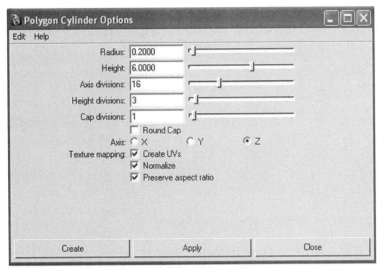

Figure 4.65 Create a new polygon cylinder for the tongue.

9. Connect the tongue with the hinge by changing Translate Y to −1.3 and Translate Z to 5.75, as shown in Figure 4.66.

Figure 4.66 Place the tongue on the hinge.

10. Change the selection mode of the cylinder to Vertex and slide the vertices in the center of the tongue toward the wagon, as shown in Figure 4.67.

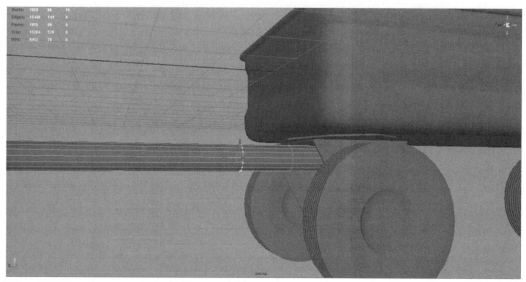

Figure 4.67 Move the vertices in the tongue toward the wagon.

11. Select the vertices at the end of the tongue near the hinge and scale them in vertically, as shown in Figure 4.68.

Figure 4.68 Scale the vertices near the hinge.

12. Next, you need to create another cylinder object for the handle. Create the cylinder in the X axis with the following options: Radius 0.2000, Height 1, Axis Divisions 16, Height Divisions 6, and Cap Divisions 1, as shown in Figure 4.69.

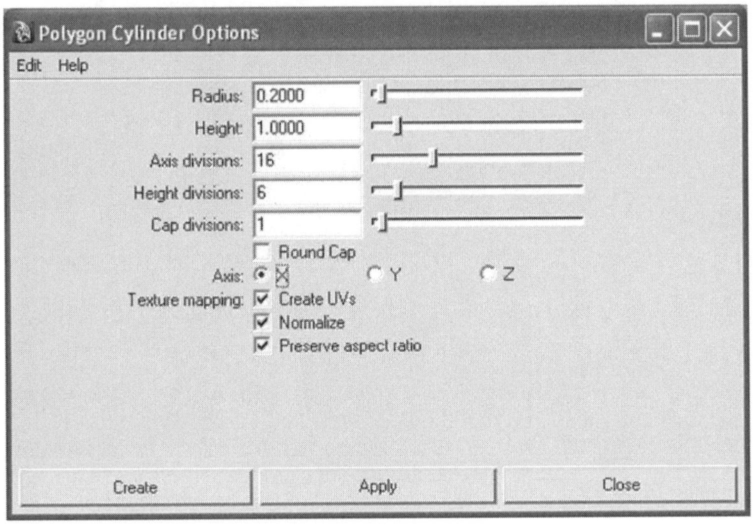

Figure 4.69 Create a cylinder for the handle

13. You will only need half of the handle right now because it will be mirrored later. Change the selection mode to Faces and select the faces on the left side of the handle, looking from the front of the wagon, as shown in Figure 4.70.

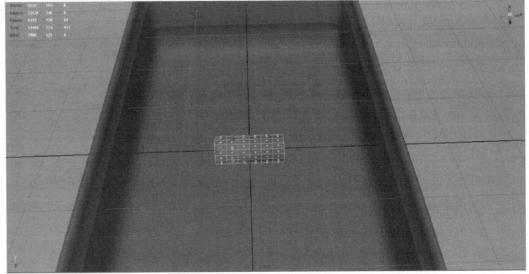

Figure 4.70 Select half of the faces on the handle.

14. Now change the selection mode to Vertex and slide the vertices of the handle toward the end of the cylinder, as shown in Figure 4.71.

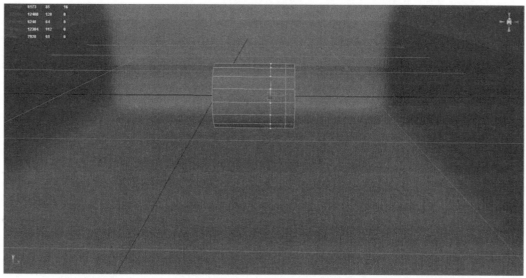

Figure 4.71 Slide the vertices of the handle to the right.

15. Select the second ring of vertices from the end of the handle and scale them in, as shown in Figure 4.72.

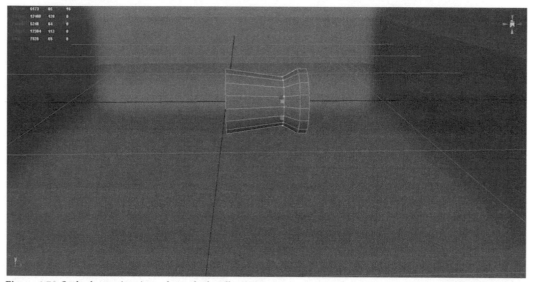

Figure 4.72 Scale the vertices in to shape the handle.

16. Now place the handle at the end of the tongue by changing Translate Y to −1.3 and Translate Z to 9.5, as shown in Figure 4.73.

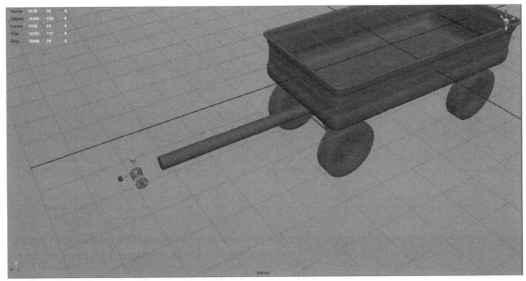

Figure 4.73 Move the handle to the end of the tongue.

17. Change the selection mode to Faces and the view to Top. Center the view over the handle.

18. Select half of the faces of the outer ring on the handle facing toward the wagon, as shown in Figure 4.74.

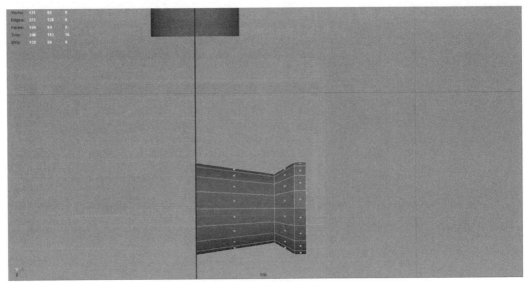

Figure 4.74 Select half of the faces of the last ring of the handle.

19. Extrude the faces and move them toward the wagon by changing Translate Z to −0.5, as shown in Figure 4.75.

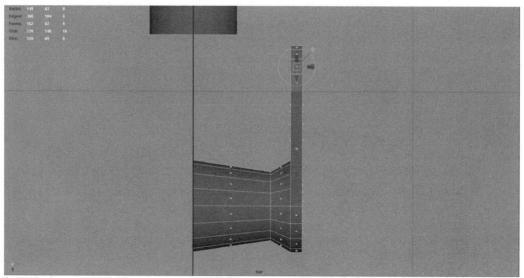

Figure 4.75 Move the extruded faces toward the wagon.

20. Use the Scale tool to scale the selected faces in the Z axis until they all line up vertically, like those in Figure 4.76.

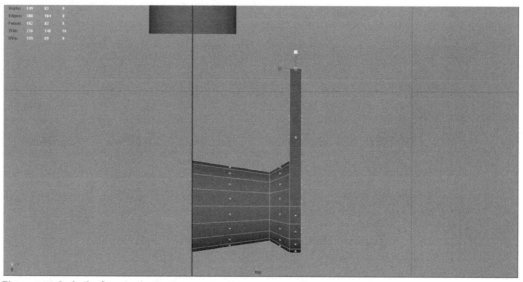

Figure 4.76 Scale the faces in the Z axis.

21. Rotate the faces toward the center to about 45 degrees, as shown in Figure 4.77.

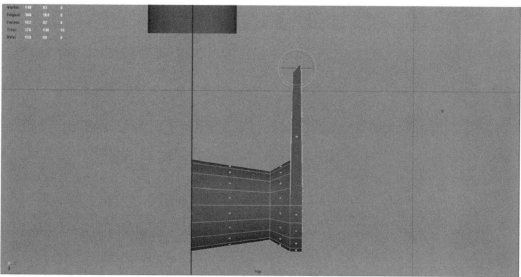

Figure 4.77 Rotate the faces of the handle.

22. Extrude the faces again and move them even with the end of the tongue by using the Extrusion manipulator, as shown in Figure 4.78.

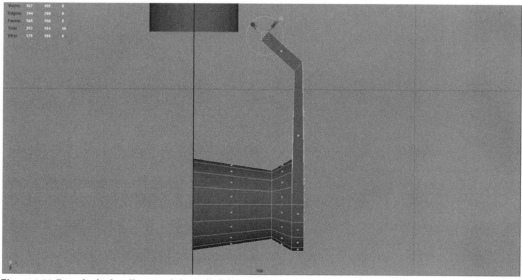

Figure 4.78 Extrude the handle toward the end of the tongue.

23. Now the handle is ready to mirror. Change the selection mode to Object.

24. Bring up the Mirror Options dialog box by going to the option box icon across from Mirror Geometry on the Polygons menu.

25. Set Mirror Direction to −X and click Apply (see Figure 4.79).

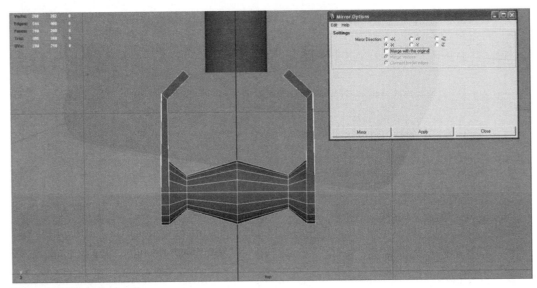

Figure 4.79 Mirror the handle.

26. Select the vertices along the seam of the mirror and merge them, as shown in Figure 4.80.

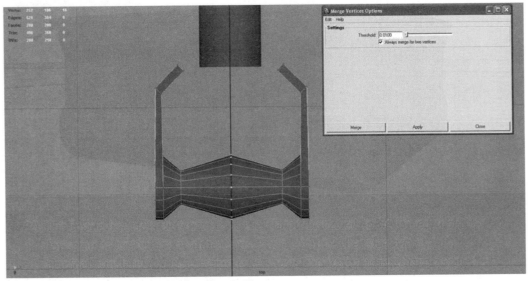

Figure 4.80 Merge the vertices between the mirrored objects.

27. Change the selection mode to Face and select the faces of the handle near the tongue.

28. Extrude the faces and use the Scale manipulator to scale the faces together, as shown in Figure 4.81.

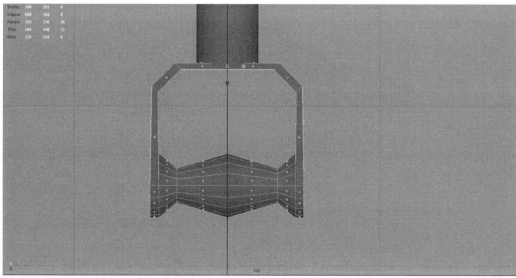

Figure 4.81 Scale the extruded faces together.

29. Select the faces along the center where the handle meets the end of the tongue (as shown in Figure 4.82) and delete them.

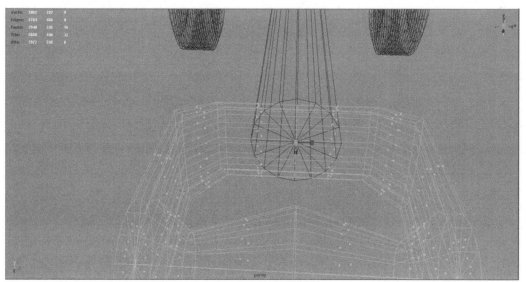

Figure 4.82 Delete the unneeded faces.

30. Change the selection mode to Vertex and merge the vertices along the seam.

31. Change the view to Perspective view. With the merged vertices selected, scale the handle to overlap the tongue, as shown in Figure 4.83.

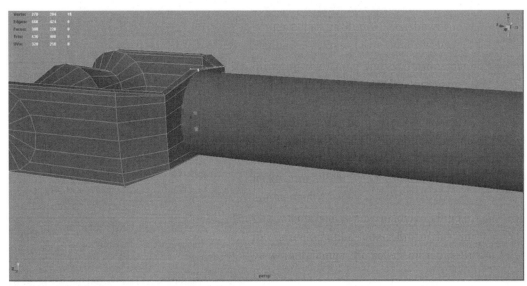

Figure 4.83 Scale the vertices to overlap the tongue.

32. Combine the handle with the tongue to make a single object, as shown in Figure 4.84.

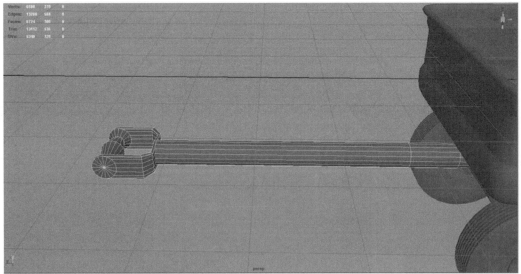

Figure 4.84 Combine the handle with the tongue.

33. Now go to the Side view and change the selection mode to Vertex. Select the handle and first row of vertices near the wagon.

34. The tongue needs to be bent near the wagon. The problem with the Rotate tool is that the pivot is in the wrong place. To change the pivot, press the Insert key with the Rotate tool chosen. A special manipulator will appear. This manipulator is used to position the pivot point by hand. Slide the pivot over the first ring of vertices, as shown in Figure 4.85.

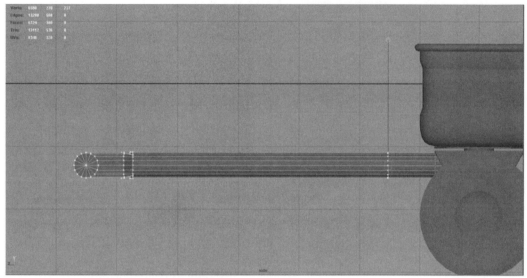

Figure 4.85 Press the Insert key to adjust the pivot.

35. Pressing the Insert key again will return the manipulator to the Rotate tool.

36. Rotate the tongue upward, as shown in Figure 4.86.

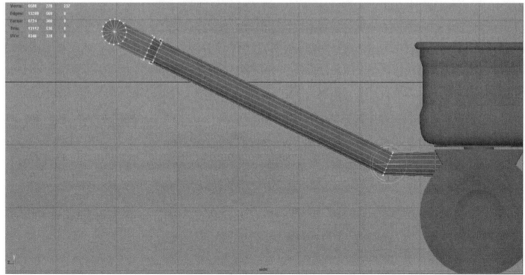

Figure 4.86 Rotate the tongue up.

37. Okay, one last thing before you are done. Change the selection mode to Edge.

38. Set all of the edges of the inner handle to 180, as shown in Figure 4.87.

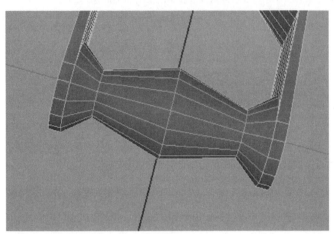

Figure 4.87 Smooth the edges of the handle.

So that is it. You have just created a nice red wagon in Maya. What? You say the wagon is not red? Later in the book, we will cover materials (shaders) and textures. Once you learn how to apply textures to objects, you will be able to come back to this model and make it red. For now, it is a gray wagon that should be red.

Figure 4.88 shows a rendering of the wagon. Your wagon should look similar to this.

Figure 4.88 A rendering of the wagon.

Well, you didn't use all of the polygon-modeling tools in this exercise, but you did use a number of them. Hopefully, you now feel comfortable with Maya's polygon-modeling tools and are ready to tackle a few of your own models. Remember that if you don't understand anything in the tools, you can look them up in Maya's online help, found in the main menu under the Help menu.

Summary

This chapter covered a number of topics related to polygon modeling in Maya. Some of the tools and functions discussed were

- Smooth Geometry
- Extrude Edge
- Extrude Face
- Duplicate Object
- Reverse Normals
- Backface Culling
- Merge Vertices
- Expand/Shrink Selection
- Harden/Soften Edges
- Selection Constraints
- Mirror Geometry

In addition, you used the Channel box for modifying and placing objects in the scene accurately.

You have just had an introduction to polygon modeling. In Chapter 5, you will learn some of the more advanced modeling methods in Maya.

Chapter 4

Polygons Anyone?

Polygons are the foundation of most 3D modeling. While there are many modeling systems (including NURBS, patches, and subdivision surfaces), most of them are output to polygons in the final steps. Polygon rendering is common with most if not all rendering engines for games and other real-time applications. Over the years and versions, 3D Studio Max has grown and tweaked its tool set to be one of the best polygon modelers out there.

In this chapter, polygon-modeling concepts will be used to further your understanding of Max. Hopefully by the end of this chapter you will begin to be comfortable with polygon modeling in Max.

Polygon Modeling

Creating a good polygon model is a process. Understanding the process and having a clear vision of the final goal are important to completing a good model. The first step is to plan your model-building process. One useful tip is to gather some reference for what you are going to build. This will really make a difference in the final product. Another tip is to go through the process in your mind first before you approach building it on the computer. For example, the project in this chapter will be to build a toy wagon. One of the challenges will be to build the wagon's bed. The bed has a lip along the top that curls out and over the edge. It also has rounded corners along the bottom. The obvious solution is to create the bed from a box, but how do you create a box that is rounded on one side and flat on the other?

In order to find a solution to the wagon bed problem, I thought about each of the tools that could be used to modify a box in the way I needed it for the end result. If I was unfamiliar with a particular tool, I did some experimenting to see what that tool could do. I also tried changing some of the tool settings to get the right result. I decided that the smoothing tools would work best for rounding the edges, but the smoothing tools rounded too much from a simple single-sided polygon box. I found that to get the rounded edges I wanted, I had to have a box that was subdivided in just the right way.

To get the flat top of the bed, I decided to delete the top of the box down to where it wasn't rounded. That meant I had to build the box high enough to compensate for the part that I would cut off. Planning and experimenting helped me find a workable solution to the wagon bed.

Note

By default, Max uses the metric scale; it measures everything in centimeters. For this tutorial and book, I will leave that as is and call out measurements in centimeters where appropriate. If you want to change the defaults to U.S. standard units, generic units, or some other custom measuring unit, you will find the dialog box to do that under Customize, Unit Setup on the main menu. At the end of this chapter, I will show you how to save settings like this so each time you start a new scene in Max, the setting will be there and ready to go.

Note

You may have noticed that when you use the Rotate Gizmo, it's hard to get the exact angle you are looking for. There are a couple solutions to this. First, with Rotate Transform selected, you can always type in a degree number in one of the desired axis boxes on the bottom-center of your screen. And second, you can set the angle snap so that when you use the Rotate Gizmo, it will "snap" to specific intervals.

To set the snap, right-click on the Angle Snap Toggle icon located near the top-center of your interface (there are four snap icons, and they all have U-shaped magnets on them).

Set Angle to 1.0 to rotate on every degree or to 0.5 to rotate on every half a degree, for example. Once you have closed the dialog box, make sure Angle Snap Toggle is on by clicking it. Refer to the end of this chapter to save Max with your preferred default setting.

Note

Although this is a small step, for this tutorial, I'm going to be setting each object's base or default colors to colors representing the actual material a toy wagon would likely have. This will help with visualization while you are working with the model but will not affect any textures you might apply later. You set the colors by clicking on the small color square located by the object's name on the Command Panel.

You can also change the name of each object you create by clicking in the text box and editing the default name, which, in the case of the wagon bed, is Box01.

I would highly recommend getting in the habit of taking these extra steps and entering descriptive names and colors. This will make life much easier as your scenes grow in complexity. You can also name lights, cameras, and helper objects with descriptive names so that when you are looking for a particular object later, you can quickly find it rather than trying to figure out if Box01, Box02, or Box03 is the one you need. The editable Name and Color boxes are pointed out in Figure 4.1.

Building the Wagon Bed

The bed of the wagon is basically a rectangular box shape. You'll begin the modeling process by creating a box. Make the box four units wide and four units deep to start. This will help when you create the lip along the top of the bed. Later, the box will be expanded to the rectangular shape of the bed.

1. Create a primitive box that is 40 cm long and wide and 20 cm high. Set Length Segs and Width Segs to 8 and Height Segs to 4, as shown in Figure 4.1.

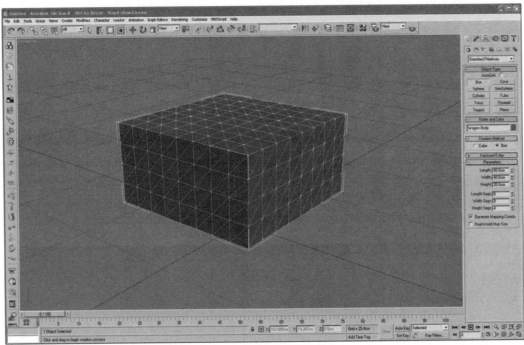

Figure 4.1 Start your wagon by creating a primitive box for the wagon bed.

Note

From this point forward in this chapter, as each primitive is created and ready for editing, I'm going to be moving to the Modify tab on the Command Panel and collapsing the stack to Editable Poly by right-clicking on the stack window and choosing Editable Poly without mentioning that step.

2. Switch to the Front view by pressing the F key, toggle the Edged Faces under the viewport label, and enter Edge Sub Object mode.

3. Select the edge shown and click the Loop button, as pointed out in Figure 4.2. This will select the entire edge loop around the model that you can delete.

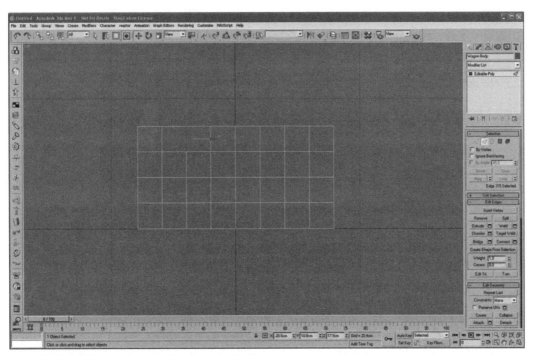

Figure 4.2 Select the edge in preparation for removing it.

Note

A good rule of thumb when creating polygon models is to keep the model as simple as possible. You don't create too many polygons, because the more polygons in a model, the longer it will take to render. In this example, the middle of the box does not need the tight subdivision but the corners do. Deleting the middle subdivisions will make the model more manageable in the future. It's also extremely easy to add polygons versus removing extra polygons at a later time. A good workflow avoids extra polygons, so as scenes grow in complexity, they will be efficient and not hog machine resources more than necessary.

4. Remove these edges by pressing the Remove button, as shown in Figure 4.3. Using the Delete key to delete the edges will also delete the associated polygons.

5. Loop by loop, select the edges indicated by the arrows in Figure 4.3 and remove them.

6. Change to Vertex Sub Object mode and select the vertices of the deleted edges, as shown in Figure 4.4.

7. Remove the selected vertices by using the Remove button again.

8. Now change to the Left view by pressing the L key, and delete the unneeded edges and vertices in the same way that you did from the Front view in Steps 4 through 6. The resulting model should now look similar to Figure 4.5.

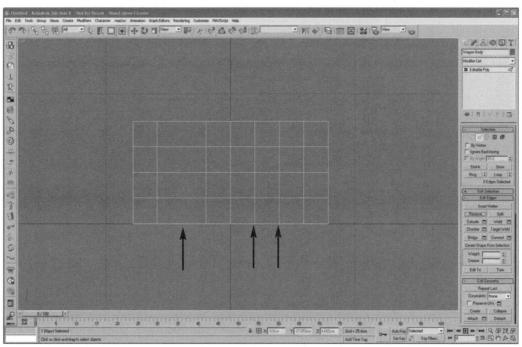

Figure 4.3 The wagon body with the first edge loop removed.

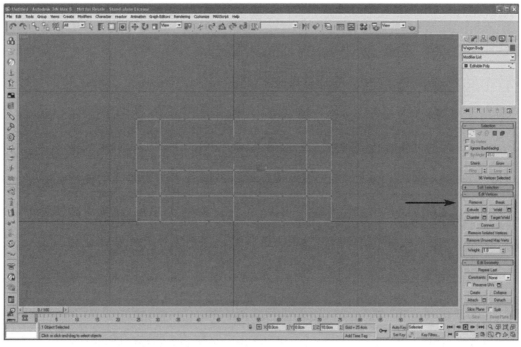

Figure 4.4 Select the vertices of the deleted edges.

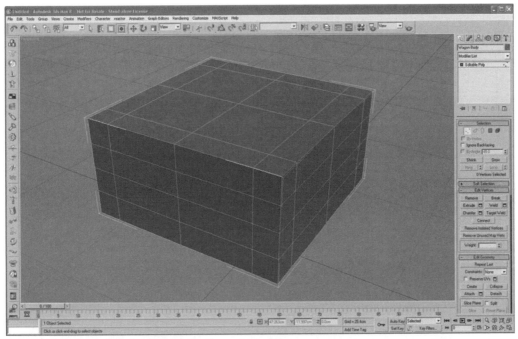

Figure 4.5 The wagon body is now ready for the next set of steps.

9. Enter Polygon Sub Object mode, and while holding the Control key, press the A key. This will select all the polygons in this object.

10. Press the MSmooth button twice to get the desired level of smoothness, as shown in Figure 4.6.

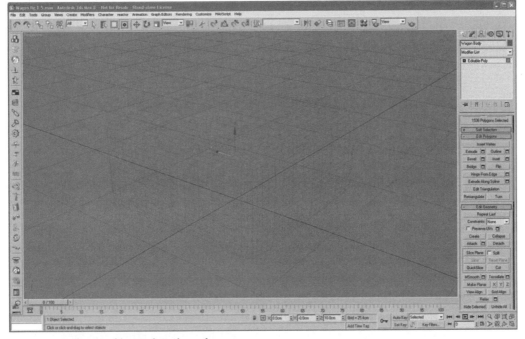

Figure 4.6 Apply smoothing to the polygon box.

Chapter 4
Max

11. Go back to the Front view by pressing the F key.

12. Deselect the entire object by holding the Control key and pressing the D key, or click on an empty area of the screen and then select the faces of the rounded top of the box, as shown in Figure 4.7.

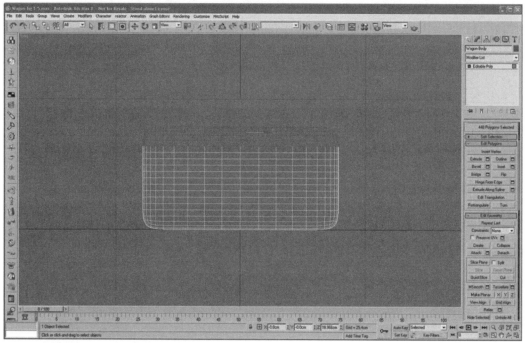

Figure 4.7 Select the faces of the top of the box.

13. Delete the faces so the top of the model is now flat.

14. The wagon will have a decorative indentation along its sides. Select five rows of faces below the top three rows.

15. Click the Scale Transform button and scale in the selected faces to create the decorative indentation, as shown in Figure 4.8. You will want to scale all sides uniformly, so click on the Gizmo or click on the selection and scale the sides in.

16. The Maya side of the book talks about using Backface Culling to view the polygons as double-sided. By default, Max only uses single-sided polygons. By pressing the P key and switching the viewport to Perspective, you can only see the outside of the wagon bed, as shown in Figure 4.9.

17. As you can see, only the outside of the bed is viewable. You could force the view to show and render the polygons double-sided, but that would give the metal of the wagon bed no thickness because polygons are flat planes with no thickness. Instead, you are going to give the bed some thickness with a new modifier called Shell. This modifier will, in effect, extrude the body of the wagon and ensure that all the polygons are facing the correct direction.

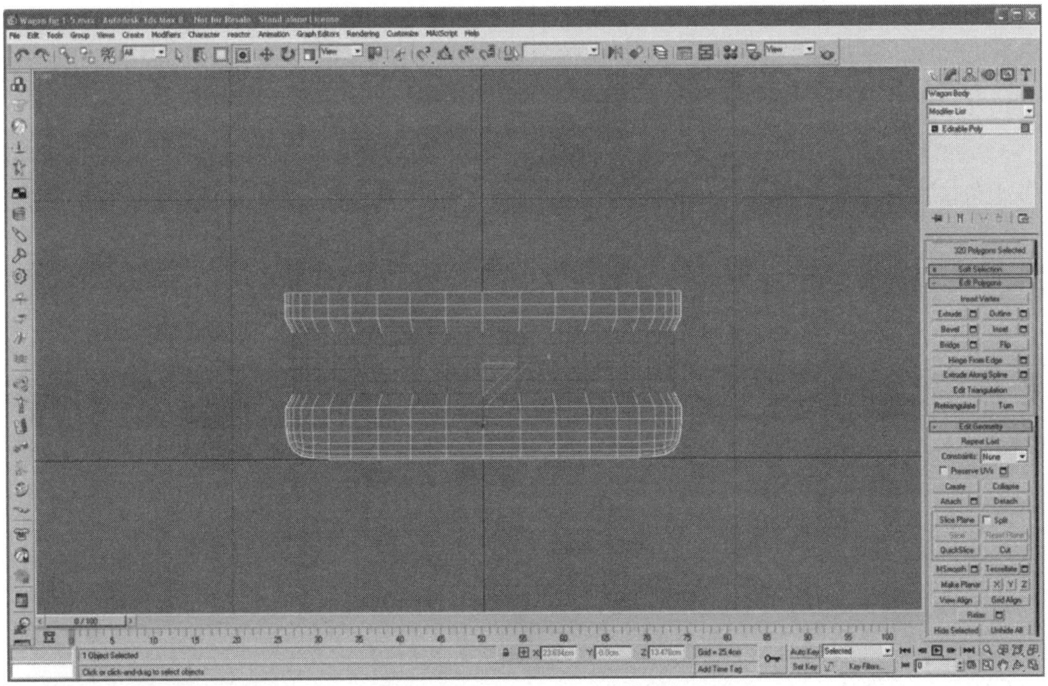

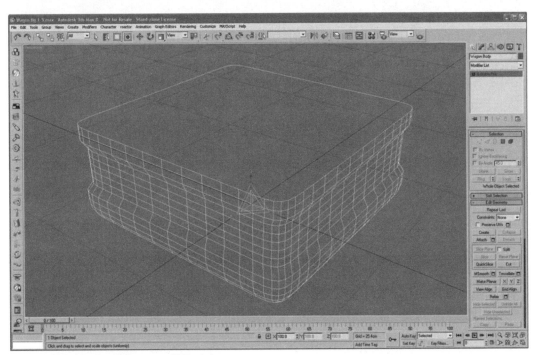

Figure 4.8 Scale the faces to create an indentation on the sides of the wagon bed.

Figure 4.9 The single-sided nature of Max polygons.

18. Make sure you are not in any Sub Object mode (but the wagon bed is selected). Using the Modifier List drop-down, select the Shell modifier under Parametric Modifier near the bottom of the drop-down (see Figure 4.10).

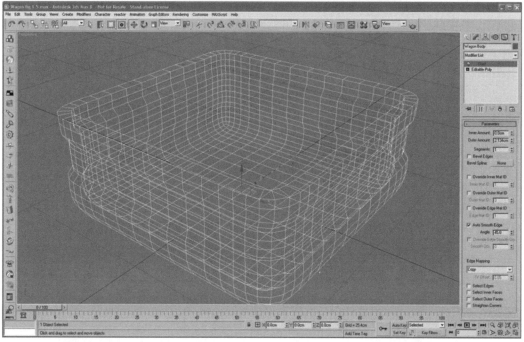

Figure 4.10 Add the Shell modifier to the stack.

19. This gives you a nice start on a hot tub, but we are making a wagon, so set the thickness to something more like the thin metal of a wagon body. Set Outer Amount to something thin, like 0.102, as shown in Figure 4.11.

20. You will want to keep the stack small and manageable and get back to a polygon-editable state, so add a new modifier called Edit Poly. At this point, you can continue to the next steps, but for this tutorial, I would recommend right-clicking on the Edit Poly modifier in the stack and choosing Collapse All so you are using less memory and have a less confusing stack. Now the wagon bed has both an inside and an outside and is ready for the next set of steps (see Figure 4.12).

21. The next process is to create a lip around the top edge of the wagon. To do that, you will be extruding the edge and curling it around. First off, prep the top part of the wagon by selecting and deleting the top, flat set of polygons that connect the inner shell with the outer shell around the top edge of the wagon to form an open edge.

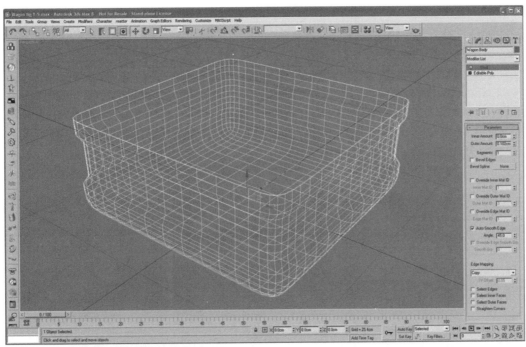

Figure 4.11 Set the thickness to a thin metal.

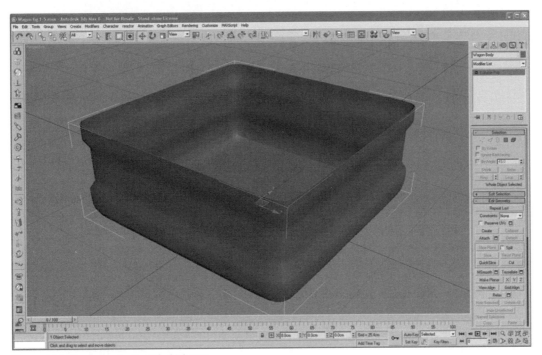

Figure 4.12 The wagon body with thickness.

Note

You are going to be using the Shift key, the Move Transform Gizmo, and the Scale Transform Gizmo to extrude the edge up and around. Using the Shift key to extrude (or *clone*, as Max calls it) the edge is very convenient, but there is one catch. The edge you are trying to extrude or clone must be "open." For example, you cannot pick an edge in the middle of a cube and extrude it. It must be an edge on the outside of a polygon with no other polygon attached to it. To open the edge, you need to extrude in the wagon, and you will need to delete some polygons in the next step.

22. In Polygon Sub Object mode and in the Front view, select the top flat polygons by drawing a marquee around the very top line of the object. Once you have the polygons selected, switch to Perspective with the P key, double-check that you have the right polygons selected, and press the Delete key (see Figure 4.13).

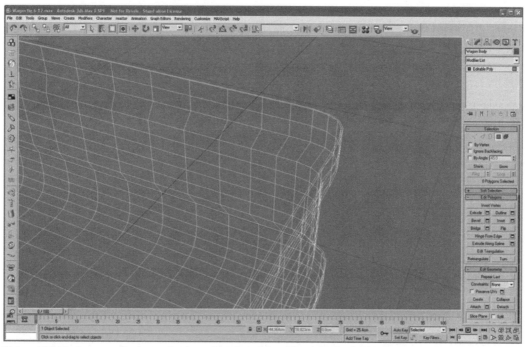

Figure 4.13 The top row of polygons has been deleted, and the object is ready for the next step.

23. For the next several steps, you will be extruding the edge of the box and forming the lip of the wagon body. First, make sure you are in the Edge Sub Object mode and select the *inside* top edges. Then click the Loop button to select the edges all the way around the wagon body. You will be extruding the edge in the Z direction by holding the Shift key as you drag the edge up, and then scaling out the new geometry.

Note

This would be an excellent time to use the Lock Selection tool. Once you have the edge selected, press the spacebar and notice the small lock icon on the bottom-center of your program turn yellow. This edge will stay selected while you do the next several steps. Don't forget to press the spacebar again to unlock it when you are ready to move on.

24. Move (using the Move Transform Gizmo) the edge up (while holding the Shift key), and then let go of the Shift key and scale the edge out slightly, as shown in Figure 4.14. Using the Scale Gizmo, make sure you are clicking on the center and all three axes are highlighted so that you are scaling uniformly.

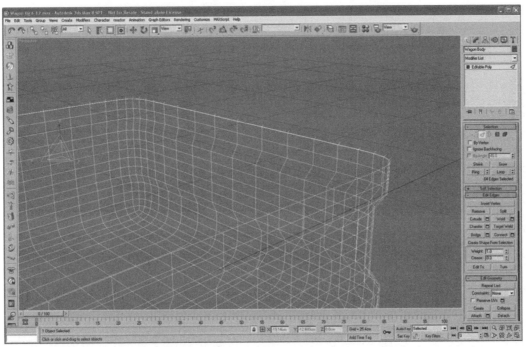

Figure 4.14 Extrude the lip up and scale outward.

25. Let's do it one more time, only this time hold the Shift key and scale it out 1 percent. In the three small coordinate windows in the bottom-center of your screen, you can see how much you have scaled, moved, or rotated an object.

26. On my model, I'm going to leave this edge where it is, as shown in Figure 4.15, but you may want to move yours up or down slightly to get a rounder edge.

27. This time I'm going to shift and scale the edge out 1 percent more, and then I'm going to move it down slightly. The model should look similar to Figure 4.16.

28. Extrude once again using the Shift-move and Scale method, and continue to form the curve, as shown in Figure 4.17.

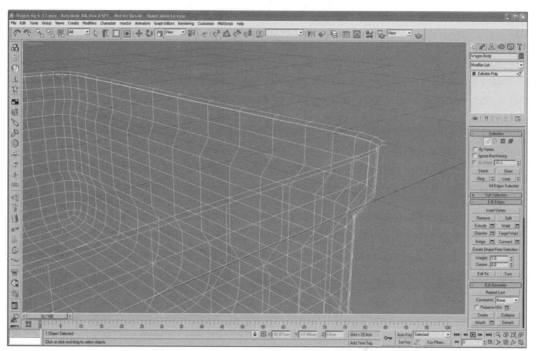

Figure 4.15 Scale and move the edges out from the wagon bed to start forming the curve of the lip.

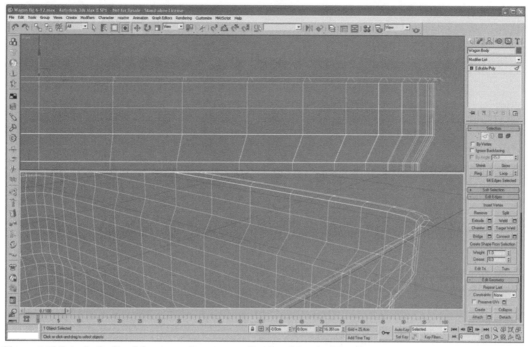

Figure 4.16 Extrude the lip of the wagon down to start forming the curl of the edge.

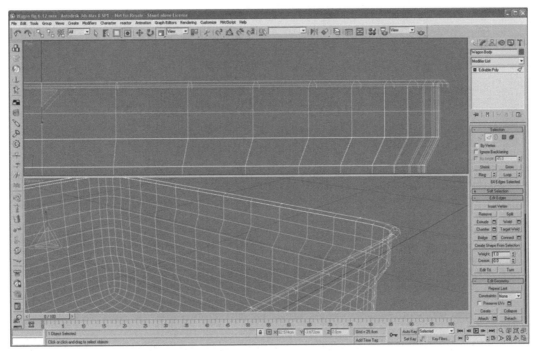

Figure 4.17 Curl the lip back toward the wagon bed.

29. Now the extrusions are starting to look like the lip of the wagon. Extrude once more and adjust the edge to start curving down (see Figure 4.18).

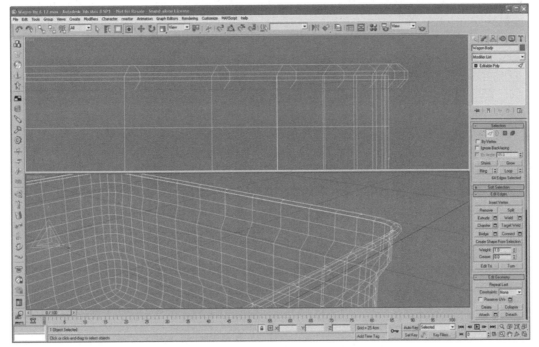

Figure 4.18 Continue the curl of the lip toward the wagon bed.

30. Extrude once more and adjust the edge to start curving back up and under (see Figure 4.19).

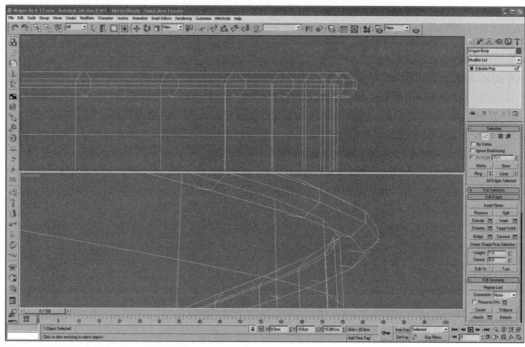

Figure 4.19 Extrude the edge up and under.

31. Now, extrude the edge one more time and adjust the edge to line it up closely with the edge of the outward-facing polygon part of the wagon bed, as shown in Figure 4.20.

32. Because you used a slightly different method of creating your wagon bed, you won't need to weld any vertices to close the mesh.

33. For this step, use the Loop tool and scale or move the edges of the lip to form a nicer curve, as shown in Figure 4.21.

34. If you find that you need more geometry, Max has a good tool for quickly splitting edges. It is the Chamfer tool.

35. Select an edge loop that you would like to split. Using the Chamfer tool will split the edge, in turn creating more geometry where it's needed. In this application, using the Chamfer tool has the added benefit of rounding the corners nicely (see Figure 4.22).

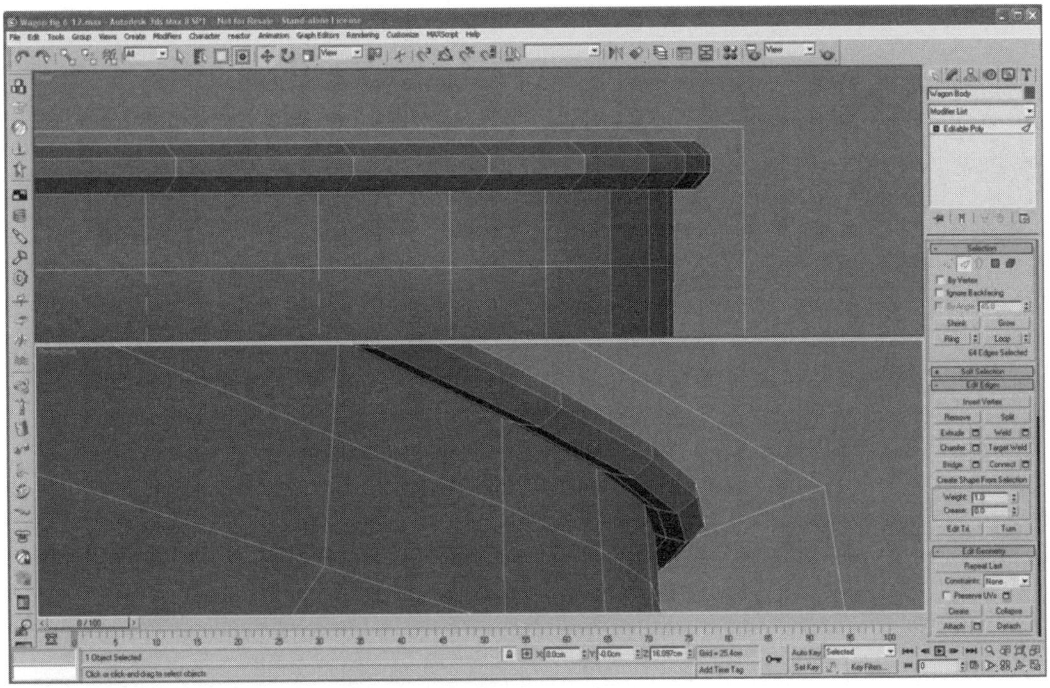

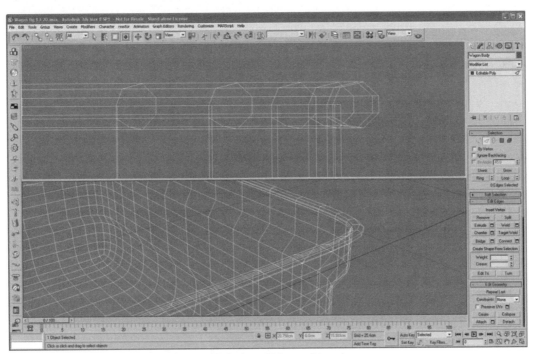

Figure 4.20 Extrude the edge and move it in toward the wagon bed.

Figure 4.21 Using Edge Loop, adjust the lip with Scale and Move so it's a nice curve.

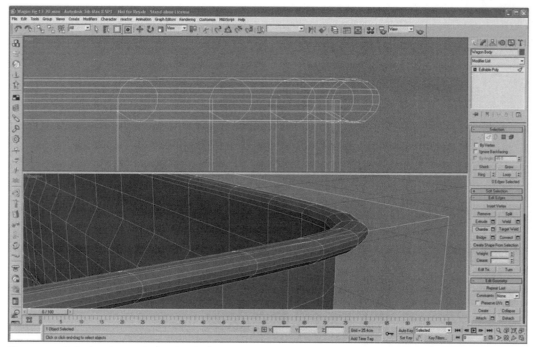

Figure 4.22 Split the edges with the Chamfer tool.

36. Let's use the Bridge tool to close the gap and complete the shell of the wagon bed. In Edge Sub Object mode, select one of the edges and use the Loop tool. While holding the Control key, select the edge on the other side of the gap and use the Loop tool again. Both edges on the gap should now be selected all the way around. Now release the Control key and simply click Bridge. This step is optional if your gap is hidden (see Figure 4.23).

37. The wagon bed is now ready to elongate into a rectangular shape. Go to the Left view and enter into Vertex Sub Object mode.

38. Select all the vertices on the right side of the wagon, excluding the center row of vertices.

39. Move the right side of the wagon bed about 25 cm to the right using the Transform Gizmo, as shown in Figure 4.24.

40. Select all the vertices on the left side of the wagon, excluding the center row of vertices.

41. Move the left side of the wagon bed about 25 cm to the left using the Transform Gizmo, as shown in Figure 4.25.

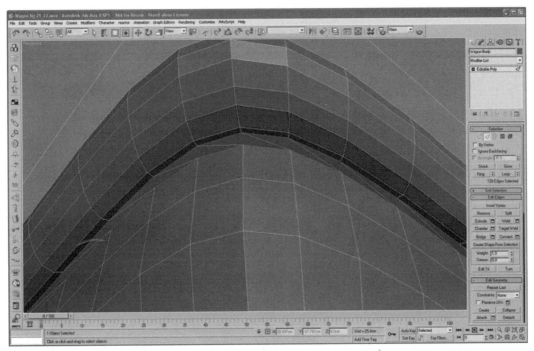

Figure 4.23 Merge the vertices of the inner and outer meshes.

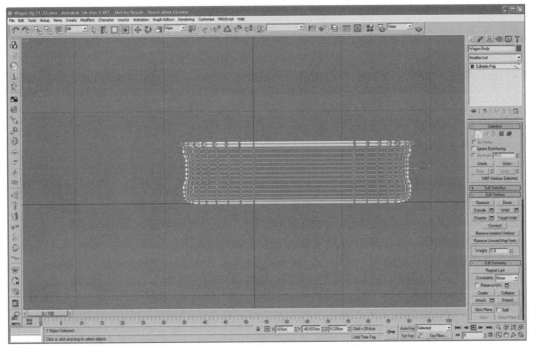

Figure 4.24 Move the selected vertices on the wagon bed toward the right of the screen.

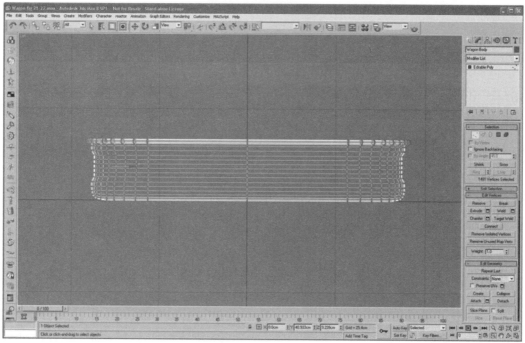

Figure 4.25 The wagon bed with the right proportions.

Note

You may have noticed that although the main body of the wagon looks smooth, the lip seems faceted. This is because the smoothing process smoothed the polygons of the body, but the lip was extruded after the initial smoothing process. You can adjust the appearance of a polygon model by changing the properties of its polygons.

42. Enter Polygon Sub Object mode and scroll down the Command Panel to the Polygon Properties rollout.

43. Select all the polygons on the wagon bed by holding the Control key and pressing the A key.

44. Click the Auto Smooth button in the rollout (see Figure 4.26). This will smooth all polygons with less than a 45-degree difference in their angles to each other. In most cases, this does a pretty good job of setting the smoothing groups.

45. Sometimes we don't want Max to make all the adjustments. The edges along the top and bottom of the indentation on the wagon bed's sides should be hard. Select the faces in the middle of the wagon, and move those to their own smoothing group so they will have a hard edge next to other polygons that are in different smoothing groups. Click on the smoothing groups 1 and 2 to remove the smoothing, and then click on 3 to set these polygons to a new and unused smoothing group, as shown in Figure 4.27.

Figure 4.26 Smooth the selected polygons with Auto Smooth.

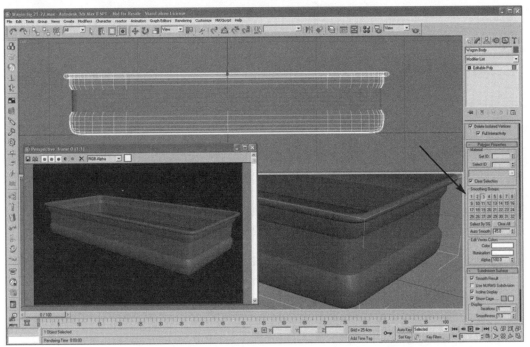

Figure 4.27 The indentation put in its own smoothing group.

The wagon bed is now complete, and it looks good. Thinking ahead saved a lot of time with building the model. We created the wagon bed as a square instead of a rectangle to help keep the smoothed corners (and indentation) symmetrical as well as the lip extrusions rounded.

Creating the Wagon Wheels

Now that you have a wagon bed, you can start creating some of the other parts of the wagon. Next will be the wagon wheels.

1. Create a primitive cylinder for the wheel. Set Radius to 10 cm and Height to 5 cm. Set Sides (which refers to sides around the axis) to 32, Height Segments to 15, and Cap Segments to 5 (see Figure 4.28).

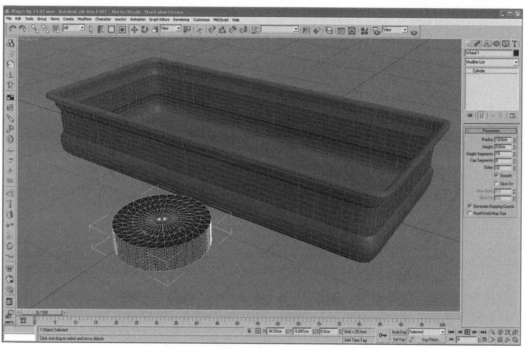

Figure 4.28 Create a new primitive cylinder object for the wheels.

2. It will be a lot easier to work on the wheel if the wagon bed is not hanging around. A simple and easy way to focus on a single object is to make it the only object visible. With the wheel selected, go to the Display tab of the Command Panel and click the Hide Unselected button, as shown in Figure 4.29.
3. Rotate the object 90 degrees and enter Polygon Sub Object mode.
4. In the Front view, select every other row of faces starting one in from the side, as shown in Figure 4.30. This is best done by holding down the Control key and drawing a marquee around the rows of polygons.

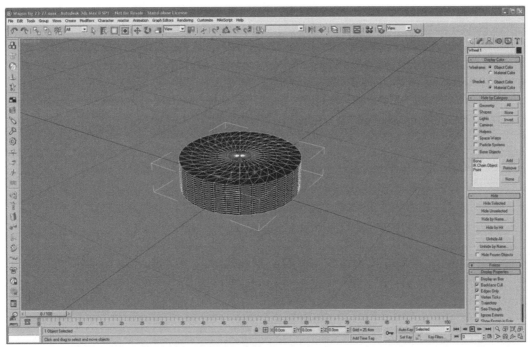

Figure 4.29 Hide Unselected isolates the selected object.

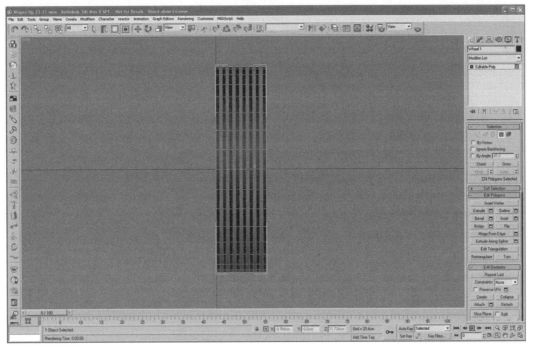

Figure 4.30 Select every other row of faces.

5. Using the Settings button next to the Extrude button, you will next extrude the tread inward by 0.20 cm. Because you have multiple rows selected and they are not connected to each other, you will need to change the Extrusion Type option to Local Normal so the extrusion happens as expected, as shown in Figure 4.31.

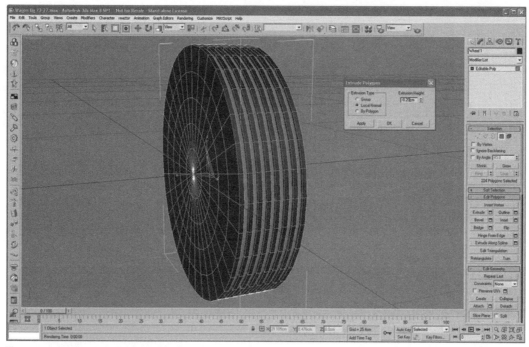

Figure 4.31 Create the tread on the tires.

6. Using the Grow button under the Selection rollout, "grow" (or expand) the selection until all of the tread is selected.

7. Next, make sure you are in Non-Uniform Scale by holding down the mouse button on the Scale icon and selecting the middle scale in the drop-down. Using the X axis on the Scale Gizmo, scale the tread by about 78 percent, as shown in Figure 4.32.

8. Press the Grow button again to expand your selection to the first ring of faces on the sidewall of the tire.

9. Scale the new selection outward in the X axis about 112 percent, as shown in Figure 4.33, to give the tire's sidewall an inflated bulge.

10. Expand the selection again and scale the tire again in the X axis to continue the taper of the tire inward to the rims (see Figure 4.34).

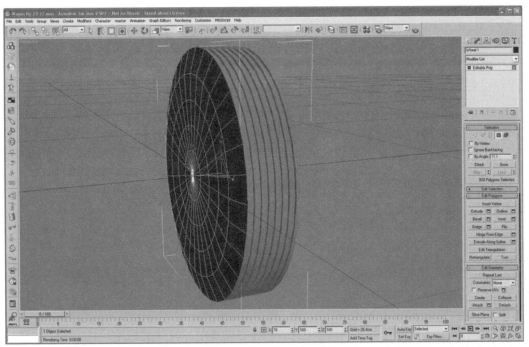

Figure 4.32 Scale the tire tread inward.

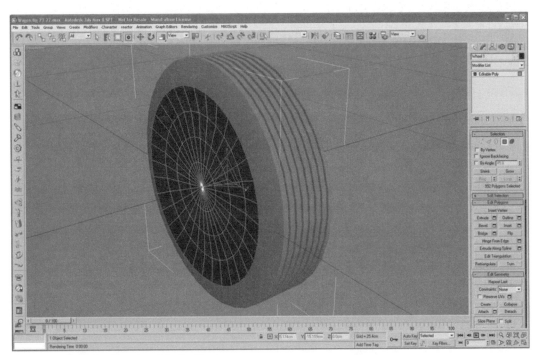

Figure 4.33 Scale the tire outward in the X axis.

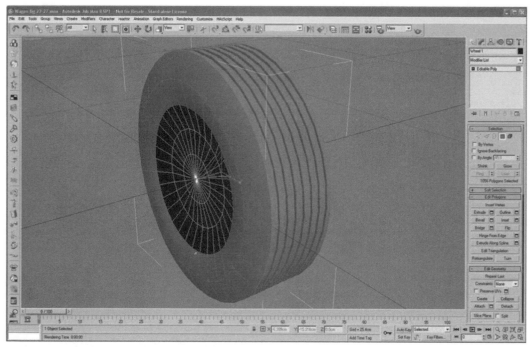

Figure 4.34 Continue the taper of the tires to the rims.

11. Expand the selection once more and invert it from the Edit menu.

12. Extrude faces 0.25 cm, using the Setting button to create a lip for the rim of the tire, as shown in Figure 4.35.

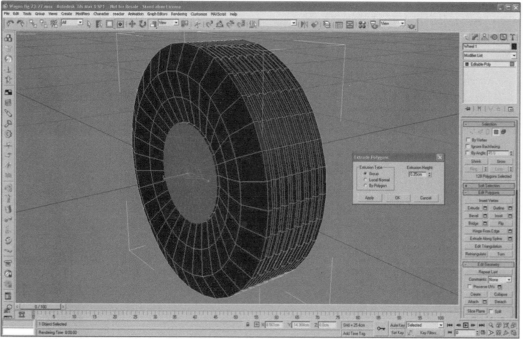

Figure 4.35 Create a ridge around the rim of the tire.

13. Invert the selection via the Edit menu and make sure the newly created rim is in the selection. Scale outward in the X axis to create a deep swell for the rim of the tire, as shown in Figure 4.36.

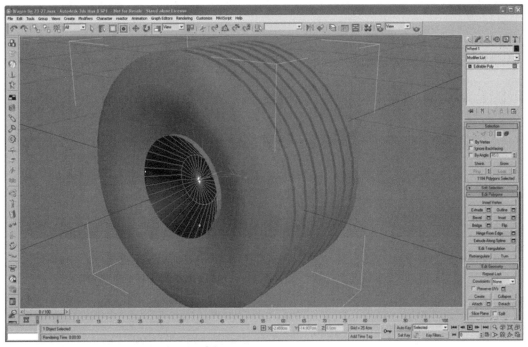

Figure 4.36 Create a deep swell for the rim of the tire.

14. Expand the selection one more time, and then scale the tire inward in the X axis to the desired thickness. The finished tire should look similar to that shown in Figure 4.37.

15. If you look around the rim of the tire, you may notice some odd shading issues. These were caused by the extrusion process; they need to be fixed. While holding the Control key, hit the A key to select all of the polygons, as shown in Figure 4.38.

16. On the Polygon Properties rollout, click the Auto Smooth button, and your wheel should look great and be ready to roll. Smoothing should fix the abnormal shading issues around the rim, as shown in Figure 4.39.

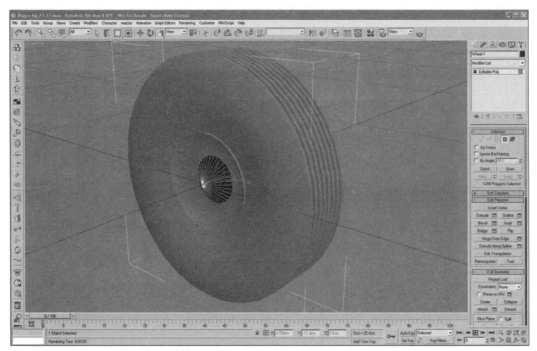

Figure 4.37 Scale in the tire to finish shaping it.

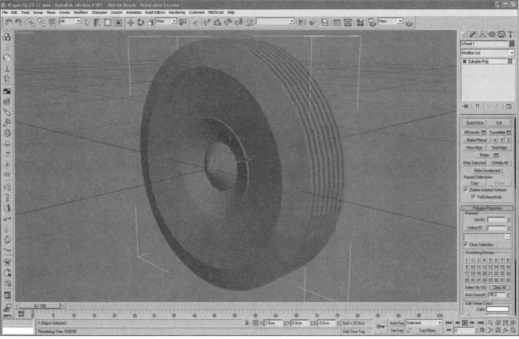

Figure 4.38 The wheel is done and ready to be smoothed.

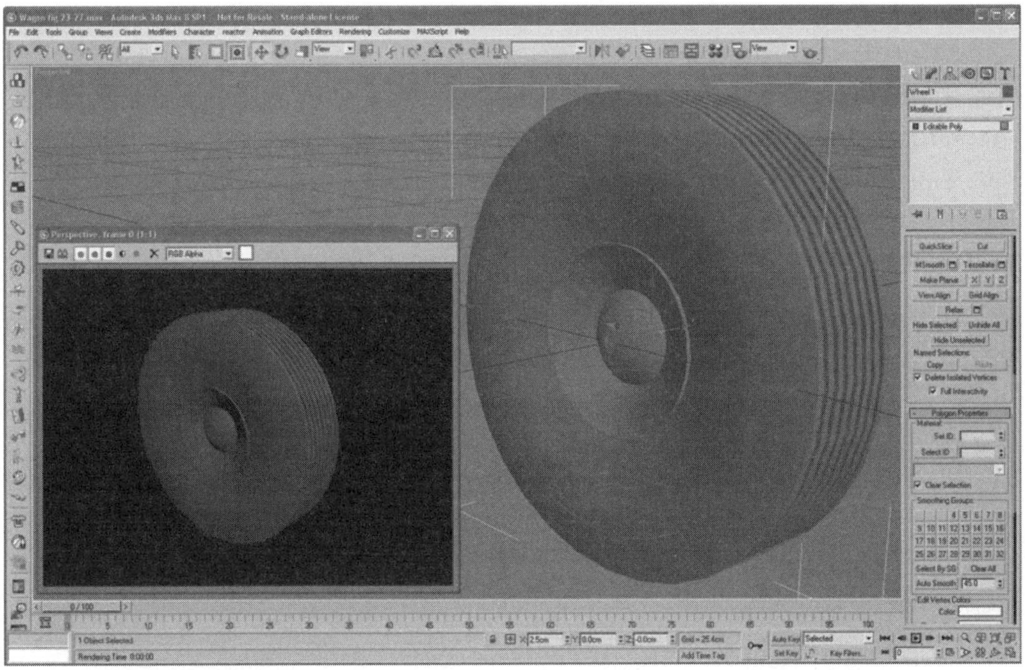

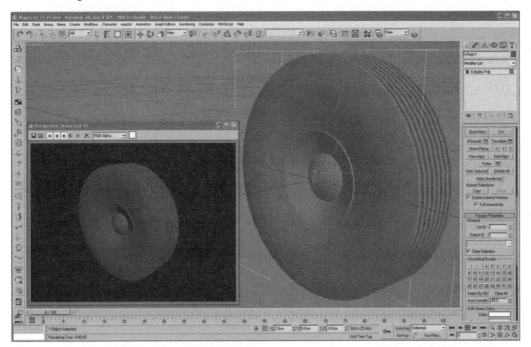

Figure 4.39 Auto Smooth results.

17. Bring the wagon bed back into the view by clicking the Unhide All button on the Display tab of the Command Panel.

18. Move the tire to where it should be located below the wagon bed, as shown in Figure 4.40.

Figure 4.40 Put the tire in place below the wagon bed.

19. Duplicate the wheel by holding the Shift key and moving the wheel to the right with the Transform Gizmo.

20. Choose Copy in the resulting dialog box.

21. In the Left viewport, draw a marquee around both front wheels to select them.

22. While holding the Shift key again, drag the new set of wheels to the back of the wagon and choose Copy in the resulting dialog box, as shown in Figure 4.41.

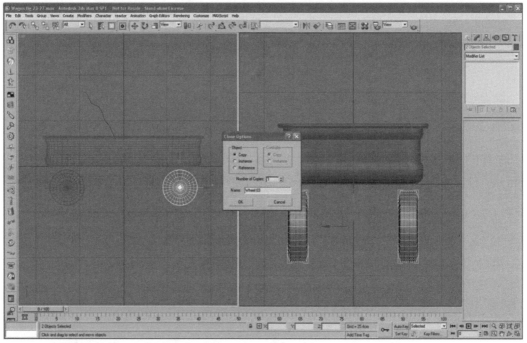

Figure 4.41 Place the wheels below the corners of the wagon bed.

The wagon is really starting to take shape. You have the wagon bed and wheels modeled. All you need to do to finish is connect the wheels to the wagon and build the tongue. In the next section, you will connect the wheels and the wagon together.

Connecting the Wheels to the Bed

To connect the wheels to the wagon bed, you will be adding many individual pieces. The wheels will connect with axles, and the axles will be attached to the wagon. The front axle will have a swivel attachment so the front wheels can be turned, while the rear axle can be attached directly to the bed because the back wheels don't swivel.

1. Start by creating an axle. Create a cylinder in the Left viewport with a radius of 0.5 cm and a height of 30 cm. Set Sides to 16, Height Segments to 4, and Cap Segments to 1, as shown in Figure 4.42.

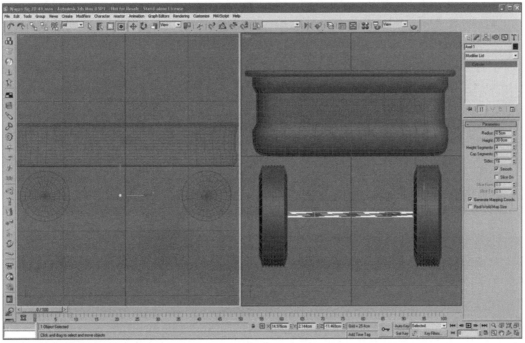

Figure 4.42 Create an axle for the wagon.

2. Move the axle to fit between the two front tires by using the Move Gizmo in the Left and Front viewports, as shown in Figure 4.43. A quick tip for centering the axle is to use the Gizmo axis lines and match the polygon edges of the wheel in the Left viewport.

3. Duplicate the axle and move the duplicate to the back wheels by holding the Shift key (see Figure 4.44).

4. Create a polygon prism with Side 1 Length set to 12.5 cm, Side 2 and 3 Lengths to 15.0 cm, and Height to 1.0 cm, as shown in Figure 4.45. Set all Segs to 1.

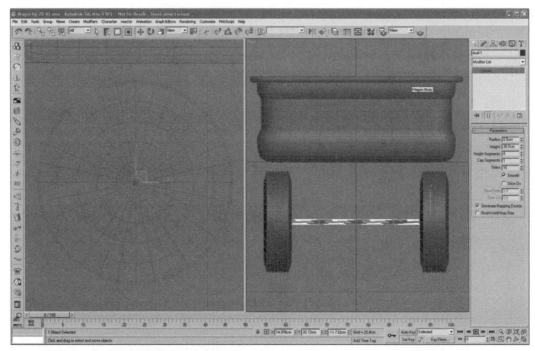

Figure 4.43 Place the axle between the two front tires.

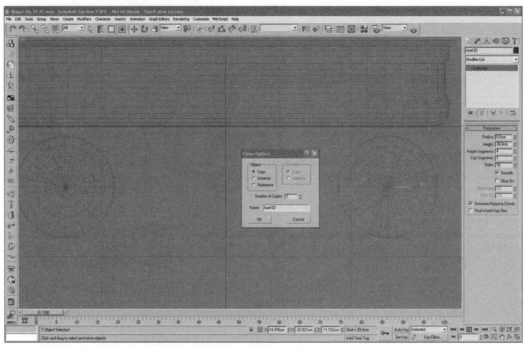

Figure 4.44 Move a duplicate of the front axle to the back.

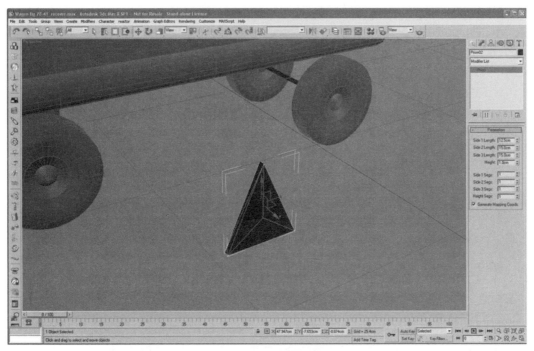

Figure 4.45 Create a polygon prism.

5. Next, in Polygon Sub Object mode, select the three outside polygons, and using the Setting dialog box for the Bevel tool, set the options to Local Normal, Height to 0.5 cm, and Outline Amount to −0.5, as shown in Figure 4.46.

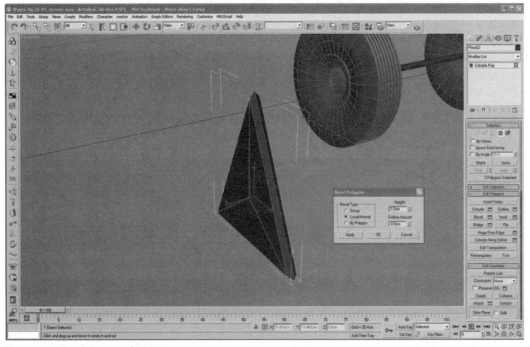

Figure 4.46 Bevel the new object.

6. Move and rotate the prism object into place on the front axle, as shown in Figure 4.47.

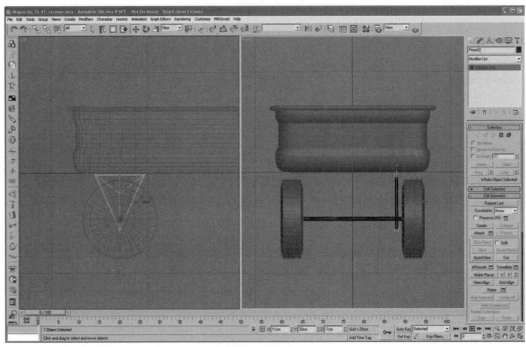

Figure 4.47 Place the new object to connect with the front axle.

7. There are several overlapping vertices that we will want to clean up; also, the corner of the triangle at the bottom of the new object is too sharp for what we need. Switch to Vertex Sub Object mode, and while holding the Control key, press the A key to select all of the points in the prism.

8. Weld these extra points into one with the Weld button. Switch to Edge Sub Object mode and select the two edges that make up the very bottom of the prism. Chamfer those edges slightly, as shown in Figure 4.48.

9. Next, draw a marquee around all of the edges that make up the bottom point of the prism to select them, and move those edges up or down slightly so the axle is near the bottom of the prism, as shown in Figure 4.49.

10. You will want to add a few extra polygons before duplicating this object.

11. In Polygon Sub Object mode, select the top two polygons and extrude them up slightly, as shown in Figure 4.49. At this point, you may need to adjust the prism so that it is still under the wagon and not poking up through the wagon bed.

12. Clone the prism to the three other wheels (using the Shift key). The results should look similar to Figure 4.50. Remember, you can select more than one object to clone, so once you have the back two axles in the perfect spot, simply select both and clone them to the front of the wagon.

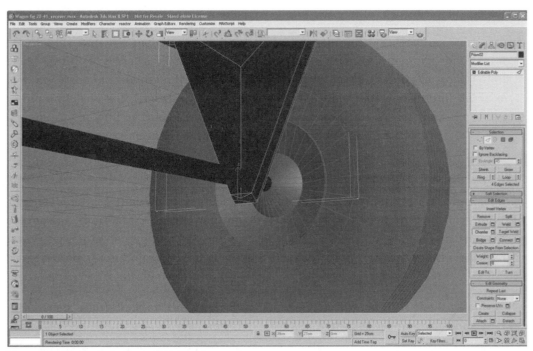

Figure 4.48 Flatten the bottom of the triangle.

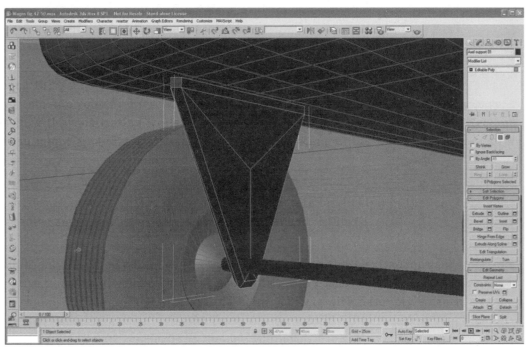

Figure 4.49 Move the bottom of the triangle up closer to the axle.

Figure 4.50 Place a prism by each wheel.

13. Let's hide the wagon bed and wheels for a few steps. Make sure you are not in a Sub Object mode and you have all four prisms selected. From the Display tab, hide Unselected Geometry.

14. Go to the back-right triangle. Make sure you are in Polygon Sub Object mode, and select the top three inside polygons, as shown in Figure 4.51.

15. Extrude the selected faces to the center of the wagon, as shown in Figure 4.52, and press the Delete key to remove the selected polygons.

16. Next merge these two back prisms into one object. Select one of the prisms and click the Attach button, then click on the opposite prism. They will join and become one object.

17. Extrude the identical faces on the opposite prism to just short of the center of the wagon, and then press the Delete key to remove the selected polygons, as shown in Figure 4.53.

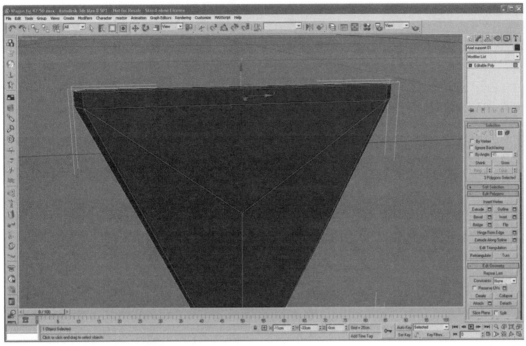

Figure 4.51 Getting ready to extrude.

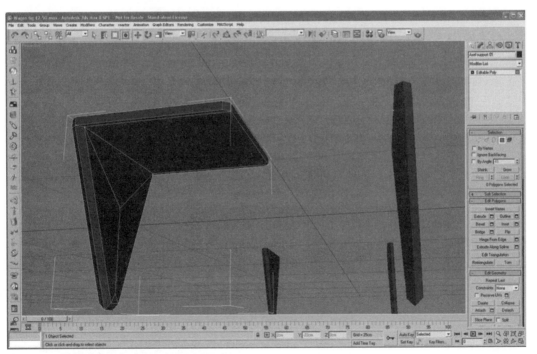

Figure 4.52 Half of the wheel mount structure.

Chapter 4
Max

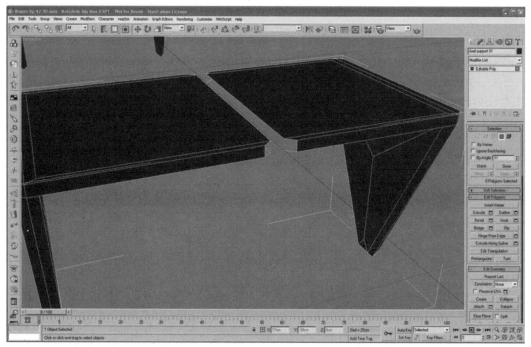

Figure 4.53 Extrude the selected faces to the center of the wagon.

18. Switch to Vertex Sub Object mode, and, using the Target Weld button, move around the vertices on the right side and weld them to the corresponding vertices on the left side to form one solid object, as shown in Figure 4.54.

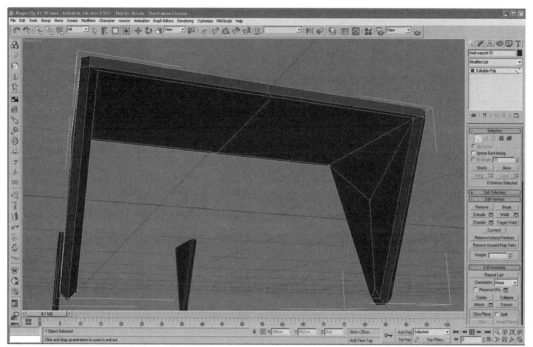

Figure 4.54 The completed rear wheel mount.

19. Repeat the process of extruding, deleting, and welding the two front wheel mounts exactly as you did the back supports. The wagon should now look similar to that shown in Figure 4.55. (You could be sneaky and delete the front two supports and clone the newly created back supports to the front.)

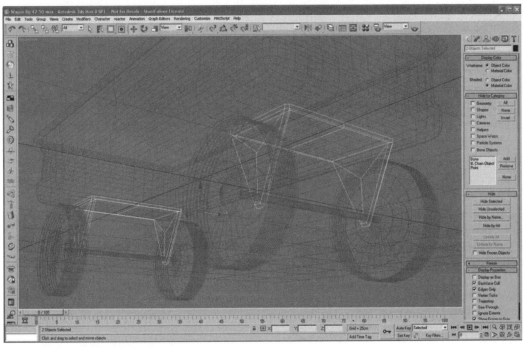

Figure 4.55 Finalize the front wheel mount.

20. Create a new primitive cylinder with the following options: Radius, 9.0 cm; Height, 0.3 cm; Height Segments, 1; Cap Segments, 2; and Sides, 8 (see Figure 4.56).

21. Move the plate into place, as shown in Figure 4.57. This plate will form the top of the swivel.

22. In the Left view, select the wheel mount, enter Vertex Sub Object mode, draw a marquee around all the top vertices, and move them down slightly below the newly placed swivel support (see Figure 4.57).

23. Create a new polygon cylinder with the following options: Radius, 2.0 cm; Height, 1 cm; Height Segments, 1; Cap Segments, 1; and Sides, 16 (see Figure 4.58).

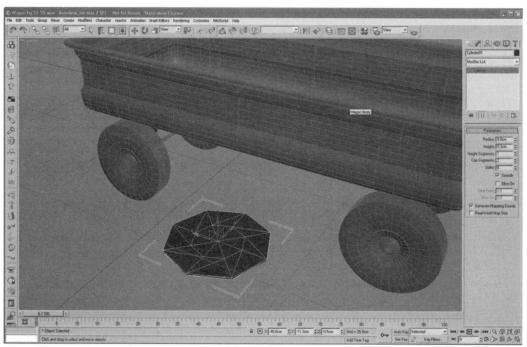

Figure 4.56 Create a new cylinder object.

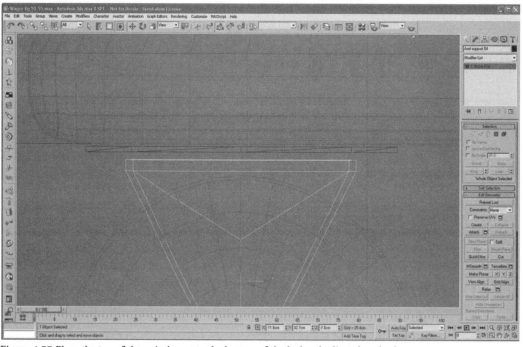

Figure 4.57 Place the top of the swivel next to the bottom of the bed and adjust the wheel mount.

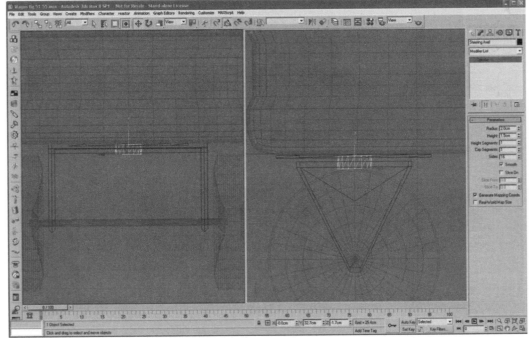

Figure 4.58 Create the middle of the swivel.

24. Move the middle of the swivel into position, as shown in Figure 4.59.

Figure 4.59 Place the middle of the swivel centered under the plate.

The main body of the wagon is now finished. All that remains is to build and attach the tongue. By now you should be starting to get the hang of creating polygon objects and placing them in a model using the Max tools. You should also be getting familiar with several of the tools used to create, modify, and extend polygon objects.

Building the Tongue

The tongue is attached to the wagon at the front swivel with a hinge, which enables the tongue to move up and down and turn the wagon left and right. You will start by creating the hinge and then building the tongue and handle.

1. You can really save time by utilizing some existing geometry to make the tongue pivot. The wheel mounts look a lot like something you would need to have for the tongue pivot. Select the front wheel mount.

2. Clone the object, as shown in Figure 4.60.

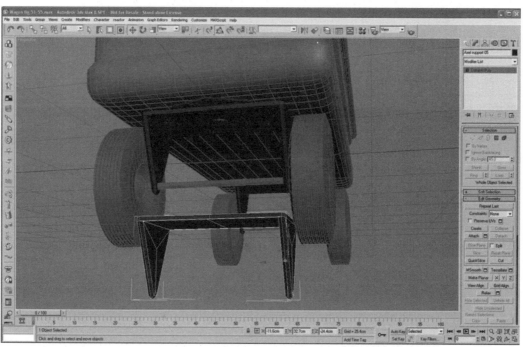

Figure 4.60 Duplicate the front wheel mount.

3. Center the pivot of the new object by selecting the Hierarchy tab and clicking Affect Pivot Only followed by Center to Object, as shown in Figure 4.61. You may also want to move the pivot up to the top of the newly created tongue pivot.

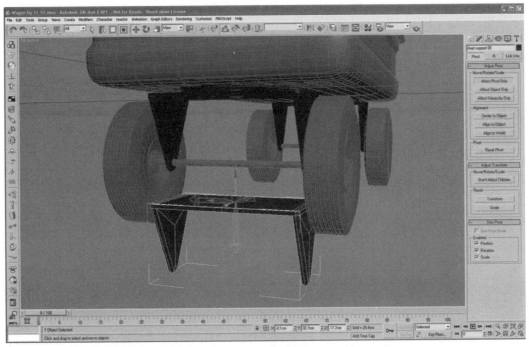

Figure 4.61 Center the pivot of the new object.

4. Scale X to 25 percent, scale Y to 15 percent, and scale Z to 25 percent so that the new object is the correct size for the tongue mount (see Figure 4.62).

Figure 4.62 Scale the new object to the correct size for the tongue.

5. Move the new object up to connect with the wheel mounts, as shown in Figure 4.63.

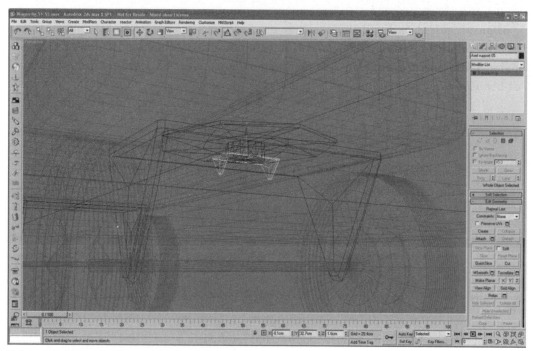

Figure 4.63 Connect the tongue mount with the swivel.

6. The tongue mount needs an axle. Clone the front wheel axle.

7. Scale the new axle to 20 percent and move it into place, as shown in Figure 4.64. (To make the scale and move process simple, you may want to center the pivot beforehand.)

8. Now to create the tongue. Create a new cylinder primitive with the following options: Radius, 1.0 cm; Height, 50.0 cm; Height Segments, 4; Cap Segments, 1; and Sides, 16 (see Figure 4.65).

9. Connect the tongue with the hinge by moving it into place, as shown in Figure 4.66.

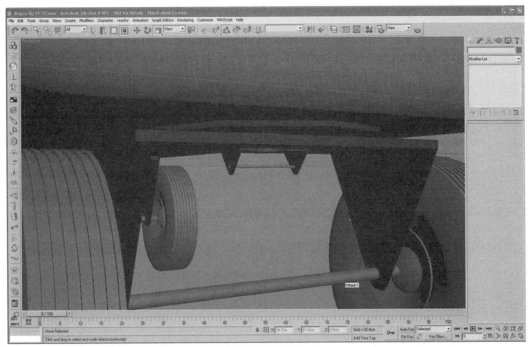

Figure 4.64 Create an axle for the hinge.

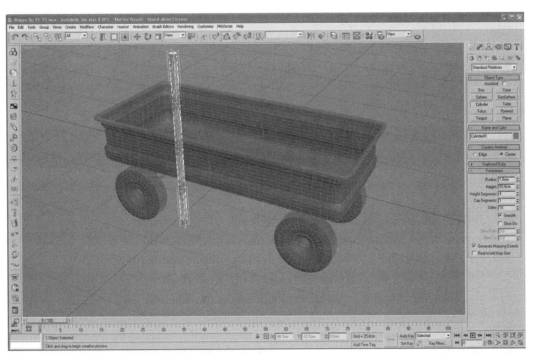

Figure 4.65 Create a new polygon cylinder for the tongue.

Chapter 4
Max

Figure 4.66 Place the tongue on the axle.

10. Enter Vertex Sub Object mode and select the loop of vertices in the center of the tongue. Slide the vertices toward the wagon, as shown in Figure 4.67.

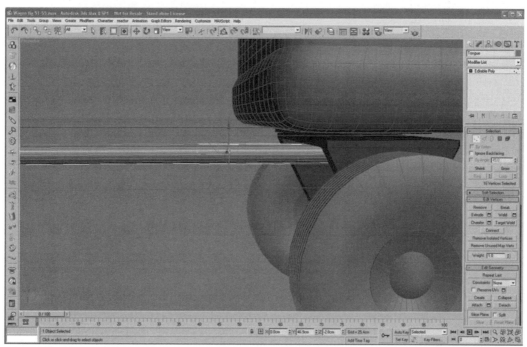

Figure 4.67 Move the vertices in the tongue toward the wagon.

11. Select the vertices at the end of the tongue near the hinge and scale them in vertically, as shown in Figure 4.68.

Figure 4.68 Scale the vertices near the hinge.

12. Next, you need to create another cylinder primitive for the handle. Create the cylinder with the following options: Radius, 1.0 cm; Height, 6.0 cm; Height Segments, 6; Cap Segments, 1; and Sides 16 (see Figure 4.69).

13. You will need only half of the handle right now because it will be mirrored later, saving you some time. Enter Vertex Sub Object mode and select the top half of the handle, not including the center row, and delete the selected vertices, as shown in Figure 4.70.

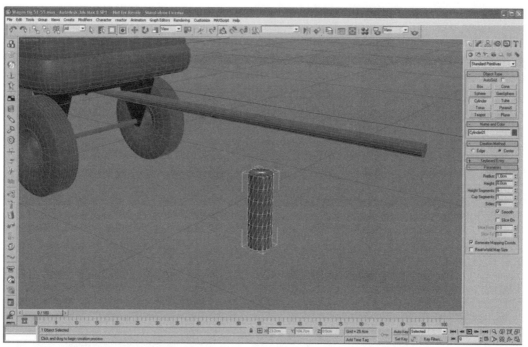

Figure 4.69 Create a cylinder for the handle.

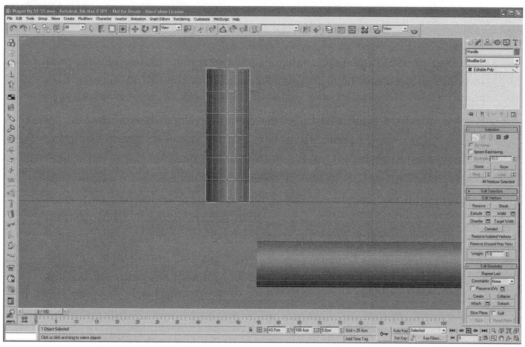

Figure 4.70 Select half of the faces on the handle.

14. Now slide the vertices of the handle toward the end of the cylinder, as shown in Figure 4.71.

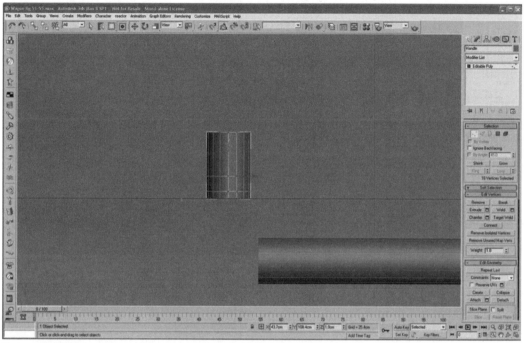

Figure 4.71 Slide the vertices of the handle toward the end of the cylinder.

15. Select the second ring of vertices from the end of the handle and scale them in, as shown in Figure 4.72.

16. Now move the handle to the end of the tongue, as shown in Figure 4.73.

17. Switch to Polygon Sub Object mode. Center the views over the handle.

18. Select half of the faces of the outer ring on the handle facing toward the wagon, as shown in Figure 4.74.

19. Extrude the faces and move them toward the tongue, as shown in Figure 4.75.

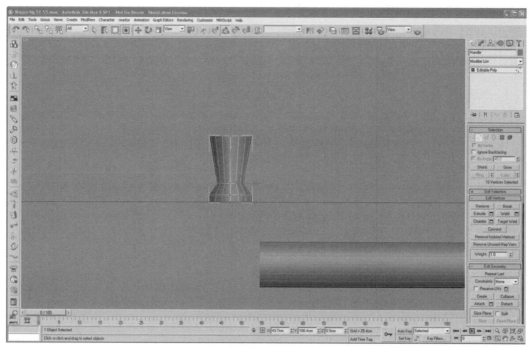

Figure 4.72 Scale the vertices in to shape the handle.

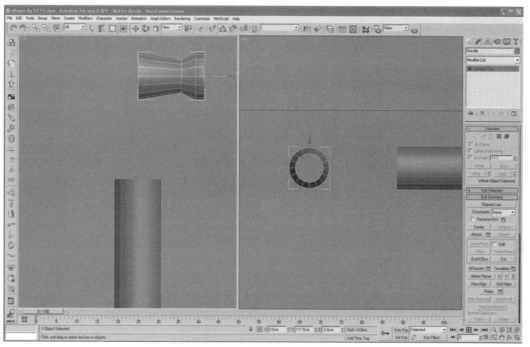

Figure 4.73 Move the handle to the end of the tongue.

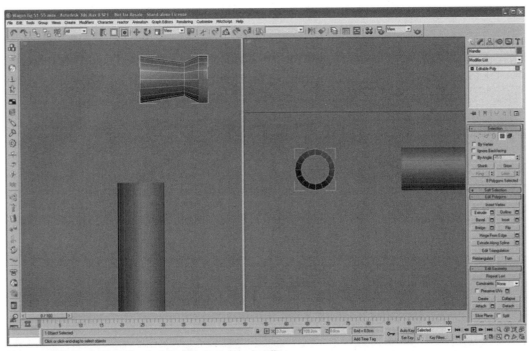

Figure 4.74 Select half the faces of the last ring of the handle.

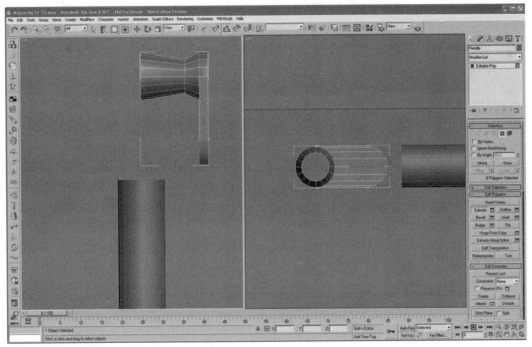

Figure 4.75 Move the extruded faces toward the wagon.

20. Using the Make Planer tool, flatten the selected faces, like those shown in Figure 4.76.

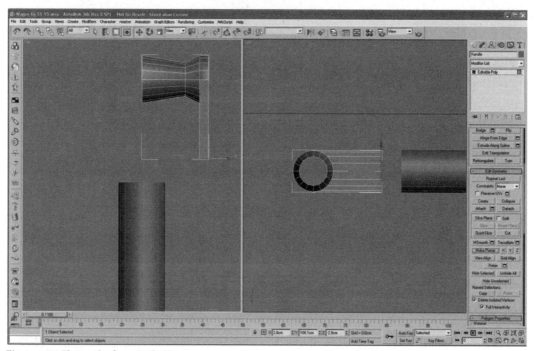

Figure 4.76 Flatten the faces in the Z axis.

21. Rotate the faces toward the center to about 45 degrees, as shown in Figure 4.77.

22. Extrude the faces again and move them so they are even with the end of the tongue by using the Extrusion tool, as shown in Figure 4.78.

23. Now the handle is ready to mirror, so let's leave Sub Object mode.

24. Bring up the Mirror dialog box, as shown in Figure 4.79.

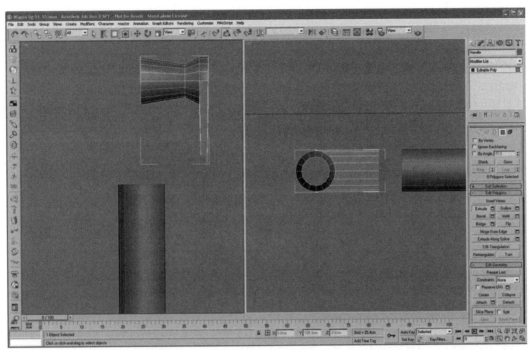

Figure 4.77 Rotate the faces of the handle.

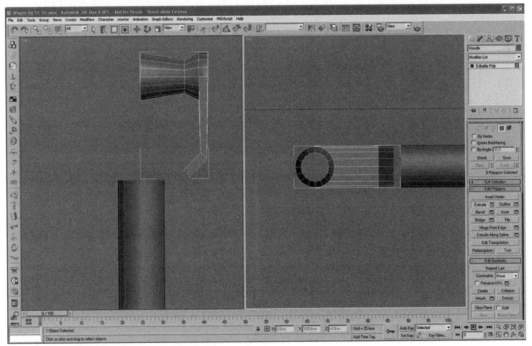

Figure 4.78 Extrude the handle toward the end of the tongue.

25. Set Mirror Axis to Z and Clone Selection to Copy. Adjust Offset so the object is in the right place. I used 6 cm. (See Figure 4.79.)

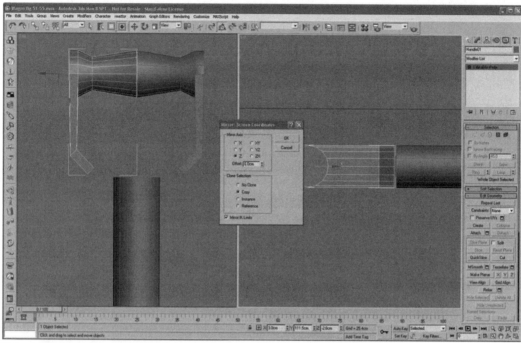

Figure 4.79 Mirror the handle.

26. Enter Vertex Sub Object mode, and, using the Attach tool, combine the two objects into one. Select the vertices along the seam of the mirror and weld them, as shown in Figure 4.80.

27. Enter Polygon Sub Object mode and select the polygons of the handle near the tongue on both sides of the handle.

28. Rotate the polygons 45 degrees and extrude the polygons to the center, as shown in Figure 4.81. With both sides selected, you should be able to rotate and extrude both sides at once, saving time and effort. (You may have to move each side individually to meet in the center.)

29. Draw a marquee around the center line to select both sides' polygons and delete them, as shown in Figure 4.82.

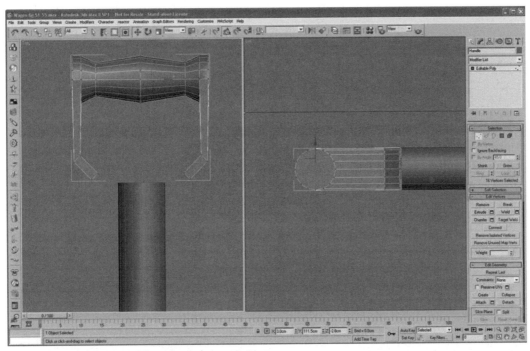

Figure 4.80 Merge the vertices between the mirrored objects.

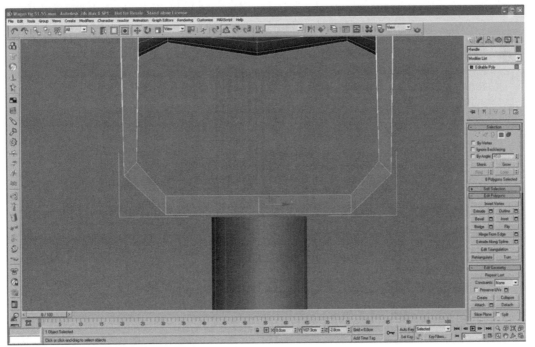

Figure 4.81 Scale the extruded faces together.

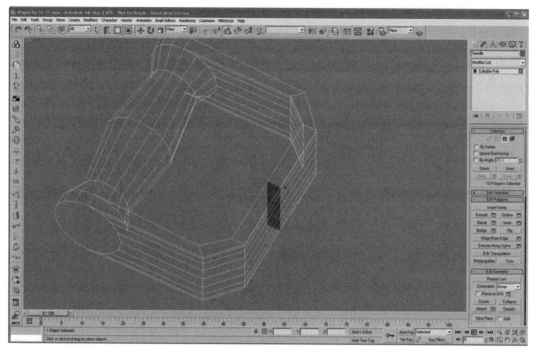

Figure 4.82 Delete the unneeded faces.

30. Enter Vertex Sub Object mode, and, using the Weld tool setting, select the vertices along the seam and weld them. (You will need to adjust Weld Threshold to something like 0.1 cm so it doesn't weld neighboring vertices.)

31. With the merged vertices still selected, scale the handle to overlap the tongue, as shown in Figure 4.83, and move the handle if needed to meet the end of the tongue.

32. Attach the handle to the tongue to make a single object, as shown in Figure 4.84.

33. You will want to set the snap so it will snap to vertices only. Do this by right-clicking on the 3D Snap button in the top center of the screen (see Figure 4.85). Set the snap only to Vertex and close the dialog box.

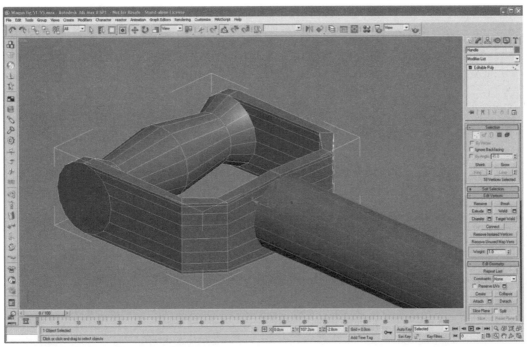

Figure 4.83 Scale the vertices to overlap the tongue.

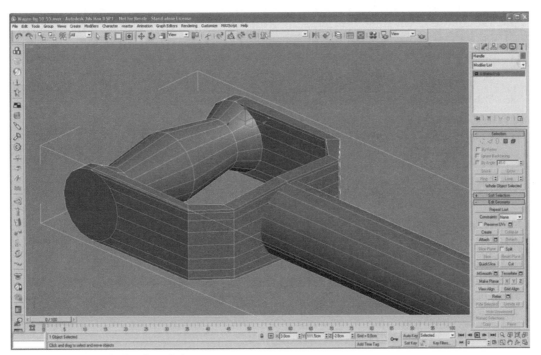

Figure 4.84 Combine the handle with the tongue.

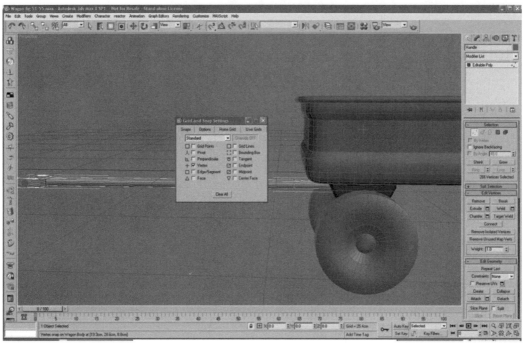

Figure 4.85 Set the snap to Vertex.

34. The tongue needs to be bent near the wagon. The problem with the Rotate tool is that the pivot is in the wrong place. To solve this, you will rotate around a selected vertex, but you have to first follow a few steps to make this work.

35. Enter Vertex Sub Object mode and select the vertices from the handle to the row nearest the wagon bed.

36. Lock the selection with the Lock icon or the spacebar.

37. Make sure the 3D Snap icon is toggled on.

38. Click the Rotate Transform icon.

39. Set the Use Center icon to Transform Coordinate Center.

40. Press F5 to set the axis to X.

41. Move the mouse over one of the vertices at the point you want to rotate around. A small blue crosshair will appear, indicating the "snap to" vertex is active. Click and rotate the tongue up so it looks right, as shown in Figure 4.86.

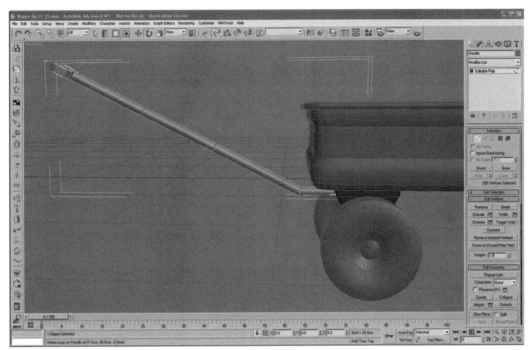

Figure 4.86 Rotate the tongue up.

42. Press the spacebar to unlock the selection and the S key to disable snapping.

43. Okay, one last thing before you are done. Switch to Polygon Sub Object mode and press Ctrl+A to select all the polygons in the tongue. Using the Auto Smooth tool, smooth the tongue so it shades correctly, as shown in Figure 4.87.

So that is it. You have just created your first wagon in Max! Figure 4.88 shows a rendering of the wagon. Your wagon should look similar to this.

Well, you didn't use all of the polygon-modeling tools in this exercise, but you did use a good number of them. Hopefully, you now feel comfortable with Max's polygon-modeling tools and are ready to tackle a few of your own models. Remember that if you don't understand anything in the tools, you can look them up in Max's extensive online help, found in the main menu under Help.

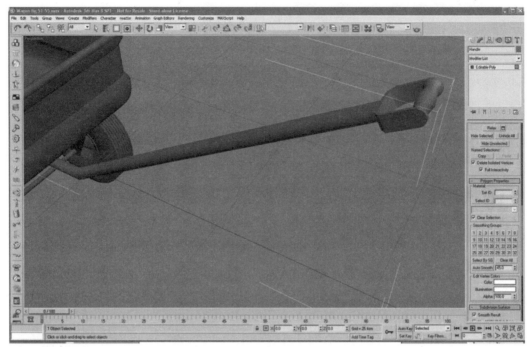

Figure 4.87 Smooth the edges of the handle.

Figure 4.88 A rendering of the wagon

Summary

This chapter covered a number of topics related to everyday polygon modeling in Max. Some of the most common concepts discussed were

- Working with Sub Object modes
- Setting object names and colors
- Locking the selection
- Smoothing geometry with MSmooth
- Extruding edges and polygons
- Removing excess geometry and keeping scenes efficient
- Cloning objects
- Welding vertices
- Expanding and shrinking selections
- Resetting the shading with Auto Smooth
- Mirroring geometry
- Using keyboard shortcuts
- Using the Snapping tools

Note

By now, you have started to develop default values for things like viewports, snaps, tools, and workflows that you might like to see set up every time you use Max. There is an easy way to set this up so that every time you start Max, these will be set by default. Start a completely new (default) scene in Max and run through each element that you want to have as a default. For example, start with things like how you want your viewports to look. Maybe you'd like one big viewport with Shading and Edged Faces turned on. Maybe you like to work in some unit other than metric, or maybe you always want to start Max with a box in the middle of the screen. Whatever it is, get Max set up so you feel most comfortable.

Once you have the default setup you desire, simply save a file called Maxstart.max in the default Scenes directory. Every time you open Max or reset the scene after this, you will get your defaults. If you want to change things over time, just resave or delete this file.

Note

As you get deeper into Max, you may find a limitation or feel you need more power here or there. The Web is a great place to look for additional plug-ins, scripts, or help. The Max community is huge and very helpful. You can find a plethora of resources (for sale or free) for every part of Max, which can really give you a huge boost. Also available is a tremendous number of tutorials that go far beyond the scope of this book, which can help you push your skills even further.

Chapter 5

Nervous About NURBS

In addition to polygon modeling, several other methods of creating digital 3D models exist. This chapter deals primarily with two of these methods: NURBS and subdivision surfaces. These two methods of modeling have advantages for building complex models depending on the type of model constructed. NURBS modeling tends to work very well for smooth, rounded shapes. Subdivision surfaces are very good for modeling forms that have both rounded surfaces and creases.

Polygon modeling is great for many applications, but sometimes polygons become difficult to deal with in models with very tight meshes. In these instances, modeling with NURBS or subdivision surfaces is often a better choice, even if the end result needs to be in polygons. The advantage of both of these systems is that the modeler can create complex smooth geometry quickly and later convert the geometry to polygons.

NURBS stands for Non-Uniform Rational B-Splines, which, unless you have a math background, might not mean much to you. Just think of NURBS as using curves to represent shapes and volumes. By controlling the shape of the curve, the modeler is able to influence the model.

Spline is an old term that goes back to the days of shipbuilding, long before the dawn of 3D modeling programs. To draw smooth curves across a series of points, shipbuilders used a thin metal or wooden beam called a *spline*, which they bent around weights called *knots*. Later, mathematical equivalents were developed for the curving of the splines, called *B-splines*, for basis splines.

NURBS Modeling

NURBS models use curves instead of flat planes to describe a 3D surface. The use of curves gives a NURBS model a smooth finish rather than the facets found in polygon models.

Maya has several tools specifically for NURBS modeling. These tools are found primarily in the Edit Curves, Surfaces, and Edit NURBS menus of the Surfaces menu set.

Like polygons, NURBS models can start with a primitive shape; however, a more common way to build NURBS models is to start with a curve. In the following example, curves and primitives are used to build a pitcher. The pitcher will be created using a CV curve, and the handles will be built from a cylinder primitive.

NURBS Primitives

Maya supports a number of primitive objects for NURBS, similar to the polygon primitives covered earlier. The supported primitives are as follows:

- Sphere
- Cube
- Cylinder
- Cone
- Plane
- Torus
- Circle
- Square

NURBS primitives differ from polygon primitives in a number of ways. For example, NURBS primitives are defined by curves rather than polygons. This makes the surfaces of a NURBS primitive smooth at any distance from the object. Because NURBS primitives are constructed based on curves, they are simpler to adjust when modeling smooth objects.

Sphere

Figure 5.1 shows the NURBS Sphere Options dialog box and the sphere that was created using the options shown.

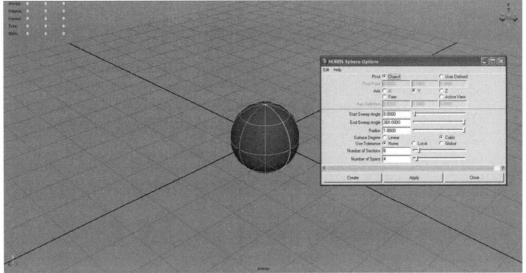

Figure 5.1 Use the NURBS Sphere Options dialog box to set options for creating spheres.

Pivot

The NURBS Sphere Options dialog box allows for the placement of the pivot, which controls the placement of the object and the scale and rotation point of the object.

Axis

Axis determines the orientation of the object along the X, Y, or Z axis. Alternately, you can select a custom orientation by selecting Free. Active view will orient the object perpendicular to the view if the view is an orthographic view.

Sweep Angles

The Start Sweep Angle and End Sweep Angle boxes are for creating full or partial spheres. For example, a start angle of 0 and an end angle of 180 will result in a half sphere.

Radius

The Radius box sets the radius of the sphere from the pivot point to the outer limit of the sphere.

Surface Degree

Surface Degree sets the surface to either Linear or Cubic. Set the option for Linear if you want to have a faceted model. Set the option to Cubic if you want a curved surface.

Use Tolerance

Use Tolerance controls the precision of a NURBS model. Global will create objects at the default precision, which can be controlled in Window, Settings/Preferences, Preferences. Local will create objects based on positional tolerance—that is, the lower the number, the tighter the mesh. None will allow the modeler to determine the number of spans and sections.

Sections

Sections are the longitudinal curves that describe an object. Setting a high number of sections will increase the surface detail of an object, but it will also increase the processing time as well.

Spans

Spans are the latitudinal curves that describe an object. As is true for sections, having more spans will increase surface detail as well as processing time.

Cube

Figure 5.2 shows the NURBS Cube Options dialog box and the cube that was created using the options shown.

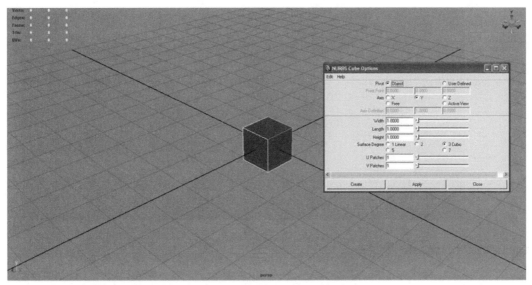

Figure 5.2 The NURBS Cube Options dialog box controls the creation of NURBS cubes.

The Pivot and Axis options are similar to those found in the NURBS Sphere Options dialog box.

Size

The Width, Length, and Height boxes control the cube's size.

Surface Degree

Surface Degree is similar to that of the sphere.

U Patches and V Patches

U Patches and V Patches control the subdivision of the cube. A patch is the rectangular area of a NURBS object bounded by curves.

Cylinder

Figure 5.3 shows the NURBS Cylinder Options dialog box and the cylinder that was created using the options shown.

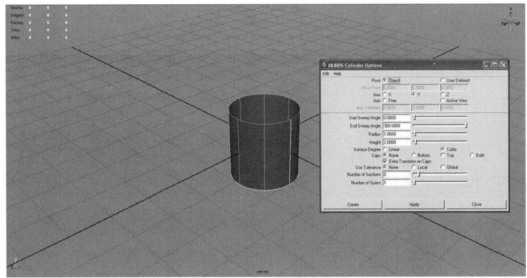

Figure 5.3 NURBS cylinders are created using the options in the NURBS Cylinder Options dialog box.

Many of the options for creating NURBS cylinders are similar to the ones used to create NURBS spheres, with a couple of exceptions.

Size

In addition to having a radius, cylinders have a height, so there is an extra option for controlling the height of the cylinder.

End Caps

Other aspects of cylinders that are different from spheres are those that deal with the end caps of the cylinder. You can select whether to have a cap on either end of the cylinder or not to have one at all. You can also choose to have the end caps as separate objects for independent manipulation.

Cone

Figure 5.4 shows the NURBS Cone Options dialog box and the cone that was created using the options shown.

The options for cones are similar to those of other previously mentioned NURBS objects, except that there is only one end cap on a cone.

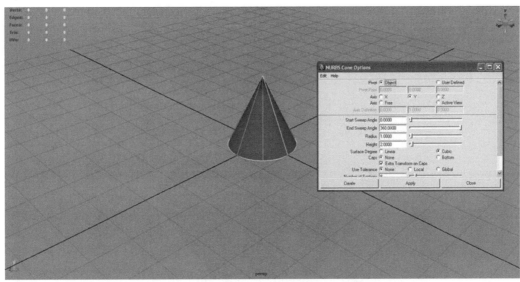

Figure 5.4 Options for NURBS cones are similar to those of other NURBS primitives.

Plane

Figure 5.5 shows the NURBS Plane Options dialog box and the plane that was created using the options shown. NURBS planes are similar to polygon planes, except that NURBS planes are made up of curves and patches instead of polygons.

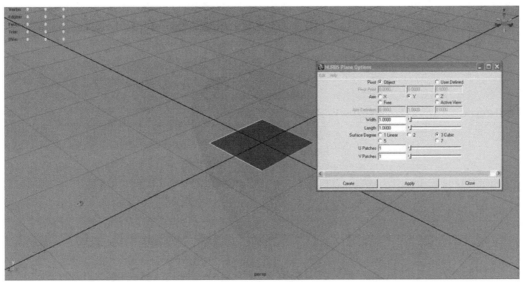

Figure 5.5 A NURBS plane is shown next to the options that created it.

The options for creating NURBS planes are similar to those for the NURBS cube, except that there is no Height option.

Torus

Figure 5.6 shows the NURBS Torus Options dialog box and the torus (or 3D ring) that was created using the options shown.

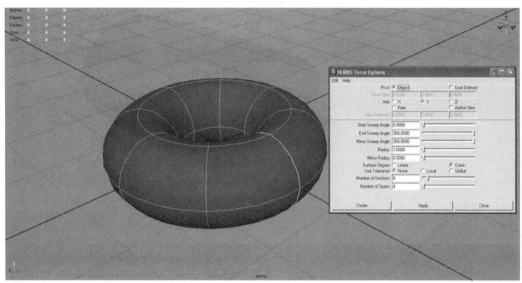

Figure 5.6 The torus is a 3D ring.

The NURBS torus has options similar to those of the NURBS sphere, cylinder, and cone, except that it has the additional options Minor Sweep Angle and Minor Radius.

Minor Sweep Angle

The Minor Sweep Angle option controls the sweep of the torus on the tube. A Minor Sweep Angle of 180 will result in an object that looks similar to the rim of a tire, as shown in Figure 5.7.

Minor Radius

The Minor Radius option controls the thickness of the ring.

Circle

A circle is a curve and not an object. Figure 5.8 shows a circle created with the option shown.

Because the circle is a curve and not a surface, it does not have any spans. The other options for creating a circle are similar to those for creating a cylinder.

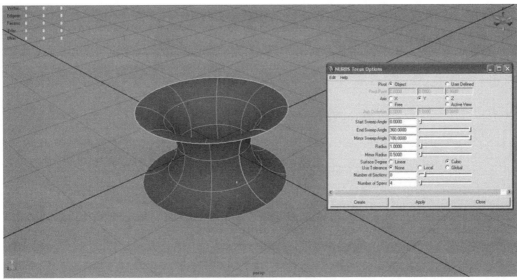

Figure 5.7 A 180 degree Minor Sweep Angle looks like the rim of a tire.

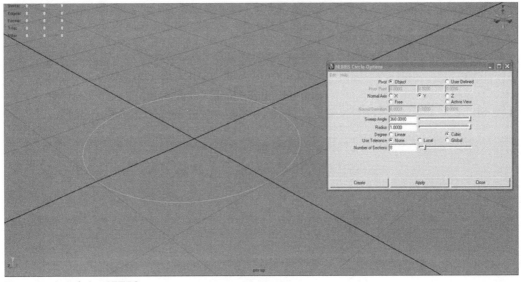

Figure 5.8 A circle is a NURBS curve.

Square

A square is also a curve and not an object. Figure 5.9 shows a NURBS square created using the options shown in the dialog box.

NURBS squares are four NURBS curves aligned to make a rectangular shape. Their options are similar to those for creating a NURBS cube.

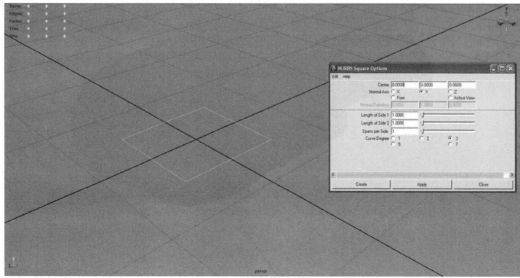

Figure 5.9 NURBS squares are curves rather than objects.

Using NURBS Primitives

NURBS primitives are great to use for creating smooth objects. In the next example, you will use NURBS primitives to create a cartoon race car.

1. Create a NURBS sphere with 16 sections and 32 spans, as shown in Figure 5.10.

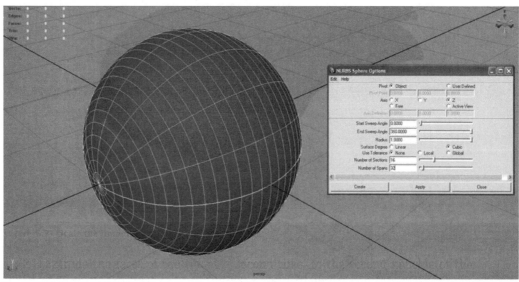

Figure 5.10 Create a NURBS sphere.

2. In the Channel box, set Scale X to 1.5 and Scale Z to 4 to form the body of the car.

3. Bring up the Sculpt Geometry Tool, found in the Edit NURBS directory. The tool will appear in the side panel, as shown in Figure 5.11.

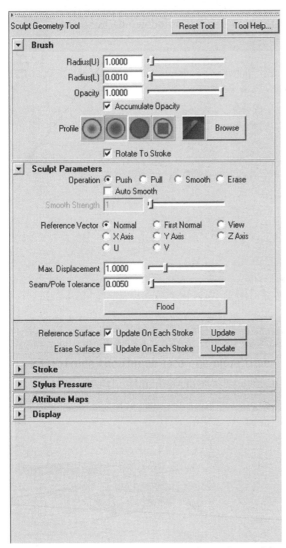

The Sculpt Geometry Tool allows the artist to sculpt NURBS objects as if they were lumps of clay. Sculpt Geometry uses Artisan brush tools. Artisan brush tools allow artists to delicately paint on 3D geometry using input devices like a stylus.

4. You will need to change the radius of the brush to work correctly in this project. Set the Radius(U) option to 0.5000. If you are using a mouse, only the Radius(U) option is available. Radius(L) is used in conjunction with Radius(U) for when you are using a pressure-sensitive stylus. Radius(U) defines the upper limit of the stylus, and Radius(L) defines the lower limit of the stylus.

5. Make sure Opacity is set to 1.0000. Opacity determines the amount of effect an Artisan brush has on an object.

Figure 5.11 The Sculpt Geometry Tool can be used to modify NURBS objects.

6. Under Sculpt Parameters, set the brush to Push. Push influences the geometry away from the brush.

7. From the Top view, push the geometry in to form the cockpit of the car, as shown in Figure 5.12.

8. Now change the brush to Pull, and pull upward in the back of the cockpit, as shown in Figure 5.13.

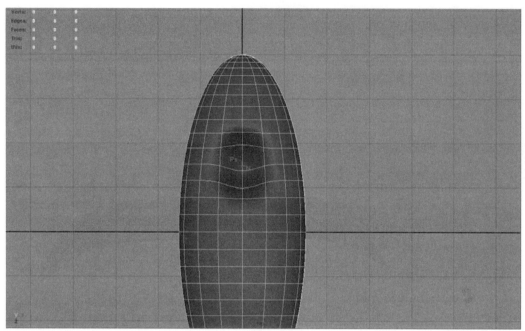

Figure 5.12 Use Push to mold the geometry for the cockpit.

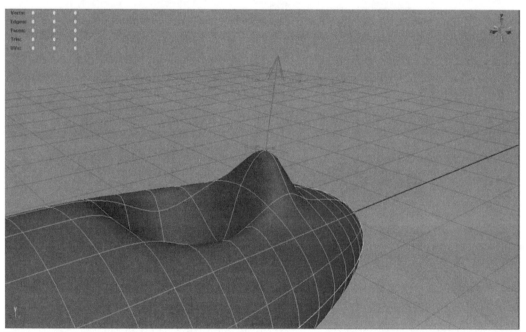

Figure 5.13 Pull the back lip of the cockpit up.

9. Push the cockpit in toward the front of the car so the driver has an area for his feet.

10. Now pull up the front of the cockpit to form a windshield for the car, as shown in Figure 5.14.

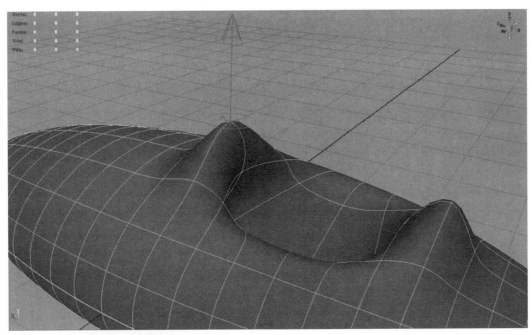

Figure 5.14 Give the car a windshield.

11. Create a NURBS torus with Radius set to 1.0000 and Minor Radius to 0.5000 for one of the wheels of the car.

12. In the Channel box, set Translate X to 2 and Translate Z to 2 so that the wheel is lined up with the front of the car.

13. Use the marking menu to change the selection mode for the wheel to Control Vertex and select the center CVs of the tire from the Front view, as shown in Figure 5.15. Control Vertices (or CVs, as they are often called) are similar to vertices on polygonal models except that they control the shape of the curves rather than directly sitting on the object itself.

14. Scale in the CVs to flatten the outer edge of the wheel, as shown in Figure 5.16.

15. Now you need to create a NURBS cylinder for the axle and rims of the tire. Make sure you have Caps set to Both. Also, set Radius to .5 and Height to 4.

16. Move the axle to the front of the car by setting Translate Z to 2 in the Channel box.

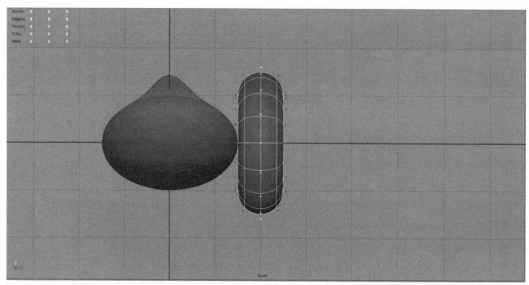

Figure 5.15 Select the CVs along the center of the wheel.

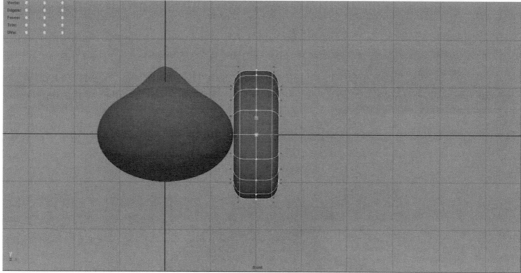

Figure 5.16 Scale in the tire.

17. From the Side view, select the center CVs of the cylinder and the first ring of CVs out from the center, as shown in Figure 5.17.

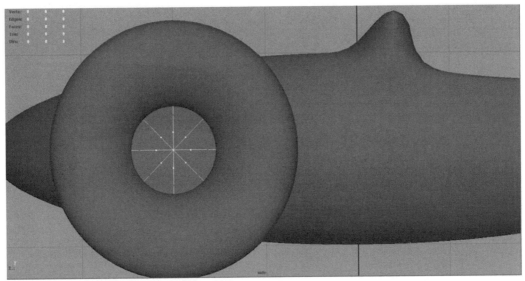

Figure 5.17 Select the center CVs of the axle.

18. Scale the CVs in the X axis outward to create the hubcaps, as shown in Figure 5.18.

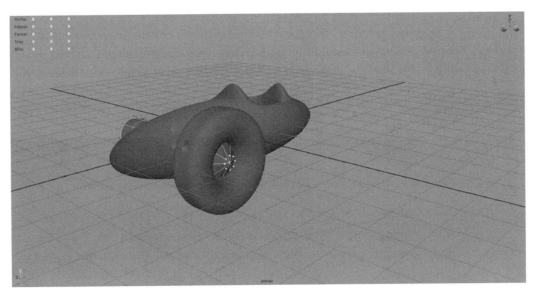

Figure 5.18 Give the tires molded hubcaps.

19. In Wireframe view, select the five rings of CVs in the middle of the axle, as shown in Figure 5.19.

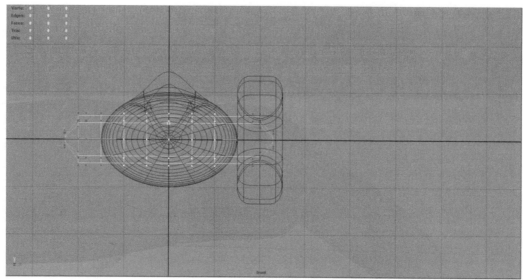

Figure 5.19 Select the five center rings of the axle.

20. Scale the CVs in all three axes, as shown in Figure 5.20.

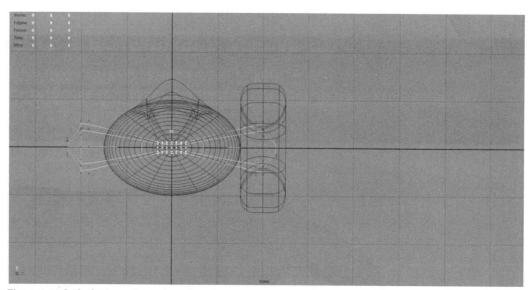

Figure 5.20 Scale the inner CVs to form the axle.

21. Now scale the CVs outward in the X axis to form the axle, as shown in Figure 5.21.

22. Duplicate the wheel and move it to the right side of the car, as shown in Figure 5.22.

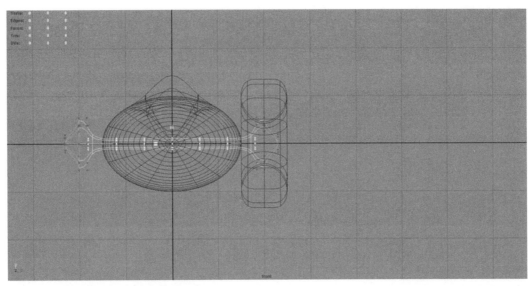

Figure 5.21 Complete the scaling of the axle.

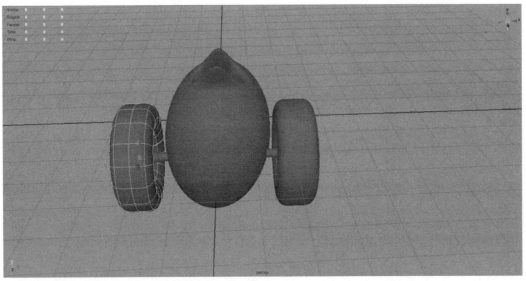

Figure 5.22 Place a duplicate wheel on the right side of the car.

23. Duplicate the axle and tires and move the duplicates −2 in Translate Z in the Channel box.

24. On the front of the body of the car, select the center CV and the first three rings of CVs outward from the center, as shown in Figure 5.23.

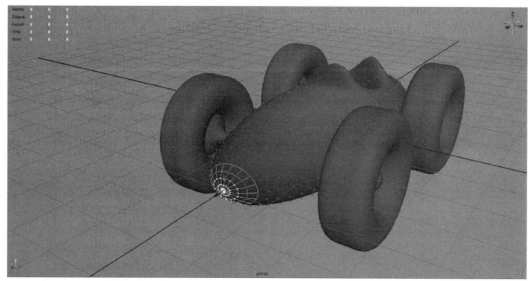

Figure 5.23 Select the CVs in the front of the car.

25. Use the Move tool to pull the CVs inward to form an air scoop, as shown in Figure 5.24. When you are working on CVs on the polar axis of a sphere, the Sculpt Geometry Tool will usually create seams. Using the Move tool is a better option for these areas.

Figure 5.24 Create an air scoop for the front of the car.

26. On the back of the car, select the first two rings and center CVs and pull them toward the center of the car, as shown in Figure 5.25.

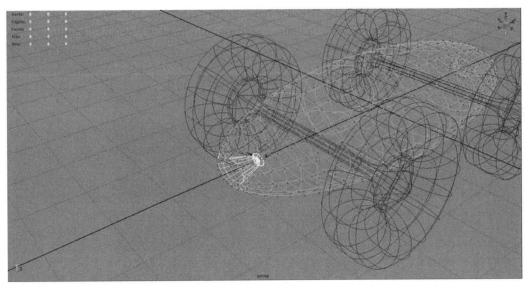

Figure 5.25 Pull the CVs toward the center of the car.

27. Now select the next four rings of CVs, as shown in Figure 5.26.

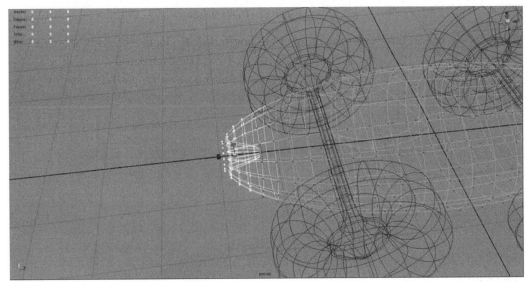

Figure 5.26 Select the next four rings of CVs.

28. Scale the CVs together in the Z axis, as shown in Figure 5.27.

29. Scale the CVs outward, as shown in Figure 5.28, to form the back of the car.

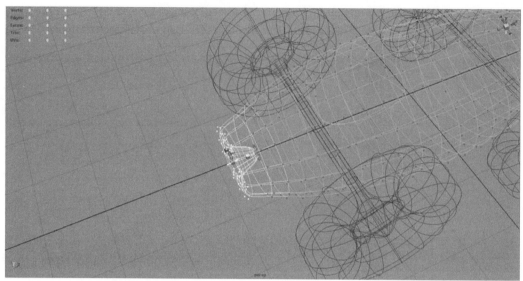

Figure 5.27 Flatten the CVs in the Z axis.

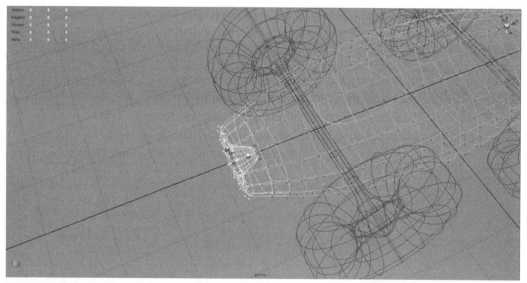

Figure 5.28 Scale the CVs to flare out on the back of the car.

Figure 5.29 shows the cartoon car. It is a very simple model. If you want to add a few more features, such as a steering wheel, feel free to modify the car as you see fit.

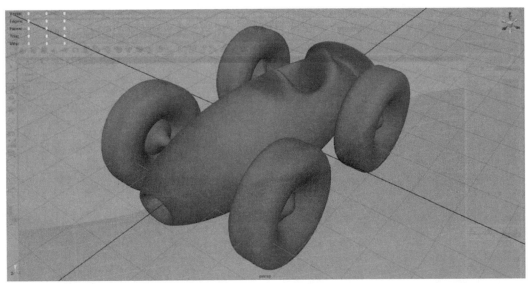

Figure 5.29 The finished cartoon car.

Using Curves

The first step to creating a model from a curve is to create a curve. You will need to change the menu set to Surfaces. The most common method of creating a curve is to use Maya's CV Curve tool. This tool is found in the Create menu of Maya's main menu.

In the last project, you used CVs to modify a NURBS primitive object. Now you will be creating your own curves by placing CVs. In this example you will be building a pitcher.

1. Select CV Curve Tool from the Create menu.

2. In the Front view, click the left mouse button with the CV Curve tool four times (see Figure 5.30). Press Ctrl+B for the first click to snap the first CV to the grid as shown.

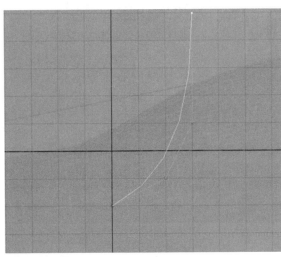

Figure 5.30 Use the CV Curve tool to create a curve.

Note

Notice that the CVs are not on the curve but rather to the side of the curve. To see how a CV affects a curve, select CV number 3 and drag it to a different position. Watch how moving the CV changes the curve. Select Undo from the Edit menu to return the CV to its original position.

3. Place another CV directly to the right of the end CV in the curve chain. This CV will establish the width of the top of the pitcher.

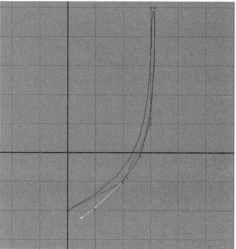

Figure 5.31 Create the outer line of the pitcher.

4. Now place another CV down along the outside of the curve staying roughly the same distance from the curve as the last two CVs. The CV curve should now curve back on itself forming a somewhat rounded lip at the top.

5. Continue to place new CVs to create the outer line of the pitcher, as shown in Figure 5.31.

6. Continue to place new CVs to create the stem of the pitcher as shown in Figure 5.32. At the highlighted point at the end of the curve shown in the figure, place three CVs directly on top of each other. This will create a sharp or hard corner in the curve.

7. Finish placing CVs until the pitcher resembles the curve in Figure 5.33. Place three CVs at the base of the pitcher to form a sharp corner on the outer edge of the base. Hit Enter on the keyboard to exit the tool.

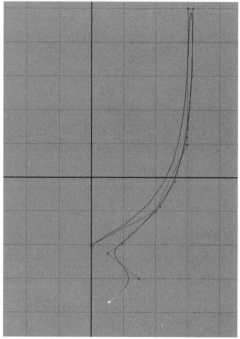

Figure 5.32 Start creating the stem of the pitcher.

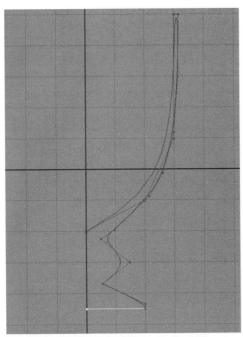

Figure 5.33 Finish placing the CVs to form the curve of the pitcher.

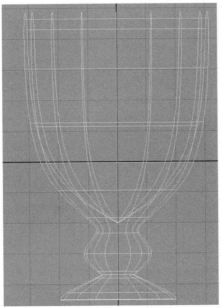

Figure 5.34 Revolve the curve to create a 3D model of the pitcher.

8. The curve should now form half the silhouette of a pitcher, as if it were cut right down the middle. It is now ready to be revolved into a full 3D model. In the main menu, go to Surface and select the dialog box next to Revolve.

9. Set the axis to Y and the segments to 16, as shown in Figure 5.34. Click Apply to revolve the curve. The model should now look similar to the one shown in the figure.

10. Next, you will need to work on the spout, but before you can do that, you need to add a little bit more detail to the top of the pitcher. Change the selection mode to Isoparm. *Isoparm* is another name for an individual segment, or span, on a NURBS object.

11. Select the second isoparm down from the top of the pitcher from the outside, as shown in Figure 5.35. It will turn yellow when selected.

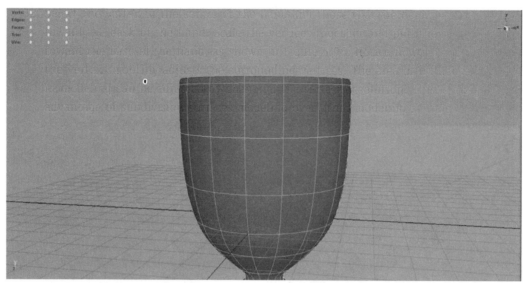

Figure 5.35 Select an isoparm on the model.

12. Click and hold down the left mouse button and drag the isoparm upward. A dotted line will appear. Release the left mouse button to place the dotted line halfway between the lower and upper isoparm, as shown in Figure 5.36.

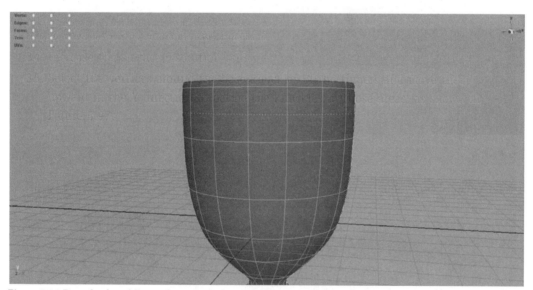

Figure 5.36 Drag the dotted line up between the lower and upper isoparm.

13. Use the Insert Isoparm function found in the Edit NURBS menu to insert an isoparm at the location of the dotted line, as shown in Figure 5.37.

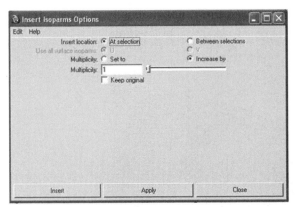

Figure 5.37 Insert an isoparm.

14. Now create another isoparm in the same way between the new one and the upper one, as shown in Figure 5.38.

15. Create two new isoparms on the inside of the pitcher so that it looks similar to Figure 5.39.

16. From the Side view, change the view mode to Wireframe and the selection mode to Control Vertex. Pull the CVs of the outer edge of the picture to the left, as shown in Figure 5.40.

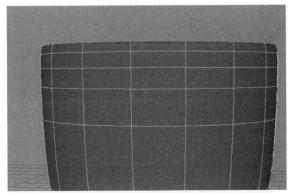

Figure 5.38 Insert another isoparm.

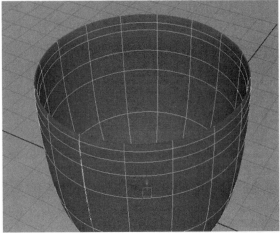

Figure 5.39 Add some more isoparms to the inside of the pitcher.

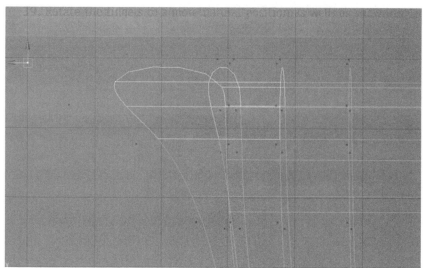

Figure 5.40 Pull the CVs on the left side to the left.

17. Pull the CVs down to form the curve of the spout, as shown in Figure 5.41.

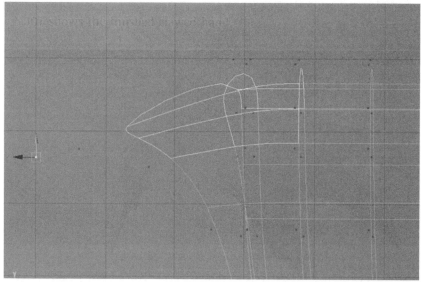

Figure 5.41 Pull the spout down.

18. Now you need to pull the CVs of the inside of the pitcher along the far left to correspond with the curve of the spout, as shown in Figure 5.42.

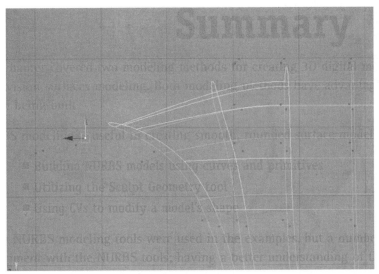

Figure 5.42 The inner curve should follow the outer curve of the spout.

19. Select the top CVs of the pitcher and scale them outward to give the top a flared look, as shown in Figure 5.43.

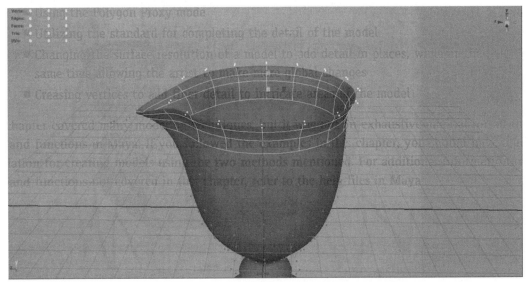

Figure 5.43 Flare the top of the pitcher.

20. Next is the handle. Create a torus object with a Radius of 1 and a Minor Radius of .25. Set the segments to 16 and the spans to 8.

21. Raise the torus four units and place it along the pitcher's edge at about Translate Z −4.34 (see Figure 5.44).

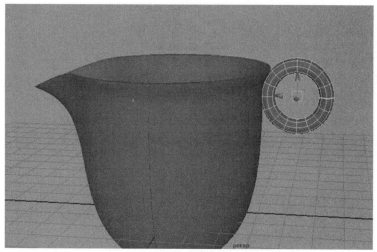

Figure 5.44 Put the torus on the back of the pitcher for the handle.

22. Change the selection mode to Isoparm and select the isoparm ring at the bottom of the torus.

23. Use the Detach Surface command to separate the torus at the selected isoparm. Detach Surface is located in the Edit NURBS menu.

24. Change the selection mode of the torus to Control Vertex and separate the CVs along the detached ends, as shown in Figure 5.45.

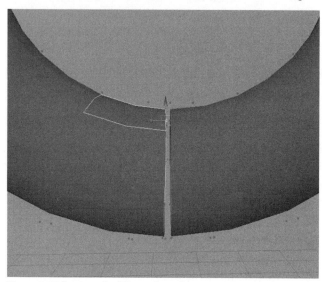

25. Pull the CVs of the right-hand end down to form the handle of the pitcher, as shown in Figure 5.46.

26. Rotate and scale the CVs of the right-hand end, as shown in Figure 5.47.

Figure 5.45 Separate the CVs on the ends.

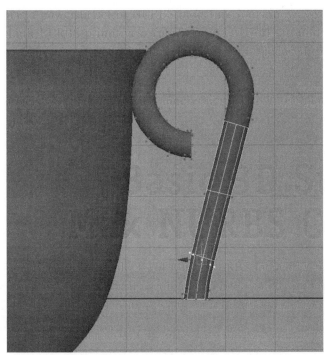

Figure 5.46 Pull the handle down from the top.

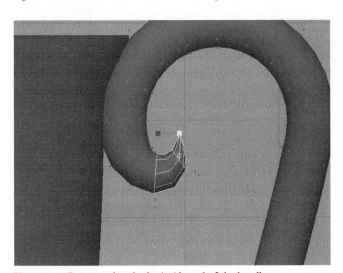

Figure 5.47 Rotate and scale the inside end of the handle.

27. Model the handle using the Move, Rotate, and Scale tools to shape it to look like the handle shown in Figure 5.48.

28. The handle is a little rough. Smooth it out by adding a few more isoparms, as shown in Figure 5.49.

Figure 5.48 Adjust the handle of the pitcher.

Figure 5.49 Smooth the handle.

29. Change the selection mode to Control Vertex and rotate the new isoparms to better follow the shape of the handle, as shown in Figure 5.50.

30. Select the original CV curve, as shown in Figure 5.51, and hide it.

Figure 5.50 Rotate the new isoparms to follow the handle.

Figure 5.51 Select the original CV curve.

Lofting Surfaces

Lofting between two curves is another way to create NURBS surfaces. Lofting can be used for a number of purposes. In this section, you will loft an organic tabletop from CV curves.

1. From the Top view, create a CV curve similar to the one shown in Figure 5.52.

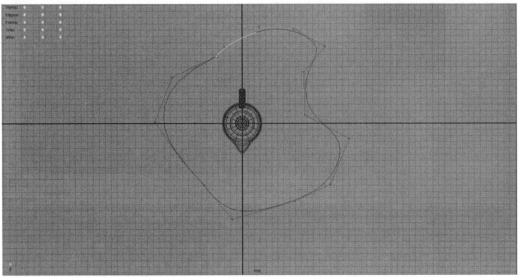

Figure 5.52 Create a CV curve for the table.

2. Close the curve using the Open/Close Curve function found in the Edit Curves menu.

3. With shapes like the tabletop, it is often a good practice to rebuild the curve so the CVs are evenly spaced around the curve. Bring up the Rebuild Curve Options dialog box by selecting it from the Edit Curves menu. Set Number of Spans to 20 and click Apply. Figure 5.53 shows the dialog box and the new CVs evenly spaced on the curve.

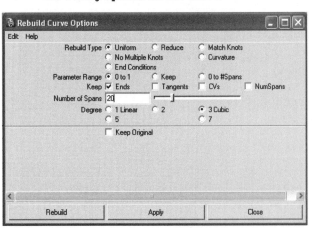

Figure 5.53 Rebuild the curve with 20 spans.

4. Place the curve at the base of the pitcher, as shown in Figure 5.54.

5. Duplicate the curve and scale it down so that it is smaller than the base of the pitcher, as shown in Figure 5.55.

Figure 5.54 Move the curve to the base of the pitcher.

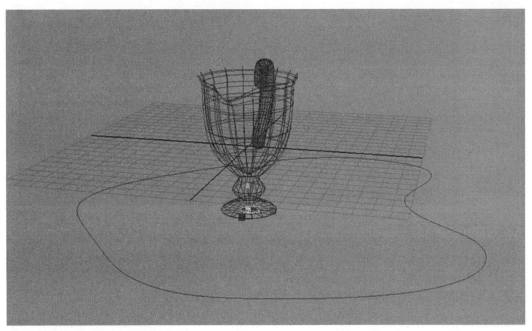

Figure 5.55 Duplicate and scale the curve.

6. Duplicate the curve again and move the duplicate down about one unit, as shown in Figure 5.56.

7. Now select the first duplicate curve and the original curve and bring up the Loft Options dialog box from the Surfaces menu.

8. Set Section Spans to 2 and click Apply to create the tabletop surface, as shown in Figure 5.57.

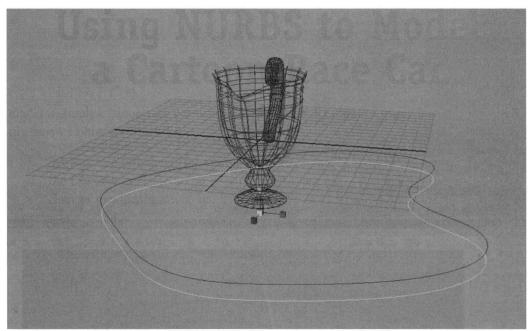

Figure 5.56 Move the duplicate curve down.

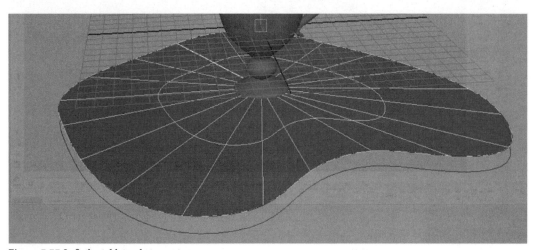

Figure 5.57 Loft the tabletop between two curves.

9. Give the table some depth by lofting between the two outside curves using only one span, as shown in Figure 5.58.

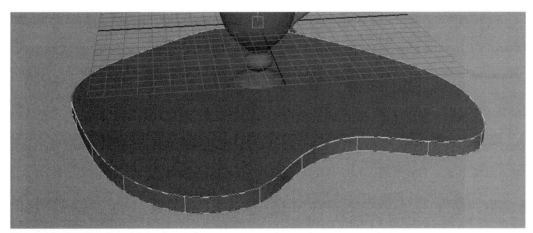

Figure 5.58 Loft the edge of the table.

You now have a pitcher sitting on a tabletop. Lofting is a great tool for building organic shapes using simple CV curves. It is also very versatile. If you leave History on, the new NURBS surfaces will remain influenced by the original CV curves. This can make editing the surfaces a lot easier. Figure 5.59 shows the CVs of the two outside curves used to change the shape of the table.

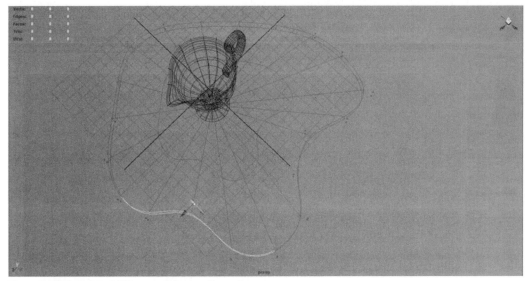

Figure 5.59 The original CV curves influence the surfaces.

Subdivision Surfaces Modeling

Subdivision surfaces modeling is an advanced modeling method used in creating models that have high surface detail. It can be used to create simple objects, but it is more useful for making complex models.

Creating models with subdivision surfaces is a little like creating a model with both polygons and NURBS at the same time. In the following example, you will build a model of a clawed hand. The process of building the hand will show many advantages of creating models using subdivision surfaces. You will create the basic model from a simple polygon cube in Polygon Proxy mode. After finishing the basic shape of the model, you will use Standard mode to refine the detail in the model. These two modes will be explained during the course of the project.

Polygon Proxy Mode

One of the biggest advantages to using subdivision surfaces is the Polygon Proxy mode. This mode is designed to give the artist access to the polygon-modeling tools while creating a smooth, rounded surface. It also allows the artist to start the model using polygons and then switch over to subdivision surfaces and back again later as needed.

1. Create a polygon cube that is 5 units wide by 5 units deep by 1.5 units high. This cube will be the basis for developing the clawed hand.

2. Open the dialog box for converting polygons to subdivision surfaces. It is located under Modify, Convert, Polygons to Subdiv.

3. Set Maximum Base Mesh Faces to 1000 and Maximum Edges Per Vertex to 32, and then click Apply to convert the model.

4. Now set the model to Polygon Proxy mode from the Subdiv Surfaces menu.

5. The model should now have a wireframe cube (of the same dimensions as the original polygon cube) around it. This cube controls the look and shape of the subdivision surfaces model. Swing around to the right side of the model in Perspective view and use the Split Polygon tool from the Edit Polygons menu to draw in four vertical lines, as shown in Figure 5.60. These lines will be used to define the fingers of the hand.

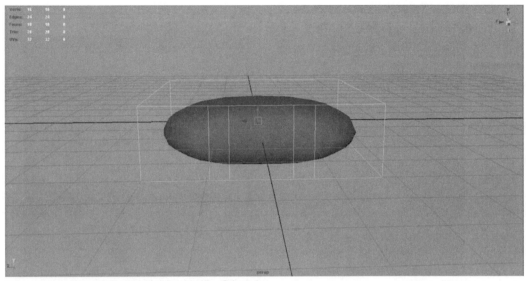

Figure 5.60 Split the polygons of the right side of the cube.

6. Now between two sets of the vertical edges, split the polygons horizontally, as shown in Figure 5.61. These polygons will be used to form webbing between the fingers.

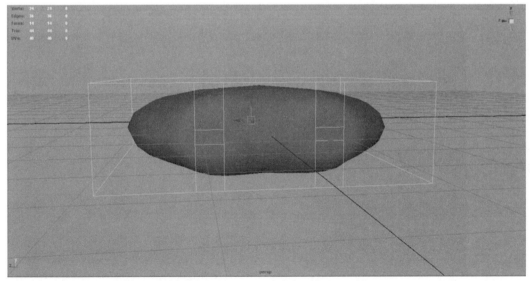

Figure 5.61 Split the polygons horizontally.

7. Change the selection mode to Faces.

8. Select the faces, as shown in Figure 5.62.

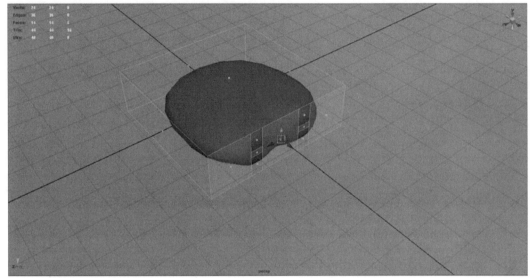

Figure 5.62 Select the polygon faces for the fingers.

9. The clawed hand will have only three fingers, in keeping with the standard for cartoon characters. Extrude the faces of the selected polygons. Extrude the selected faces and move the extruded faces in the X direction 1.5 units, as shown in Figure 5.63. Notice how the subdivision surfaces model follows the polygon proxy.

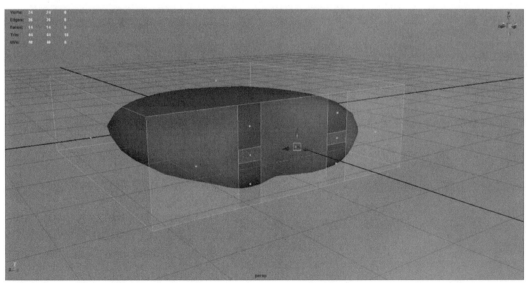

Figure 5.63 Extrude the fingers of the hand.

10. The fingers should not all be the same length. This first extrusion will be to the first knuckles. Select the polygon for each finger and move it in the X direction to take into account the differing lengths of the fingers, as shown in Figure 5.64.

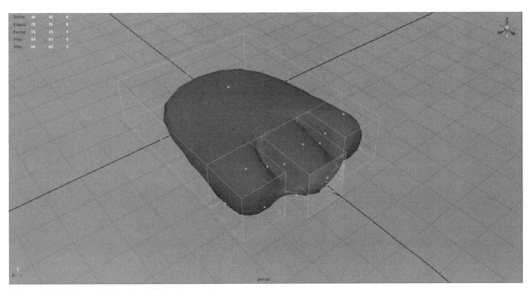

Figure 5.64 Adjust the lengths of the fingers.

11. Now reselect the polygons of the fingers and webbing and extrude them again, as shown in Figure 5.65.

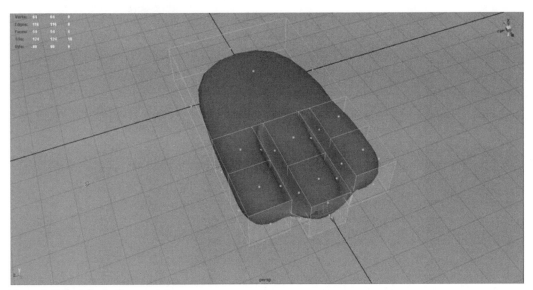

Figure 5.65 Extrude the fingers again.

12. Adjust the fingers as needed for placement of the second knuckles so that the center finger's knuckle extends farther than the other two.

13. Extrude the fingers again, except this time don't include the webbing.

14. Adjust the ends of the fingers, as shown in Figure 5.66.

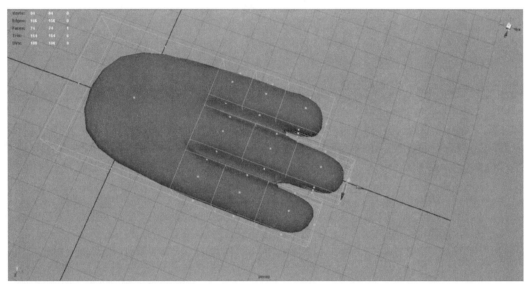

Figure 5.66 Adjust the ends of the fingers.

15. Each finger will now need a clawed end. Select one of the fingers and extrude the end polygon. Rotate the extruded polygon and move it down, as shown in Figure 5.67.

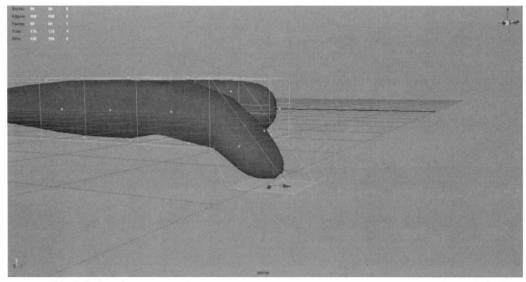

Figure 5.67 Extrude the claw of the finger.

16. It doesn't look much like a claw now, but it will before the project is done. Use the Channel box to set the scale to 0.01 for the X, Y, and Z to bring the claw to a point, as shown in Figure 5.68.

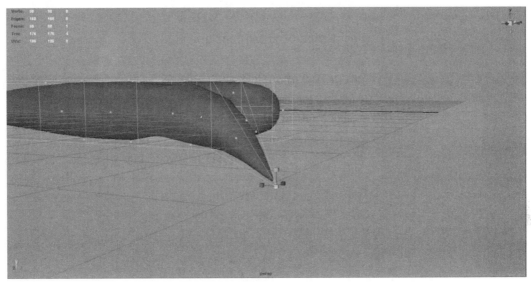

Figure 5.68 Give the claw a point by scaling the polygon.

17. Repeat the process for the claw on each of the remaining fingers.

18. Next, the hand needs a thumb. Split the polygons in the Front view of the model, as shown in Figure 5.69.

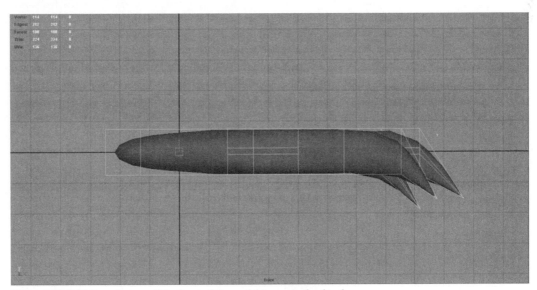

Figure 5.69 Split the polygons of the front of the model to create the thumb.

19. Extrude the newly split faces, as shown in Figure 5.70.

Figure 5.70 Extrude the thumb to the first knuckle.

20. Use the Scale tool to pull the vertices together, tapering the thumb from the hand, as shown in Figure 5.71.

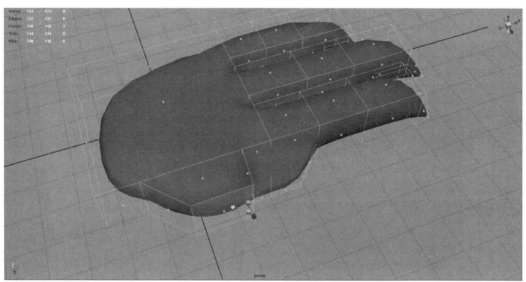

Figure 5.71 Scale the thumb.

21. Extrude the faces of the thumb a second time, to the second knuckle of the thumb. Taper the thumb again.

22. The webbing for the thumb needs to be simplified. Snap the vertices of the webbing to the thumb and merge them with the vertices of the thumb, as shown in Figure 5.72. Changing to Wireframe view will help you locate the vertices of the webbing to snap to the thumb vertices.

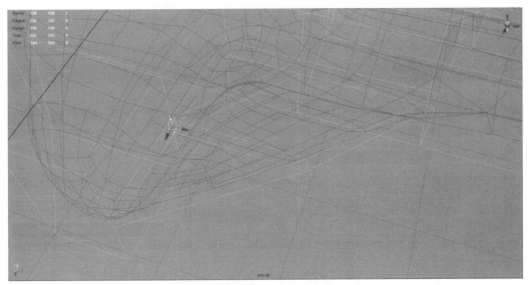

Figure 5.72 Adjust the shape of the webbing between the thumb and the fingers.

23. Extrude the thumb face one more time.

24. Now give the thumb a claw, as shown in Figure 5.73.

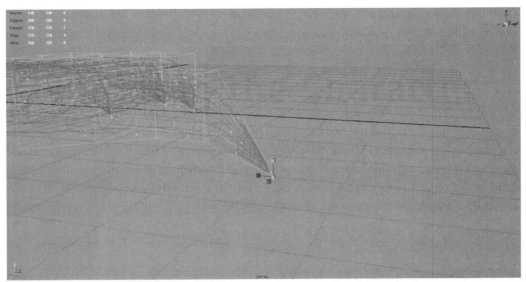

Figure 5.73 Give the thumb a claw as well.

25. Change the polygon proxy to Vertex Selection mode using the marking menu.

26. Use the Scale tool to refine the shape of the fingers, as shown in Figure 5.74.

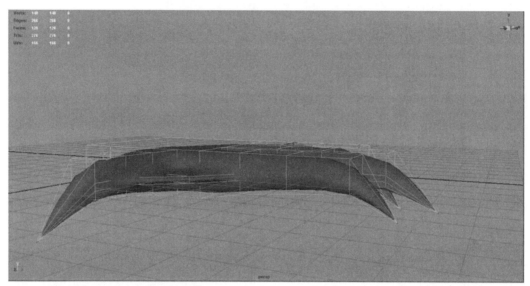

Figure 5.74 Refine the shape of the fingers.

Each finger should taper from the base to the end.

27. Select the face at the base of the hand.

28. Delete the face. This will open up the base of the hand, as shown in Figure 5.75. Opening the base of the hand will allow the hand to connect to an arm.

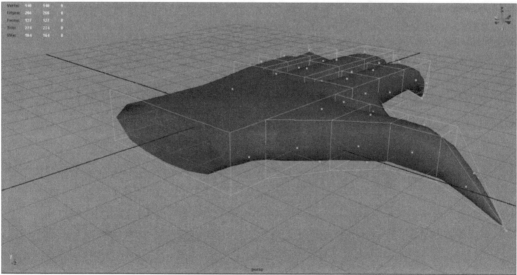

Figure 5.75 Delete the face at the base of the hand.

Using Polygon Proxy mode, you were able to quickly construct the hand. It lacks refinement, but the basic shape is in place. From here on out, you will complete the model in Standard mode.

Standard Mode Modeling

To convert the model to Standard mode, you must first change to Object Selection mode. Once the model is in Object Selection mode, change to Standard mode by selecting it in the Subdiv Surfaces menu.

You may encounter a loss of resolution along one or more of the fingers. Figure 5.76 shows a loss of detail in the small middle fingers and in the thumb.

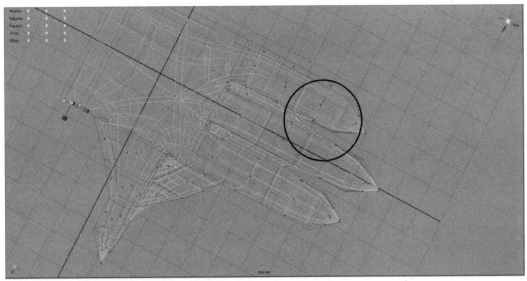

Figure 5.76 Loss of detail in the fingers and thumb.

If your model has this problem, convert the object to faces and select the faces that correspond to the problem areas. Then select Refine Selected Components from the Subdiv Surfaces menu. This should fix the problem.

Now the model is ready for modeling using standard subdivision surfaces tools and options.

1. Change the selection mode to Vertex using the marking menu.
2. Subdivision surfaces have several levels of resolution. Zero is the lowest level. This level is good for making larger changes to the model. Smaller refinements need to have higher resolutions. Change the resolution of the model to 1 by using the marking menu and selecting Finer, just above Vertex.

3. Select the vertices around one of the fingers between the joints, as shown in Figure 5.77. Use the Scale tool to reduce the circumference of the finger.

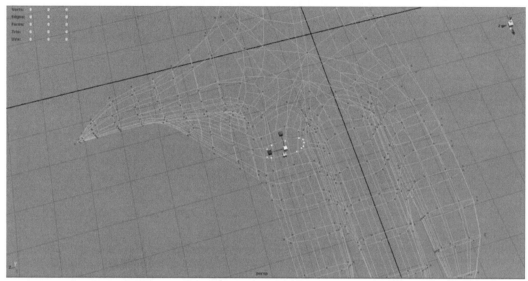

Figure 5.77 Reduce the circumference of the finger between the joints.

4. Continue to similarly reduce the circumference of the other fingers and the thumb between the joints.

5. Select the vertices around the base of the hand and scale them to look more natural, as shown in Figure 5.78.

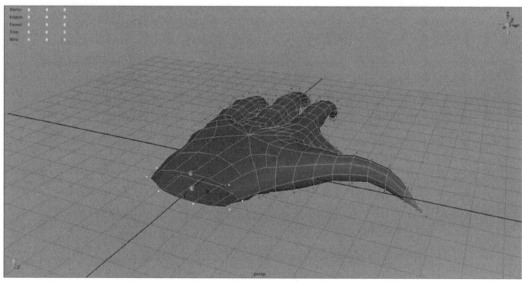

Figure 5.78 Scale the base of the hand.

6. Now that you have made most of the major adjustments, it is time to move on and add detail to the hand. Move in close to the tip of the thumb. Select the vertices of the claw and use the Rotate tool to adjust the claw to look more natural, as shown in Figure 5.79.

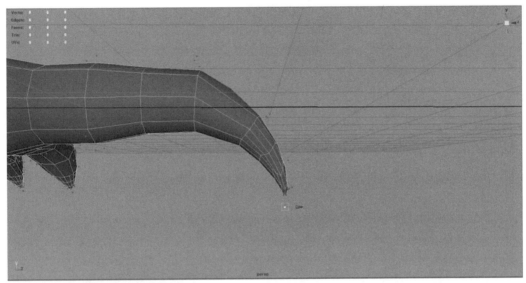

Figure 5.79 Adjust the vertices in the claw.

7. Change the selection mode to Edges.

8. Select all of the edges of the claw and the end of the thumb.

9. Refine the surfaces to level 2 by selecting Finer in the marking menu.

10. The surface needs to crease where the claw extends from the end of the thumb. The Subdiv Surfaces menu has a tool for creating creases in models. Select the edges of the model, as shown in Figure 5.80. Make sure to select only the edges around the claw and none of the edges that run the length of the claw.

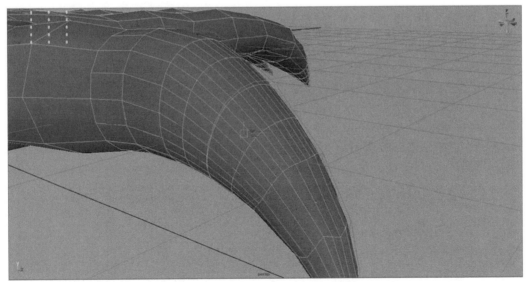

Figure 5.80 Select the edges where the claw extends from the end of the thumb.

11. With the edges selected, use the Full Crease Edge/Vertex function in the Subdiv Surfaces menu to crease the selected edges.

12. The selected edges will change to a dotted line. Scale the edges inward and move them toward the end of the thumb, as shown in Figure 5.81.

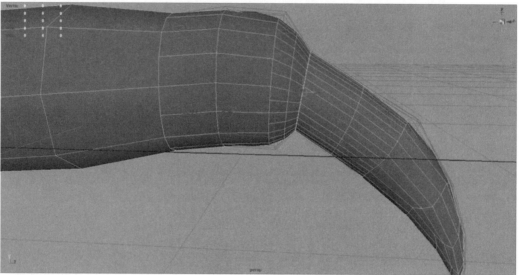

Figure 5.81 Scale the edges and move them closer to the end of the thumb.

13. Now change the selection mode to Vertex.

14. Use the Scale, Rotate, and Move tools to refine the shape of the thumb, as shown in Figure 5.82.

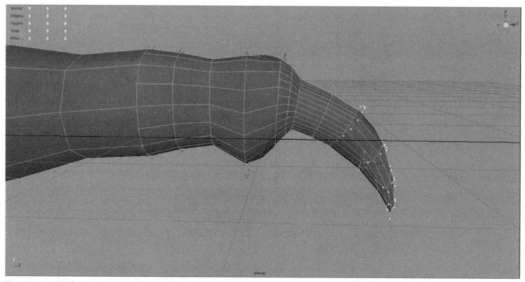

Figure 5.82 Refine the shape of the thumb.

15. It is time to refine the shape of the rest of the thumb. Go back to level 1 by using the marking menu and selecting Courser, just below Vertex.

16. Select the vertices between the base of the thumb and the end of the thumb.

17. Select Subdiv Surfaces, Refine Selected Components. This should increase the resolution of the selected area to 2, as shown in Figure 5.83..

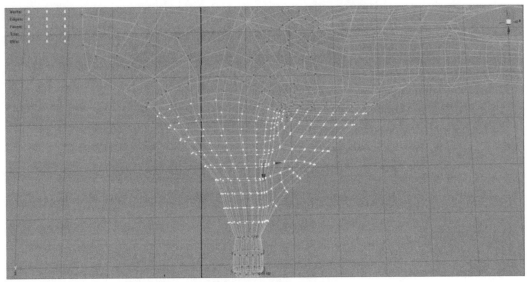

Figure 5.83 Refine the resolution of the remaining surfaces of the thumb

18. The surfaces of the model need to be refined even more in a few areas to add detail to the top of the thumb. Change the selection mode to Faces and select the faces between the second and third joints of the thumb, as shown in Figure 5.84.

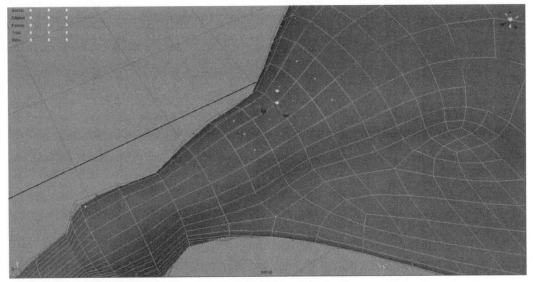

Figure 5.84 Select the faces between the second and third joints of the thumb.

19. Now go back to Vertex selection mode and move the vertices of the area between the joints to create a defined tendon between the joints, as shown in Figure 5.85.

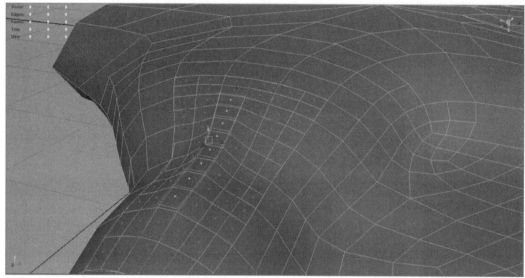

Figure 5.85 Define the tendon along the top of the thumb.

20. Repeat the process to define the tendon between the third joint and the end of the thumb.

21. Refine the surface resolution of the knuckles of the thumb to level 4, as shown in Figure 5.86.

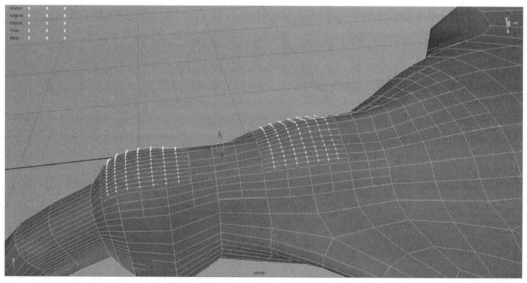

Figure 5.86 Refine the surface resolution of the knuckles.

22. Change the selection mode to Edges and select the line of edges shown in Figure 5.87. These edges will be used to simulate the creases at the top of the joints.

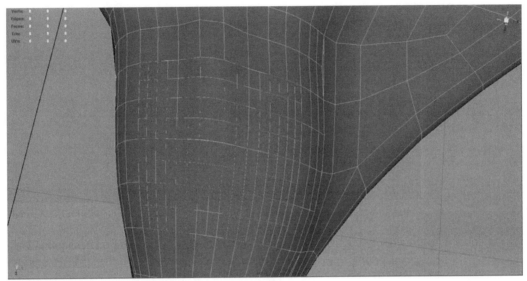

Figure 5.87 Select a line of edges along the top of the knuckle.

23. Crease the edges similar to what you did before in Step 12, and use the Scale tool to first flatten the curve of the edges, and then use the Move tool to move the edges downward, as shown in Figure 5.88.

Figure 5.88 Move the creased edges down.

24. Change the selection mode back to Vertex and scale the vertices on either side of the crease together, as shown in Figure 5.89.

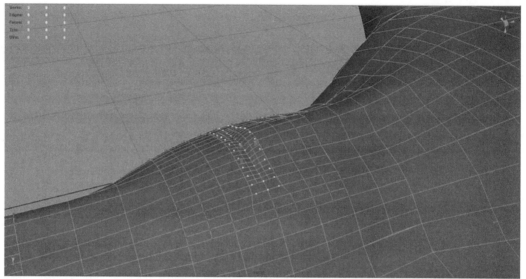

Figure 5.89 Pull in the vertices on either side of the crease.

Note

Currently, the thumb is at a 90-degree angle from the hand. Even though this is not a natural position for the thumb, having the thumb in this position makes it easier to perform operations like scaling components in one direction. If the thumb were in its natural position, the scale function would have been more difficult to use. After the thumb is finished, it will be an easy process to move the thumb into its natural position.

25. Now crease and adjust the two lines of edges on either side of the original crease, as shown in Figure 5.90. These two creases do not go as deep as the center crease.

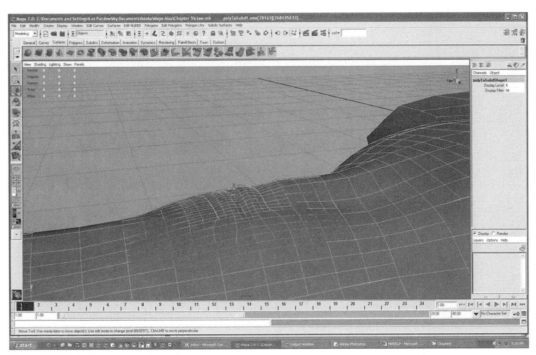

Figure 5.90 Make two more creases.

26. Now select individual rows of vertices perpendicular to the creases and move them along the length of the thumb to give the area a more organic look. The results should be similar to what's shown in Figure 5.91.

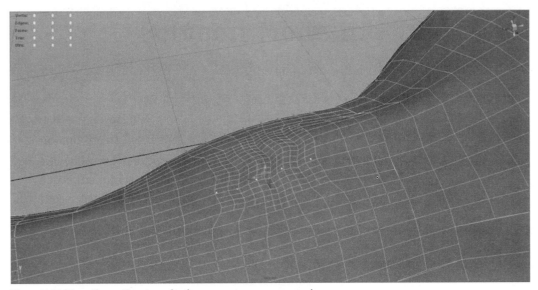

Figure 5.91 Move the vertices to make the creases seem more organic.

27. Add a crease underneath the knuckle, as shown in Figure 5.92.

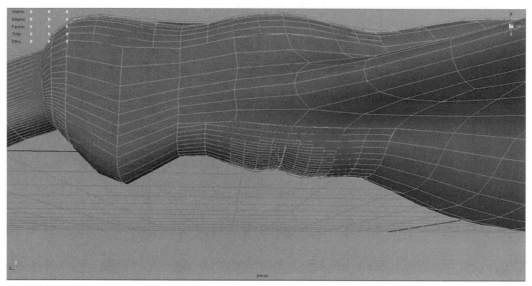

Figure 5.92 Add a crease underneath the knuckle.

28. The process of adding tendons and creases to the fingers is the same as it is for the thumb. Move over to the fingers and modify each in the same way as the thumb, first creating the claw and then defining the surface qualities of the finger. Figure 5.93 shows the fingers after the refinements have taken place.

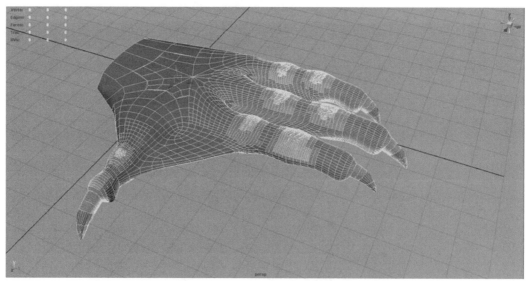

Figure 5.93 Add surface definition to the fingers.

29. Next, move on to the palm and back of the hand. First, increase the surface resolution of that area, as shown in Figure 5.94.

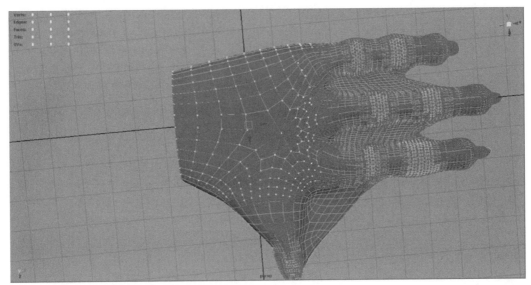

Figure 5.94 Increase the surface resolution of the hand.

30. Turn the hand over and add some creases to the palm, as shown in Figure 5.95.

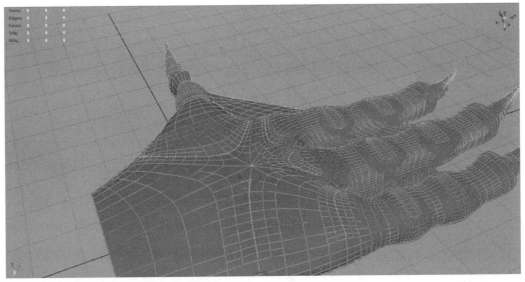

Figure 5.95 Add creases to the palm of the hand.

31. After creasing the palm, move the edges of the creases to look more natural for the surface of the palm.

32. Turn the hand over to view the top. Change the surface resolution to 1 using the marking menu.

33. Select the vertex in the center of the hand and those that are below it toward the back of the hand. Scale the vertices together and pull them toward the base of the hand, as shown in Figure 5.96. Notice how moving the vertex smoothly adjusts the surrounding vertices. The area of influence in modeling can be adjusted by changing the surface resolution. This is a big advantage of subdivision surfaces modeling over other modeling methods.

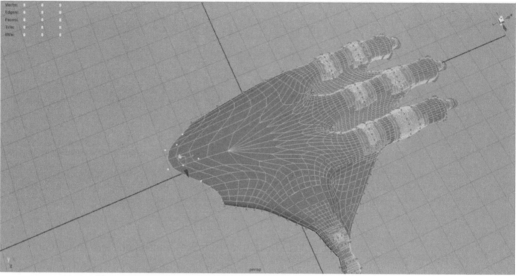

Figure 5.96 Move the center vertex to the base of the hand.

34. Increase the surface resolution to 3.

35. Select the vertices around the base knuckles of the fingers and move them upward in the Y direction to define the knuckles in those areas, as shown in Figure 5.97.

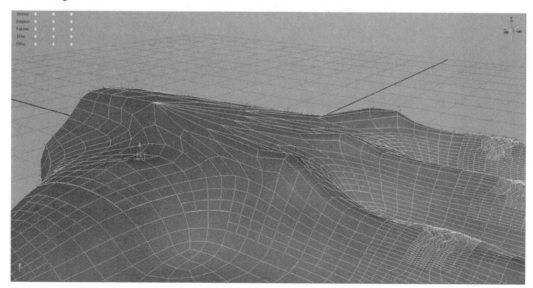

Figure 5.97 Define the base knuckles of the fingers.

36. Define the tendons that run from the base knuckles to the wrist area, as shown in Figure 5.98.

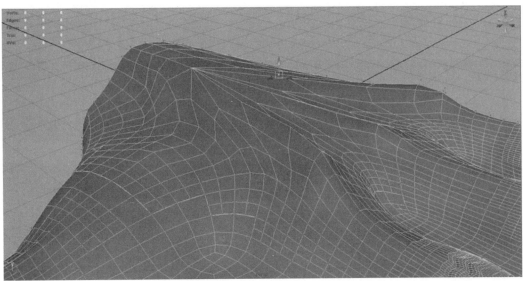

Figure 5.98 Define the tendons on the back of the hand.

37. Now that most of the surface detail is completed, the thumb can be adjusted to a more natural position. Change the surface resolution to 1.

38. Select the vertices near the base of the thumb toward the base of the hand and move them to form a more natural thumb muscle, as shown in Figure 5.99.

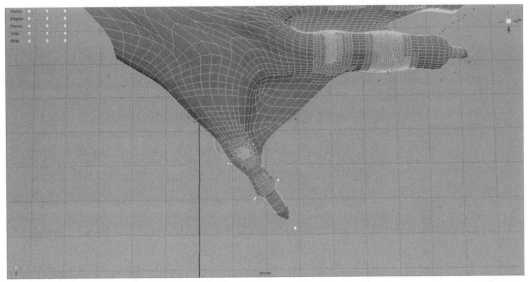

Figure 5.99 Reshape the muscle of the thumb.

39. Rotate the fingers to a more natural position as well, as shown in Figure 5.100.

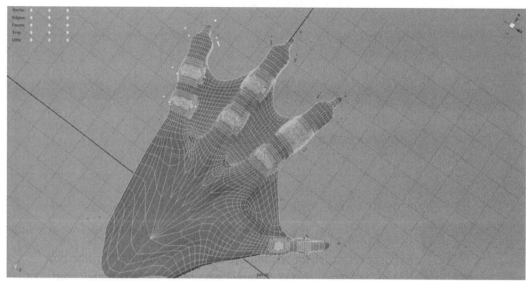

Figure 5.100 Put the fingers into a more natural position.

Figure 5.101 shows the finished clawed hand.

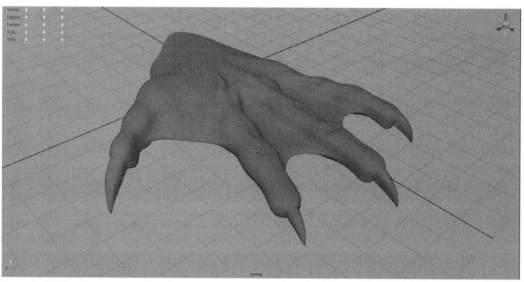

Figure 5.101 The finished clawed hand.

It was relatively easy to use subdivision surfaces to complete a complex model with lots of surface detail. Subdivision surfaces is one of the best modeling methods for creating complex organic shapes.

Summary

This chapter covered two modeling methods for creating 3D digital models: NURBS modeling and subdivision surfaces modeling. Both modeling methods have advantages, depending on the type of model being built.

NURBS modeling is useful in creating smooth, rounded surface models. The chapter covered

- Building NURBS models using curves and primitives
- Utilizing the Sculpt Geometry tool
- Using CVs to modify a model's shape

Many NURBS modeling tools were used in the examples, but a number of them were not. Experiment with the NURBS tools; having a better understanding of the tools will increase your ability to create models using NURBS.

Subdivision surfaces modeling is useful in creating complex models, particularly organic models that have a high degree of surface detail. The chapter covered the following:

- Using the Polygon Proxy mode
- Utilizing the standard for completing the detail of the model
- Changing the surface resolution of a model to add detail in places, while at the same time allowing the artist to make more global changes
- Creasing vertices to add finer detail to intricate areas of the model

This chapter covered many modeling techniques, but it was not an exhaustive manual for all the tools and functions in Maya. If you followed the examples in this chapter, you should have a good foundation for creating models using the two methods mentioned. For additional information on the tools and functions not covered in this chapter, refer to the help files in Maya.

Chapter 5

Nervous About NURBS

In addition to polygon modeling, several other methods of creating digital 3D models exist. This chapter deals primarily with two of these methods: NURBS and subdivision surfaces. These two methods of modeling have advantages for building complex models, depending on the type of model constructed. NURBS modeling tends to work very well for smooth, rounded shapes. Subdivision surfaces are very good for modeling forms that have both rounded surfaces and creases.

Polygon modeling is great for many applications, but sometimes polygons become difficult to deal with in models with very dense meshes. In these instances, modeling with NURBS or subdivision surfaces is often a better choice, even if the end result needs to be in polygons. The advantage of both of these systems is that the modeler can create complex smooth geometry quickly and later convert the geometry to polygons.

NURBS stands for Non-Uniform Rational B-Splines, which, unless you have a math background, might not mean much to you. Just think of NURBS as using curves to represent shapes and volumes. By controlling the shape of the curve, the modeler is able to influence the model.

Spline is an old term that goes back to the days of shipbuilding, long before the dawn of 3D modeling programs. To draw smooth curves across a series of points, shipbuilders used a thin metal or wooden beam called a *spline*, which they bent around weights called *knots*. Later, mathematical equivalents were developed for the curving of the splines, called *B-splines*, for basis splines.

NURBS Modeling

NURBS models use mathematical curves instead of flat planes to describe a 3D surface. The use of curves gives a NURBS model a smooth finish rather than the facets found in polygon models.

The complexity of NURBS in Max is way beyond the scope of the following few tutorials. If you find that NURBS are an important part of your workflow, then you will require a much more detailed guide, as we will barely be scratching the surface of this complex subject.

Max has a powerful set of NURBS modeling tools; however, it differs from Maya in that there are no default NURBS primitives. There are a few work-arounds that we will employ for this, but the following primitives section and tutorials will be focused on building NURBS models mainly from scratch rather than primitives.

The models will end up looking much the same as those made with Maya, but the steps will vary in many places.

Basic 3D Studio Max NURBS Concepts

The four basic building blocks of Max's NURBS modeling are composed of two surface types and two curve types. You can also convert primitives and splines to NURBS objects. We will be using curves and converting primitives or splines in the following tutorials.

The four types of surfaces and curves fall into two control categories: points and CVs. Point surfaces and curves are controlled by manipulating the points directly on the surface or curve. CV surfaces and curves are manipulated by working with points on a control lattice. You can see this control lattice in the first two figures.

For the most part, we will be using the CV surfaces and curves in the following tutorials; however, you may find that point surfaces and curves work better for tighter, more detailed work.

Figure 5.1 shows the two surface types side by side, with the point surface on the left and the CV surface on the right.

You will find the NURBS surfaces on the Create tab of the Command Panel under the Geometry icon and in the Type drop-down, as shown in Figure 5.1. Try making a few surfaces and then manipulating the points so you can get a feel for how it works.

Curves are also found on the Create tab under the Shapes icon and in the Type drop-down. In Figure 5.2, you will see the two types of curves, with the point curve on the left and the CV curve on the right.

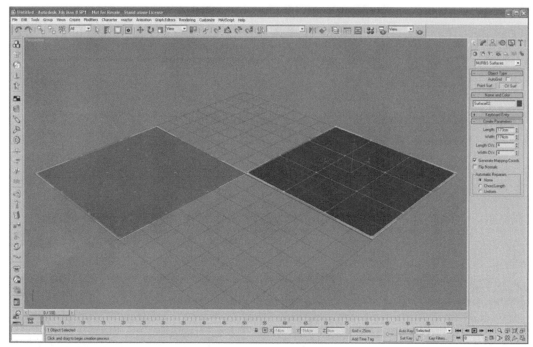

Figure 5.1 Point and CV surface examples.

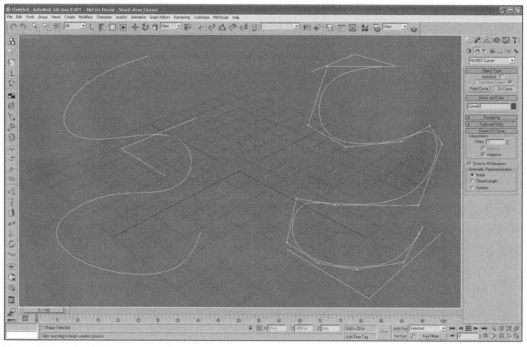

Figure 5.2 Point and CV curve examples.

We can also use splines (Max refers to splines as *shapes*) in the following tutorials. Splines are an important building block and tool for modeling in Max. You can use them for building complex outlines (for extruding/lofting into complex objects), paths for animation, and outlines for lathing cylindrical objects. You may find them useful for creating perfect circles, squares, or other shapes, and then converting them to NURBS.

Controlling the curve of a spline works in three basic ways: Bezier (the curve is controlled with tangents), Smooth (the curve is controlled with a math formula), and Corner (there is no curve).

Figure 5.3 shows some of the basic splines and where to find them in Max.

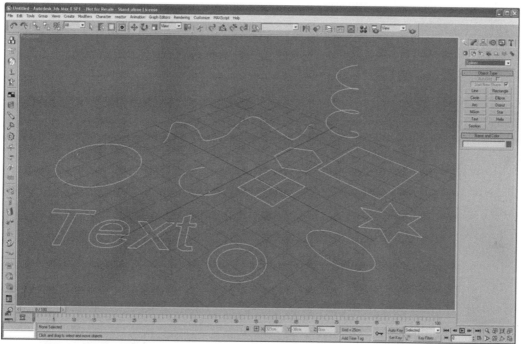

Figure 5.3 The basic splines in Max.

Several parts of working with NURBS in the Command Panel are useful to note. When you are working with a NURBS object and you want to create new surfaces or curves, you will need the toolboxes or rollouts shown in Figure 5.4. The toolbox in the upper-left corner contains all the creation tools available when working with NURBS. You can turn this toolbox on or off by pressing the noted icon on the far-right middle of the Command Panel. The three rollouts noted toward the bottom of the Command Panel contain the same tools as found in the toolbox, if you prefer to use the Command Panel rather than the toolbox.

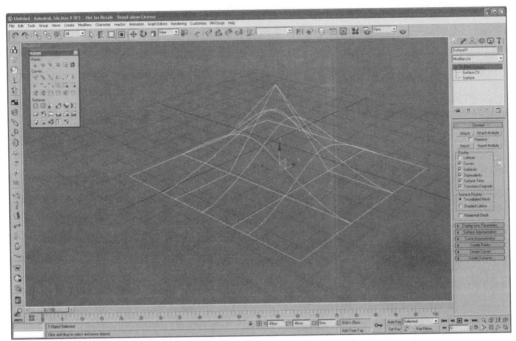

Figure 5.4 Creating NURBS surfaces and curves.

The next useful tool is the Weight setting. The Weight setting tells the surface or curve how much to conform to the CV. Try moving a CV on a surface or curve and adjust the weight amount to see the effect. The Weight setting is shown in Figure 5.5. The surface on the left has Weight set at 20 and the one on the right has Weight set at 1. Point surfaces and curves don't have Weight settings.

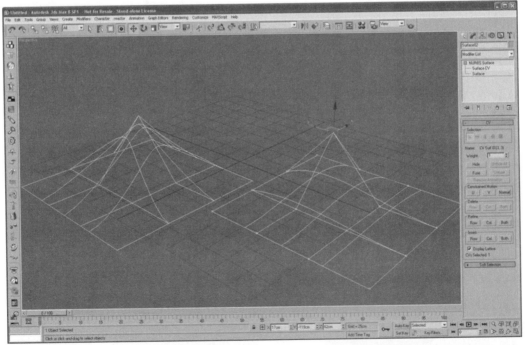

Figure 5.5 The Weight setting for CV surfaces and curves.

The last thing I want to point out before moving on to the tutorials are normals. Often when you are creating surfaces from curves, the normals are flipped and the surface will be invisible from the side you are viewing it from or will look "inside out." In most of the surface-creating tools, like U Loft, you will find a check box labeled Flip Normals.

This setting is tied to the surface, so if you forget to check it while creating the surface, look for it under the Surface Sub Object. Simply check this box, and you should see the expected results, as shown in Figure 5.6.

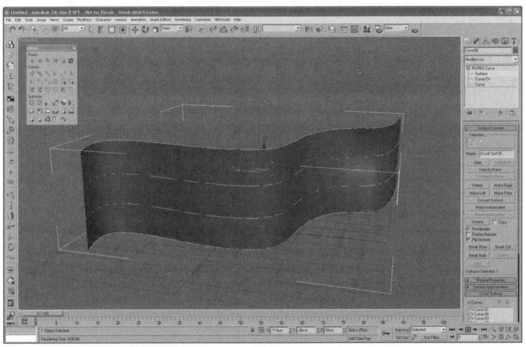

Figure 5.6 The Flip Normals setting for a newly created U Loft surface.

That's about it for a very short intro to NURBS. There are, of course, many more tools and options for creating NURBS models, and I will touch on some of them as we work through the following tutorials. But I hope this simple primer will make the following tutorial more easily understood.

Note

Per the Max users' guide, avoid using the Non-Uniform Scale on NURBS curves and surfaces as it may cause instabilities when modeling in NURBS.

Using NURBS to Model a Cartoon Race Car

Let's model a simple cartoon race car using the same practices and tools we have been using thus far, only now combined with NURBS.

1. Set Max to a full-screen Top viewport and create a CV curve that is similar to the CV curve in Figure 5.7. It doesn't have to be exact—you will have several chances to adjust it as you go.

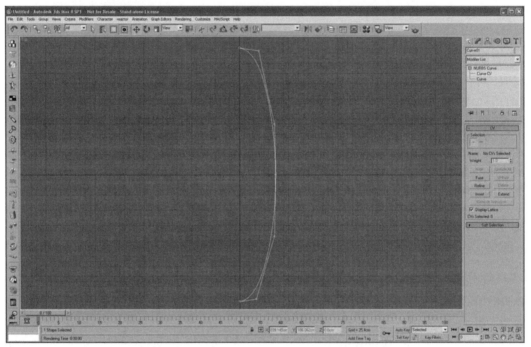

Figure 5.7 Create the basic shape of the car body.

2. Using the Lathe tool, turn the CV curve into the NURBS surface that you will use for the car body (see Figure 5.8).

3. At this point, you can switch to a full-screen Perspective view and turn the grid off by pressing the G key.

4. Switch to Surface Sub Object mode and select the body of the car.

5. Press the Make Independent button. You should now have something that looks like what you see in Figure 5.9.

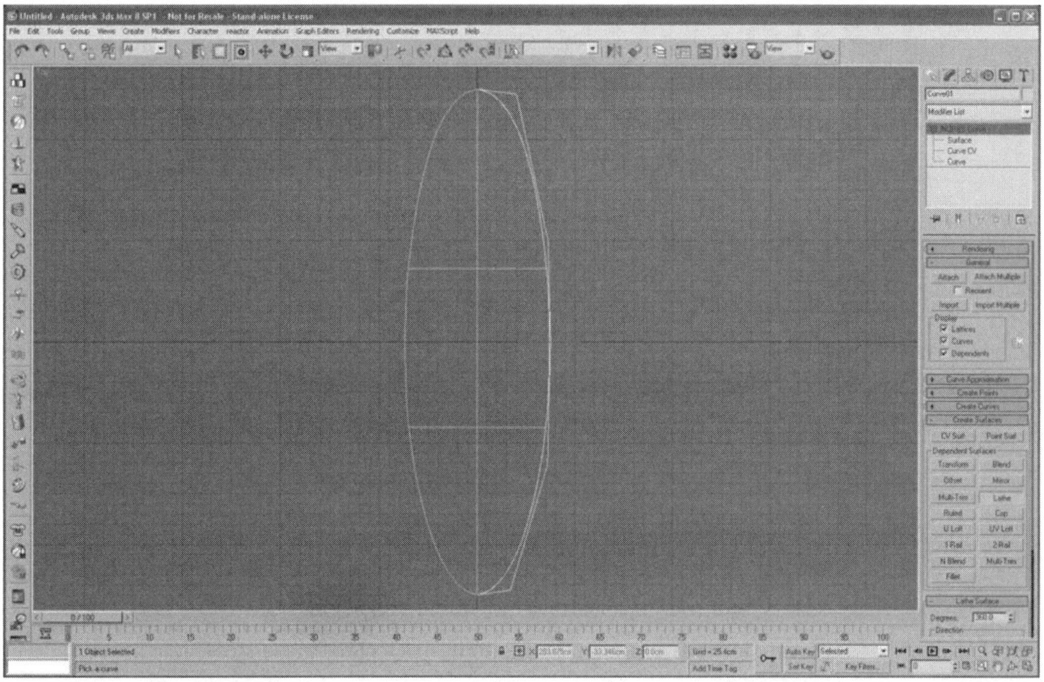

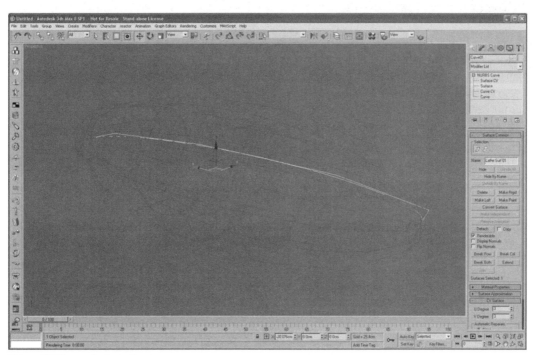

Figure 5.8 Converted to NURBS.

Figure 5.9 The car body surface.

6. Switch to Curve Sub Object mode and select and delete the original curve used to make the NURBS surface.

7. The conversion to a surface has left an odd number of CV rows in the lattice, so rotate the surface 90 degrees. This will set you up better for adding the cockpit. Rotate the surface so the three close rows of CVs are on the top of the model, as shown in Figure 5.10.

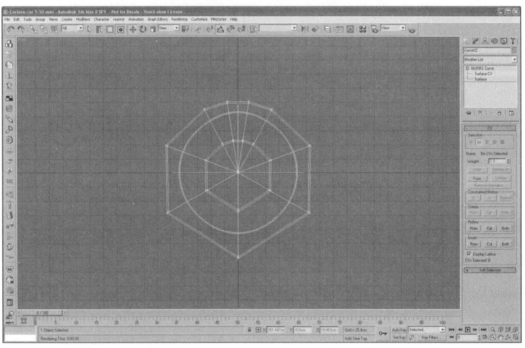

Figure 5.10 Car body rotated 90 degrees.

8. Switch to the full-screen Left view and Surface CV Sub Object mode.

9. It's not good to use Max's Non-Uniform Scale in NURBS, per the users' guide, so adjust the points in groups by moving them to achieve a slightly squashed car body that looks similar to that shown in Figure 5.11.

10. Now add the driver's seat to the car body. Switch back to Perspective view, as shown in Figure 5.12, and start refining the CV lattice and adding the cockpit, windscreen, and seat back.

11. Using the Col. button in the Insert box, add several CV columns by sliding the cursor across the surface and clicking to define an area where you will push the points in to make a seat. You will see where the new columns will be as you slide the cursor around the surface.

12. Select the four points on the top middle of the CVs you just added and push them down into the car body, as shown in Figure 5.13. This will start the cockpit and give you a place to begin forming the windscreen and seat back.

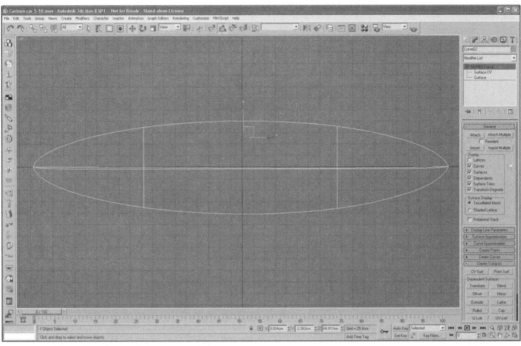

Figure 5.11 A squashed car body.

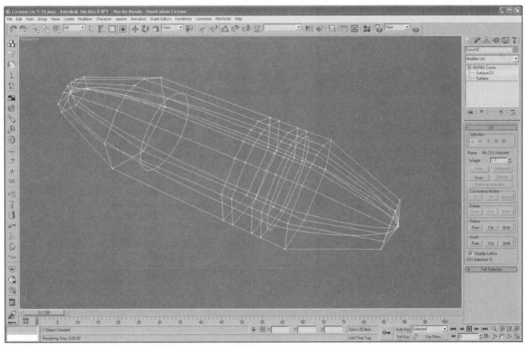

Figure 5.12 Adding extra CVs in preparation to create the seat.

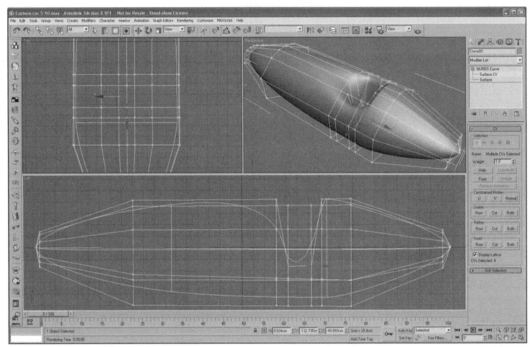

Figure 5.13 Push in the seat of the cockpit.

13. Now insert a few more columns and start forming the windscreen, as shown in Figure 5.14. You may also want to add a few more row CVs to the lattice to give yourself more CVs to work with.

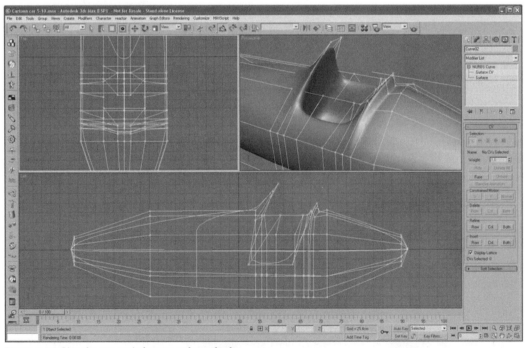

Figure 5.14 Give the car a windscreen and seat back.

Note

I used the Weight spinner on several of the CVs to create more or less pull on the surface.

Note

Now that you have the basics for adding and manipulating CVs, feel free to adjust or add details to the car body as we move through the tutorial.

14. Next, create and position a torus primitive about the size of a wheel, as shown in Figure 5.15.

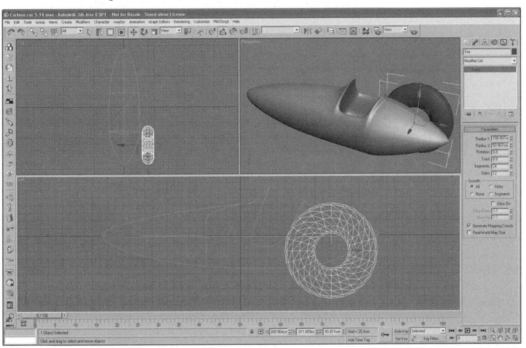

Figure 5.15 Create one of the wheels for the car.

15. Right-click on the stack window and convert the torus to a NURBS surface (see Figure 5.16).
16. Using the Column of CVs selection tool, select the center row of CVs that define the outside center of the tire and scale them so the tire is flat, as shown in Figure 5.17.

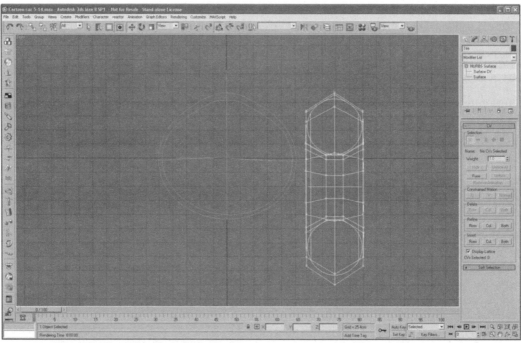

Figure 5.16 The torus converted to a NURBS surface.

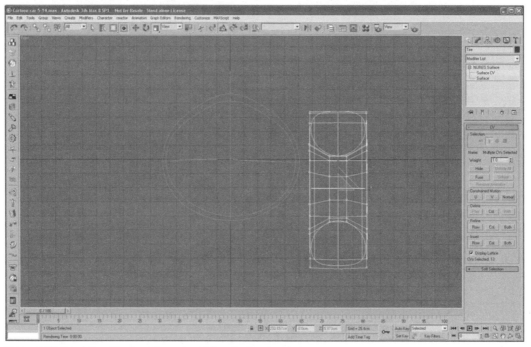

Figure 5.17 Select the CVs along the center of the wheel and scale.

17. Now create a CV curve that you can lathe to create the axle (see Figure 5.18). (The Lathe is a tool that will take a shape and duplicate it around an axis, building an object by "skinning" the shapes that is has duplicated.)

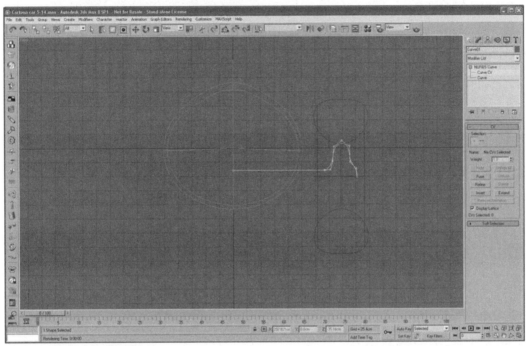

Figure 5.18 CV curve for the axle.

18. Switch out of Sub Object mode and lathe the axle. It's likely that you will need to change the lathe surface direction to X to get the desired results. It's also likely that you will need to adjust the lathe center. In Surface Sub Object mode, select the line and move it up or down to get the lathe looking just right, as shown in Figure 5.19.

19. Exit Sub Object mode and move the axle into place, as shown in Figure 5.20.

20. With the axle in place and selected, you will now attach the wheel. Click on the Attach button and select the wheel.

21. In the Hierarchy tab in the Command Panel, click Affect Pivot Only and move the pivot to the end of the axle. Take care to get it right on the end, as Max will be using this point to mirror the axle.

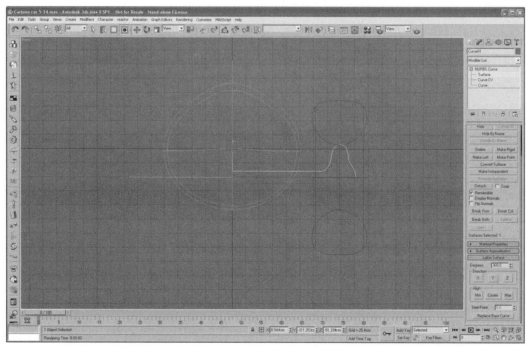

Figure 5.19 Final axle with adjustments.

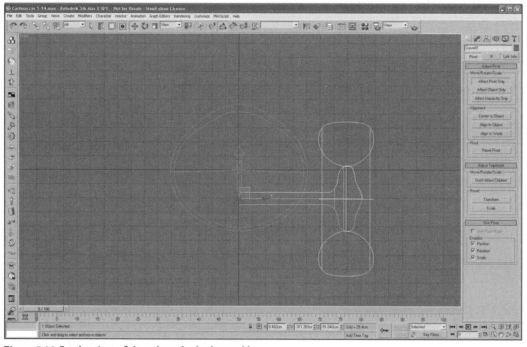

Figure 5.20 Set the pivot of the axle-and-wheel assembly.

22. Next, duplicate the axle-and-wheel assembly using the Mirror command, as shown in Figure 5.21.

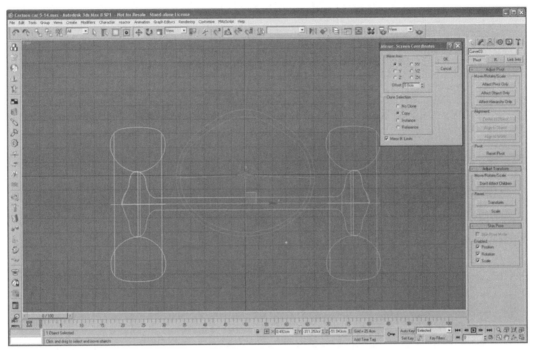

Figure 5.21 Both rear wheels in place.

23. Select both wheel assemblies and, using the Shift key, clone them to the front of the car, as shown in Figure 5.22.

Figure 5.22 All four tires in place.

24. Now create an air scoop, as shown in Figure 5.23. Select the car body and switch to Surface CV Sub Object mode.

25. Add a few columns to the lattice with the Insert Col. button.

26. Select the front column of CVs with the Column of CVs selection tool, push them into the car body, and scale them down a bit to form the air scoop, as shown in Figure 5.23. (I also rotated the front set of CVs slightly for a better look.)

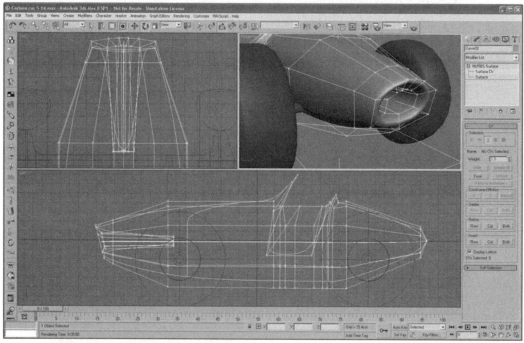

Figure 5.23 Create an air scoop for the front of the car.

27. Next, you will create much the same shape to the back of the car by adding three columns to the lattice and moving/scaling the columns to get the same look as in Figure 5.24.

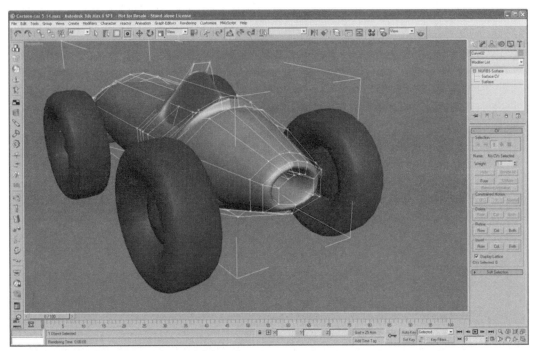

Figure 5.24 Back of the car with the start of the exhaust.

28. Add two more columns to the CV lattice, as shown in Figure 5.25.

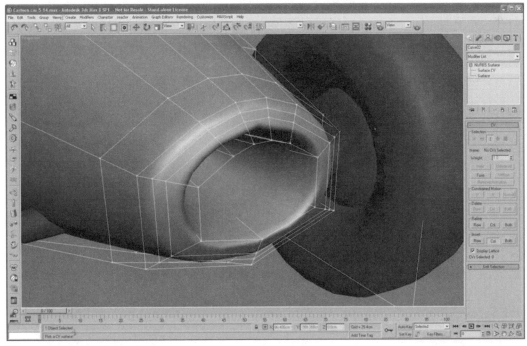

Figure 5.25 Add two more columns.

29. Select these two columns and scale them up, as shown in Figure 5.26.

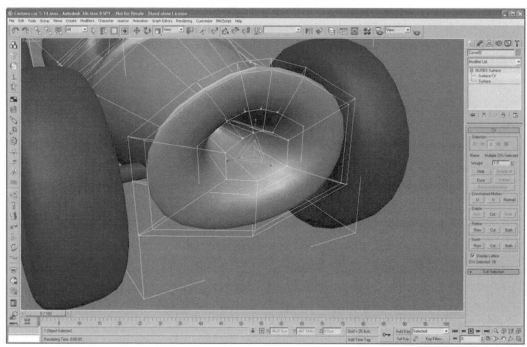

Figure 5.26 Scale up the flange.

30. Scale and move the selected CVs, as shown in Figure 5.27, to form the back of the car.

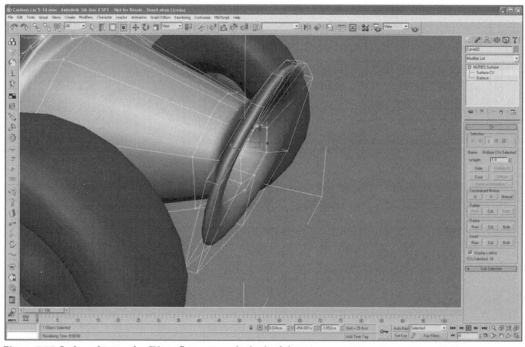

Figure 5.27 Scale and move the CVs to flare out on the back of the car.

Figure 5.28 shows the finished cartoon car. It is a very simple model. If you want to add a few more features, like a steering wheel, feel free to modify the car as you see fit.

Figure 5.28 The finished cartoon car.

Using Curves

Let's try one more quick NURBS tutorial so you can get a good feel for NURBS modeling in Max, especially with curves.

1. Select CV Curve from the Create, Shapes, NURBS Curves menu.
2. In the Front view, click the left mouse button with the CV Curve tool four times, from the center to the upper right (see Figure 5.29).
3. Place another CV directly to the right of the end CV in the curve chain. This CV will establish the width of the top of the pitcher.
4. Now place another CV down along the outside of the curve, staying roughly the same distance from the curve as the last two CVs. The CV curve should now curve back on itself, forming a somewhat rounded lip at the top.
5. Continue to place new CVs to create the outer line of the pitcher, as shown in Figure 5.30.

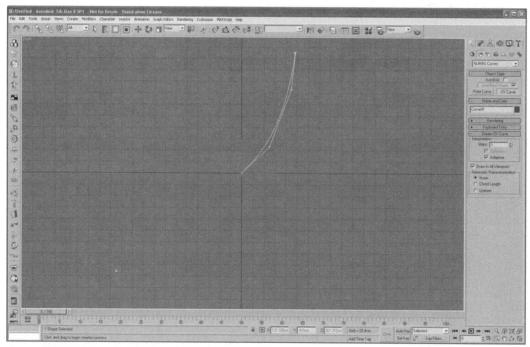

Figure 5.29 Use the CV Curve tool to create a curve.

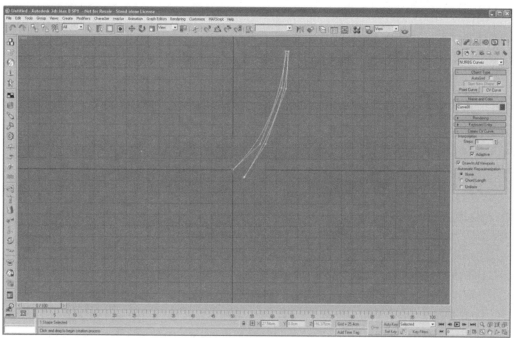

Figure 5.30 The top half of the pitcher outline defined in a curve.

6. Continue to place new CVs to create the stem of the pitcher, as shown in Figure 5.31. Don't worry about getting it just perfect. We will be refining the curve in a few steps.

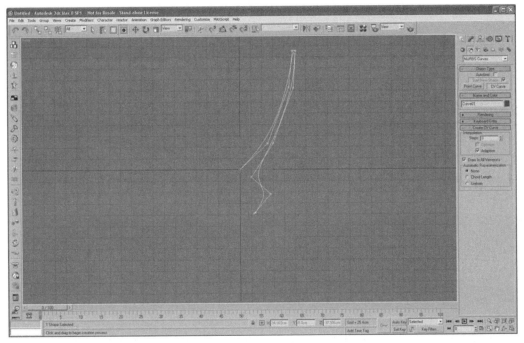

Figure 5.31 Start creating the stem of the pitcher.

7. Finish placing CVs until the pitcher roughly resembles the curve in Figure 5.32.

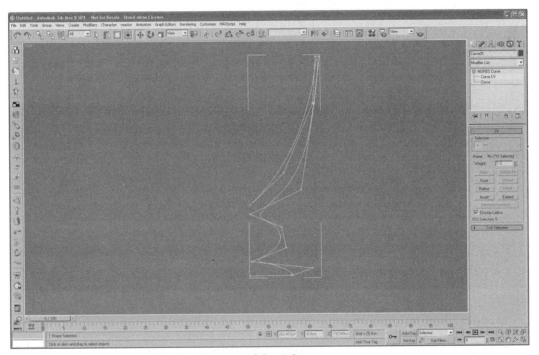

Figure 5.32 Finish placing the CVs to form the curve of the pitcher.

8. Now that you have the curve representing the profile of the pitcher, you can edit it so that it's just perfect. Using the Refine button, add a point or two, and then move them so that the curve is just how you like it. You can also use the Insert button; however, that has a different result than the Refine tool. The Refine tool tries to keep your curve the way you had it while adding points. The Insert doesn't respect the curve and adds a point.

Note

Notice that the CVs are not on the curve but rather to the side of the curve. To see how a CV affects a curve, select one of the CVs and drag it to a different position. Watch how moving the CV changes the curve. Select Undo from the Edit menu to return the CV to its original position.

9. The curve should now form half the silhouette of a pitcher, as if it were cut right down the middle. It is now ready to be lathed into a NURBS surface. You will find the Lathe tool in the NURBS toolbox, or you can exit Sub Object mode and use the Lathe tool found under the Create Surfaces rollout. Once you have the tool selected, simply click the curve to create the pitcher.

10. Once you have the surface created, you can go back and adjust the curve if it didn't turn out quite right. Enter Curve CV Sub Object mode and tweak the curve while watching the surface change. You will also notice a vertical yellow line that you can click on to adjust the center (rotation point) of the lathe. And lastly, you will find options for adjusting the lathe in the Command Panel while the Lathe tool is active. The model should now look similar to the one shown in Figure 5.33.

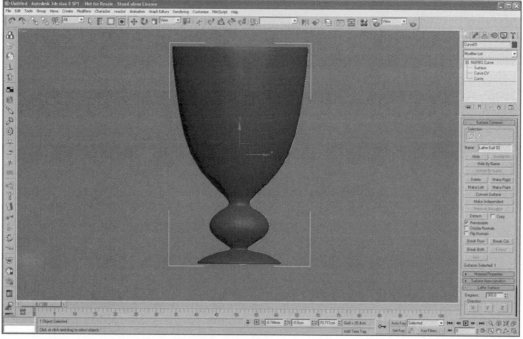

Figure 5.33 Lathe the curve to create a 3D model of the pitcher.

11. Next, you will need to add the spout, but before you can do that, you need to add a little bit more detail to the top of the pitcher. We need to perform a couple of steps to prep the surface for easy adjustments. While in Surface Sub Object mode, select the surface and click Make Independent (see Figure 5.34). This will separate the surface from the curve and allow for editing. It will also stop the curve from affecting the surface further.

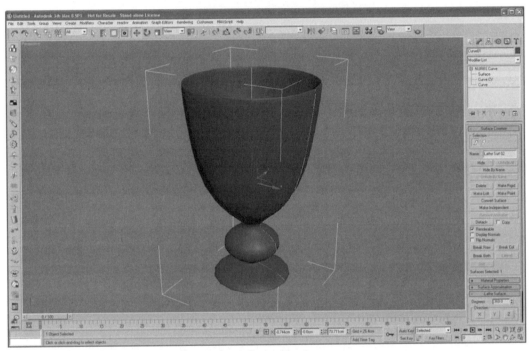

Figure 5.34 The model is now independent and not influenced by the curve.

12. Notice that Max has almost randomly placed the vertical CVs around the pitcher. You will want to rebuild the lattice so that it is much easier to work with. In Surface Sub Object mode, click on the Convert Surface button, set the CV Surface tab to 20 in the U and 20 or so in the V, and then click OK (see Figure 5.35). This will rebuild the lattice.

13. In Surface CV Sub Object mode and in the Front viewport, start to move the points out to create the spout, as shown in Figure 5.36. Don't forget the Weight spinner, where you can adjust the amount of "pull" the CV has on the affected surface area.

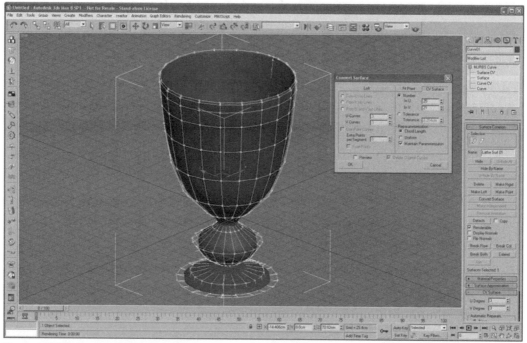

Figure 5.35 The Convert Surface dialog box.

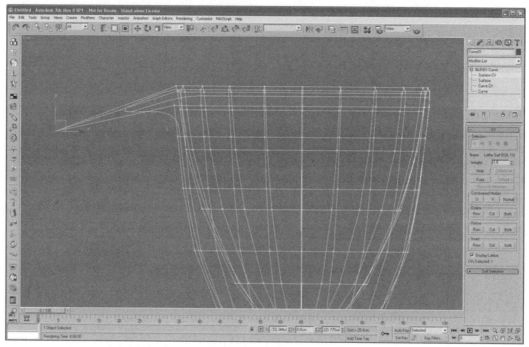

Figure 5.36 The start of the spout.

14. Continue to adjust points around the outside of the spout to form the shape of the spout, as shown in Figure 5.37.

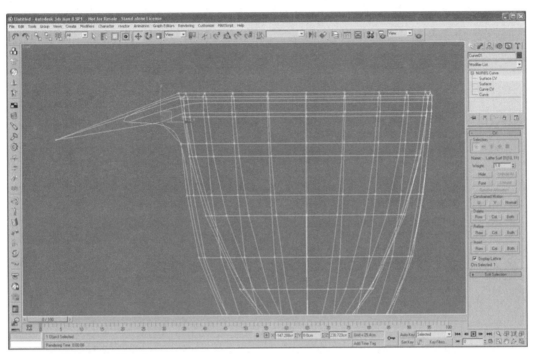

Figure 5.37 The spout taking shape.

15. Occasionally, it is useful to use the Shaded view or the Perspective viewport to visualize your progress (see Figure 5.38).

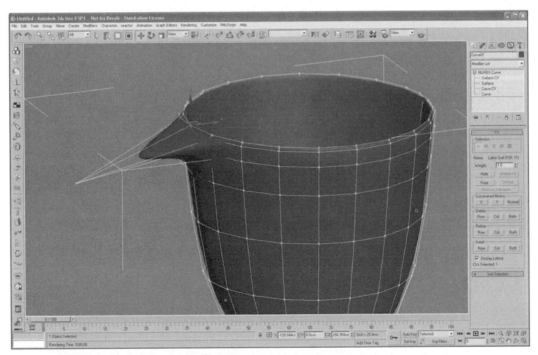

Figure 5.38 Using the Shaded view to visualize progress.

16. Once you are happy with the general shape of the spout, adjust the inside of the pitcher, as shown in Figure 5.39.

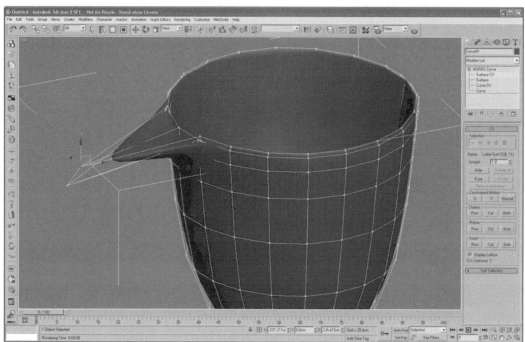

Figure 5.39 Pull the spout down.

17. Continue to shape the spout until you are happy with the results. Consider the thickness, angle, and shape of the final spout (see Figure 5.40).

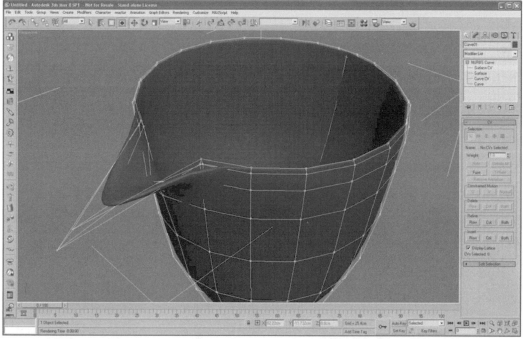

Figure 5.40 The final spout.

18. Now select the top CVs of the pitcher and scale them outward to give the top a slightly flared edge, as shown in Figure 5.41.

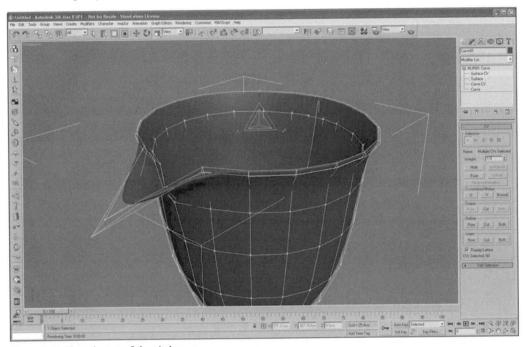

Figure 5.41 Flare the top of the pitcher.

19. Next is the handle. Create a torus primitive similar to the one shown in Figure 5.42 and move it into place accordingly.

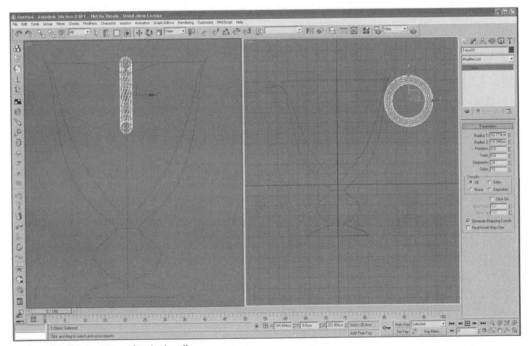

Figure 5.42 Create a torus for the handle.

20. Convert the torus to a NURBS object by right-clicking in the stack window and choosing NURBS (see Figure 5.43).

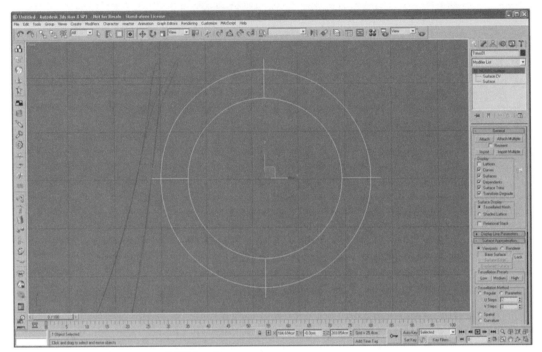

Figure 5.43 Convert the torus to a NURBS surface.

21. You need to make a break in the torus so you can manipulate it into the shape of the handle. Switch to Surface Sub Object mode and toggle the Break Row button (see Figure 5.44).

22. Click on the bottom CV row and click once. This should make a separation there.

23. Switch to Surface CV Sub Object mode and separate the CVs along the detached ends by moving the CVs, as shown in Figure 5.45.

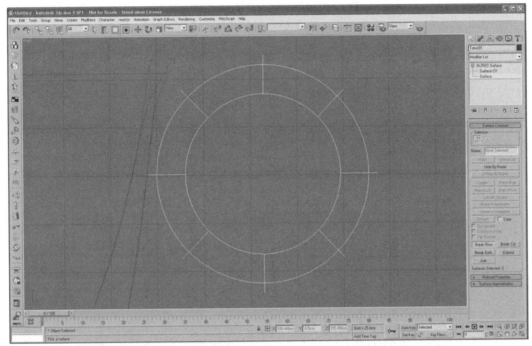

Figure 5.44 Use the Break Row tool to make a separation.

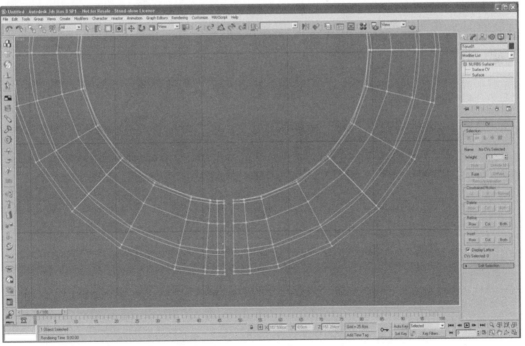

Figure 5.45 Separate the CVs on the ends.

24. Move and Rotate the CVs of the right-hand end down to form the handle of the pitcher, as shown in Figure 5.46.

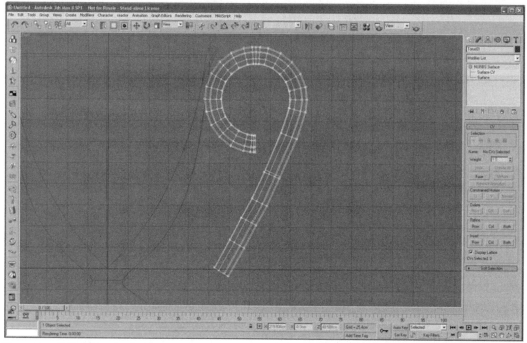

Figure 5.46 Pull the handle down from the top.

25. Rotate and scale the CVs of the right-hand end, as shown in Figure 5.47.

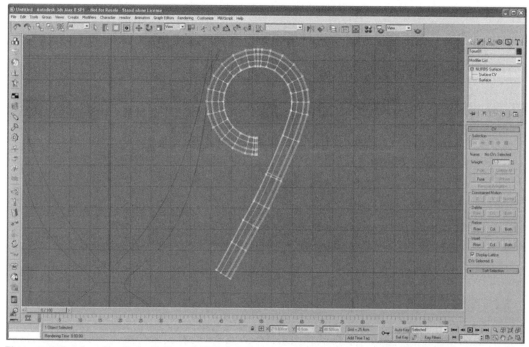

Figure 5.47 Rotate and scale the inside end of the handle.

26. Model the handle using the Move, Rotate, and Scale tools to shape it to look like the handle shown in Figure 5.48.

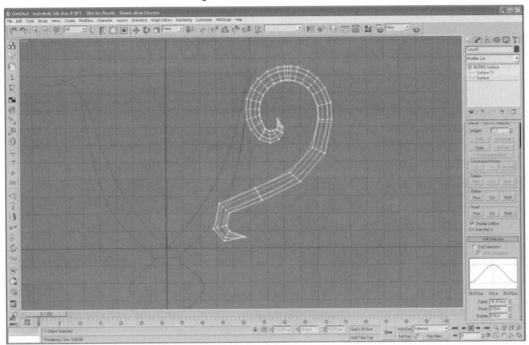

Figure 5.48 Finish the bottom of the handle.

27. The handle is a little rough. Smooth it out by using the Refine Row tool, as shown in Figure 5.49.

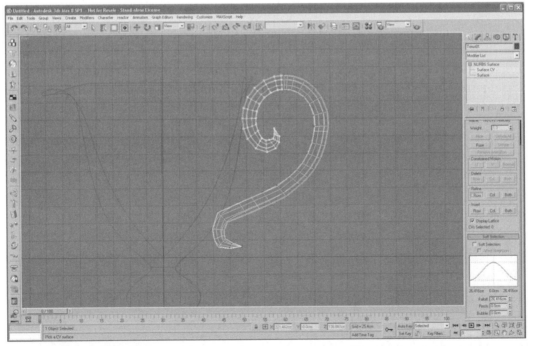

Figure 5.49 Smooth the handle.

28. Rotate the new CV rows to better follow the shape of the handle, as shown in Figure 5.50.

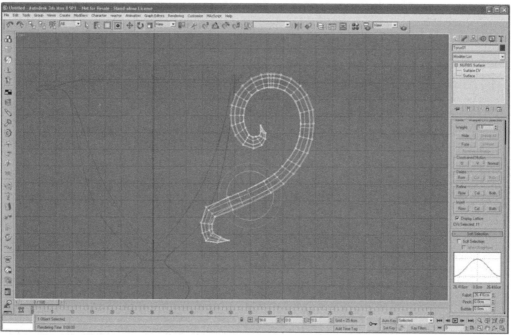

Figure 5.50 Rotate the new rows to follow the handle smoothly.

29. Exit Sub Object mode and select the pitcher. Enter Curve Sub Object mode and select the original curve you used to lathe with, as shown in Figure 5.51, and hide it.

Figure 5.51 Select the original CV curve.

There, now you have a nice model of a pitcher using just one CV curve to start and a NURBS torus for the handle. Figure 5.52 shows the final model.

Figure 5.52 The final pitcher.

Lofting Surfaces

Lofting between two curves is another way to create NURBS surfaces. Lofting can be used for a number of purposes. In this section, you will loft an organic tabletop from CV curves.

1. From the Top view, create a CV curve similar to the one shown in Figure 5.53.

2. Close the curve by clicking the last point on top of the first point you created. Figure 5.54 shows the resulting option box for closing the curve.

3. With shapes like the tabletop, it is often a good practice to rebuild the curve so the CVs are more evenly spaced around the curve. You can also refine the curve by adding or removing CVs at this point. Switch to Curve Sub Object mode and select the curve you just created. Figure 5.55 shows the option box. Choose the Number option and set it to 20.

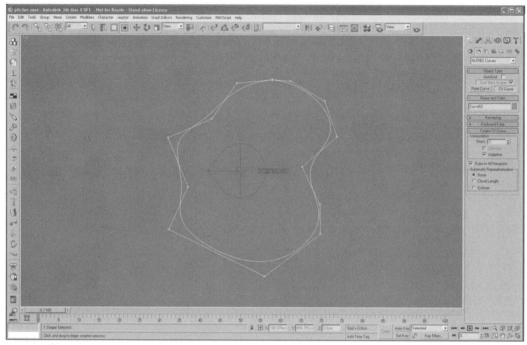

Figure 5.53 Create a CV curve for the table.

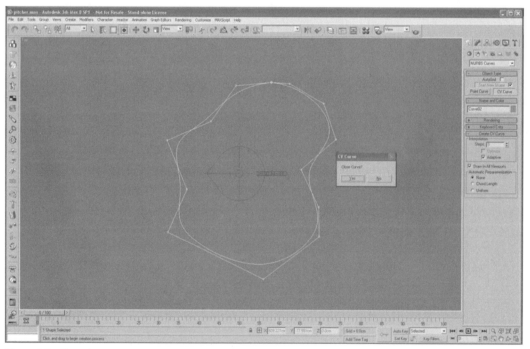

Figure 5.54 Close the curve.

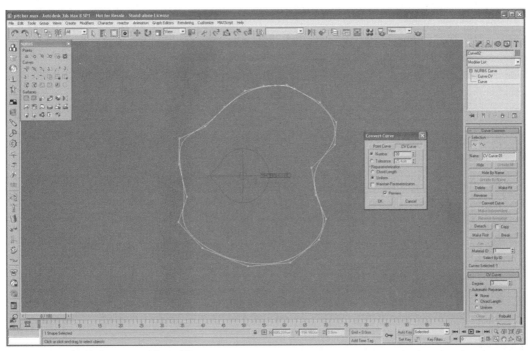

Figure 5.55 Rebuild the curve with 20 CVs.

4. Move the curve to the base of the pitcher, as shown in Figure 5.56.

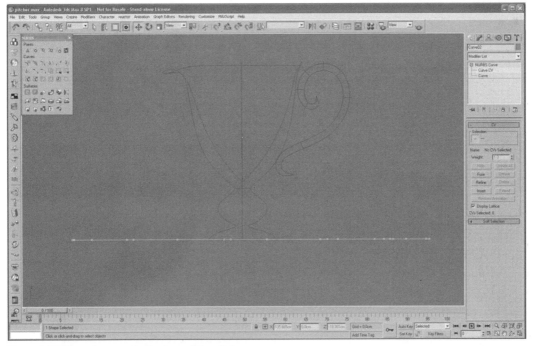

Figure 5.56 Move the curve to the base of the pitcher.

5. Exit Sub Object mode and clone the curve by holding the Shift key and scaling the curve down so that it is smaller than the base of the pitcher, as shown in Figure 5.57.

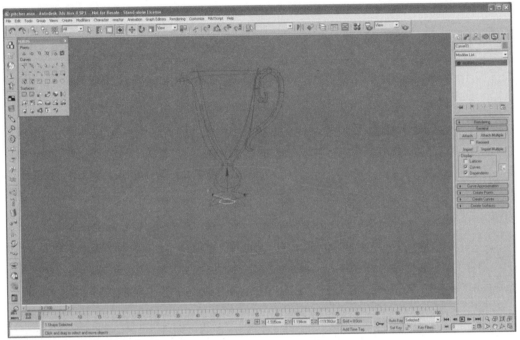

Figure 5.57 Clone and scale the curve.

6. Clone the original curve again by holding the Shift key and moving the curve straight down, as shown in Figure 5.58.

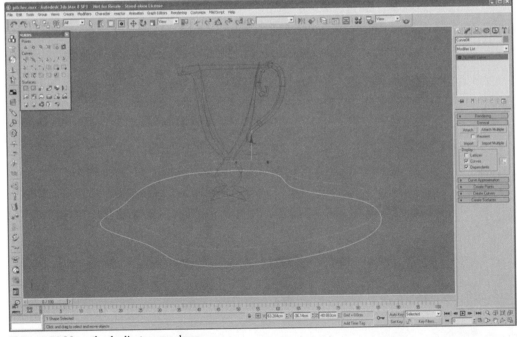

Figure 5.58 Move the duplicate curve down.

7. Select the curve under the pitcher and, using the Attach tool, select the other two curves. Once you have one object, select the Loft tool from the Create Surfaces rollout or the NURBS toolbox dialog box.

8. Starting with the curve under the pitcher and moving to the outside top curve, build the top of the table (see Figure 5.59). Right-click to disable the U Loft tool.

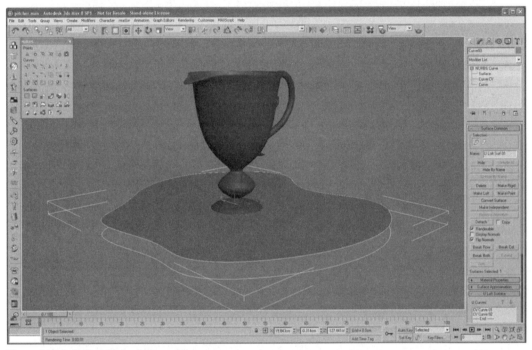

Figure 5.59 Loft the tabletop between two curves.

9. Give the table some depth by reselecting the U Loft tool and clicking the top curve of the table followed by the bottom curve. This gives the table thickness, as shown in Figure 5.60. Right-click to disable the U Loft tool. You may need to check the Flip Normals box under the U Loft options rollout at the bottom of the Command Panel. If you missed this in the U Loft options, you can find the option under Surface Sub Object mode.

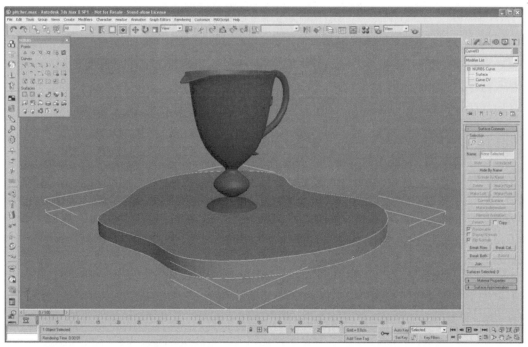

Figure 5.60 Loft the edge of the table.

You now have a pitcher sitting on a tabletop. Lofting is a great tool for building organic shapes using simple CV curves. It is also very versatile. Until you use the Make Independent tool on the new NURBS surfaces, they will remain influenced by the original CV curves. This can make editing the surfaces a lot easier. Figure 5.61 shows the CVs of the two outside curves used to change the shape of the table.

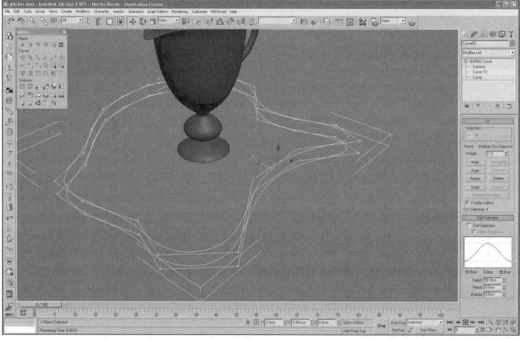

Figure 5.61 The original CV curves influence the surfaces.

Subdivision Surfaces Modeling

Subdivision surfaces modeling is an advanced, yet very easy, polygon-modeling method used in creating models that have high surface detail. It can be used to create simple objects, but it is really useful for making complex models.

Creating models with subdivision surfaces is a little like creating a model with both polygons and NURBS at the same time. We will be using a polygonal cage to control a dense polygonal mesh similar to the way a CV lattice controlled the NURBS surface in the previous tutorials.

In the following example, you will build a model of a clawed hand. The process of building the hand will show many advantages of creating models using subdivision surfaces. You will create the basic model from a single polygon cube in NURMS subdivision mode. Max has a couple of ways to model subdivision surfaces, but we will be focusing on the NURMS method, which is very simple yet powerful. After finishing the basic shape of the model, you will use Standard mode to refine the detail in the model. These two modes will be explained during the course of the project.

Polygon Proxy Mode

One of the biggest advantages to using subdivision surfaces is the Polygon Proxy mode. This mode is designed to give the artist access to the polygon-modeling tools while creating a smooth, rounded surface. It also allows the artist to start the model using polygons, and then switch over to subdivision surfaces and back again later as needed.

1. Create a polygon box that is roughly 150 cm wide by 150 cm long by 50 cm high, as shown in Figure 5.62. This cube will be the basis for developing the clawed hand.

2. Now convert it to an Editable Poly object and get ready to model with subdivision surfaces. Once you have collapsed the stack to Editable Poly, look for the Subdivision Surface rollout and check Use NURMS Subdivision, as shown in Figure 5.63.

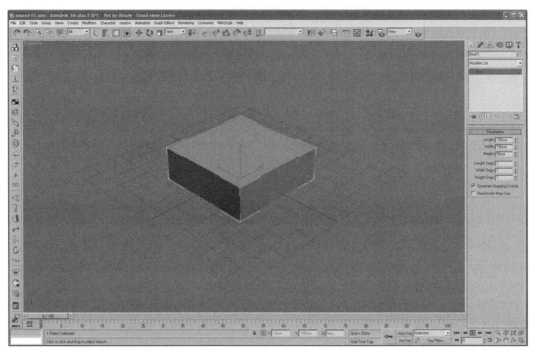

Figure 5.62 Create a polygon cube.

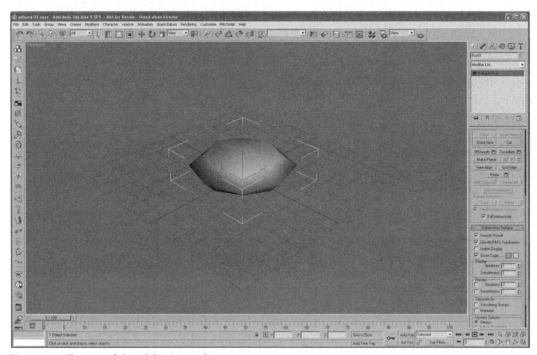

Figure 5.63 The start of the subdivision mesh.

3. There are a few options that you should note (see Figure 5.64). Right under where you selected the NURMS tool are boxes labeled Display and one labeled Render. These options control how dense the mesh is in the display (while you are working with it) and how many times to subdivide at render time. For now I would set Iterations at 2 or 3 for each box. Another setting to take note of is the Isoline Display check box. This affects how the mesh is displayed in the viewport. Checking it off will show the polygonal mesh, while leaving it on will show a simplified version of the mesh. All three of these settings are personal preferences and depend on how you like to work, as well as how fast your machine is. Set Display Iterations low, like 1 or 2, and Render Iterations high if you have a slow machine. For this tutorial, I will leave Isoline Display unchecked so you can see the mesh as we are working. Isoline will reduce the number of polygons displayed in very dense meshes and can be useful for clarity.

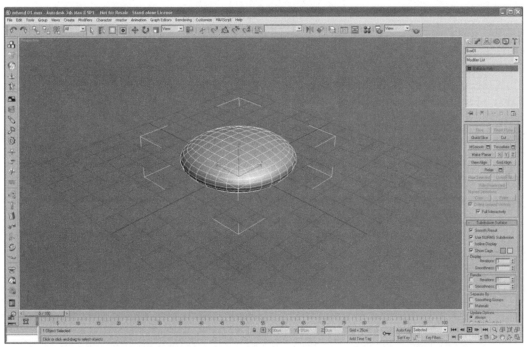

Figure 5.64 The base options for how the model is displayed and rendered.

4. Switch to Polygon Sub Object mode and hit the G key to turn the grid off.

5. The model should now have a wireframe cube (of the same dimensions as the original polygon cube) around it. This box controls the look and shape of the subdivision surfaces model very much like the CV lattice did with NURBS. Swing around to the right side of the model in Perspective view and use the Cut tool, found under the Edit Geometry rollout, to draw in four vertical lines, as shown in Figure 5.65. You will have to right-click after each cut to start a new vertical line. These lines will be used to define the fingers of the hand.

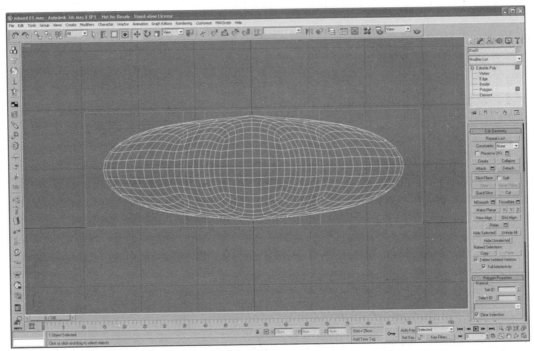

Figure 5.65 Split the polygons of the right side of the cube.

6. Now between two sets of the vertical edges, split the polygons horizontally, as shown in Figure 5.66. These polygons will be used to form webbing between the fingers.

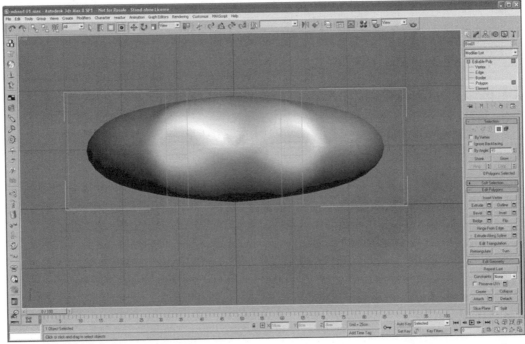

Figure 5.66 Split the polygons horizontally.

7. Select the faces as shown in Figure 5.67. Max displays the selected "cage" polygons in yellow and the affected polygons on the subdivided mesh in red. I have used the F2 key to toggle the selection view mode to Outline.

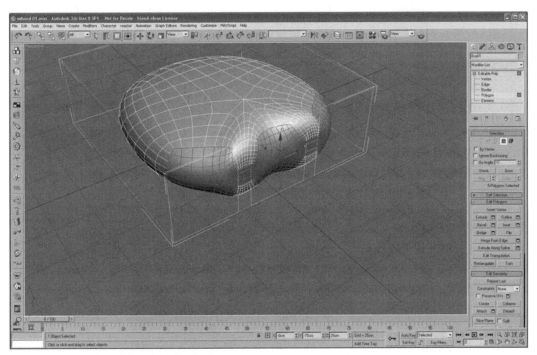

Figure 5.67 Select the polygon faces for the fingers.

Note

Don't forget the F3 and F4 keys! They make it very easy to change the view modes. F3 toggles between Shaded and Wireframe mode, and F4 toggles between displaying the wireframe in Shaded mode.

It is also important to note that you are working on the "cage" of the model. The subdivided mesh is a representation of what the model will look like when you convert or render the model. At any point, you can go back to the original model that was started by the box primitive by checking the Use NURMS Subdivision box, as long as you have not collapsed the stack again.

8. The clawed hand will only have three fingers, in keeping with the standard for cartoon characters. Using the Extrude tool, click on the selected polygons and drag the fingers out of the hand, as shown in Figure 5.68. Notice how the subdivision surfaces model follows the rough geometry, or the "cage," that we are working with.

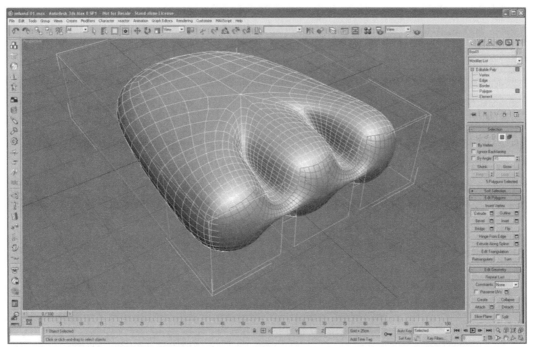

Figure 5.68 Extrude the fingers of the hand.

9. The fingers should not all be the same length. This first extrusion will place the first knuckles. Using your own fingers as a guide, select the polygons for each finger and move the joints in the X direction to take into account the differing lengths of the fingers, as shown in Figure 5.69.

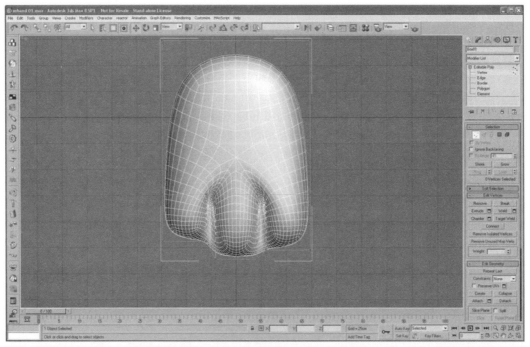

Figure 5.69 Adjust the lengths of the fingers.

10. Now reselect all of the polygons for fingers and webbing and extrude them again, as shown in Figure 5.70.

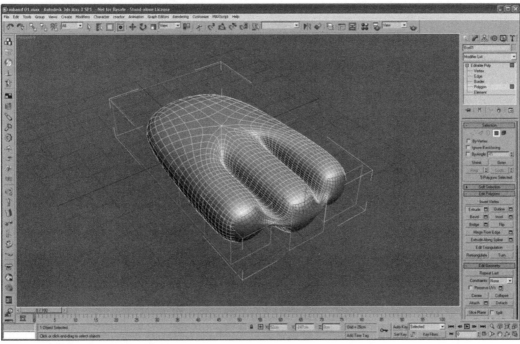

Figure 5.70 Extrude the fingers again.

11. Adjust the fingers as needed for placement of the second knuckles so that the center finger's knuckle extends farther than the other two.

12. Extrude the fingers again, except this time don't include the webbing.

13. Adjust the ends of the fingers, as shown in Figure 5.71.

14. Each finger will now need a clawed end. Select one of the fingers and extrude the end polygon. Rotate the extruded polygon and move it down, as shown in Figure 5.72.

15. It doesn't look much like a claw now, but it will before the project is done. Scale the selected polygon close to 0% to bring the claw to a point, as shown in Figure 5.73. You could also collapse the polygon, but you wouldn't get quite the point needed for this tutorial.

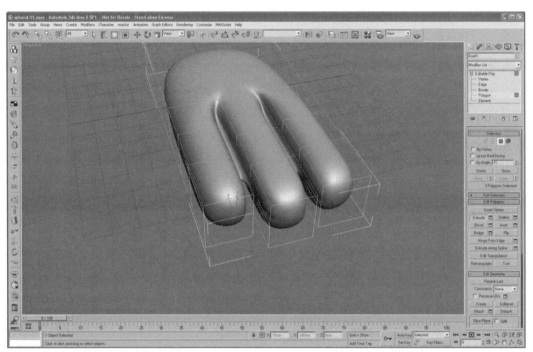

Figure 5.71 Adjust the ends of the fingers.

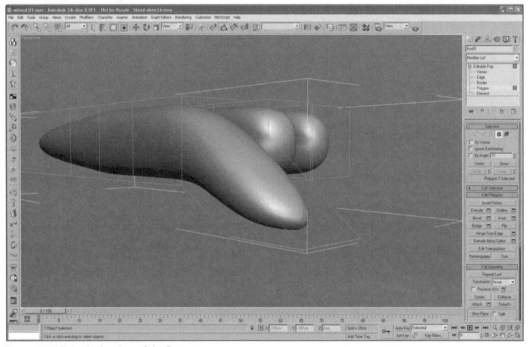

Figure 5.72 Extrude the claw of the finger.

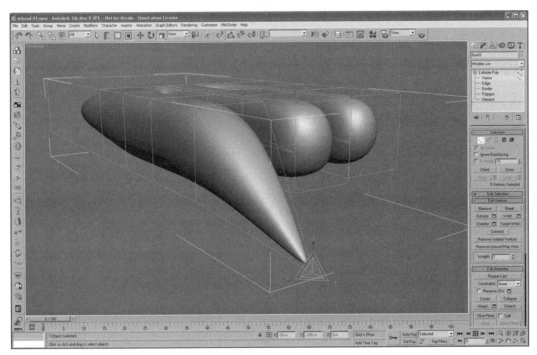

Figure 5.73 Give the claw a point by scaling the polygon.

16. Repeat the process for the claw on each of the remaining fingers. The model should now look similar to what is shown in Figure 5.74.

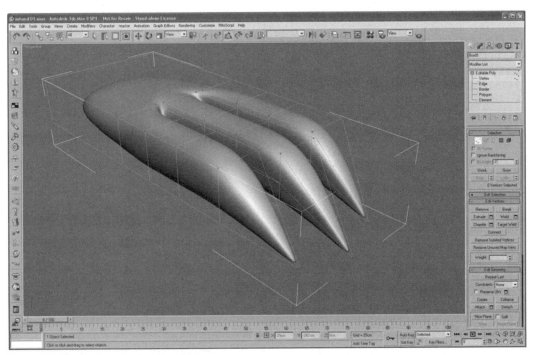

Figure 5.74 Create claws for the other fingers.

17. Next, the hand needs a thumb. Split the polygons in the Front view of the model, as shown in Figure 5.75.

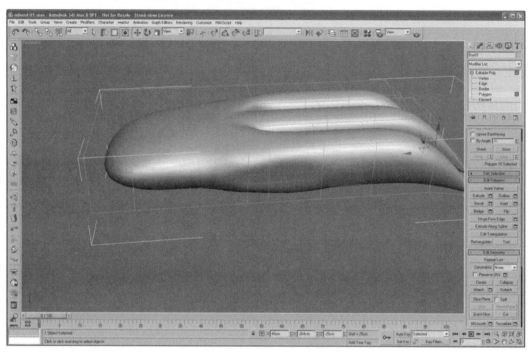

Figure 5.75 Split the polygons of the front of the model to create the thumb.

18. Extrude the newly split faces, as shown in Figure 5.76.

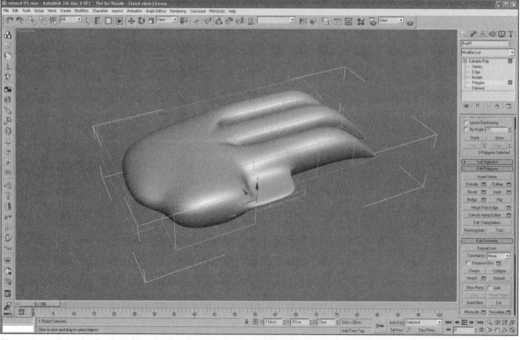

Figure 5.76 Extrude the thumb to the first knuckle.

19. Use the Scale Gizmo to scale the vertices together, tapering the thumb from the hand, as shown in Figure 5.77.

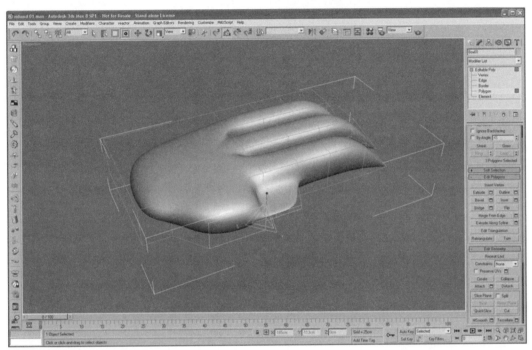

Figure 5.77 Scale the thumb.

20. Extrude the faces of the thumb a second time, to the second knuckle of the thumb. Taper the thumb again by scaling it.

21. The webbing for the thumb needs to be simplified. Using the Target Weld tool in Vertex Sub Object mode, weld the vertices of the webbing to the thumb and merge them with the vertices of the thumb, as shown in Figure 5.78. Changing to Wireframe view may help you locate the vertices of the webbing to weld to the thumb vertices.

22. Extrude the thumb face one more time.

23. Now give the thumb a claw by extruding, rotating, and scaling, as shown in Figure 5.79.

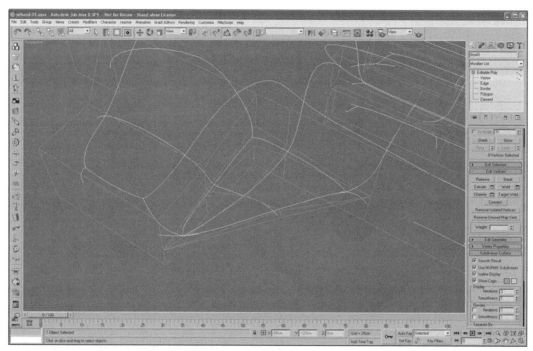

Figure 5.78 Adjust the shape of the webbing between the thumb and the fingers.

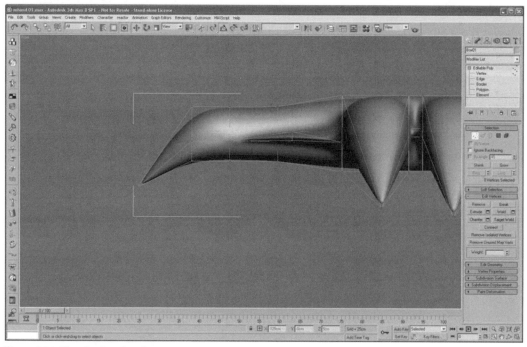

Figure 5.79 Give the thumb a claw.

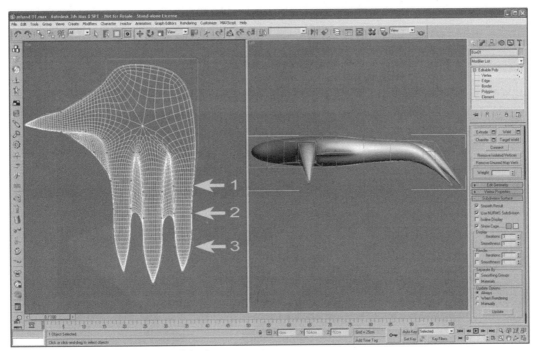

Figure 5.80 Start to refine the shape of the fingers.

24. Switch to Vertex Sub Object mode.

25. Use the Scale Gizmo to refine the shape of the fingers, as shown in Figure 5.80. Each finger should taper from the base to the end. I scaled the points around the first, second, and third knuckles to 75 percent, 65 percent, and 60 percent, respectively. I also scaled the thumb joint down so it looked correct and adjusted the thumb webbing area a bit.

26. Select the face at the base of the hand, as shown in Figure 5.81.

27. Delete the face. This will open up the base of the hand, as shown in Figure 5.82. Opening the base of the hand will allow the hand to connect to an arm.

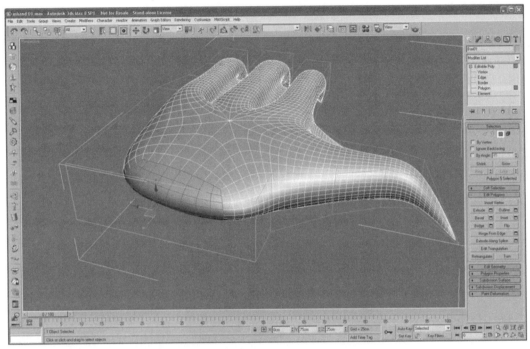

Figure 5.81 Select the face at the base of the hand.

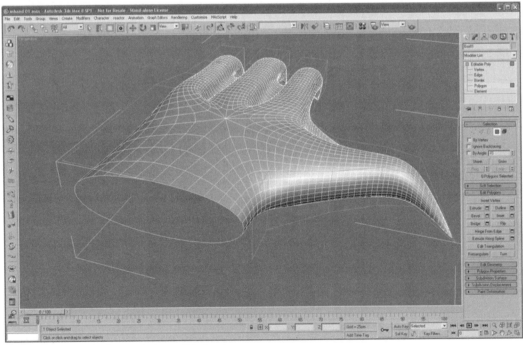

Figure 5.82 Delete the face at the base of the hand.

Using subdivision modeling, you were able to quickly construct the hand. It lacks refinement, but the basic shape is in place. We will follow along much the same way as we have been, just adding refinement to the hand with the standard Max polygon-modeling tools.

More Subdivision Modeling

At this point on the Maya side tutorial, the author switches to something called *Standard mode*. Max does not have a mode change at this point; we will continue to model and refine the hand until it is finished. At that point, you may want to convert it from a subdivision model to the final mesh or leave it as a subdivision model for speedy animation or more refinement.

1. Let's add a little bit of resolution to the subdivision cage. In Polygon Sub Object mode, select all the polygons on the cage and press the MSmooth button once to subdivide the mesh.

2. Because of the added resolution to the mesh, you may want to set the NURMS iterations down a bit if your machine is bogging down. I also switched to Isoline Display for clarity.

3. Select the vertices around one of the fingers between the joints, as shown in Figure 5.83. Use the Scale tool to reduce the circumference of the finger.

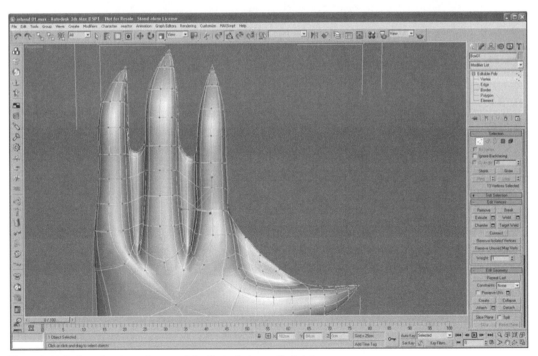

Figure 5.83 Reduce the circumference of the finger between the joints.

4. Continue to similarly reduce the circumference of the other fingers and the thumb between the joints.

5. Select the vertices around the base of the hand and scale them to look more natural, as shown in Figure 5.84. You may want to adjust a vertex here or there to help shape the hand a little more.

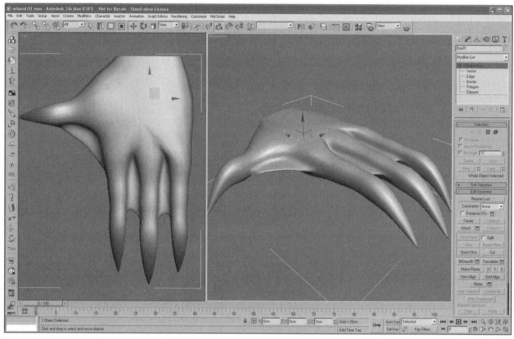

Figure 5.84 Scale the base of the hand.

6. Now that you have made most of the major adjustments, it is time to move on and add detail to the hand. Move in close to the tip of the thumb. Select the vertices of the claw and use the Rotate tool to adjust the claw to look more creepy, as shown in Figure 5.85.

7. Switch to Polygon Sub Object mode and select all of the polygons of the claw and the end of the thumb.

8. Using the MSmooth tool once again, subdivide the mesh. The end of the thumb should now look similar to that shown in Figure 5.86.

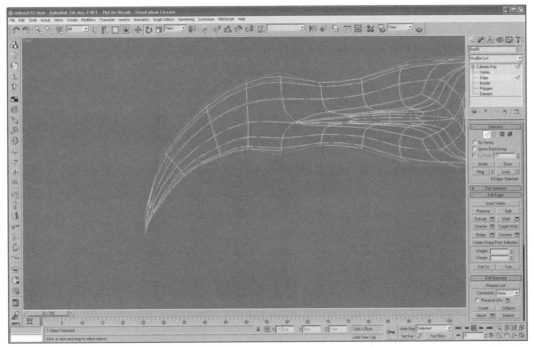

Figure 5.85 Adjust the vertices in the claw.

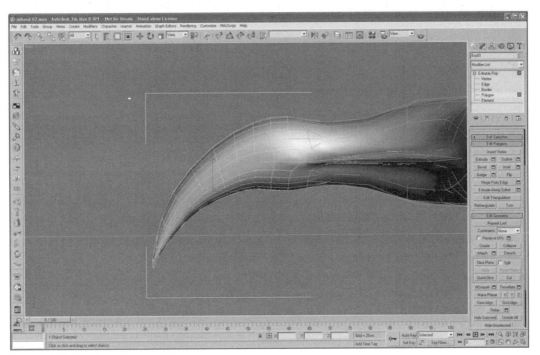

Figure 5.86 Refine the surface resolution.

9. You may want to check the Isoline Display under the Subdivision Surface rollout now that you are starting to get a denser mesh. This will show less detail in the mesh and make it easier to see what's going on.

10. The surface needs to crease where the claw extends from the end of the thumb. Select the edge loop at the thumb tip and use the Chamfer tool to split the edge in two, as shown in Figure 5.87.

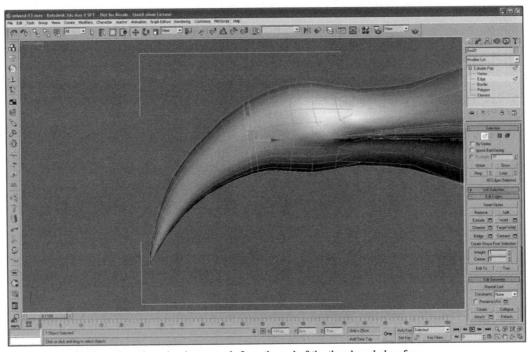

Figure 5.87 Select the edges where the claw extends from the end of the thumb and chamfer.

11. Select the new edge where the claw meets the thumb and adjust the value in the Crease spinner to 1 so you will have a nice sharp edge.

12. Switch to Polygon Sub Object mode and select the claw polygons, as shown in Figure 5.88.

13. Scale the claw down to about 70 percent and move it into place.

14. Switch to Vertex Sub Object mode and, using the Scale, Rotate, and Move tools, refine the shape of the thumb, as shown in Figure 5.89. Now would also be a good time to shape the three remaining fingers (and claws).

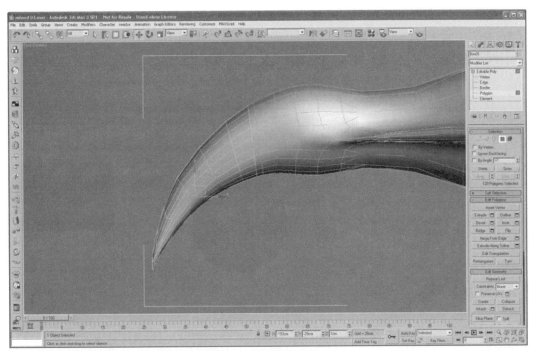

Figure 5.88 Scale the edges and move them closer to the end of the thumb.

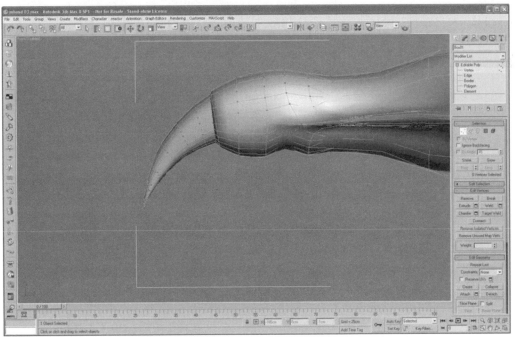

Figure 5.89 Refine the shape of the thumb.

15. It is time to refine the shape of the rest of the thumb.

16. Select all of the polygons, excluding the thumb area where you previously added resolution.

17. Use the MSmooth tool once to double the resolution, as shown in Figure 5.90.

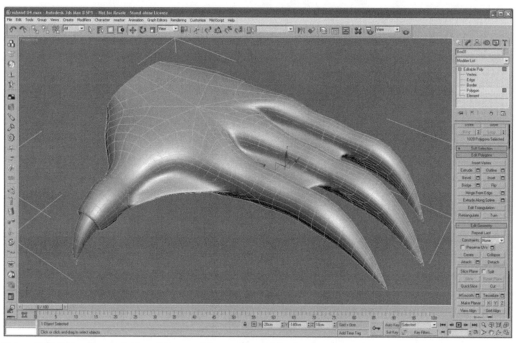

Figure 5.90 Refine the resolution of the remaining surfaces of the hand.

18. As you can see, there is a bit of odd geometry around the middle of the thumb where you smoothed earlier. You'll want to clean up that geometry and rebuild the polygons so the mesh stays in nice order and is easy to work with. To do this, select all of the polygons around the area you want to delete, as shown in Figure 5.91, and press Delete. Deleting polygons can also be done one by one, rather than by selecting a group. Be careful when you get to the webbing. You may want to leave much of that and not rebuild it. Don't worry if you miss a few—you can catch them after you delete the selected set.

19. Now that the area is clear and cleaned up, it's time to rebuild the polygons. Select the Create tool under the Edit Geometry rollout and, in a counterclock-wise order, click on the four vertices that make up a polygon and double-click on the last one of the four to end the polygon. Quickly run around the opening you created and rebuild the remaining polygons (see Figure 5.92).

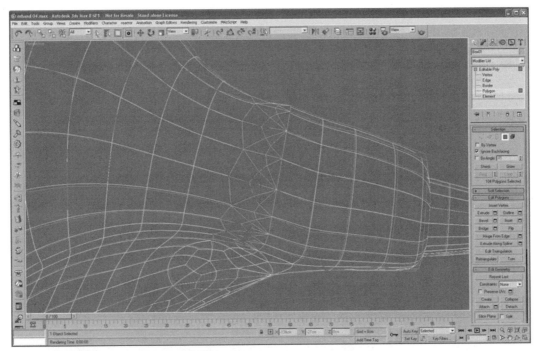

Figure 5.91 The area you are going to rebuild.

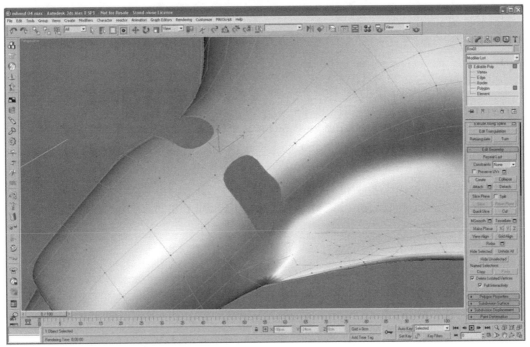

Figure 5.92 The first polygon re-created.

20. The surfaces of the model need to be refined even more in a few areas to add detail to the top of the thumb. Change the selection mode to Faces and select the faces between the second and third joints of the thumb, as shown in Figure 5.93.

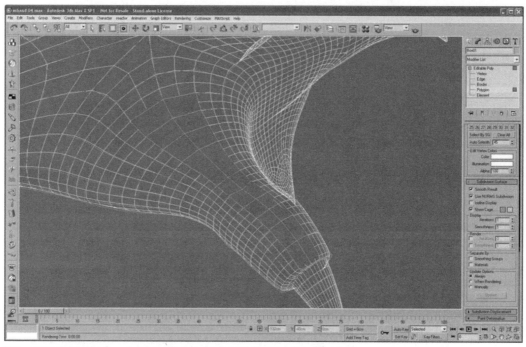

Figure 5.93 Select the faces between the second and third joints of the thumb.

21. Raise the selected polygons of the area between the joints to create a defined tendon between the joints, as shown in Figure 5.94. You may want to jump back and forth between Polygon and Vertex Sub Object modes and adjust the ends via vertex moving to get a nice blend into the hand.

22. Repeat the process to define the tendon between the third joint and the end of the thumb, as shown in Figure 5.95.

23. Refine the surface resolution of the knuckles of the thumb, as shown in Figure 5.96.

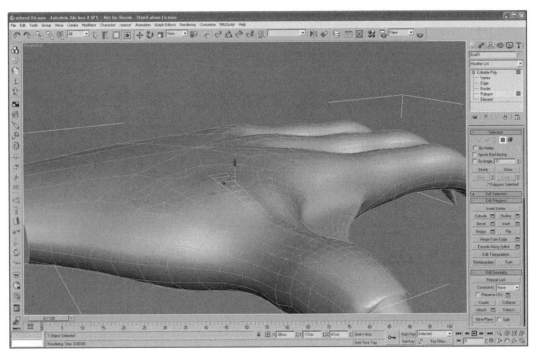

Figure 5.94 Define the tendon along the top of the thumb.

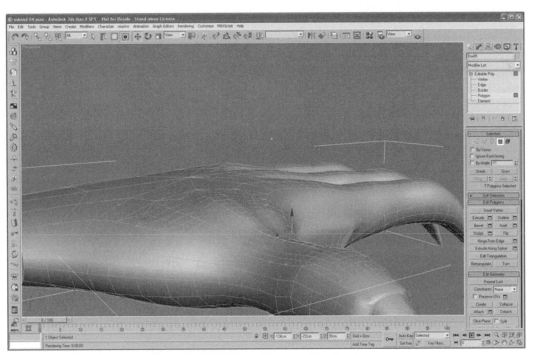

Figure 5.95 Define the tendon between the third joint and the end of the thumb.

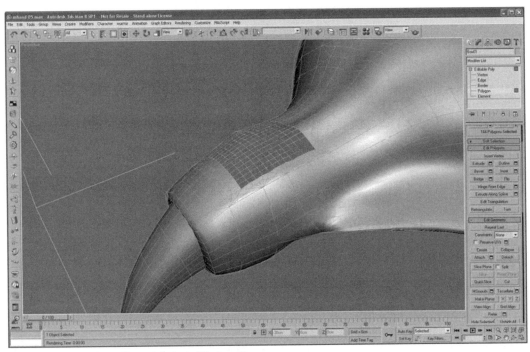

Figure 5.96 Refine the surface resolution of the knuckles.

24. Switch to Edge Sub Object mode and select the line of edges shown in Figure 5.97. These edges will be used to simulate the creases at the top of the joints.

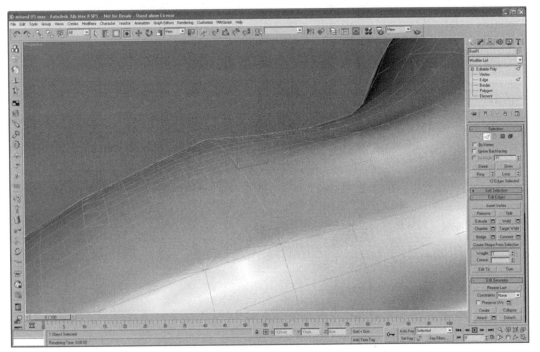

Figure 5.97 Select a line of edges along the top of the knuckle.

25. Crease the edges by setting the crease amount to 1, and use the Scale tool to first flatten the curve of the edges, then use the Move gizmo to move the edges downward, as shown in Figure 5.98.

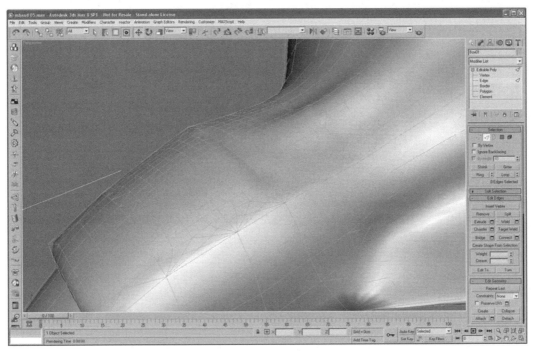

Figure 5.98 Move the creased edges down.

26. Change the selection mode back to Vertex and scale the vertices on either side of the crease together, as shown in Figure 5.99.

Note

Currently, the thumb is at a 90-degree angle from the hand. Even though this is not a natural position for the thumb, having the thumb in this position makes it easier to perform operations like scaling components in one direction. If the thumb were in its natural position, the scale function would have been much more difficult. After the thumb is finished, it will be an easy step to move the thumb into its natural position.

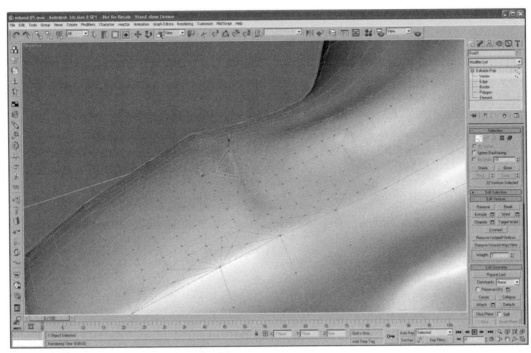

Figure 5.99 Pull in the vertices on either side of the crease.

27. Now crease and adjust the two lines of edges on either side of the original
crease, as shown in Figure 5.100. These two creases do not go as deep as the
center crease.

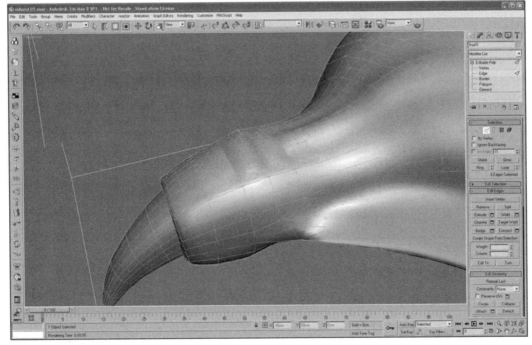

Figure 5.100 Make two more creases.

28. Scale the vertices on either side of the creases, as shown in Figure 5.101.

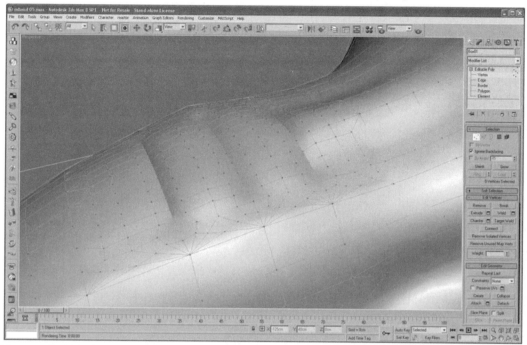

Figure 5.101 Scale the vertices on either side of the creases.

29. Now select individual rows of vertices perpendicular to the creases and move them along the length of the thumb to give the area a more organic look. The results should be similar to what's shown in Figure 5.102.

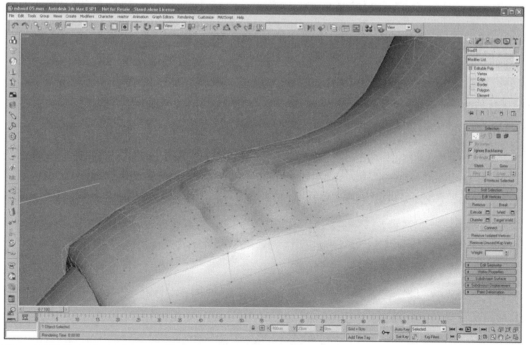

Figure 5.102 Move the vertices to make the creases seem more organic.

30. Add a crease underneath the knuckle, as shown in Figure 5.103, by following the same steps as for the top of the thumb. I had a nicely placed line that I was able to crease without adding the extra geometry.

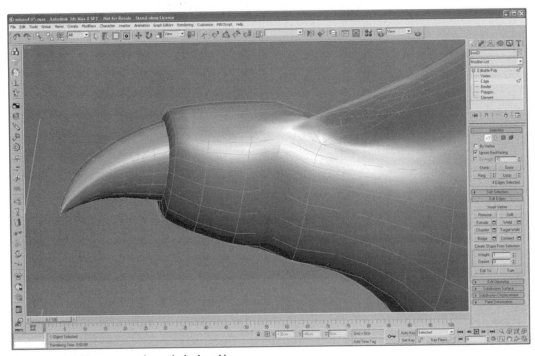

Figure 5.103 Add a crease underneath the knuckle.

31. The process of adding tendons and creases to the fingers is the same as it is for the thumb. Move over to the fingers and modify each in the same way as the thumb. Figure 5.104 shows the fingers after the refinements have taken place.

32. Next, move on to the palm and back of the hand. First, increase the surface resolution of that area, as shown in Figure 5.105.

33. Turn the hand over and add some creases to the palm, as shown in Figure 5.106.

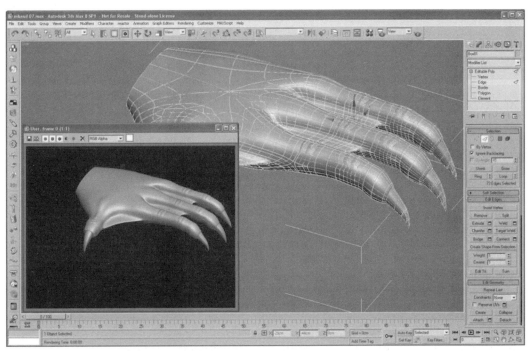

Figure 5.104 Add surface definition to the fingers.

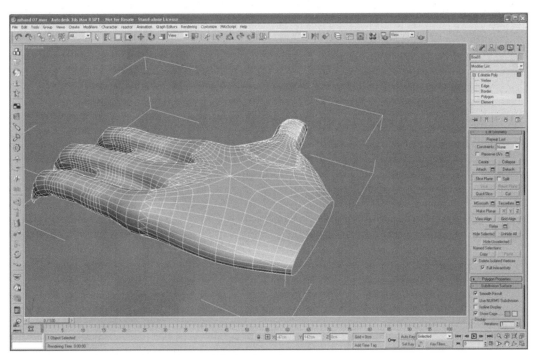

Figure 5.105 Increase the surface resolution of the hand.

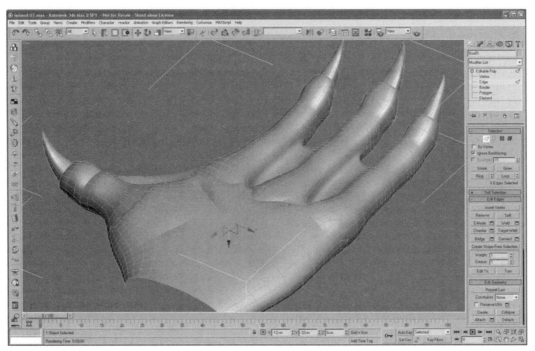

Figure 5.106 Add creases to the palm of the hand.

34. After creasing the palm, move the edges of the creases to look more natural for the surface of the palm.

35. Turn the hand over to view the top.

36. Let me introduce you to a new tool, the Soft Selection rollout. (See the Command Panel in Figure 5.107.) Switch to Vertex Sub Object mode and pick the center point on the back of the hand. Turn on Use Soft Selection, turn off Affect Backfacing, and toggle Shaded Face Toggle. Adjust Falloff up until you get something that looks like the selection shown in Figure 5.107. Notice how moving the vertex smoothly adjusts the surrounding vertices. Move the center point and middle wrist point to something resembling Figure 5.107.

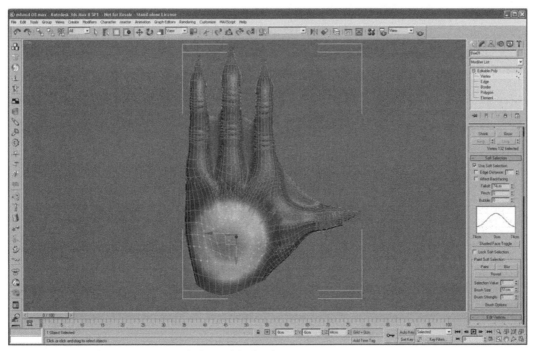

Figure 5.107 Move the center vertex to the base of the hand.

Note

If you're planning on moving the vertex a longer distance, it's helpful to move the points in smaller amounts and let go of the mouse button so Soft Selection will update between vertex moves. Otherwise, only the original soft selection will move, leaving you with a "shelf."

37. Select the vertices around the base of the knuckles and adjust Falloff so it only affects the desired area.

38. Move the selected vertices upward in the Y direction to define the knuckles in those areas, as shown in Figure 5.108.

39. Define the tendons that run from the base knuckles to the wrist area, as shown in Figure 5.109.

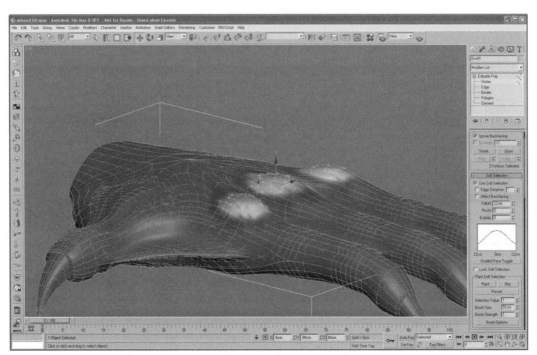

Figure 5.108 Define the base knuckles of the fingers.

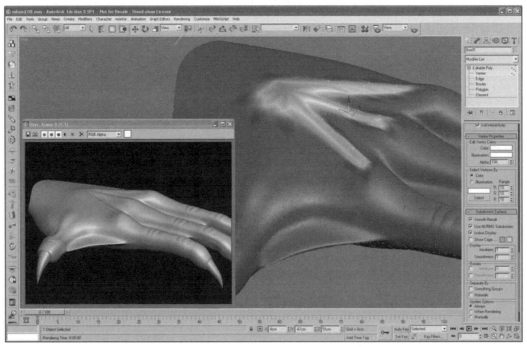

Figure 5.109 Define the tendons on the back of the hand.

40. Now that most of the surface detail is completed, the thumb can be adjusted to a more natural position.

41. Check Affect Backfacing on the Soft Selection rollout, select the vertices near the base of the thumb toward the base of the hand, and move them to form a more natural thumb muscle, as shown in Figure 5.110. It may take a few smaller rotations and movements to get it in the right place.

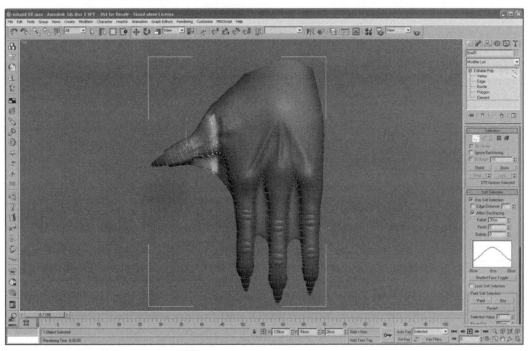

Figure 5.110 Reshape the muscle of the thumb.

42. Rotate the fingers to a more natural position as well, as shown in Figure 5.111.

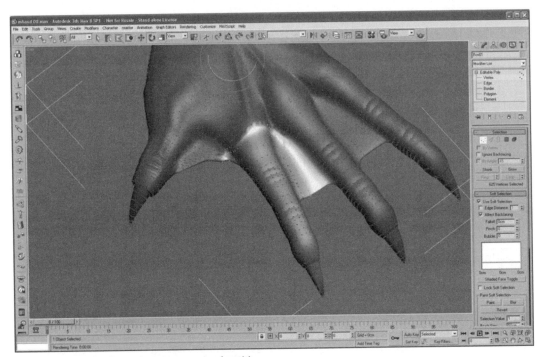

Figure 5.111 Put the fingers into a more natural position.

Figure 5.112 shows the finished clawed hand.

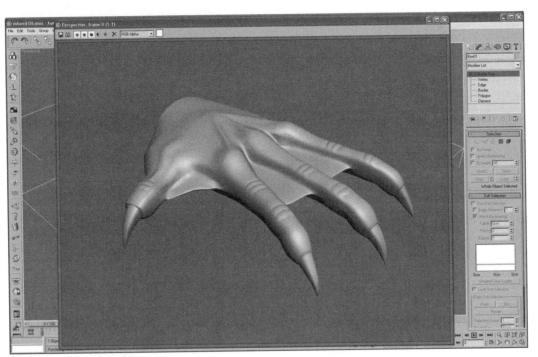

Figure 5.112 The finished clawed hand.

It was relatively easy to use subdivision surfaces to complete a complex model with lots of surface detail. Subdivision surfaces are one of the best modeling methods for creating complex organic shapes.

Summary

This chapter covered two modeling methods for creating 3D digital models: NURBS modeling and subdivision surfaces modeling. Both modeling methods have advantages, depending on the type of model being built.

NURBS modeling is useful in creating smooth, rounded surface models. The chapter covered

- Building NURBS models using curves and primitives
- Understanding CVs and how they are used to modify a model's shape

Many NURBS modeling tools were used in the examples, but a number of the deeper tools were not covered. Experiment with the NURBS tools; having a better understanding of the tools will increase your ability to create models using NURBS.

Subdivision surfaces modeling is useful in creating complex models, particularly organic models that have a high degree of surface detail. The chapter covered the following:

- Creating complex models starting from a box
- Changing the surface resolution of a model to add detail in places
- Creasing edges to add finer detail to intricate areas of the model

This chapter covered many modeling techniques, but it was not an exhaustive manual for all the tools and functions in Max. If you followed the examples in this chapter, you should have a good foundation for creating models using the two methods mentioned. For additional information on the tools and functions not covered in this chapter, refer to the help files in Max.

Chapter 6

Made in the Shader

This chapter is about surfaces. Building 3D geometry is only part of the total process for creating 3D models. 3D models also need to have surfaces. Every object in real life has a surface. For example, this page has a surface made up of paper and printed ink. If you wanted to accurately reproduce this page from the book in a 3D program, you would need to first build the 3D geometry, and then define the surface qualities of the page. Surface quality definitions are contained in shaders.

Maya Shaders

Maya defines shaders as materials. The two words are somewhat interchangeable, and you will see both terms used in this chapter. Materials in Maya contain all of the surface information for all or part of a 3D model. Some 3D models only have a single material, but many have multiple materials, each containing its own surface definitions. For example, the glass in a window is transparent while the molding is not. Transparency is a surface quality. The glass and the molding need to have separate materials because the surface definitions are different.

The best way to understand materials or shaders in Maya is to learn how to make them and apply them to 3D models to see what they do. To prepare for learning about creating materials, you will build a simple scene with two 3D objects.

1. Start by creating a polygon sphere. Set Radius to 2.0000 and Axis Divisions and Height Divisions to 32.

2. Move the sphere up 2 units so it is sitting on top of the grid.

3. Now create a polygon cube. The cube should be 1 unit high by 10 units wide and 10 units deep. Set Width and Depth Divisions to 10 and Height Divisions to 1.

4. Move the cube down in the Y axis 0.5. Your scene should now look similar to what you see in Figure 6.1.

5. Light is required to see any surface. Create a point light with an intensity of 1 and place it above the polygon objects, as shown in Figure 6.2.

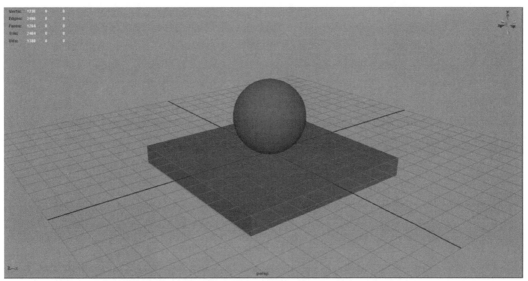

Figure 6.1 Move the cube down so the sphere looks like it is sitting on it.

6. Next, create an ambient light with an intensity of 0.3, as shown in Figure 6.3. You will need a light so you can see the scene. Maya has default lighting, but I like to have a little more control over my scenes, so I usually define my own lights in a scene. Move the ambient light as shown.

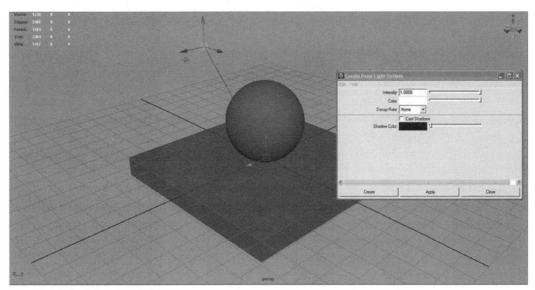

Figure 6.2 Put a light in the scene.

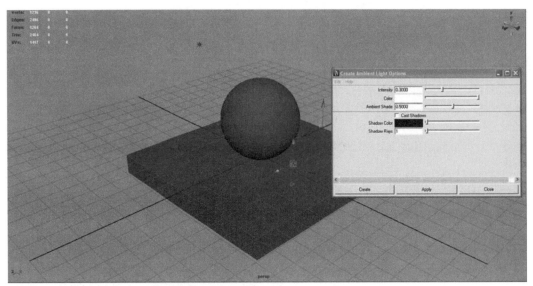

Figure 6.3 Add an ambient light as a second light source.

Okay, the scene is ready for you to start experimenting with some materials. The first step will be to create a material, and then apply the material to a model. Go to a two-panel display with the Perspective view on the right and Maya's material tool, Hypershade, on the left. The easiest way to do this is to select it from the Quick Layout buttons on the left side of the screen. It is the fifth from the top.

Hypershade has three panels: two stacked on the right and one on the left. The top panel on the right, the Work Area tab, contains information about shading networks. The bottom panel on the right, the Shader Library tab, contains specific shader nodes and connections. The panel on the left, the Create bar, contains tools for creating materials different types of rendering effects.

In the Create bar, find and click Lambert to create a new material, as shown in Figure 6.4.

With the material selected, click on the Attribute Editor button or press Ctrl+A to edit the attributes of the new material. In the box next to Lambert in the Attribute Editor, change the material name to Ball. It is always a good practice to rename materials for easy sorting, particularly when creating complex scenes with multiple materials. Create another Lambert material and name it Block.

Under Common Material Attributes, click on the swatch next to Color. This will bring up a color palette called the Color Chooser. You can change the color of a material by changing the colors in the Color Chooser. For this material, change the color to white by using the slider bar to the left, as shown in Figure 6.5. Set the color for the ball and the block to white.

Materials are applied to 3D objects through Hypershade. First, select the object in the Workspace, and then press the right mouse button over the top of the material you want to apply in Hypershade. This will bring up the marking menu. Select Apply Material to Selection and release the mouse button. The material will be applied to the selected object.

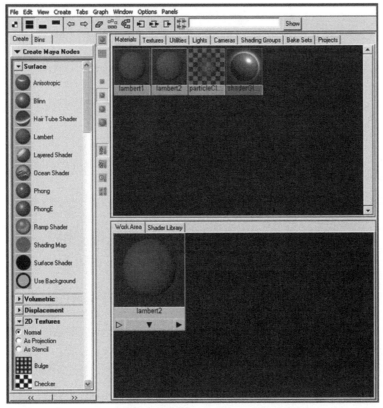

Figure 6.4 Create a new Lambert material.

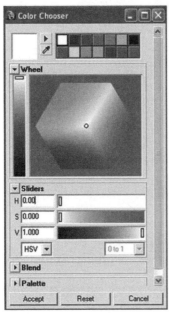

Figure 6.5 Change the material to white.

Apply the Ball material to the ball in the Workspace and the Block material to the block in the Workspace, as shown in Figure 6.6.

The ball and block now have a surface material or *shader* applied. Figure 6.7 shows the ball and block rendered with the new materials.

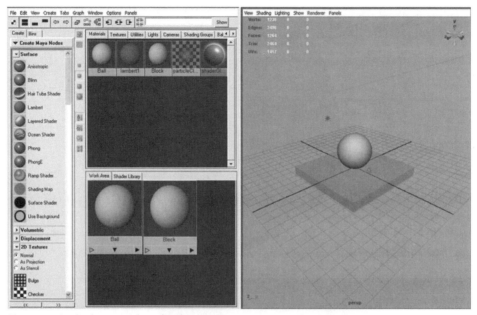

Figure 6.6 Apply the materials to the objects.

Figure 6.7 The picture shows a rendering of the scene with the new materials.

Material Attributes

There are just too many features and functions in Maya to cover them completely in one volume. Instead, attention will be given to a basic set of material attributes that will give you a working knowledge of the functions and procedures for working with shaders in Maya. From this foundation you will then be better equipped to explore deeper knowledge.

Common Material Attributes

You just worked with one of the basic attributes of a material in the last section when you applied a color to the ball and block. Select the Ball material in Hypershade and bring up the Attribute Editor. Look down the editor to Common Material Attributes. Within this section are material attributes that are common across material types. The top one is Color. You have already used this section by changing the color using the Color Chooser. Now let's take a look at some other aspects of the Common Material Attributes in the Attribute Editor shown in Figure 6.8.

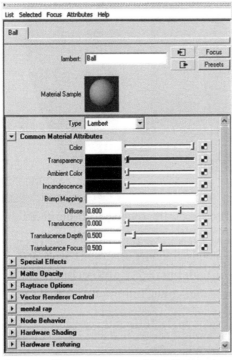

Let's first look at how each attribute is organized. On the left side is the name of each attribute. To the right of the name is either a color swatch or a text box. Clicking on the color swatch will bring up the Color Chooser. The text boxes are for accurate input of data.

The next item to the right is a slider bar for manual input and adjustments. All of the attributes except for Bump Mapping have this slider bar. To the right of the slider bars is a checkered icon. Clicking on this icon gives access to more advanced editing of each attribute. For example, if you want to load a texture into the material, you can import it by clicking the checkered icon and using the more advanced editing options.

Figure 6.8 Many common material attributes can be found in the Attribute Editor.

Transparency

Below Color is the Transparency attribute. Slide the Transparency slider bar to the right about halfway. Notice that the ball in the Workspace changes to indicate the ball is now semitransparent. The Material Sample in the Attribute Editor also changes to a transparent ball with a checkered background. This is also true for the material in Hypershade.

When rendered, the ball is now transparent, as shown in Figure 6.9.

The slider bar's range is from full opaque on the left to completely transparent on the right. Move the slider bar back to full opaque to continue to the next section.

Figure 6.9 Changing the Transparency attribute will make the object appear transparent.

Ambient Color

The word *ambient* means "surrounding," or "encircling." Ambient Color is a material attribute that simulates color reflected on an object from its surroundings. Slide the slider bar to the right about halfway. Notice the changes to the Material Samples in Hypershade and in the Attribute Editor.

When the scene is rendered, the ball now looks brighter, as shown in Figure 6.10.

Figure 6.10 The ball appears brighter in the scene.

The default for ambient light is off. Use ambient light as a subtle effect to increase the appearance of universal lighting on an object.

Move the slider bar back to the left to move on to the next section.

Incandescence

Incandescence is the internal brightness of an object, as if it were a light source. Although incandescence does not emit light and will not light surrounding objects, it does cause an object to appear bright. Incandescence is often used when modeling something bright in a scene, such as lava or a light bulb. Move the slider bar all the way to the right. Again, notice the difference in the Material Samples.

Figure 6.11 shows the effects of increasing the material's incandescence.

Figure 6.11 Incandescence makes an object appear to emit light.

Move the Incandescence slider bar back to the left to move on to the next section.

Bump Mapping

Bump mapping is used to give a material the appearance of a surface roughness. It is often used where geometry is impractical. Although a bump map may appear to have surface deformations, it does not change the underlying geometry.

There is no slider bar next to Bump Mapping. That is because bump maps require the creation of a new render node. Before going farther, save the scene so it can be loaded later. Click on the checkered icon to the right of Bump Mapping. A Create Render Node dialog box will appear, with options for creating pre-made 2D and 3D textures in addition to import options for files or movies. Select Cloth from the pre-made 2D textures.

A simulated cloth bump map is now applied to the Ball material. Notice in the rendering of the scene, shown in Figure 6.12, that although the ball now appears to have surface deformation, it does not affect the actual geometry of the ball, as seen around the edges of the model.

Figure 6.12 The bump map does not affect the geometry of the ball.

Figure 6.13 The connected nodes for the bump map will appear in the Shader Library tab.

You should also notice that there are a few new items in the Shader Library tab (see Figure 6.13). These are the connected nodes that form the bump map.

Load the saved file of the ball and block to continue on to the next section.

Diffuse and Translucence

The next few items deal with the translucent quality of a material. Translucence is the material attribute that controls the appearance of light passing through an object. It is different from transparency in that it transmits and scatters light. This effect is similar to how light passes through a lampshade or the wax of a lit candle. The following is an explanation of how each item works:

- **Diffuse.** This causes light to be reflected in all directions. The higher the value, the closer the color is to the actual color settings.
- **Translucence.** This gives a material the ability to absorb and diffuse light from a light source.

- **Translucence Depth.** This controls the depth to which light passes through an object before it is reduced to nothing.
- **Translucence Focus.** This controls the angle of translucent light passing through an object. Thinner materials have a higher focus value than thicker materials.

To see how translucence works, move the point light from above the ball to the center of the ball.

Select the Ball material again and slide the Translucence slider all the way to the right and Translucence Focus about halfway to the right.

Figure 6.14 shows the results of the changes in translucence when rendered.

Figure 6.14 The ball now transmits the light from the point light.

Now slide the Translucence Focus slider back to the left.

Figure 6.15 shows the rendered results of the difference in translucence focus.

Play around with the Common Material Attributes and see how each affects the models.

To continue, reload the saved ball scene.

Figure 6.15 The ball now glows more evenly from the light.

Specular Shading

The Lambert material is a basic flat material. It is kind of like flat wall paint; it has no shininess. The material attributes that make a material shiny are contained in the Specular Shading group. To see how these attributes work, you will need to change the material type to a material that supports shiny surfaces. In the Type pull-down menu, change the material from Lambert to Blinn. Blinn materials are great for metallic objects, but they can also be adjusted to simulate other shiny surfaces as well. When you change the material, you will have to rename it Ball again.

Figure 6.16 shows the new Blinn material rendered.

Figure 6.16 The Blinn material simulates a shiny surface.

Eccentricity

The first item in the Specular Shading group is Eccentricity. Eccentricity controls the size of highlights on an object. For example, change Eccentricity to 0.100.

Figure 6.17 shows the scene rendered with the lower eccentricity. Notice how small the highlight on the object is. Smaller, brighter highlights tend to make objects look shinier.

Figure 6.17 Lower eccentricity reduces the size of the highlight.

Specular Roll Off

Specular Roll Off controls the amount of oblique angle reflection of an object's surroundings. It also increases or decreases the intensity of the specular highlight. Change Specular Roll Off to 0.100.

Figure 6.18 shows the scene rendered with Specular Roll Off reduced.

Figure 6.18 Reducing Specular Roll Off reduces the intensity of the highlight.

Specular Color

Specular Color controls the color of the highlight. Change Specular Roll Off to 0.3. Click the color swatch next to Specular Color and change the highlight color to red using the Color Chooser. Notice that the highlight color changes in the Workspace and in the Material Samples as well.

Figure 6.19 shows the rendered version of the scene with the red specular highlight (although obviously the red isn't visible to you, given that this book is not in color).

Figure 6.19 The ball now has a red highlight.

Change Specular Color back to a neutral gray.

Reflectivity

Reflectivity is similar to Specular Roll Off. It allows the material to reflect its surroundings or a color. To reflect its surroundings, Raytracing has to be turned on. To turn Raytracing on, you will need to bring up the Render Settings dialog box. To access the Render Settings dialog box, click on its icon on the right side of the status line.

Once you have the Render Settings dialog box up, go to the Maya Software tab and down to Raytracing. Click the Raytracing check box.

Now when the scene is rendered, the ball will reflect its surroundings, as shown in Figure 6.20.

Figure 6.20 The ball is now reflective.

Reflected Color

Reflected Color applies a color or an image as reflections. You can use Reflected Color to simulate reflections similar to an environment map. You can also use Reflected Color to add a color to the reflection. When Raytracing is turned on, Reflected Color is combined with the reflection to tint the color of the reflection. Click the checkered icon to the far right of Reflected Color to bring up the Create Render Node dialog box.

For this example, use the Ramp texture. It is the bottom 2D texture in the first column. Ramp textures are similar to applying color to a material except that instead of a color, you are applying a gradient that ramps from one color to another.

Once the Ramp texture is chosen, you can edit the colors in the Attribute Editor using the Color Chooser, as shown in Figure 6.21.

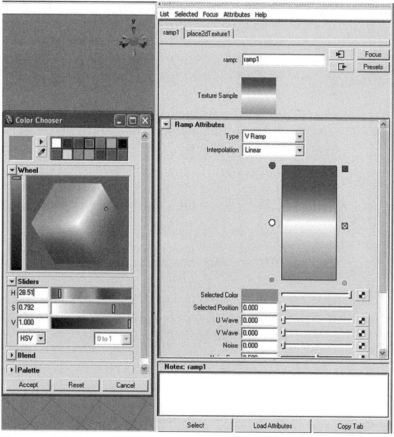

Figure 6.21 Edit the ramp in the Attribute Editor.

The large color swatch in the Attribute Editor indicates the colors for the texture. You can turn new colors on or eliminate colors from the ramp by clicking the squares on the right side of the ramp. The circles on the left side can be used to position colors in the ramp. Set up your ramp so it is similar to that shown in Figure 6.21. Figure 6.22 shows the rendered results of the reflected color.

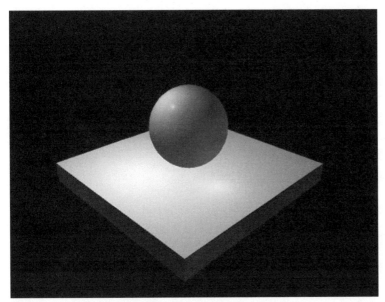

Figure 6.22 Reflected color is added to the reflection on the ball.

Putting It Together

Now that you understand a few of the many attributes used in creating materials in Maya, let's take a look at how to put these together to create a more complex scene. For the next example, load the original ball and block scene. If the ball is not already a Blinn material, change it to Blinn now.

1. In this example, a File texture will be used on the ball. Click the checkered icon to the far right of Color to bring up the Create Render Node dialog box. File is the second 2D texture from the top of the second column.

2. In the Attribute Editor, click the file folder icon to browse for a File texture to load. For this example, I used a marble tile I took from the standard tiles that come with Corel Draw. It doesn't really matter what you use other than that it needs to be a 2D bitmap picture that is compatible with Maya. Maya accepts most standard bitmap file formats, including .iff, .bmp, .jpg, .tga, .tif, .gif, .psd, and .pic, among others. Figure 6.23 shows the new File texture loaded into the material for the ball. If you don't see it in the scene, press the 6 key for Smooth Shaded mode.

3. Next, change the Block material to Blinn and give it a File texture as well. I again used a tile from Corel Draw, that of a wood texture.

   Figure 6.24 shows the scene rendered with the File textures added to the materials of the ball and the block.

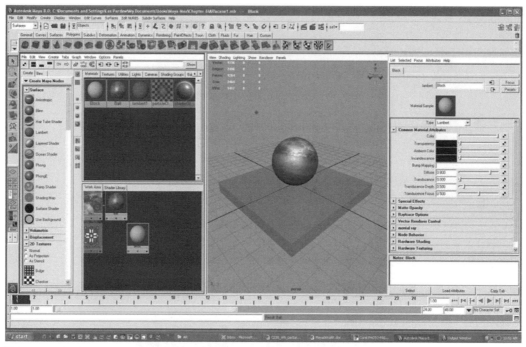

Figure 6.23 A File texture is added to the material.

Figure 6.24 The File textures make the scene seem more realistic.

4. Now add Raytracing in the Render Settings dialog box to give the scene a more natural look with real reflections.

5. Let's also add a cast shadow to make the scene look more real. To turn on cast shadows, select the point light and, in the Attribute Editor, go into the Shadow

section. Scroll down to Raytrace Shadow Attributes and click on the check box titled Use Ray Trace Shadows. Figure 6.25 shows the scene rendered with Raytracing turned on.

Figure 6.25 Raytracing adds reflections to the scene.

6. Now let's add some variation to the surface of the ball by adding a bump map. For this example, I added a file bump map that roughly follows the colors of the material. File bump maps are most effective if they are grayscale pictures. The lighter areas bump upward and the darker areas bump downward. See the results in the rendering with the bump map in Figure 6.26.

Figure 6.26 A bump map is added to the ball.

As you can see, when you combine just a few elements of the many attributes in a material, the model can look more and more real when rendered. As you become more familiar with the different attributes of the materials in Maya, try experimenting to see how they affect each other.

Cartoon Shaders

Maya has a fun feature called Toon. Toon is a cartoon shader system built into Maya for creating cartoon ink and paint effects. The following is a quick example of how it works.

1. Load the cartoon race car you built in Chapter 5.
2. Change the main menu from Polygons to Rendering.
3. Maya has a number of Toon Shader styles. We will only be covering a few of them in this book. Select the body of the car, and then select Toon, Assign Fill Shader, Circle Highlight.
4. Many of the Toon Shaders work similarly to the way the ramp shader works. Change the left color swatch on the Circle Highlight shader to dark red, as shown in Figure 6.27.
5. Change the lighter color to a light red, as shown in Figure 6.28.

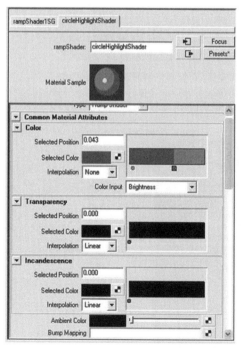

Figure 6.27 Change the darker color to dark red.

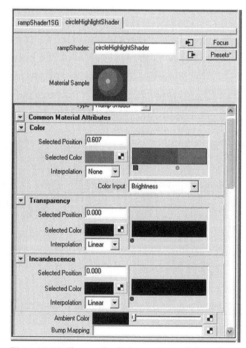

Figure 6.28 Change the lighter color to light red.

6. Select all four wheels.
7. Apply a Shaded Brightness Three Tone fill shader to the wheels from the Assign Fill Shader list.

8. Change the three colors to range from dark gray to light gray, as shown in Figure 6.29.

9. Select the axles and wheel hubs for the front and back tires.

10. Apply a Dark Profile fill shader.

11. Change the colors to dark and light gray, as shown in Figure 6.30.

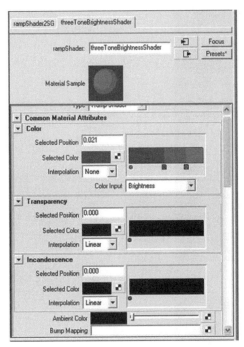

Figure 6.29 Use three tones of gray for the wheels.

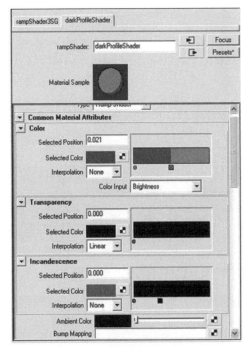

Figure 6.30 Give the axles a gray fill shader.

12. Render the scene to see how the fill shaders affect the model. Your scene should look similar to that shown in Figure 6.31.

13. Now for the Toon lines. Select all of the objects, and then select Toon, Assign Outline, Add New Toon outline.

The model is now Toon shaded. Wasn't that easy? Take a look at the rendered results shown in Figure 6.32.

Figure 6.31 Render the image to see the fill shaders on the model.

Figure 6.32 The model looks like a cartoon.

3D Paint

Another way to apply materials to a surface is to paint on the models directly using a feature in Maya called 3D paint. The 3D paint tool is also located in the Rendering menu set in the Texturing menu. Load the clawed hand model you created in Chapter 5.

1. Convert the model from subdivision surfaces to polygons by using the conversion tool found in Convert in the Modify menu. Use Adaptive Tessellation. Set Divisions Per Face to 1, and check Replace.

2. You will need to divide all of the polygons that are five-sided or more. Go back to the Polygons menu set and use the Cleanup tool found in the Mesh menu. Cleanup is a tool that fixes problems in polygon meshes. It has a number of features. The default settings will work fine for this model for tessellating polygons with more than four sides.

3. For 3D paint to work properly, the model has to be mapped within the 0 to 1 texture area with no overlapping UVs. The easiest way to ensure that the model is mapped correctly is to use Automatic Mapping (see Figure 6.33).

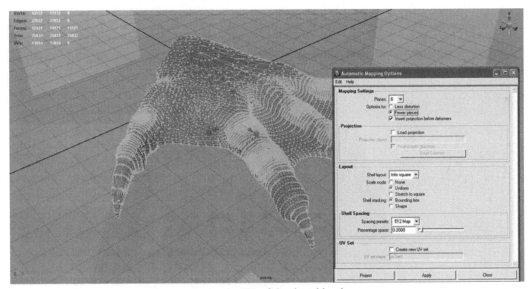

Figure 6.33 Use Automatic Mapping to organize the UVs of the clawed hand.

You can see the results of Automatic Mapping in the UV Texture Editor, as shown in Figure 6.34.

4. Create a solid green texture that is 1,024 pixels by 1,024 pixels in a 2D paint program.

5. Create a Blinn material and load the green texture into the color of the Blinn material. Apply the texture to the clawed hand model.

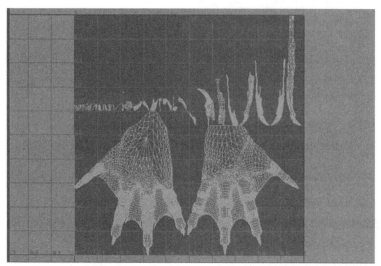

Figure 6.34 Automatic Mapping lays out the UVs for painting.

6. You will need to make several adjustments to the Blinn material to get it to look more like flesh and less like metal. Set Translucence to 0.800, Translucence Focus to 0.500, Eccentricity to 0.500, Specular Roll Off to 0.500, and Reflectivity to 0.100.

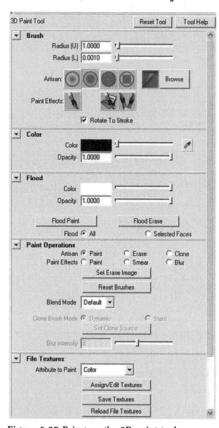

Figure 6.35 Bring up the 3D paint tool.

7. Now bring up the 3D Paint tool from the Texturing menu. The tool is in the Tool area to the right side of the screen, as shown in Figure 6.35.

Note

The 3D Paint tool has two types of brushes that can be used to paint on 3D surfaces: Artisan brushes and Paint Effects brushes. Artisan brushes are represented by the blue icons with red circles. Paint Effects brushes can be loaded using the Paint Effects icons below the Artisan brushes.

You can control the size of a brush by using either the slider bars at the top of the tool or the text boxes next to them. 3D Paint is made for using a digitizing pad and a pressure-sensitive stylus. The two size controls are for the upper and lower sizes of the brush based on the pressure on the stylus. If you are using a mouse, only the upper radius applies.

Use the Color Chooser to change the color of the brush.

8. Start painting by setting the color to that of the hand. Change the lighting to Use No Lights in the Lighting menu of the Panel menu. This will flatten the image to the single color of the green material.

9. Now use the eyedropper in the Color Chooser to select the color of the green texture, as I have done in Figure 6.36.

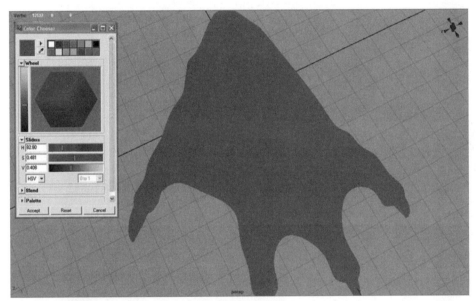

Figure 6.36 Change the current color to that of the green texture.

10. Now paint some tonal qualities on the hand by first painting a lighter tone over the knuckle areas.

11. Next, paint a darker green color in between the ligaments and sides of the fingers (see Figure 6.37).

12. Paint a lighter green in the webbing between the fingers, (see Figure 6.38).

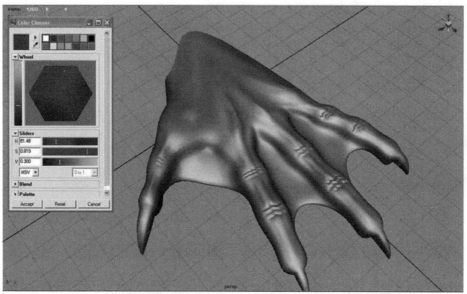

Figure 6.37 Add some tonal qualities to the hand.

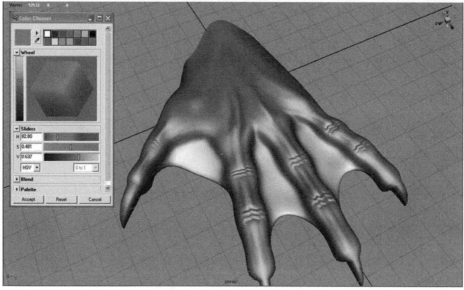

Figure 6.38 Lighten the webbing between the fingers.

13. Paint the individual claws black, as shown in Figure 6.39.

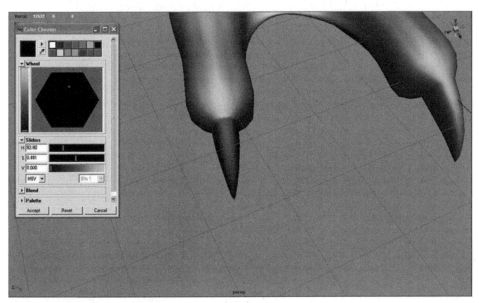

Figure 6.39 Paint the claws black.

The scene should look like Figure 6.40 when you are finished painting each claw.

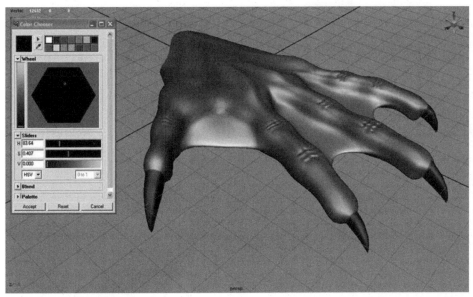

Figure 6.40 Finish painting the claws.

14. Now let's add some paint effects. Click on the icon with the double brushes in the Paint Effects brushes. This will bring up the Visor.

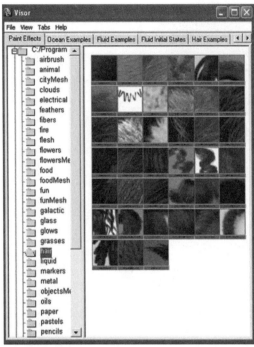

Figure 6.41 Choose a Paint Effects brush.

15. There are a number of predefined Paint Effects brushes. Choose hair from the list and BodyFurBlack.Mel from the displayed brush types. It is the second one from the left in the top row of brushes (see Figure 6.41).

16. Set the brush size to 0.2 and lightly lay in an upward stroke from the base of the wrist (see Figure 6.42). This is an easy way to paint in body hair.

Figure 6.43 shows a rendered version of the clawed hand.

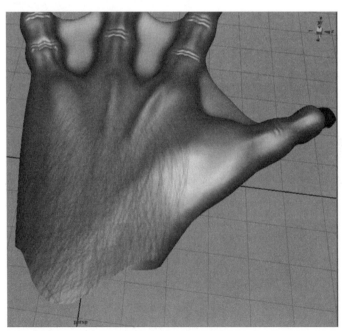

Figure 6.42 Paint on some body hair.

3D Paint is a very powerful way to create textures for models in Maya. It gives the artist the ability to paint directly onto a model, almost like painting an object in real life. With the powerful addition of Paint Effects brushes, there are almost endless possibilities.

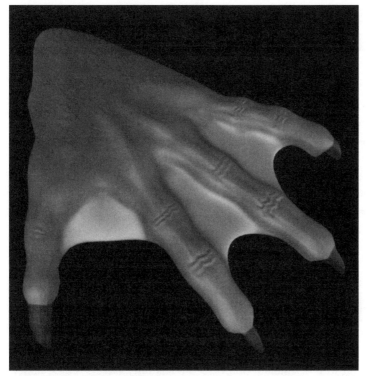

Figure 6.43 The clawed hand rendered.

In addition to being able to paint in the Color attributes of a material, 3D Paint can also work in other attributes, such as Transparency, Incandescence, Translucence, and even Bump. Try some experiments of your own with different material attributes. Also try a few of the many Paint Effects brushes.

Summary

This chapter was an overview of some of the many aspects of shaders in Maya. Maya has one of the most robust and extensive shader systems of any 3D software. In this chapter, you should have become familiar with the following aspects of Maya's shader system:

- Material types
- Material attributes
- Applying materials to models
- 2D and 3D textures
- Toon Shaders
- 3D Paint

Shaders—or materials, as they are called in Maya—are an essential part of creating believable 3D models. In this chapter, you have just scratched the surface of learning how to develop surface shaders. However, hopefully you now have a good foundation that you can use as a base for further exploration.

Chapter 6

Made in the Shader

This chapter is about surfaces. Building 3D geometry is only part of the total process for creating 3D models. 3D models also need to have surfaces. Every object in real life has a surface. For example, this page has a surface made up of paper and printed ink. If you wanted to accurately reproduce this page from the book in a 3D program, you would need to first build the 3D geometry and then define the surface qualities of the page. Surface quality definitions are contained in shaders.

Max Shaders

Max defines shaders as *materials*. The two words are interchangeable. Materials in Max contain all of the surface information for all or part of a 3D model. Some 3D models only have a single material, but many have multiple materials, each containing its own surface definitions. For example, the glass in a window is transparent while the molding is not. Transparency is a surface quality. The glass and the molding need to have separate materials because the surface definitions are different.

The best way to understand materials or shaders in Max is to learn how to make them and apply them to 3D models to see what they do. To prepare for learning about creating materials, you will build a simple scene with two 3D objects.

1. Start by creating a sphere primitive. Set Radius to 45.0 cm and Segments to 32.
2. Now create a box primitive. The cube should be about 300 cm long by 300 cm wide by 15 cm tall. Set Width Segs and Length Segs to 10 and Height Segs to 1.
3. Move the sphere up so it is sitting on top of the box primitive.
4. Set the default color of both primitives to a medium gray. Your scene should now look similar to that shown in Figure 6.1.
5. Light is required to see any surface. Create an Omni light and place it above the objects, as shown in Figure 6.2. You will find the Omni light under the Create tab of the Command Panel under Lights. Set Shadows to On and Multiplier to 1.5. If you forget to set these values before you create the light or you want to adjust them, you can always change values in the Modify tab. Just select the light and switch to the Modify tab.

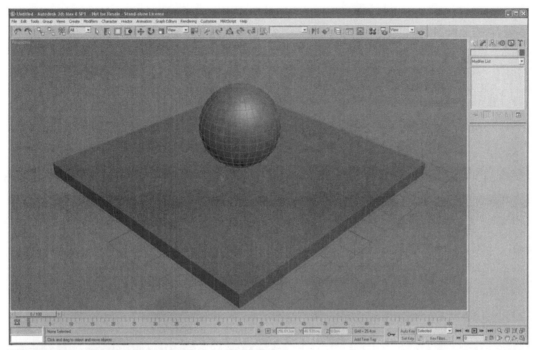

Figure 6.1 Move the sphere up so it is sitting on top of the box.

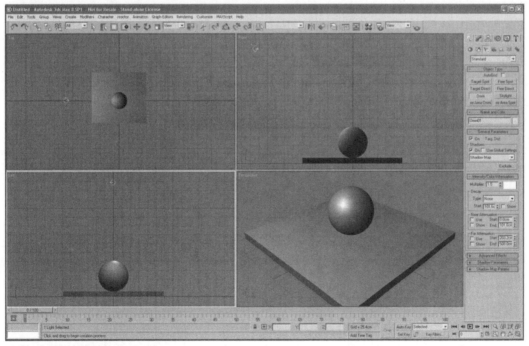

Figure 6.2 Put a light in the scene.

6. Next, create an ambient light, as shown in Figure 6.3. Set the intensity to 0.5 and make sure the shadows are off for this light source.

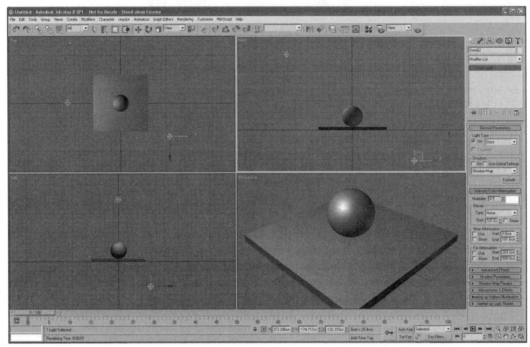

Figure 6.3 Add an ambient light as a second light source.

Okay, the scene is ready for you to start experimenting with some materials. The first step will be to create a material, and then apply that material to an object. You will be creating all of your materials in the Material Editor. You can access this by pressing the M key.

Note

Here are some common terms found in the Material Editor and a brief definition for each:

Diffuse—color

Specular—highlight color and/or strength

Glossiness—spread of the specular highlight

Blinn/Phong/Metal/Anisotropic/...—shader types (usually named after the original author)

UVs—mapping coordinates

Wire—renders the object in wireframe

2-Sided—forces Max to render polygons as two sided

Face Map—renders the texture on each face and ignores the UVs

Faceted—renders the object without smooth shading

At first glance, the Material Editor seems simple; however, the Material Editor is quite deep and can get confusing. Figure 6.4 shows common areas you will be using. They are described here:

1. The material preview balls will give you a small preview of the material you are creating. Double-clicking on one of these will bring up a resizable window that can give you a better idea of the material you are creating.

2. This vertical bar of icons consists of settings for the Material Editor. Run your mouse over the icons for an idea of the types of things you can do with each icon.

3. This horizontal bar of icons mainly deals with assigning, viewing, saving, and moving through the individual materials (balls). You will use the icons on this bar a lot, so take a minute to get familiar with them by mousing over the icons and noting what each does.

4. You will also frequently use the three items in this horizontal section. They are (left to right) Pick Material from Object, the material's name, and the material's type.

5. This section has the most basic properties of the shader. They are the shader type and some basic rendering modes.

6. The next section deals with more basics of a material, like color, transparency, and specular highlights.

7. And the final section is the Maps rollout. Here you can assign things like color texture maps as well as bump maps. You can also set the strength of those maps.

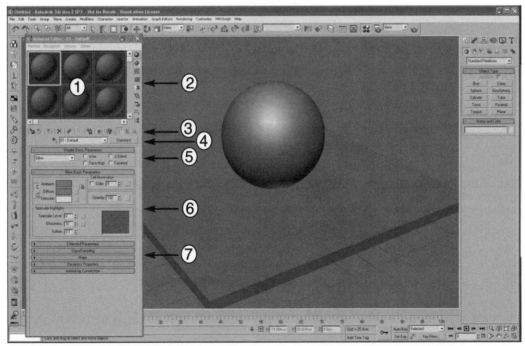

Figure 6.4 The Material Editor basics.

Let's assign the first material ball to the sphere in the scene. You can do this a couple different ways. You can drag and drop the material ball to the object, or you can select the object and click Assign Material to Selection (found in section 3, as shown in Figure 6.4).

Note

It is always good practice to rename materials for easy sorting, particularly when you are creating complex scenes with multiple materials. I have named the first material ball "Ball" and the second material ball "Block."

Go ahead and assign the first material ball to the sphere and the second material ball to the box primitive. Now adjust the material properties for these two new materials. Under the Blinn Basic Parameters rollout, click on the color swatch next to Diffuse. This will bring up the Color Selector, where you can adjust the color. Set the color for this material to white by using either the slider bars on the right or the color picker on the left, as shown in Figure 6.5. Set the color for the sphere and the box to white.

Figure 6.5 Change the material to white.

Notice the four small triangles that appear around the material ball you just assigned (see Figure 6.6). These indicate that the material is assigned to something in the scene. These markers have two states, either dark gray or solid white. The solid white state indicates that the assigned material is on an object that is currently selected in the scene, and the darker gray state indicates that it's assigned to an object but that object is not currently selected. This is useful information to have when you are working with complex scenes.

It also seems that the scene is lit too brightly. I have adjusted the main Omni light back to a multiplier of 1. When you are setting up materials for a scene, it is common to go back and forth with adjusting the material properties as well as lighting. Both have a direct effect on how the object looks and feels.

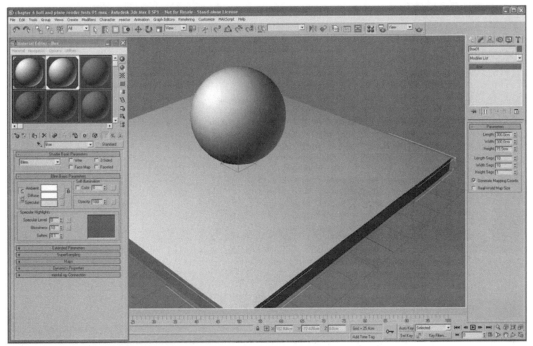

Figure 6.6 Note the small triangle indicators.

The ball and block now have separate surface materials or shaders applied. Figure 6.7 shows the ball and block rendered with the new materials.

Figure 6.7 A rendering of the scene with the new materials.

Material Attributes

As with much of this book, we will just be scratching the surface of the materials and rendering, so I would encourage you to explore this further with the Max help feature, online tutorials, and more extensive books on the subject.

Common Material Attributes

You just worked with one of the basic attributes of a material in the last section when you applied a color to the sphere and box. Select the Ball material by clicking on the first material ball. You have already changed the color using the Color Selector. Now let's take a look at some other aspects of the Blinn Basic Parameters.

Transparency

To the right of where you set the color is the Opacity spinner. Set Opacity to about 50 percent. Notice that the ball in the viewport changes to indicate that the ball is now semitransparent. The material ball in the Material Editor also changes to a transparent ball. (I have toggled on the Background icon, shown as a checkered icon to the right of the material balls. This will show a checkered background behind the material ball for clarity.)

When rendered as shown in Figure 6.8, the ball is now transparent.

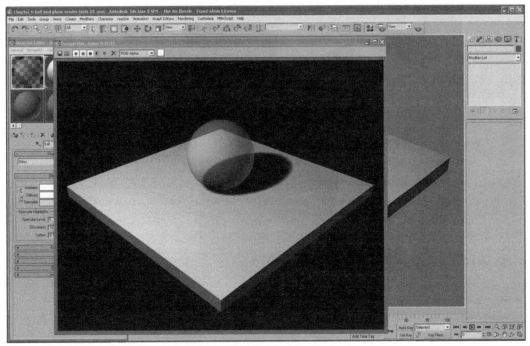

Figure 6.8 Changing the Transparency attribute will make the object appear transparent.

The slider bar's range is from 100 percent opaque on the left to completely transparent. Move the slider bar back to 100 percent opaque for the next example.

Ambient Color

The word *ambient* means "surrounding," or "encircling." Ambient Color is a material attribute that simulates color reflected on an object from its surroundings by affecting the shadow color and/or value. The Ambient value in the Material Editor is tied to the global ambient setting found in the Environment and Effects dialog box shown in Figure 6.9. To see the ambient change, you will need to bring up the Environment and Effects dialog box by pressing 8 and unlock the Ambient value from the Diffuse value by toggling the small yellow icon next to the Ambient and Diffuse settings. Set the Ambient value to a mid-gray, and then adjust the Ambient value in the Material Editor to your liking. (I used blue.) Notice the changes to the Material Samples in the Material Editor and in the viewport.

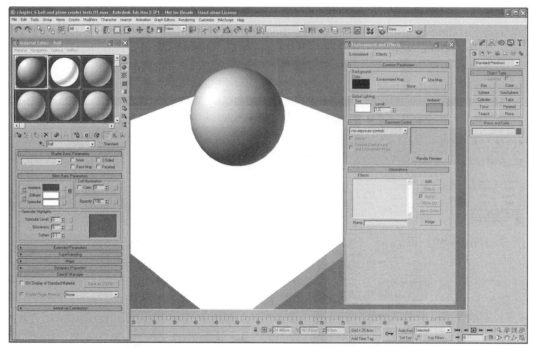

Figure 6.9 Increase the ambient color of the ball.

When the scene is rendered, the ball looks brighter, as shown in Figure 6.10.

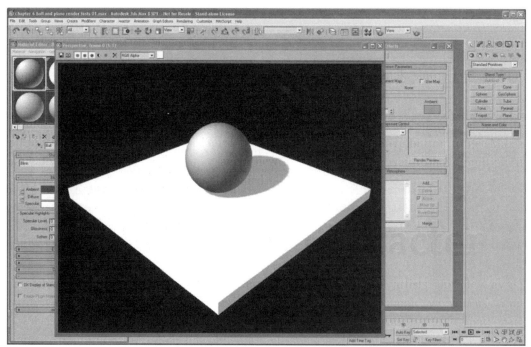

Figure 6.10 The ball appears brighter in the scene.

It's best not to use the ambient color changes because they are faking lighting, and you can end up with a flat scene. It's a much better practice to use lights to achieve the desired affect. An even better solution would be to use some of the advanced lighting techniques, such as Radiosity or Global Illumination. Many advancements have been made in consumer 3D software in recent years to achieve better, more realistic lighting/renders. The Ambient settings in Max are a holdover from the early years, when faking advanced lighting with Ambient values was necessary.

Set the Ambient values that you changed in the Environment and Effects dialog box back to black, and relock the Ambient and Diffuse settings in the Material Editor for the next example.

Self-Illumination (Incandescence)

Self-illumination is the internal brightness of an object as if it were a light source. Although self-illumination does not emit light and will not light surrounding objects, it does cause an object to appear bright. Self-illumination is often used when modeling something bright in a scene, like lava or a light bulb. Set the spinner to about 65 percent. Again, notice the difference in the Material Samples. You can set a color for self-illumination by checking the small check box next to the spinner.

Figure 6.11 shows the effects of increasing the material's self-illumination.

Figure 6.11 The sphere's Self-Illumination attribute set to 65 percent.

Set the Self-Illumination spinner back to 0 for the next example.

Bump Mapping

Bump mapping is used to give a material the appearance of a surface roughness. It is often used where geometry is impractical. Although a bump map may appear to have surface deformations, it does not change the underlying geometry.

Normally, we would use a texture map for the bump; however, for this example we will use one of the basic procedural textures from Max called Cellular. Click on the Maps rollout to expand it and click on the long bar labeled None next to the Bump label. Select Cellular from the Material/Map Browser dialog box. The small icon that is pointed out will toggle on or off the maps display in the viewport.

A Cellular bump map is now applied to the Ball material. Notice in the rendering of the scene, shown in Figure 6.12, that although the ball now appears to have surface deformation, it does not affect the actual geometry of the ball, as seen around the edges of the model.

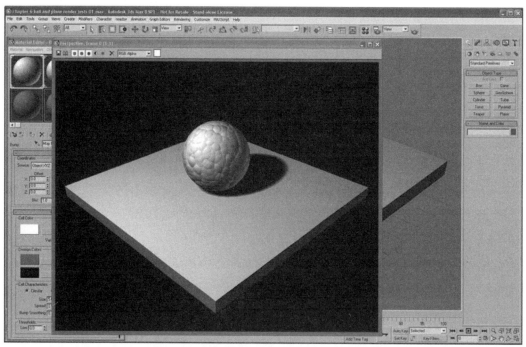

Figure 6.12 The bump map does not affect the geometry of the ball.

You should also notice that you are now in a different area of the Material Editor, as shown in Figure 6.13. These new options are for the Cellular texture you just applied. You are effectively one step lower in the Ball material hierarchy. Max refers to this as a *child*. The icon that looks like an arrow pointing up and labeled Go to Parent will take you back up the chain to the top level, or the parent. Pressing on the button labeled Cellular will bring up the Material/Map Browser dialog box, where you can choose a different bump material or map. The rollout labeled Cellular Parameters contains items that affect the Cellular material.

Figure 6.13 The Cellular material applied.

Click on the Go to Parent icon to go back to the parent material, where you can remove the Cellular bump. In the Maps rollout, simply drag the button labeled None onto the Bump button, and the Cellular material will be gone.

Diffuse and Translucence

The next few items deal with the translucent quality of a material. Translucence is the material attribute that controls the appearance of light passing through an object. It is different from transparency in that it transmits and scatters light similar to a lampshade or the wax of a candle; however, it does not make the object transparent.

For this and the next couple examples, you are going to switch your material type from Standard to Raytrace. Click on the Standard button and choose Raytrace from the resulting browser. The Raytrace material has more options than the Standard material, at the expense of speed. Standard is fast and works well for many applications. Occasionally, though, you will need to use a more advanced material.

Now that you have reset the scene to the original sphere and box, go ahead and save the scene with the Raytrace material so you can quickly get back to the original state on upcoming examples.

To see how translucence works, move the point light from above the ball to the center of the ball, as shown in Figure 6.14. Select the fill light and turn it off via the Modify tab. The ball is now dark, but the light is still shining on the block.

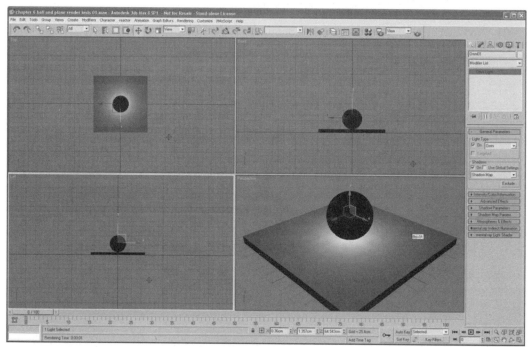

Figure 6.14 Move the point light to the center of the ball.

Select the Ball material and set the Translucency color to white. Max does not have a Translucence Focus. Figure 6.15 shows the results of the changes in translucence when rendered.

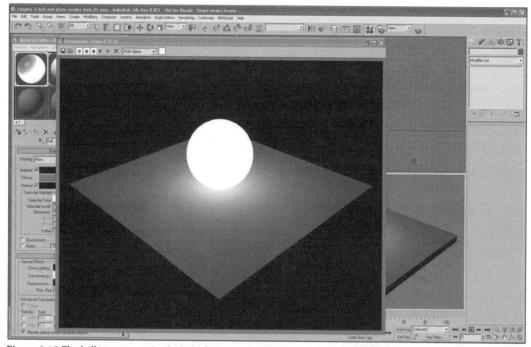

Figure 6.15 The ball now transmits the light from the point light.

Now move the light outside the sphere to its original place and set the Translucency color to a bright gray. Figure 6.16 shows the rendered results of the light move.

Figure 6.16 The results of the light shining on the sphere.

Note

If you have shadows for your light turned on, you must make sure they are set to Ray Traced Shadows. The default shadows in Max are Shadow Map Shadows; these cause harsh artifacts with translucency. To change the shadow-rendering method from Shadow Map Shadows to Ray Traced Shadows, select the light and change the option in the Modify Panel.

Play around with the Raytrace material attributes and see how each affects the models. To continue, reload the saved ball scene.

Specular Shading

Max has several shading methods that demonstrate Specular highlights. The Blinn shader has nice circular highlights and is easy to control. The Phong shader is similar to the Blinn shader, but does not demonstrate the same nice highlights; however, it renders much more quickly. The Anisotropic shader is known for its elongated highlights. The Multi Layer shader has two layers of anisotropic highlights. The Oren-Nayar-Blinn shader is good for cloth; the Metal shader is useful for highly polished metals, such as car bodies; the Strauss shader is another metal shader; and finally, there is a Translucent shader that has similar values to the previous example but without the Raytracing. For this example, we will continue to the use the Blinn shader.

Specular Level

There are three main controls for adjusting specular highlights: Specular Color, Specular Level, and Glossiness. They all work together to form the highlight, but let's start with the Specular Level. This controls the intensity of the highlight. For example, change the level to something like 150.

Figure 6.17 shows the scene rendered with Specular Level set to 150. Notice how small and focused the highlight on the object is. Smaller, brighter highlights tend to make objects look shinier.

Figure 6.17 Higher Specular Levels increase the intensity of the highlight.

Glossiness

This value adjusts the sharpness of the highlight. Set Glossiness to 15 and Specular Level to 103. Figure 6.18 shows the scene rendered with Glossiness reduced.

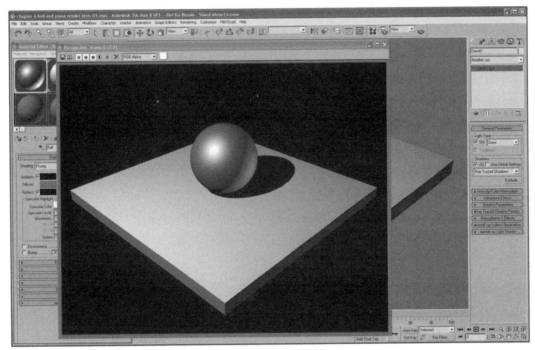

Figure 6.18 Reducing Glossiness reduces the sharpness of the highlight.

Specular Color

Specular Color controls the color of the highlight. Click the color swatch next to Specular Color and change the highlight color to red. Notice that the highlight color changes in the viewport and in the Material Samples as well. Figure 6.19 shows the rendered version of the scene.

Change Specular Color back to white. Let's also change the highlight in preparation for the next few steps. Set Specular Level to 125 and Glossiness to about 40 for the next step.

Figure 6.19 The ball now has a red highlight.

Reflectivity

The Reflect color allows the material to reflect its surroundings or a color. To reflect its surroundings you have to use the Raytrace material. Set the Reflect color to a light gray. Now when the scene is rendered, the ball will reflect its surroundings, as shown in Figure 6.20.

Reflect Color (Reflected Color)

You can use Reflect color to add color to tint the reflection. When Raytracing is turned on, the Reflect color is combined with the reflection to tint the color of the reflection, as shown in Figure 6.21.

Let's add an environment map for this example. An environment map is a bitmap that Max and other 3D programs use for simulating reflections in an object. Use a bitmap that shows the scene you want reflected in your object. For example, if you are rendering a glass cup on a kitchen table, you would want a picture of a kitchen so you would see familiar objects reflected in the glass. Set Reflect back to a light gray and click on the None button next to the Environment setting (below the Specular Highlight area). Choose Gradient Ramp from the resulting dialog box.

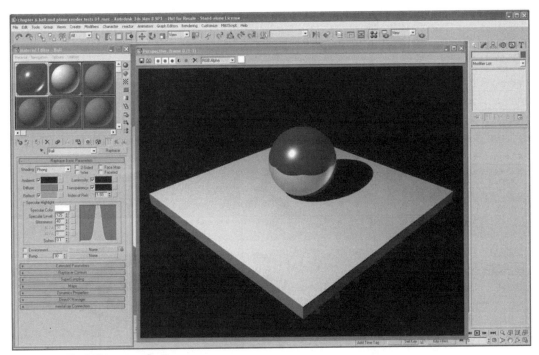

Figure 6.20 The ball is now reflective.

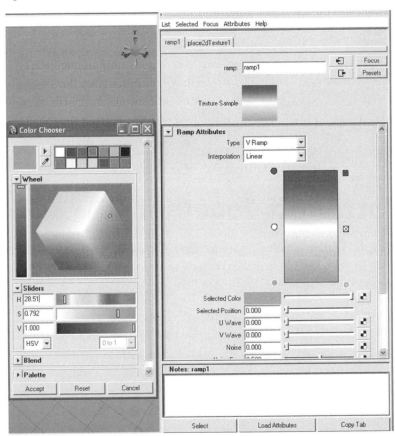

Figure 6.21 A tinted Reflect color.

The Gradient Ramp texture is similar to applying a color to a material, except that the colors can ramp from one color to another across the texture.

Once the Gradient Ramp texture is chosen, you can edit the colors by double-clicking on the little arrows along the bottom of the gradient. You can also add, delete, or move the little triangles. Set your ramp to look like something you think looks cool. There are a couple more steps. First, under Angle, edit W to −90 degrees so the gradient is sitting the right way. Next, change Mapping to Screen in the drop-down.

Figure 6.22 shows the rendered results of the reflected color.

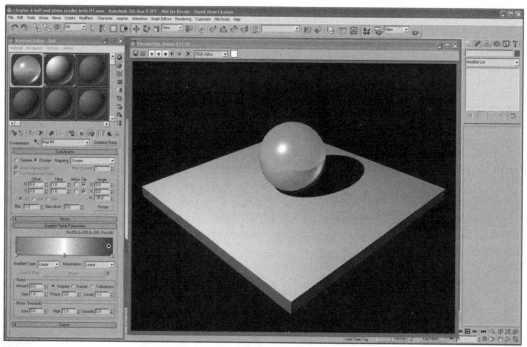

Figure 6.22 The environment color is added to the reflection on the ball.

Putting It Together

Now that you have used the Material Editor, hopefully you are seeing a few of the many possibilities you can use in creating materials in Max. Let's take a look at how to put these together to create a more complex scene. For the next example, load the original sphere and box scene.

1. In this example, a texture map will be used on the sphere and box. Click the small box next to the Diffuse color swatch to bring up the Material/Map Browser dialog box. This is a shortcut to adding maps to the Diffuse channel. Choose the Bitmap texture and browse to the Maps/Metals directory inside the Max Install folder. Choose the MtlPlat2.jpg file or choose a bitmap from your hard drive. (It doesn't really matter what you use other than that it needs to be a bitmap picture that is compatible with Max. Max accepts most

standard bitmap file formats, including .bmp, .jpg, .tga, .tif, .gif, and .psd, among others.)

2. Once you have that selected, make sure you toggle on the Show Map in Viewport icon, as shown. Figure 6.23 shows the new texture loaded into the Diffuse channel on the ball.

Figure 6.23 A File texture is added to the material.

3. Next, click on the Block material ball to select it. Change the material type from Standard to Raytrace so you can render with reflections. Repeat the last two steps to give the box a texture map. The one I used was the diamond check plate texture from the same directory.

   Figure 6.24 shows the scene rendered with the file textures added to the materials of the ball and the block.

4. Now let's give the scene a more natural look with real reflections. You will need to click on the Go to Parent icon to go back up the chain and set the Reflect value to a medium gray on both material balls. Figure 6.25 shows the scene rendered with Raytracing turned on.

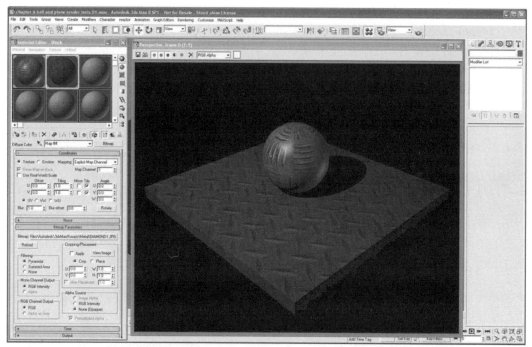

Figure 6.24 The texture maps make the scene seem more realistic.

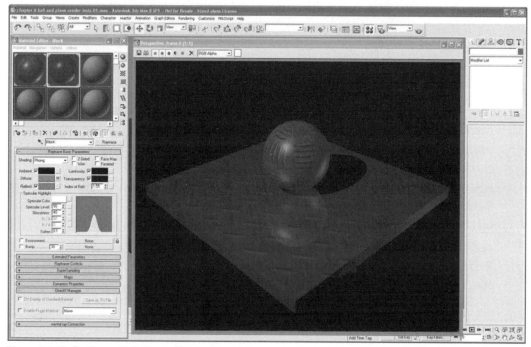

Figure 6.25 Reflections add further realism to the scene.

5. Now let's add some variation to the surface of the ball by adding a bump map. For this example, I added the matching bump map (MtlPlat2_Bump.jpg) from the Metals directory to the Bump channel found under the Maps rollout. Bump maps are most effective if they are grayscale pictures; however, in a pinch you can use the same color map in the Bump channel that you used in the Diffuse channel (as I did for the box). The lighter areas bump upward and the darker areas bump downward. See the results in the rendering with the bump map in Figure 6.26.

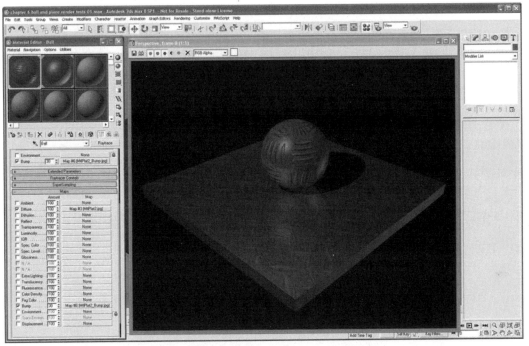

Figure 6.26 A bump map is added to the sphere and box.

As you can see, by just combining a few elements of the many attributes in a material, the model can look more and more real when rendered. As you become more familiar with the different attributes of the materials in Max, try experimenting to see how they affect each other.

Cartoon Shaders

Max has a fun material type called Ink 'n Paint. Ink 'n Paint is a Cartoon shader system built into Max for creating cartoon ink and paint effects. The following is a quick example of how it works.

Note

It's a good idea to review the Max help feature under Ink 'n Paint. There you'll find lots of good tips that can make rendering cartoon images fun and easy. For example, Ink 'n Paint does not render correctly in any view except Perspective and Camera.

You will also have access to a nice visual overview of the various options and can quickly get help for creating the look you are after.

1. Load the cartoon race car you built in Chapter 5.
2. Make sure you are in the Perspective view.
3. Select the body, and under the Surface Approximation rollout, choose High so you have a nice smooth mesh. Do the same for the wheels individually.
4. Open the Material Editor and assign the first material ball to the body and the second to the wheels, as shown in Figure 6.27. It's also a good time to rename the materials.

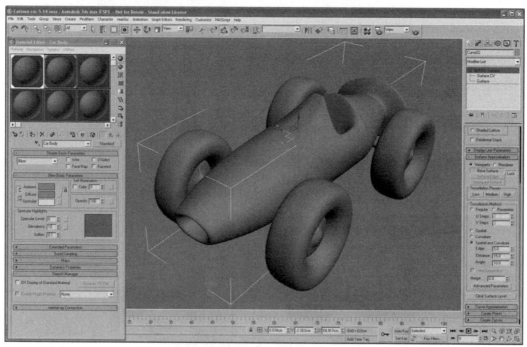

Figure 6.27 The first two material balls are assigned to the car.

5. On both materials, click the button labeled Standard, and choose Ink 'n Paint from the resulting browser. Both will default to a light blue shade.
6. Choose the car body material and change the Lighted color to a nice red.
7. Adjust Paint Levels to 4.
8. Check the box next to Highlight to get white highlights.

9. Make a test render to see the results, as shown in Figure 6.28.

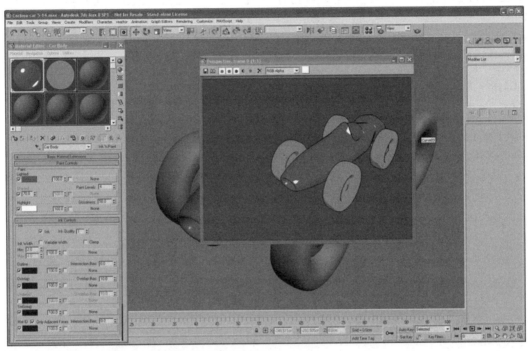

Figure 6.28 Test render the car and make any adjustments.

10. Select the wheel material and change the color to a dark gray.

11. Check the Highlight box and set Paint Levels to 4.

12. So that you can get a more dramatic shade to the tires, set the number in the Shaded box to about 20.0.

13. Render the scene to see how the tires look. Your scene should look similar to that shown in Figure 6.29.

The model is now Toon shaded. Make any last adjustments and render the final product. Take a look at the rendered results shown in Figure 6.30.

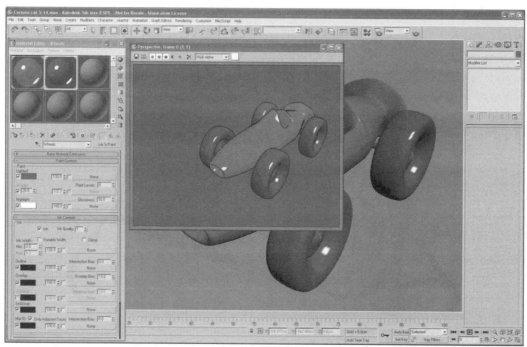

Figure 6.29 Check the tires.

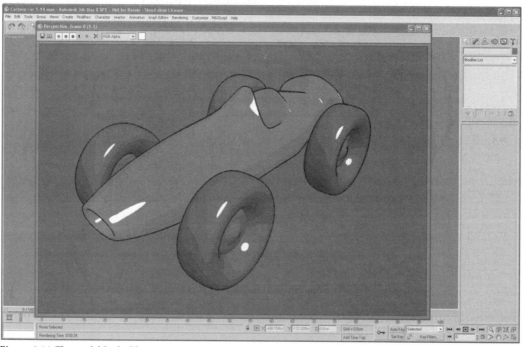

Figure 6.30 The model looks like a cartoon.

3D Paint

Max does not have the native 3D Paint capability that Maya has (unless you purchase a third-party plug-in), so I will show you a more common mapping technique. This will be a simplified version; more study is recommended on the subject of mapping and UVs. Max has a very competent and deep mapping setup, but the complexity of those tools is beyond the scope of this book.

1. Load the clawed hand model you created in Chapter 5, and set the subdivision iterations to 0 so you have a very low-res mesh (see Figure 6.31). This will make the next few steps easier.

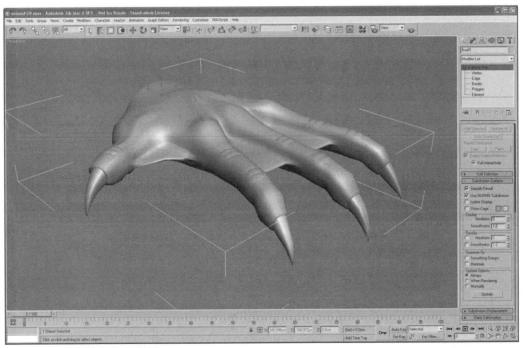

Figure 6.31 Load the monster hand.

2. Switch to Polygon Sub Object mode and select all the polygons by pressing Ctrl+A. For the next few operations, it will be easier if you are in Shaded Select mode, so press the F2 button. Set all the polygons to ID 1, as shown in Figure 6.32.

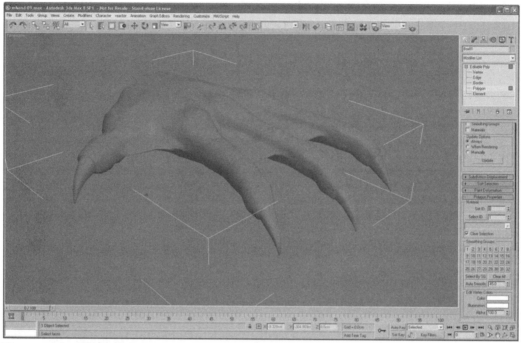

Figure 6.32 Set all the polygons to ID 1.

You are going to be setting six IDs so that when you add mapping coordinates (UVs), you will easily be able to select groups of polygons and apply the UVs.

3. Deselect the hand and select only the thumb claw. For that claw, set the ID to 2 (see Figure 6.33).

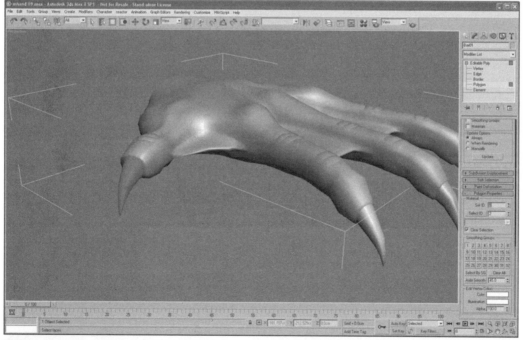

Figure 6.33 Assign individual IDs to the claw.

4. Now select the other three claws individually and set the IDs to 3, 4, and 5.

5. Put the number 1 in the Select ID box and press the Select ID button. Only the hand (minus the claws) should be selected, as shown in Figure 6.34.

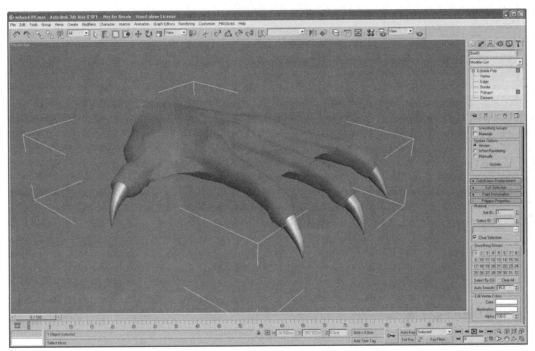

Figure 6.34 Polygons assigned to ID 1 are selected.

6. Invert the selection by pressing Ctrl+I.

7. Hide the claws temporarily by using the Hide Selection button found under the Edit Geometry rollout.

8. Deselect the bottom half of the hand by holding the Alt key (Minus Selection) and dragging a box around the bottom half of the hand, as shown in Figure 6.35. After the initial deselection, move around the hand and either add to the selection by holding the Control key or subtract from the selection by holding the Alt key to get a nice selection of just the top half of the hand. This is where the solid shaded selection will be very handy. After this step, you can switch back to a different mode with the F2 key.

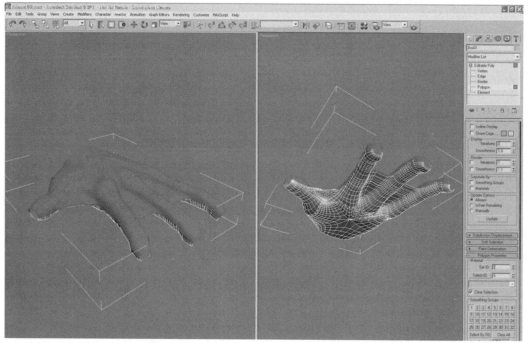

Figure 6.35 Select the top half of the hand.

9. Set the top half of the hand to ID 6.

10. Unhide the claws by clicking the Unhide All button.

11. Now that you have the hand grouped into IDs, set the hand subdivision iterations to 1.

12. Exit Sub Object mode and add the Unwrap UVW modifier to the stack, as shown in Figure 6.36.

13. Switch to Face Sub Object mode in the Unwrap UVW modifier.

14. Use the Select MatID button with 1 in the spinner box to select the bottom of the hand, as shown in Figure 6.37.

15. Click the Planer button, and then the Fit button to apply mapping coordinates to this selection, as shown in Figure 6.38.

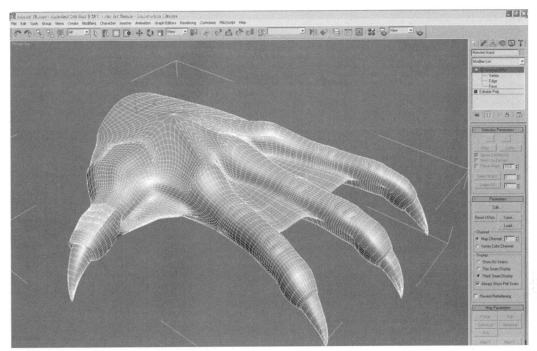

Figure 6.36 Apply the Unwrap UVW modifier.

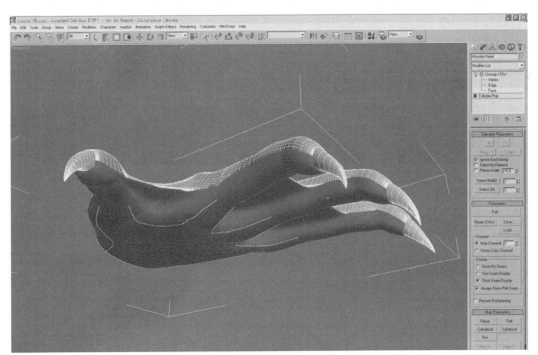

Figure 6.37 Select the bottom of the hand in preparation to refine the UVs.

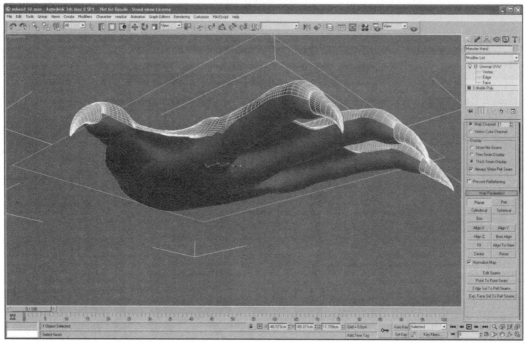

Figure 6.38 Apply the first mapping coordinates to the bottom of the hand.

16. Now set the ID to 6 and press the Select MatID button to highlight the top of the hand.

17. Click the Planer button, and then the Fit button to apply mapping coordinates to this selection.

18. Set the ID to 2 and press the Select MatID button to highlight the thumb claw. Click the Cylindrical button and the Best Align button to fit the Mapping Gizmo to the claw, as shown in Figure 6.39. The green line on the Mapping Gizmo indicates where it will "split" and unwrap. You can rotate the Mapping Gizmo around its local axis if you want it to split somewhere else. The green lines you see are the seams where the model is split into sections for mapping.

19. Quickly map the other three claws in the same way.

20. Press the Edit button to bring up the Edit UVWs dialog box, as shown in Figure 6.40.

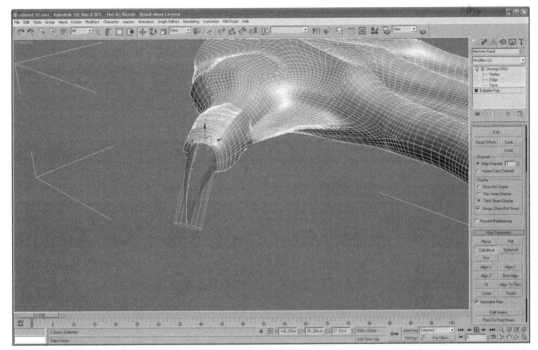

Figure 6.39 The Mapping Gizmo on the thumb claw.

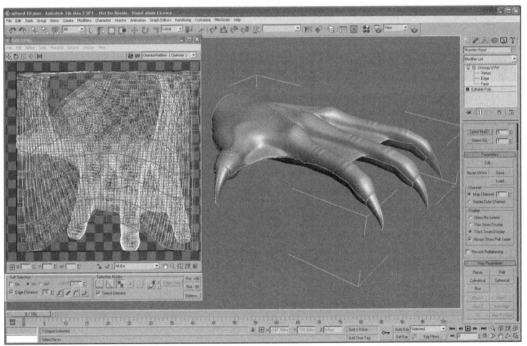

Figure 6.40 The Edit UVWs dialog box.

21. At first this dialog box may seem a bit confusing, but once you move a few things around, it should make sense. What you are seeing are all the parts of the hand you just added UVs to, but they are all stacked on top of each other. What you'll want to do is move them apart so they are ready to paint a map for the hand. Zoom out the Edit UVWs view a bit and spread out the individual pieces. To do this easily, make sure the Face Selection mode is set and the Select Element box is checked. It's also helpful to be in Move mode. You will now clearly see the hand (top and bottom) and the claws all splayed out, as shown in Figure 6.41.

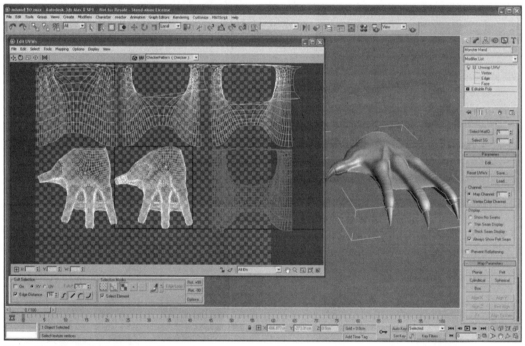

Figure 6.41 The UVs for the hand all spaced out.

22. The claws don't need to have such a big UV space. Grab the individual pieces and arrange them so that they roughly occupy a square area.

23. Drag a marquee around all the parts of the hand and scale them down as a group so they fit in the black outline, as shown in Figure 6.42.

24. Under the Tools menu, choose Render UVs. Set Width and Height each to 1024 and click Render UV Template. This will pop up a picture that you can save for use in a painting program, such as Photoshop, Paint Shop Pro, or Painter.

25. Save the bitmap as a BMP or TGA file (see Figure 6.43).

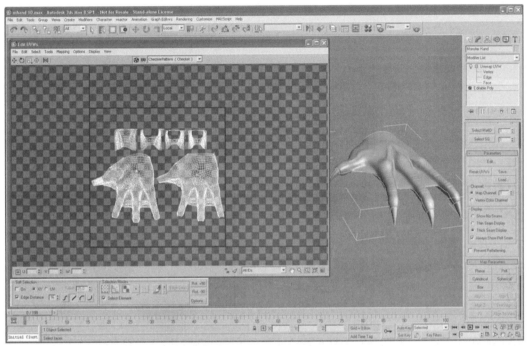

Figure 6.42 The final UVs for the hand and claws.

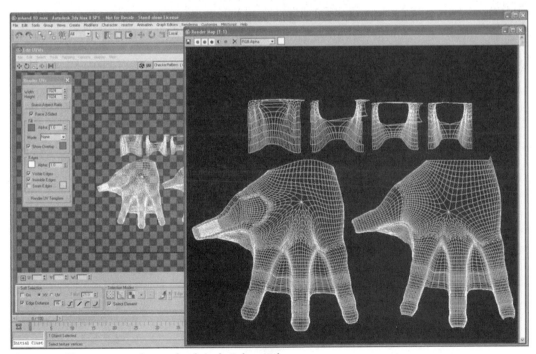

Figure 6.43 The texture template rendered, ready to be saved..

26. Close the UV render and Unwrap dialog boxes and open the Material Editor.

27. Assign the first material ball to the hand.

28. Click on the small square next to the Diffuse color swatch and choose Bitmap from the resulting dialog box.

29. Find and load the texture template that you just saved in Step 25.

30. Click the Show in Viewport icon. You should see a perfectly mapped hand.

Figure 6.44 shows a rendering of the clawed hand with the template applied. Now all that is left is to paint a cool texture on the template and render the results! I'm not a great artist, so I will leave the fun to you.

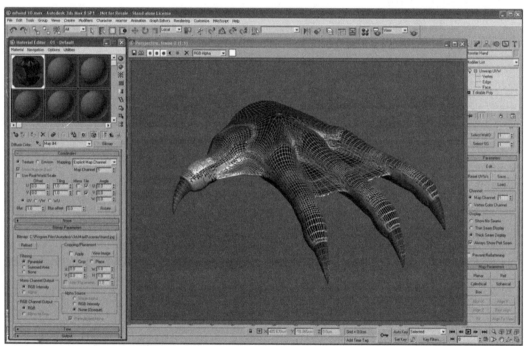

Figure 6.44 The clawed hand rendered.

One tool we did not cover (in the interest of simplicity) is the Relax tool. Before saving the template, you may want to relax, or "flatten," some of the finger and thumb vertices that are vertical and stacked on top of each other in the 2D view of the UVW Editor. The results of not flattening those vertices are smearing on the sides of the fingers and thumb. You can also relax after the fact, but you will need to resave the template, and it's best to do it before you start working on the texture itself.

Once you have started painting a texture in a 2D program, you can jump back to Max frequently and see the results. There is a fairly simple way to do this. Just save your work in the 2D program (don't change the name or location of the map). Switch back to Max and click the Reload button. This will grab the work you have just saved in 2D; you can see the results quickly either in the Material Editor or by rendering the scene.

Summary

This chapter was an overview of some of the many aspects of materials in Max. Max has a very deep and capable Material Editor; with some work, you can achieve incredible results. In this chapter, you should have become familiar with the following aspects of Max's shader system:

- Material types
- Material attributes
- Applying materials to models
- 2D and 3D textures
- Toon shaders
- Texturing an organic object

Shaders—or materials, as they are called in Max—are an essential part of creating believable 3D models. In this chapter, you have just scratched the surface of learning how to develop materials. However, hopefully you now have a good foundation that you can use as a base for further exploration.

Chapter 7

Gaining Character

Character development is one of the most demanding and exciting aspects of 3D art. Maya has a great array of tools and features specifically designed for the development and animation of characters. There is so much involved in developing and animating characters that one chapter is not enough to cover the subject. Therefore, this chapter, along with the next two, will deal specifically with the creation of a character—from a drawing to animation. This chapter will deal with building the character, Chapter 8 will cover texturing and rigging the character, and Chapter 9 will delve into character animation.

It All Starts with a Drawing

Character models are complex and often difficult to complete unless you have some visual clues. A common practice among character artists is to create a character template that they can use as a guide when building a character. The template is similar to a drafting drawing done by architects or product designers. It has at least three, and sometimes more, orthogonal views. They are isometric drawings in that there is no perspective used. Figure 7.1 shows the front view of a character. The character is a young cartoon-style ninja. He is in an open pose, with the legs slightly apart and the arms held out from the body. This is a good pose for animating characters.

Figure 7.2 shows the back view of the character. The back view needs to be an exact duplicate of the proportions of the front view.

When you are creating the back view of a character, a good way to ensure that the proportions and position of the character are exactly correct is to flip the front view and trace it, though changing it from a front to a back view.

Figure 7.1 Having the legs apart and the arms out from the body helps with animation.

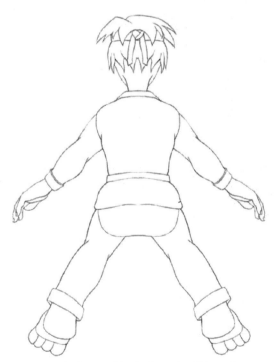

Figure 7.2 The front and back views should have the same proportions.

The side view is shown in Figure 7.3.

Figure 7.3 The side view needs to be proportional to the front and back views.

The side view is a little harder to create because you can't get it from tracing another view, like you can for the back view. It still needs to be exact proportionally. Drawing the side view overlaying the front and back views can help to get things lined up correctly.

On human or other two-legged characters, three views are usually sufficient. Four-legged creatures may need a top view and in some cases a bottom view as well.

Make sure the drawings are centered on the image. If they are drawn on paper, scan them into a 2D paint package and crop them so they are exactly square. You are welcome to scan the drawings from the book to follow along with this project, or you can draw your own character. The original files are on the CD that accompanies the book.

Setting Up the Template

Once the drawings are ready, you can load them into Maya and begin using them for building the model. If you're ready, let's get started.

1. Start by creating a single polygon plane that is 10 units high by 10 units wide in the Z axis.

2. Use the Channel box to move the polygon plane to 0.01 in the Z axis.

3. Create another polygon plane using the same settings as Step 1, and rotate it 180 degrees in the Y axis and move it −0.01 in the Z axis.

4. Create one more polygon plane and rotate it 90 degrees. Your scene should now look similar to that shown in Figure 7.4.

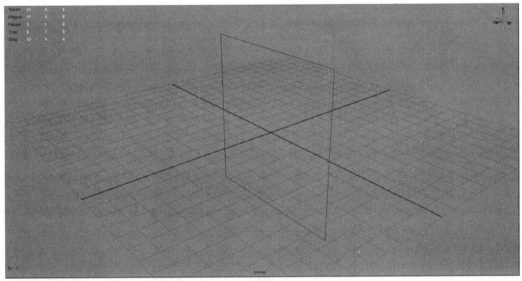

Figure 7.4 Create a third polygon plane.

5. Create three Lambert materials and load the template drawings one each into the new materials. Rename the materials "Front," "Back," and "Side," as shown in Figure 7.5.

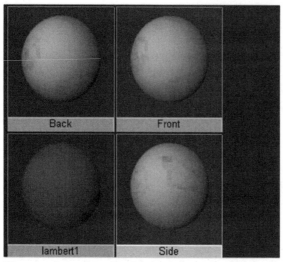

Figure 7.5 Create three materials for the template drawings.

6. Now apply the drawing of the front of the character to the polygon where the polygon normal is facing in the Z axis, the drawing of the back of the character to the polygon where the polygon normal is facing in the −Z axis, and the drawing of the side of the character to the polygon where the polygon normal is facing in the X axis, as shown in Figure 7.6.

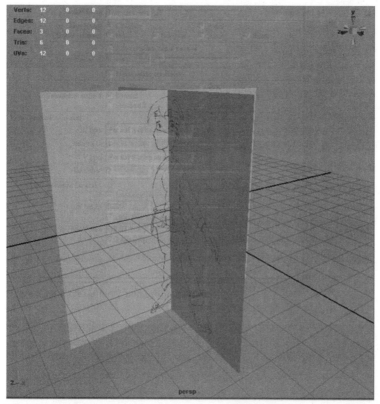

Figure 7.6 Apply the three materials to the three polygons.

7. To get the template to work correctly, you will need to call two menu commands. First, select Backface Culling from the Shading menu in the Panel menu, as shown in Figure 7.7.

Figure 7.7 Turn on Backface Culling.

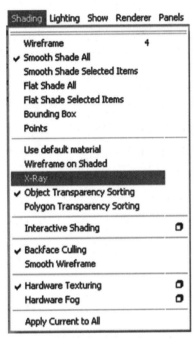

Figure 7.8 Select the X-Ray view option.

8. Next, select X-Ray from the same menu, as shown in Figure 7.8.

Now the template is finished and ready to use. Rotate around the model to make sure that everything is lined up as it should be.

Building the Character

There are about as many ways to build characters in 3D as there are 3D artists. No one way is necessarily wrong unless it creates problems in the geometry. In this example, we will use what I call NURBS-assisted polygonal modeling. The model will end up in polygons, but NURBS and curves will be used to assist in the construction of the model. You will need to go to the Surfaces menu to create the curves.

1. Use the Create CV Curve tool starting at the top of the eye, as shown in Figure 7.9.

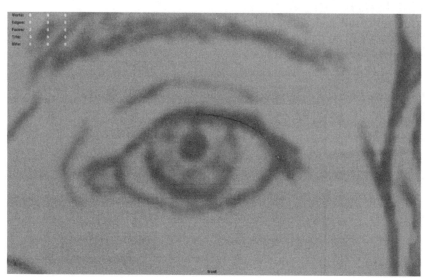

Figure 7.9 Draw a CV curve around the upper eyelid.

2. Place three CVs at the outer corner of the eye for a hard turn in the spline, and continue drawing around the edge of the eyelids and around the tear duct, as shown in Figure 7.10.

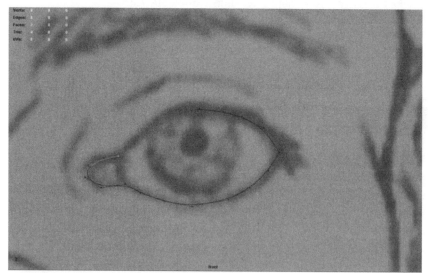

Figure 7.10 Continue to draw in the shape of the eye.

3. Join the curve onto itself by using the Open/Close Curve option in the Edit Curves menu. The finished curve should look like that shown in Figure 7.11. The curve in the figure has 22 spans. Yours may have a different number of spans, but it is important to make note of how many spans you have.

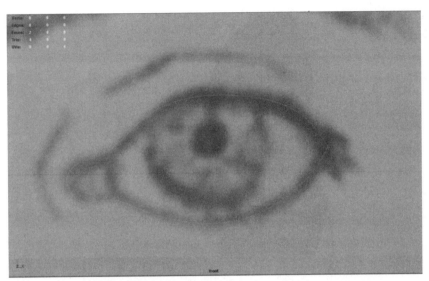

Figure 7.11 Finish drawing the curve around the eye.

4. From the Side view, move the curve to the outer edge of the eyelids, as shown in Figure 7.12.

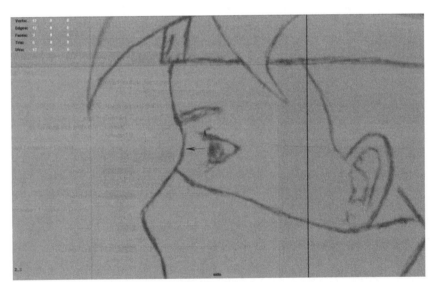

Figure 7.12 Move the curve into place from the Side view.

5. Change the selection mode to CVs and fine-tune them to the shape of the eyelids.

6. The eyelids follow the shape of the eyeball, which is basically a sphere. Round the curve to follow a spherical shape, as shown in Figure 7.13.

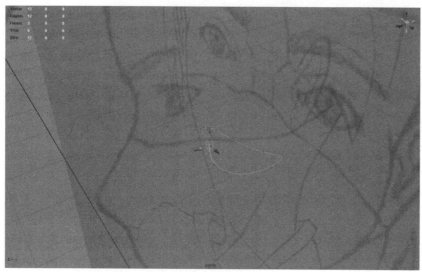

Figure 7.13 Change the curve to follow the shape of an eye.

7. Duplicate the eye and scale it in, as shown in Figure 7.14.

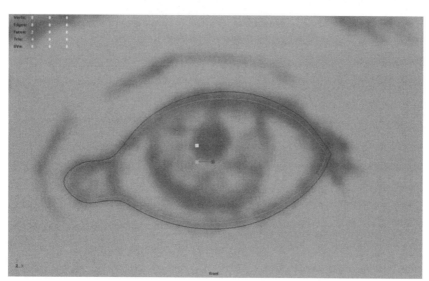

Figure 7.14 Duplicate the curve.

8. This second curve will be the inside edge of the eyelids. Adjust it to fit the eyelids, as shown in Figure 7.15.

Figure 7.15 Adjust the second curve to fit the inside edge of the eyelids.

9. Duplicate the original curve and expand it to the area where the eyelids join
   the face, as shown in Figure 7.16.

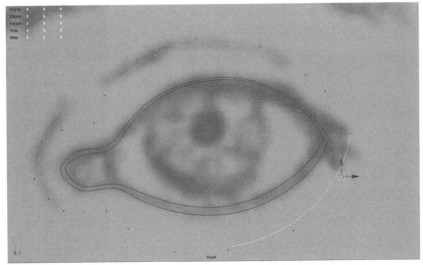

Figure 7.16 Expand the duplicate curve to fit where the eyelids meet the face.

10. Adjust the CVs in the Perspective view to match the contours of the face, as
    shown in Figure 7.17. The curve should recede in the middle and stay close
    to the same plane as the original curve on either side, as shown.

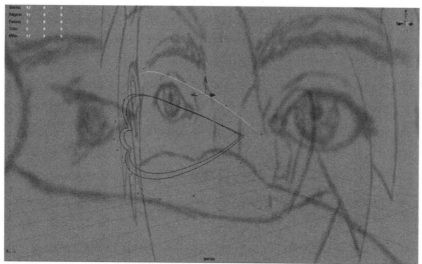

Figure 7.17 Have the curve follow the contour of the eyelids.

11. The curve no longer needs the sharp corner where the eyelids meet. Rebuild the curve to eliminate the corner, as shown in Figure 7.18. Remember to make sure the number of spans is identical to the original curve, or you will have problems when you loft the polygons later. The Rebuild Curve options are in the Edit Curves menu of the main menu.

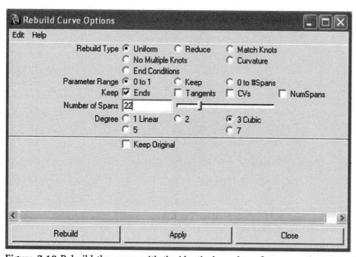

Figure 7.18 Rebuild the curve with the identical number of spans as the original curve.

12. Now it's time to loft some polygons to start building surfaces. Bring up the Loft tool found in the Surfaces menu and set it to Polygons. Set Type to Quads and Tessellation Method to General. Under Initial Tessellation Controls, set U Type to Per Surf # of Iso Params and the value (Number U) to 40. Set V Type to Per Surf # of Iso Params in 3D and the value (Number V) to 2. Loft the polygons between the inner two curves, as shown in Figure 7.19. If the faces are facing the wrong direction, undo the loft, select the two curves in the opposite order, and loft again.

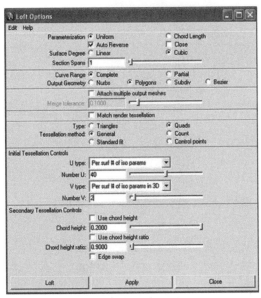

Figure 7.19 Loft polygons between the two inner curves.

13. Use the same settings to loft between the two outer curves, as shown in Figure 7.20.

14. You probably notice that the polygons are not matching up very well, giving a few of them some irregular shapes. Because the lofted polygons are influenced by the CV curves, you can adjust the polygons to better emanate from the eye by moving the CV curves. Adjust the polygons using the CV curves, as shown in Figure 7.21 to line them up more directly.

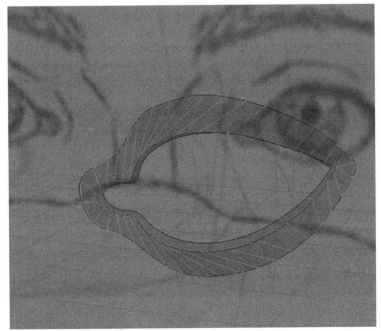

Figure 7.20 Loft polygons for the eyelids.

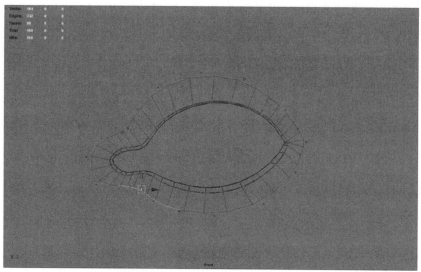

Figure 7.21 Line up the polygons emanating from the eye.

15. As long as you have History turned on, you can adjust the model by adjusting the CVs of the curves. This gives you an easier way to make smooth adjustments to the model. Moving individual vertices is a lot more time consuming. Fine-tune the shape of the eyelids by adjusting the CVs, as shown in Figure 7.22.

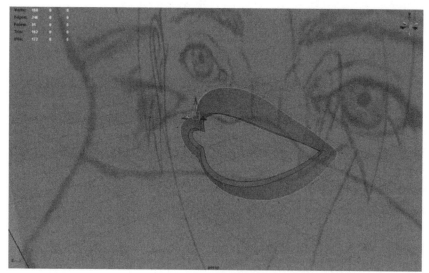

Figure 7.22 Adjust the eyelids.

16. Continue to construct the area around the eye by duplicating the outer curve and scaling it outward and lofting the polygons in the same way as earlier. Adjust the curve to fit the contour of the face (see Figure 7.23).

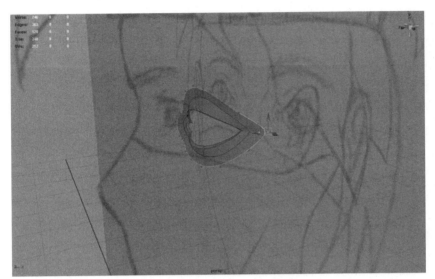

Figure 7.23 Create another band of polygons outward from the eye.

17. Repeat the process again, going yet farther from the eye following the bridge of the nose, brow, and cheekbone, as shown in Figure 7.24.

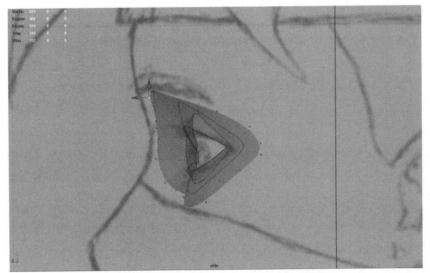

Figure 7.24 Continue to create bands of polygons outward from the eye.

18. Create another band of polygons in the same manner, going still farther from the eye. Continue this process. When you reach the center of the nose, line up the CVs with the centerline, as shown in Figure 7.25. With only a few exceptions, the character is symmetrical, so there is no need to model both sides. We will model only one side and mirror the model later.

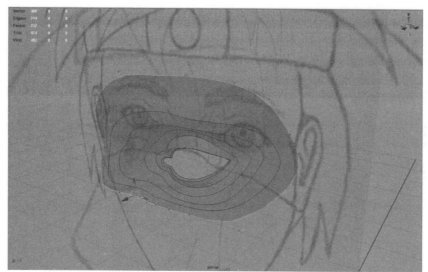

Figure 7.25 Line up the CVs with the centerline of the nose.

19. When your model looks similar to that shown in Figure 7.26, select all of the
CV curves, as shown, and press Ctrl+H to hide them for now.

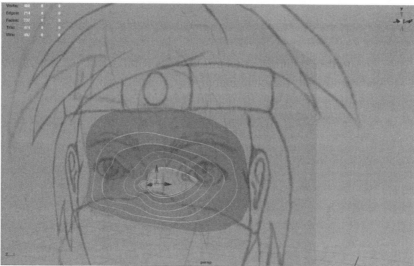

Figure 7.26 Hide the CV curves.

20. Select all of the lofted polygons and combine them into a single model, as
shown in Figure 7.27. The Combine feature is found in the Mesh menu, so
you will have to go back to the Polygons menu set.

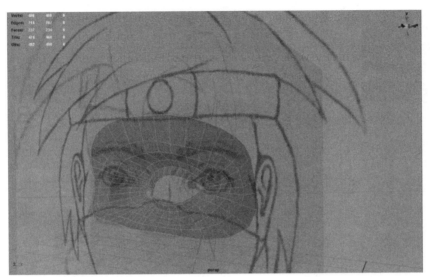

Figure 7.27 Combine the polygons.

21. The single polygon model has several duplicate vertices. Change the selection mode to Vertex, select all of the vertices in the model, and then select Edit Mesh, Merge to merge the duplicate vertices. Set the threshold to .001 so you only merge duplicate vertices. If the setting is too high, it could cause neighboring vertices to merge as well.

The curves should only come to the center of the bridge of the nose and no farther.

Polygon Modeling

Rather than using curves to complete the rest of the face, you will use polygon modeling techniques, as covered in this section.

1. Select the top edges of the model, and from the Front view, extrude them upward to the headband.

2. You will need additional polygons to fill in the top of the forehead just above the bridge of the nose. Extrude edges and merge vertices to match those shown in Figure 7.28.

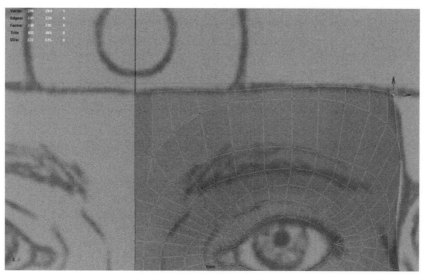

Figure 7.28 Construct the forehead by extruding edges.

3. Follow the same procedure for the nose. Extrude the edges above the nose to the mask. Extrude extra edges on the bridge of the nose like you did with the forehead.

4. Now the model should follow the headband above and the mask below. Extrude the edges along the side of the model, as shown in Figure 7.29.

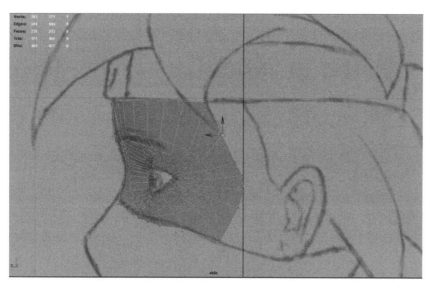

Figure 7.29 Extrude the edges on the side toward the back of the face.

5. Adjust the extrusion by moving vertices to follow the headband and mask.

6. Extrude the edges again, as shown in Figure 7.30. The new extruded polygons should reach to the edge of the character's hair.

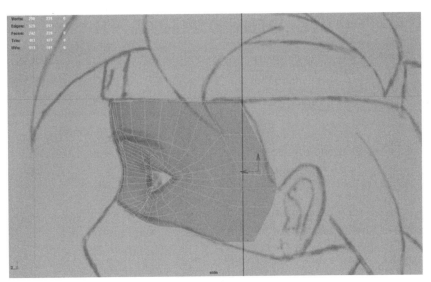

Figure 7.30 Extrude the edges to the character's hair.

7. Again adjust individual vertices to fit the contour of the face.

8. Extrude the edges again and adjust them for the hair and front of the ear, as shown in Figure 7.31.

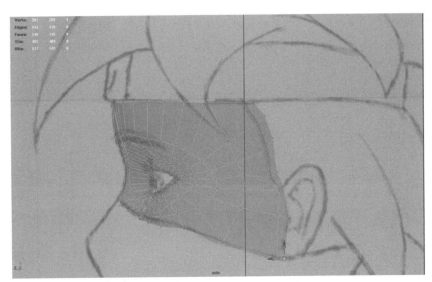

Figure 7.31 Extrude the edges and adjust for the hair.

9. Continue to extrude the edge of the model toward the back of the head. Between each extrusion, move vertices to fit the contour of the face and ear.

10. Once past the ear, extrude the edge one more time and adjust the vertices so they fit the back of the skull, as shown in Figure 7.32.

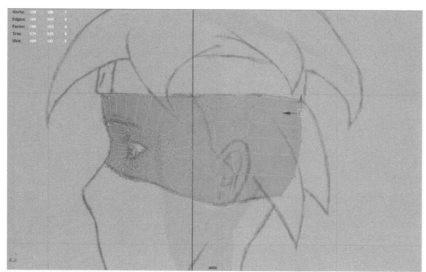

Figure 7.32 Move vertices to fit the back of the skull from the Side view.

11. Maya does not have a default Back view, so you will need to make one. Go to Panels, Orthographic, New, Front to establish a new orthographic camera.

12. Rename the camera in the Channel box to "Back."

13. In the Channel box, change Rotate Y to 180 and Translate Z to −100.

14. Select the vertices at the back of the head and move them to the centerline, as shown in Figure 7.33.

Figure 7.33 Move the back vertices to the center.

15. Now use the Split Polygon Tool to divide the polygons, as shown in Figure 7.34.

Figure 7.34 Split the polygons on the back of the head.

16. Make two more splits in the polygons so that there are four columns of polygons, as shown in Figure 7.35.

Figure 7.35 Create four columns of polygons.

17. Change the selection mode to Vertex and move the vertices of the newly created polygons to roughly follow the shape of the back of the head, as shown in Figure 7.36.

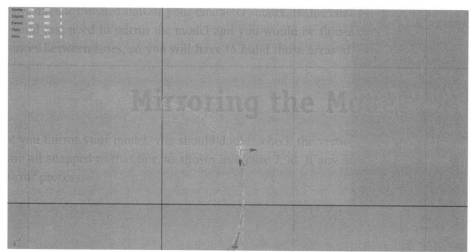

Figure 7.36 Move the vertices to follow the shape of the head.

You will probably need to move around the model in Perspective view to get the polygons to look right (see Figure 7.37).

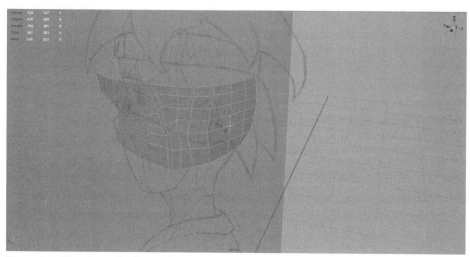

Figure 7.37 View the model from different angles to get the adjustments correct.

The Ear

Next up for this model will be the ear. The ear is attached to the side of the head just a little more than halfway from the front of the face. Use the Side view drawing to position it correctly.

1. Use the Split Polygon Tool to divide the polygons where the ear attaches to the head, as shown in Figure 7.38.

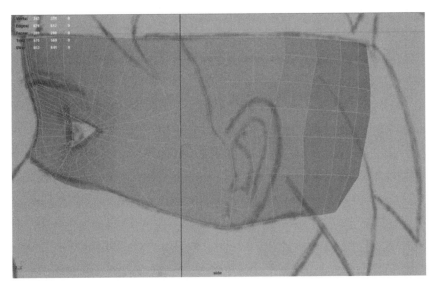

Figure 7.38 Split the polygons near the base of the ear.

2. Now select the polygon faces of the ear and extrude them outward, as shown in Figure 7.39.

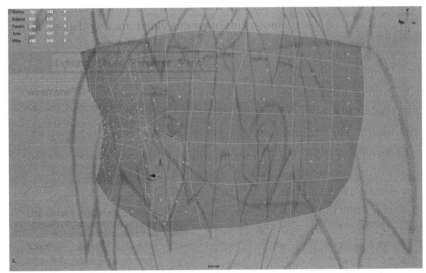

Figure 7.39 Extrude the ear out from the head.

3. The extrusion will need to be adjusted to the shape of the base of the ear, as shown in Figure 7.40.

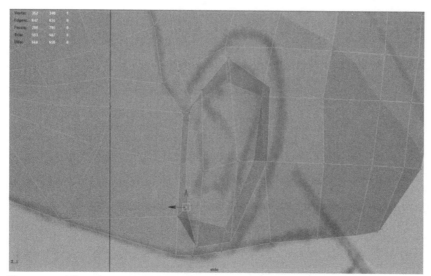

Figure 7.40 Adjust the new polygons to fit the shape of the base of the ear.

4. Extrude the ear polygons again and adjust this second extrusion to again follow the shape of the ear, as shown in Figure 7.41.

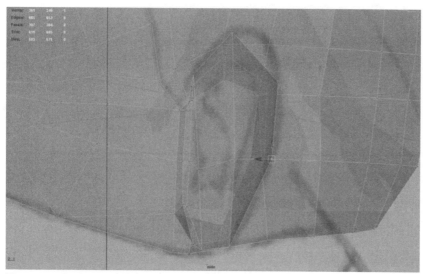

Figure 7.41 Continue to follow the basic shape of the ear.

5. Now extrude the ear outward again to create the basic shape of the ear, as shown in Figure 7.42.

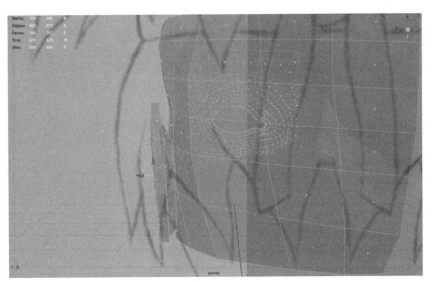

Figure 7.42 Extrude the ear again outward.

6. After extruding the ear, go back in and move the vertices of the inside of the ear and the front of the ear to pull them in closer to the head, as shown in Figure 7.43.

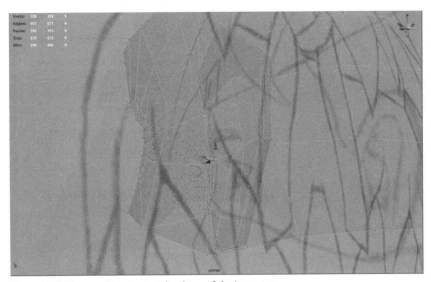

Figure 7.43 Move vertices to start the shape of the inner ear.

7. Extrude the face at the top and back of the ear to round off that area. Scale the extrusion and position it as shown in Figure 7.44.

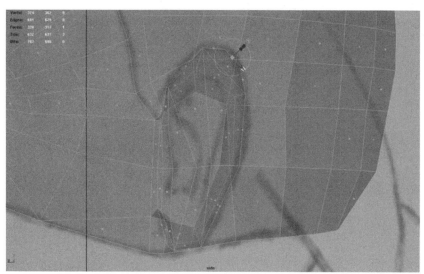

Figure 7.44 Round off the back of the ear.

8. Split the polygons on the inside of the ear to follow the shape of the ear, as shown in Figure 7.45.

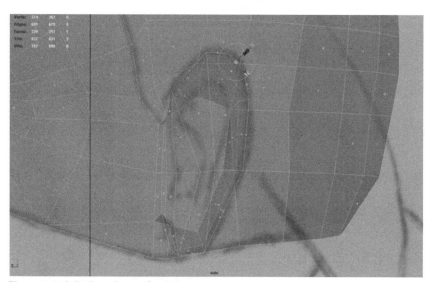

Figure 7.45 Split the polygons for the inner ear.

9. Select the faces of the inner ear area and extrude them back toward the head, as shown in Figure 7.46.

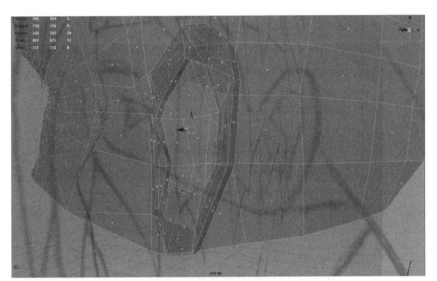

Figure 7.46 Extrude the inner ear area in toward the head.

10. Now move and adjust vertices to get the shape of the ear and its inner area, as shown in Figure 7.47.

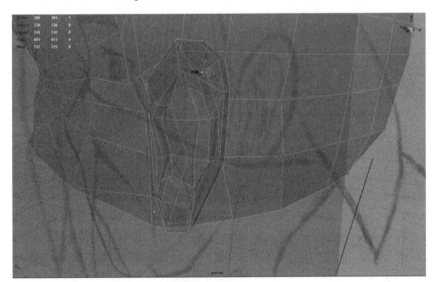

Figure 7.47 Finish modeling the basic shape of the ear.

11. Now select the faces of the ear and the head near those faces and use the Smooth tool found in the Polygons menu to smooth the ear, as shown in Figure 7.48.

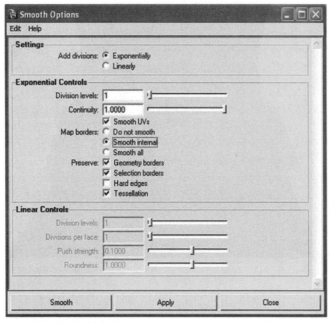

Figure 7.48 Smooth the ear to give it a more natural appearance.

12. Go back to Vertex selection mode and move vertices in the ear as needed to make it look more natural, as shown in Figure 7.49.

There may be easier and better ways to create an ear, but this method works just fine for the purposes of this book. Smooth will create a number of five-sided polygons around the ear. Use Snap to Vertex to move the vertices and merge them to get rid of any five-sided polygons. Five-sided polygons don't render well.

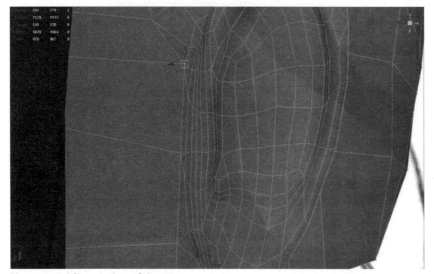

Figure 7.49 Adjust vertices of the ear.

The Top of the Head

Next will be the top of the head, including the headband. Start with the headband.

1. Select the edges at the top of the model along the headband. Extrude those edges outward, as shown in Figure 7.50.

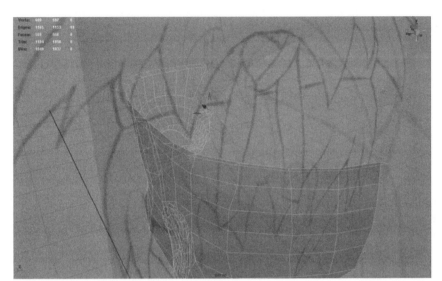

Figure 7.50 Create the lower edge of the headband.

2. Pull the vertices of the headband out in the back to make room for adding hair later, as shown in Figure 7.51.

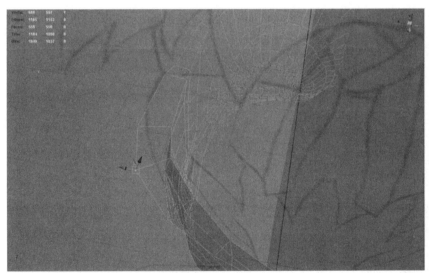

Figure 7.51 Expand the headband in the back.

3. Select the edges again and extrude them upward to form the headband, as shown in Figure 7.52.

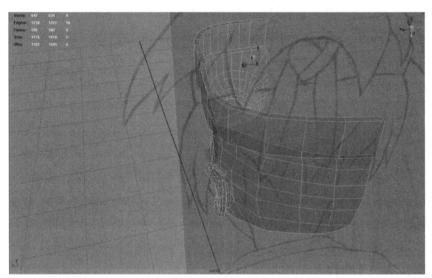

Figure 7.52 Extrude the headband upward.

4. Extrude the headband again as before and scale it in to form its upper lip, as shown in Figure 7.53.

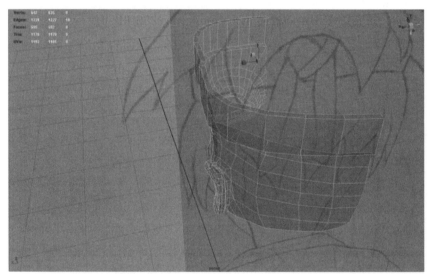

Figure 7.53 Create the upper edge of the headband.

5. Now you need to form the top of the skull, disregarding the hair. Extrude the edges and scale them after each extrusion to create a rounded head, as shown in Figure 7.54.

Figure 7.54 Extrude the edges to form the top of the head.

6. At the very top of the head, merge the vertices to a single vertex.

7. Now move to the bottom of the model and extrude the bottom edge outward to form the upper lip of the mask, as shown in Figure 7.55.

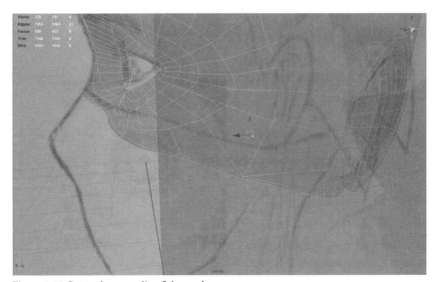

Figure 7.55 Create the upper lip of the mask.

8. Several vertices will not line up accurately with the centerline. Adjust these vertices one by one using the Snap to Coordinates function (Ctrl+X), as shown in Figure 7.56.

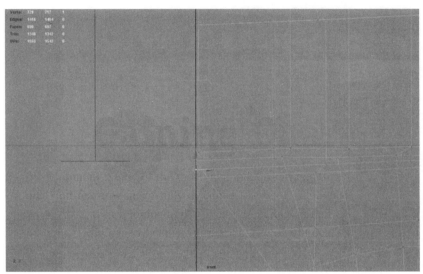

Figure 7.56 Snap vertices to the centerline.

Now that you have the top of the head modeled, all you need to do is to continue downward to finish the model. The next section will cover modeling the bottom of the face and the torso using curves and lofted surfaces.

Lofting the Head and Torso

The model is now ready for finishing the face and neck. In this section, you will use curves and lofted surfaces to construct the model. The curves will allow for greater modeling flexibility than extruding polygons.

1. Draw a CV curve along the lower edge of the model. Snap the CVs to the vertices of the edge. Make sure you click twice on the beginning and ending vertex to line up the CVs with the vertices for lofting later. The drawn curve should look like that shown in Figure 7.57.

2. Duplicate the curve and move the duplicate down.

3. Loft polygons between the two curves using the Per Span # of Iso Params for both U and V, as shown in Figure 7.58. Set the number for both U and V to 1.

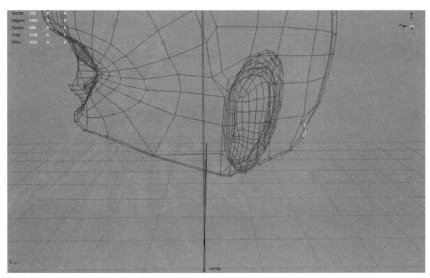

Figure 7.57 Draw a CV curve along the lower edge.

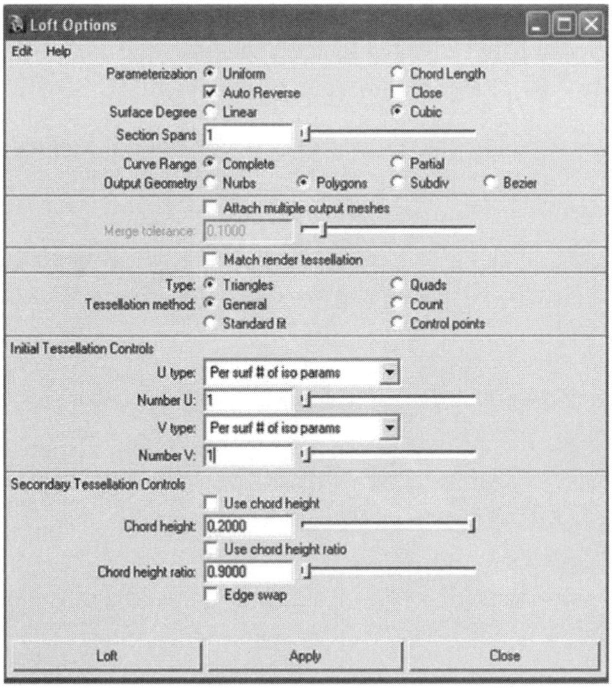

Figure 7.58 Loft polygons between the two curves.

4. Change the selection mode for the lower CV curve to CVs and adjust the CVs to fit that part of the face, as shown in Figure 7.59.

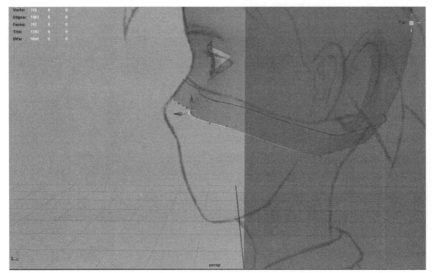

Figure 7.59 Adjust the CVs of the lower curve.

5. Continue to duplicate the lower CV curves and move them down, adjusting them as you go and lofting polygons between them to form the chin and neck of the character. Use Figure 7.60 as a guide for your modeling.

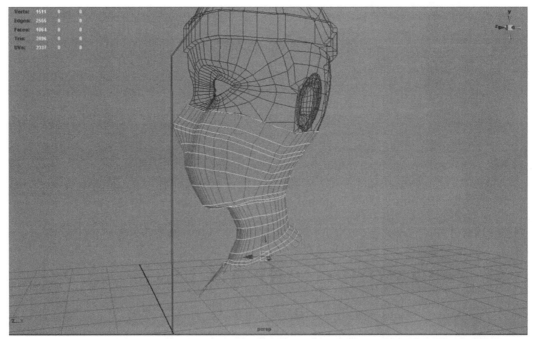

Figure 7.60 Model the chin and neck.

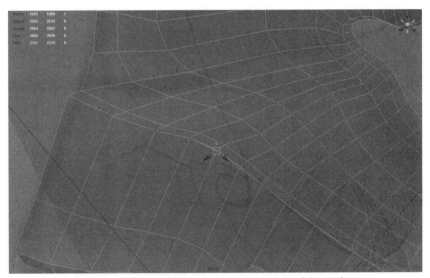
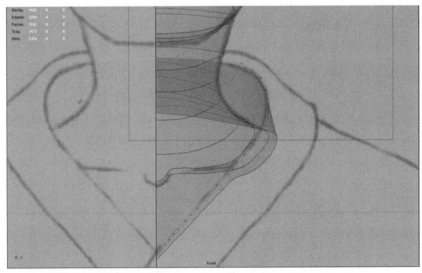

6. Combine all of the polygons into one model.

7. The vertices created with the curve will not be exactly the same as those of the mask's upper lip. You will need to snap the vertices together, as shown in Figure 7.61.

Figure 7.61 Snap the edge of the mask together with the vertices of the mask.

8. Now merge all of the duplicate vertices of the head and neck that overlap each other so there are no extra vertices.

9. Next, you need to create the character's gi (karate uniform). Start by duplicating the bottom curve and adjusting it to follow the bottom edge of the collar.

10. Loft between the two curves, as shown in Figure 7.62.

Figure 7.62 Loft between the two curves to create the bottom of the collar.

11. Continue to duplicate the curve and build the collar of the gi, as shown in Figure 7.63.

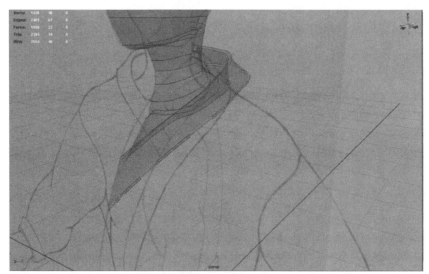

Figure 7.63 Create the collar of the gi.

12. Continue to duplicate the curve and build outward toward the character's shoulder, as shown in Figure 7.64.

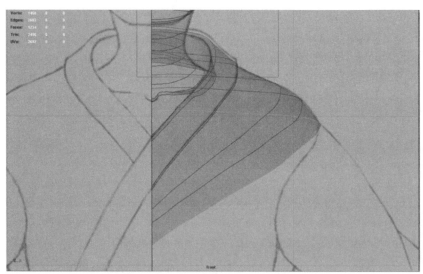

Figure 7.64 Build the model down to the shoulder.

13. Build the torso down to the belt, as shown in Figure 7.65.

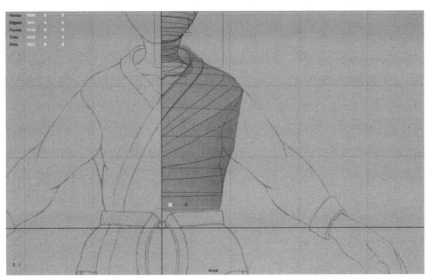

Figure 7.65 Build the torso to the belt.

14. Continue down the character, creating first the belt and then the rest of the gi. Use Figure 7.66 as a guide to how the gi should look when finished. The last curves will be up under the gi where the pants will start.

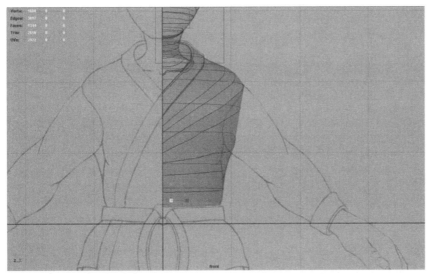

Figure 7.66 Finish building the gi.

15. As you continue to build the model, you will need to make a special adjustment for the area where the legs connect. Pull the CVs of the curves around the top of the leg, as shown in Figure 7.67.

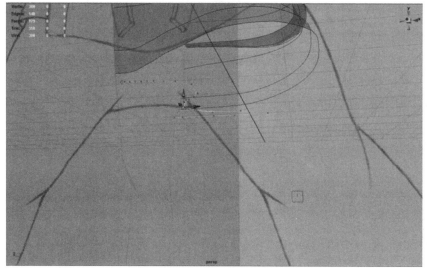

Figure 7.67 Make a special adjustment of the model near the top of the legs.

16. When you loft this special area, set Number V to 2, as shown in Figure 7.68.

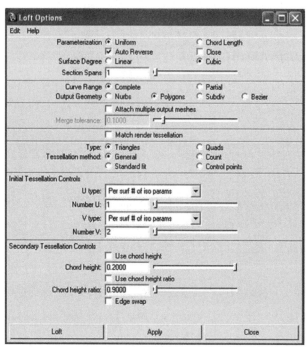

Figure 7.68 Increase the V number on the loft.

17. Line up the last curve that completes the crotch area with the centerline, as shown in Figure 7.69.

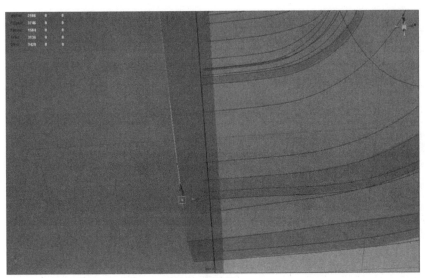

Figure 7.69 The last curve lines up with the centerline.

The basic shape for the torso is now complete. Later, you will need to make adjustments where the gi overlaps, but that will come after the object is mirrored.

Building the Arms and Legs

For the most part, the arms and legs of the character are cylindrical. The project will use a revolved NURBS surface to create cylindrical shapes that will later be converted to polygons and attached to the model.

1. From the Front view, draw a curve following the profile of the arm and hand, as shown in Figure 7.70.

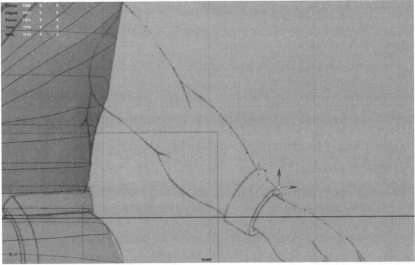

Figure 7.70 Draw a CV curve for the arm.

2. Bring up the Revolve Options dialog box and set Axis Preset to Free. Change the X Axis to −.90. Surface Degree should be Cubic. Set Start Sweep Angle to 0.0000 and End Sweep Angle at 360.0000. Change the number of segments to 4. Set Curve Range to Complete and select Nurbs for Output Geometry. Your revolved NURBS surface should look similar to that shown in Figure 7.71.

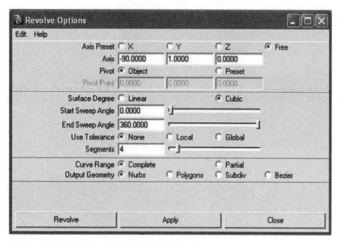

Figure 7.71 Revolve a NURBS surface for the arm.

3. Change the selection type to CVs and adjust the NURBS surface to follow the contour of the arm from the Front view, as shown in Figure 7.72.

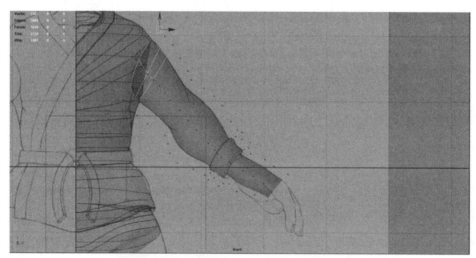

Figure 7.72 Adjust the NURBS surface to fit the arm.

4. Now go to the Side view and move the CVs to fit the arm from that view, as shown in Figure 7.73.

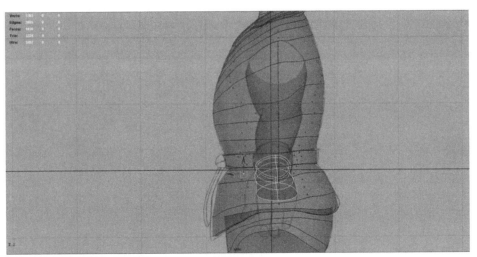

Figure 7.73 Adjust the CVs of the arm from the Side view.

5. Bring up the Convert NURBS to Polygons Options dialog box. It is found under Modify, Convert in the main menu. Under Initial Tessellation Controls, select Per Span # of Iso Params for both U and V. Set the number of U spans to 1 and V spans to 4. Then click Apply. The result should look like that shown in Figure 7.74.

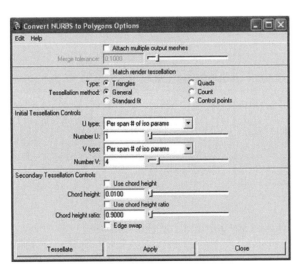

Figure 7.74 Convert the NURBS surface to polygons.

6. Now go to the leg and draw a CV curve along the inside of the leg from the Front view, as shown in Figure 7.75.

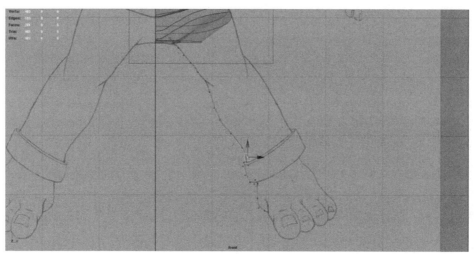

Figure 7.75 Draw a CV curve for the leg.

7. Use the same setting that you did for the arms with the exception that the X axis needs to be set at −.55 instead of −.90. The revolved surface should look similar to that shown in Figure 7.76.

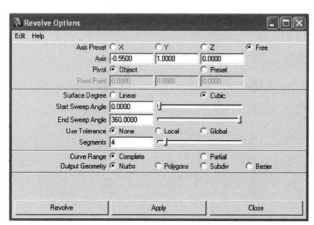

Figure 7.76 Revolve a NURBS surface for the leg.

8. Adjust the CVs of the leg from the front like you did for the arm (see Figure 7.77).

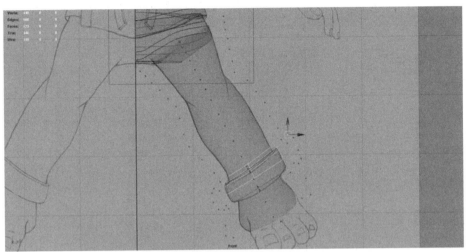

Figure **7.77** Move the CVS to match the shape of the leg.

9. Again go to the Side view and adjust the CVs of the leg there, as shown in Figure 7.78.

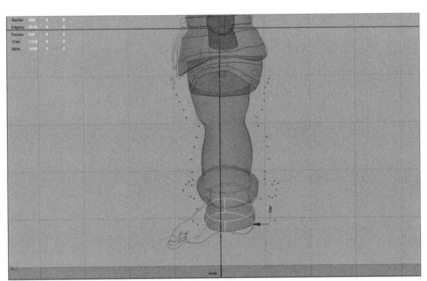

Figure **7.78** Adjust the shape of the leg from the side.

10. Move the CVs of the bottom of the leg to form the heel of the foot, as shown in Figure 7.79.

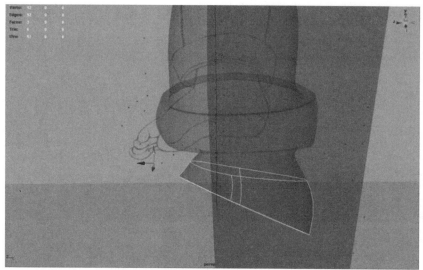

Figure 7.79 Give the character a heel to his feet.

11. Convert the NURBS surface for the leg to polygons using the same settings as you did for the arm, as shown in Figure 7.80.

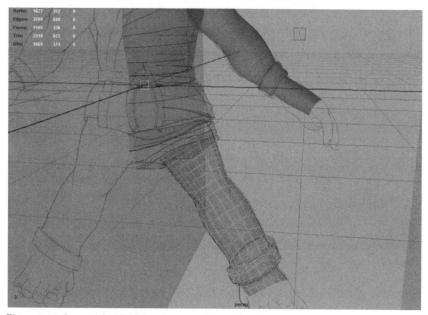

Figure 7.80 Convert the NURBS surface to polygons for the leg.

Okay, you are getting close to having a finished character. Hang in there. You only have a few more things to do, like making hands, feet, and a few other items.

Creating the Hands and the Feet

The character is a cartoon character, so we will be using the cartoon-standard three-fingered hand (plus thumb). Go to the area of the hand first. You will use polygon-modeling techniques to create the thumb and fingers.

1. Select three polygon faces on the side of the palm and extrude them outward, as shown in Figure 7.81.

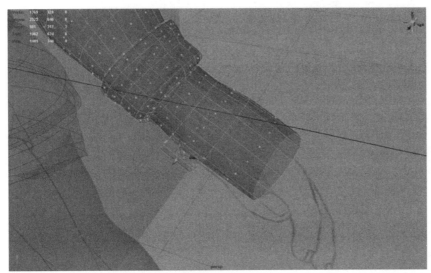

Figure 7.81 Extrude polygons for the thumb.

2. Move the vertices of the extrusion to fit the contour of the base of the thumb, as shown in Figure 7.82.

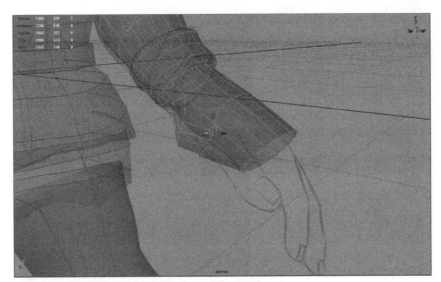

Figure 7.82 Adjust the vertices of the base of the thumb.

3. Extrude the polygon faces of the base of the thumb to form the thumb, similar to what you see in Figure 7.83. Use the Front and Side views to help define its shape. You will need to extrude the faces several times and adjust the vertices after each extrusion.

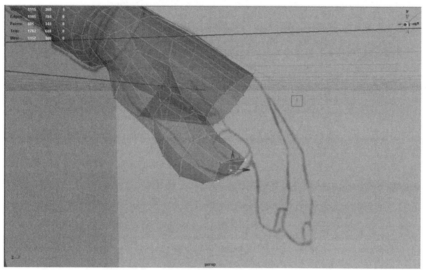

Figure 7.83 Create the thumb by extruding faces from the base.

4. Split the polygons on the tip of the thumb to give it a more rounded look, as shown in Figure 7.84.

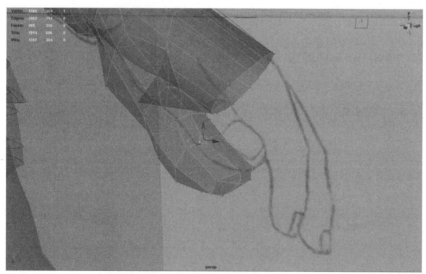

Figure 7.84 Add polygons to the tip to finish the thumb.

5. Select the edges for the first finger and extrude them outward, as shown in Figure 7.85.

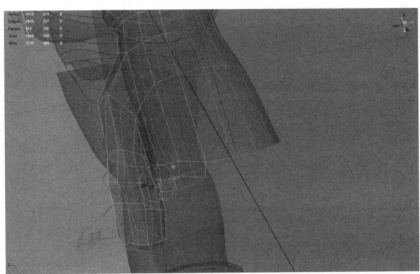

Figure 7.85 Start extruding the first finger.

6. The finger does not have an inside surface. Select the inner edges and extrude them together, as shown in Figure 7.86.

Figure 7.86 Extrude edges for the inside of the first finger.

7. Join the inside polygons of the finger by merging their vertices. Now you should have a surface that extends all the way around the first finger.

8. Select the edges of the first finger and extrude them similar to what you did with the thumb to form the finger, as shown in Figure 7.87.

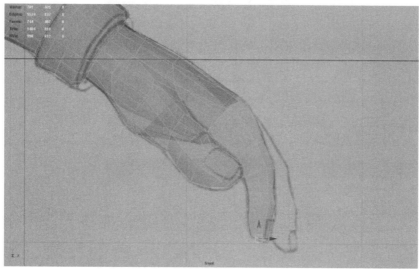

Figure 7.87 Extrude the first finger.

9. Create a base for the second finger in a similar fashion to what you did with the first finger. Your result should look like that shown in Figure 7.88.

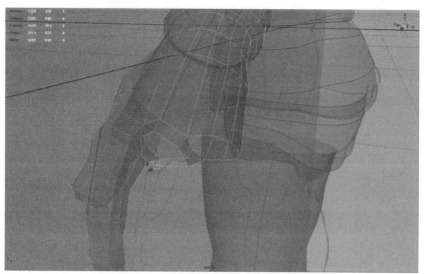

Figure 7.88 Create a base for the second finger.

10. Now extrude the second finger and complete it, similar to how you created the first finger.

11. Finally, create the third finger in the same way that you did the first and second fingers. Your result should look similar to that shown in Figure 7.89.

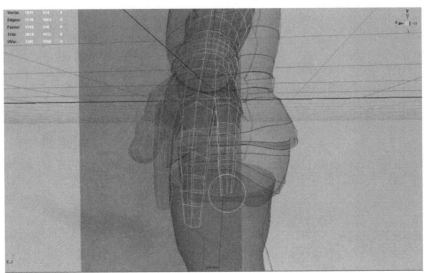

Figure 7.89 Extrude the third finger.

12. Because the fingers were created from extruding edges, they lack tips. Extrude the bottom edges of the fingers to fill in the holes at the end of the fingers. Join them by merging vertices, as shown in Figure 7.90.

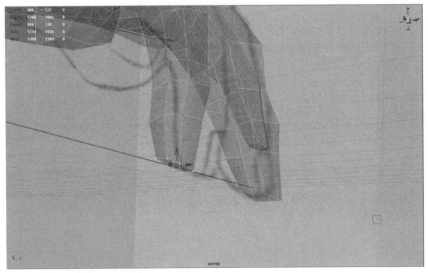

Figure 7.90 Add tips to the fingers.

13. Now go down to the feet. Select the edges around the end of the model and extrude the base of the foot, as shown in Figure 7.91.

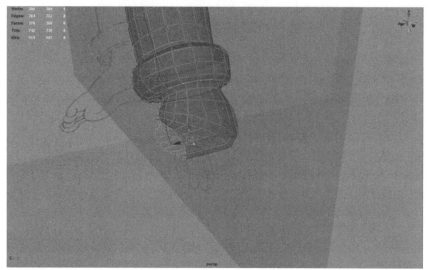

Figure 7.91 Extrude the base of the foot.

14. Extrude the toes in the same way you did the fingers of the hand. Figure 7.92 shows the finished foot after the toes are completed.

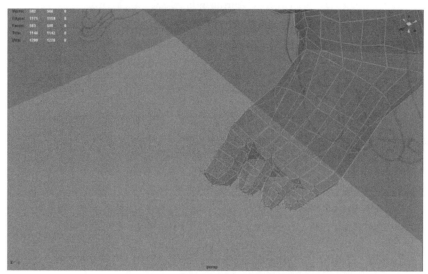

Figure 7.92 Extrude the toes of the foot.

The character is starting to take shape. He is almost to the stage where he can be mirrored to form the other half.

Attaching and Smoothing

Before the character can be mirrored, you will need to attach the legs and the arms to the torso. Also, you should do some smoothing to blend the attached areas.

1. Hide all nonpolygon geometry and curves so you are only looking at the polygons.
2. Select all of the geometry and combine it into one polygon object.
3. Select all of the vertices of the model. Merge vertices to join into a single surface.
4. Snap the vertices of the arm to the corresponding vertices of the shoulder, as shown in Figure 7.93. Note that in a few cases where there are more arm vertices than shoulder vertices you may need to snap two of the arm vertices to one shoulder vertex.

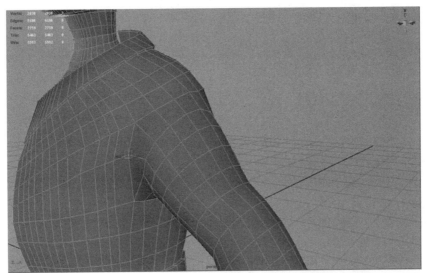

Figure 7.93 Snap vertices from the arm to those on the shoulder to join the arm to the shoulder.

5. Where the arm and shoulder join, delete the unneeded faces of the shoulder, as shown in Figure 7.94.

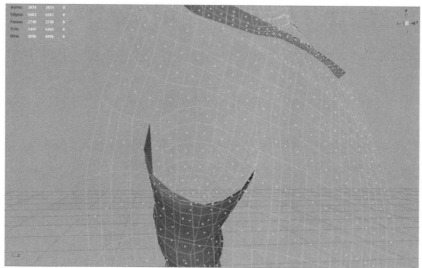

Figure 7.94 Delete the unneeded faces of the shoulder.

6. Merge the vertices of the arm with those of the torso.

7. Now go to the leg. You may notice that there are a lot of faces in the crotch area of the character. Many of these faces are unnecessary and can be removed by merging vertices with adjoining faces so they are closer to the number of faces on the leg. Look at Figure 7.95 as an example of how the joining of the leg and the torso should look for the crotch area.

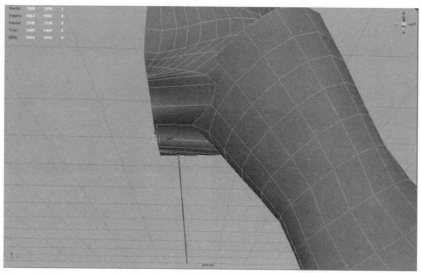

Figure 7.95 Remove some of the faces in the crotch area to better join it with the leg.

8. Join the leg to the torso in the same way you did the arm and torso by snapping vertices to the torso and then removing the unneeded geometry covered by the leg.

9. Merge the vertices of the leg and torso.

10. Soften the edges of the model using the Soften Edge function found in the Normals menu.

11. Use the Sculpt Geometry Tool to smooth the areas where the arm and leg join with the torso, as shown in Figure 7.96. Be careful not to smooth any polygons near the centerline, or you will cause problems when the model is mirrored.

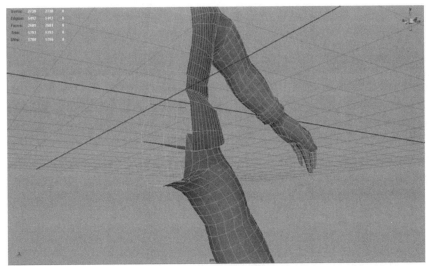

Figure 7.96 Smooth the model where the leg meets the torso.

Figure 7.97 shows the smoothing of the shoulder area.

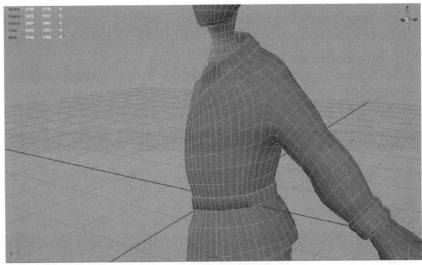

Figure 7.97 Smooth the model where the arm meets the torso.

You now have a finished half of your character model. If this character were completely symmetrical, you would just need to mirror the model and you would be finished. This character, however, has differences between sides, so you will have to build those areas after mirroring.

Mirroring the Model

Before you mirror your model, you should double-check the vertices along the centerline to make sure they are all snapped to that line, as shown in Figure 7.98. If any are off, it will cause problems with the mirror process.

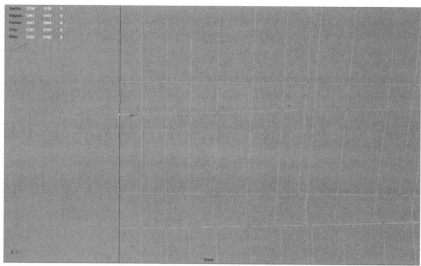

Figure 7.98 Make sure all vertices are directly on the centerline.

Use the Polygon Mirror options found in the Polygons menu to mirror your model. Select −X for the mirror direction.

You will now need to join the two halves of the model by merging the vertices, as shown in Figure 7.99. I like to merge the vertices after the mirror process because it is a little cleaner than using the Merge With Original option in the Mirror function.

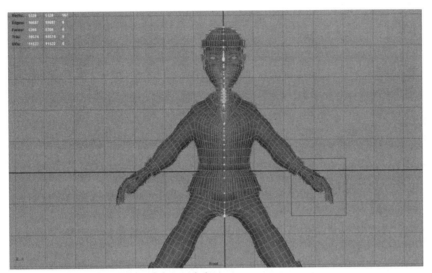

Figure 7.99 Merge the vertices of the two halves.

Adding Unique Geometry

Several areas of the character—like his hair and the gi—are not symmetrical. Now that you have both sides of the model, you are ready to create this geometry. We will start with the gi.

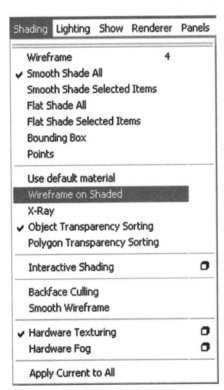

Figure 7.100 Change the shading to Wireframe on Shaded.

1. Create a NURBS plane with a width of 0.2 and a length of 3. Set Axis to Z, Surface Degree to 3 Cubic, U Patches to 1, and V Patches to 10.

2. Move the plane to just in front of the model.

3. Go to Shading in the Panel menu and select Wireframe on Shaded, as shown in Figure 7.100.

4. Snap the CVs of the top of the NURBS plane to the vertices of the collar, as shown in Figure 7.101.

5. Move the CVs of the plane to follow the contour of the gi, as shown in Figure 7.102. Notice that the CVs are snapped to the vertices of the belt.

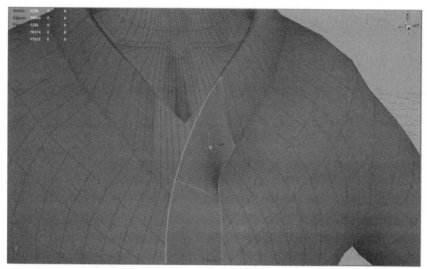

Figure 7.101 Snap the NURBS plane to the collar.

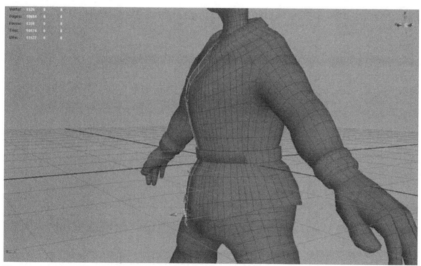

Figure 7.102 Model the plane to the contour of the gi.

6. Convert the NURBS plane to polygons, setting the U value to 1 and the V value to 2.

7. Change the selection mode to Edge and use the Select Using Constraints tool to select the border edges.

8. Extrude the edges into the body, as shown in Figure 7.103.

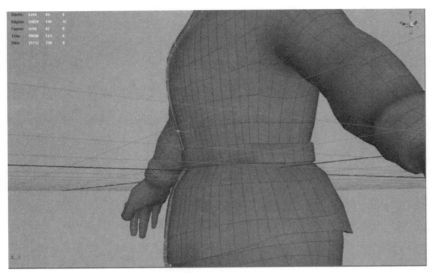

Figure 7.103 Extrude the edges of the polygon plane.

9. Adjust the vertices of the gi to follow the new geometry, as shown in Figure 7.104.

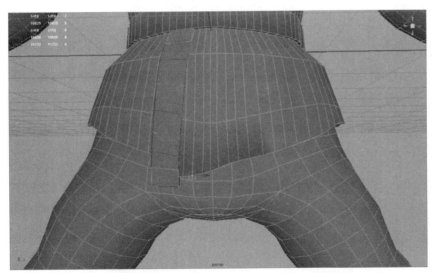

Figure 7.104 Adjust the gi's vertices.

10. Extrude the bottom inside edge of the new geometry to seal it, as shown in Figure 7.105.

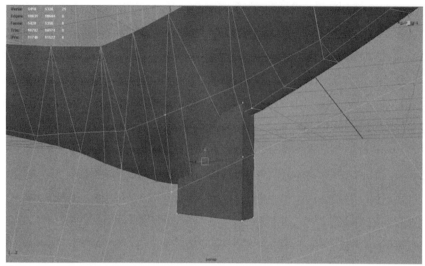

Figure 7.105 Seal the new geometry.

11. Create a polygon sphere for the belt knot. Set Radius to 0.1500, Axis Divisions to 8, and Height Divisions to 4.

12. Place the sphere so it is in the belt, as shown in Figure 7.106.

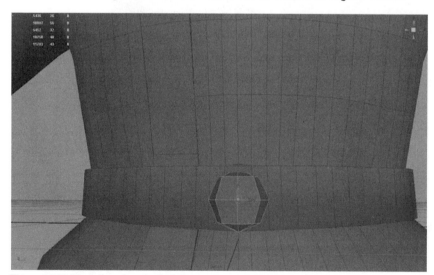

Figure 7.106 Move the sphere to the belt.

13. Extrude and scale the faces of the top of the sphere outward, as shown in Figure 7.107.

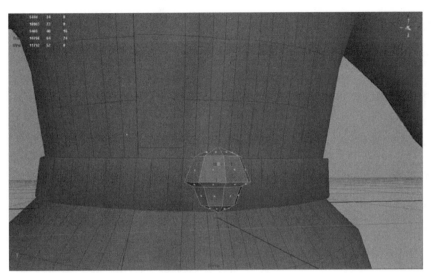

Figure 7.107 Extrude the top of the sphere.

14. Select two faces on the bottom of the sphere and extrude them downward, as shown in Figure 7.108.

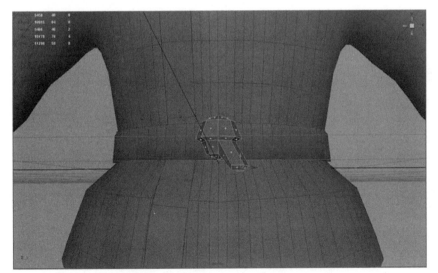

Figure 7.108 Extrude the belt from the knot.

15. Extrude the polygons to form the belt coming out of the knot, as shown in Figure 7.109.

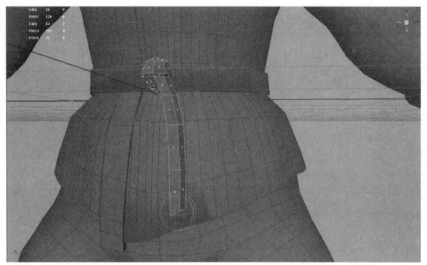

Figure 7.109 Create one side of the belt so it comes out of the knot.

16. Extrude the other side of the belt coming from the knot also, as shown in Figure 7.110.

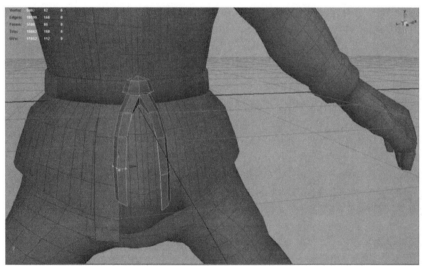

Figure 7.110 Extrude the other side of the belt.

17. Move to the character's eyes. You have not yet created the tear ducts. They need to be in place before you can add the eyeballs. Create them by extruding the edges and merging the vertices, as shown in Figure 7.111.

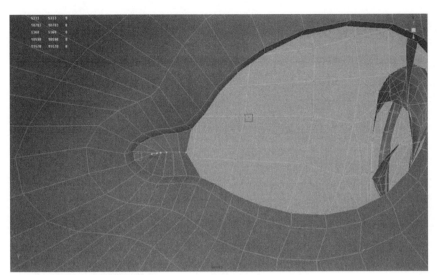

Figure 7.111 Create the tear ducts.

18. For the eyeball, create a polygon sphere in the Z axis with a radius of 0.135. Set Axis Divisions to 24 and Height Divisions to 12.

19. Place the eyeball in the eye socket, as shown in Figure 7.112. You may need to adjust vertices of the eyelids to get the eye to fit properly.

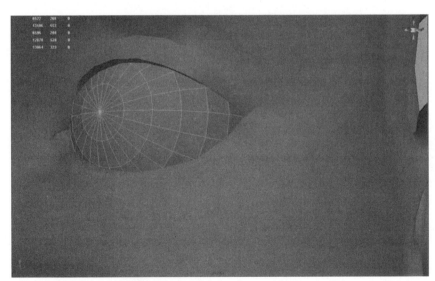

Figure 7.112 Place the eyeball in the eye socket.

20. Create a NURBS cone. Set Start Sweep Angle to 0.0000, End Sweep Angle to 360.0000, Radius to 0.2000, and Height to 0.8000, Number of Sections to 8, and Number of Spans to 1.

21. Move the cone to the character's hair, and place and adjust the cone to form a lock of the character's hair, similar to that shown in Figure 7.113.

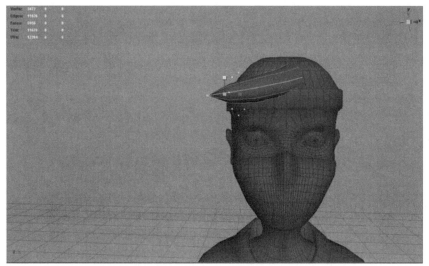

Figure 7.113 Turn the cone into a lock of hair.

22. This character has wild hair, so duplicate the cone and randomly place locks of hair around his head and in the back of the head beneath the headband. Your finished hairstyle should look similar to that shown in Figure 7.114. Convert the NURBS cones into polygons, with the U value set to 8 and the V value set to 1.

You're done! You have just completed building the geometry for the character. Your finished model should look similar to the model in Figure 7.114.

Figure 7.114 The finished character model.

Summary

Well, it was a long process, but I hope you hung in there and created a model. You will need the model for the next chapter, where we will cover texturing and rigging the character.

In this chapter, you created a character using a number of techniques, including the following:

- NURBS-assisted polygon modeling
- Polygon modeling
- NURBS modeling
- NURBS to polygons
- Mirroring polygons

The methods you used for creating the model varied greatly so that you could get some experience using Maya's many features for blending NURBS and polygon-modeling techniques. As stated toward the beginning of the book, there is any number of ways to create character models. Hopefully, you can use what you learned in this chapter to find your own favorite way to model your characters.

Chapter 7

Gaining Character

Character development is one of the most demanding and exciting aspects of 3D art. Max has a nice array of tools and features specifically designed for the development and animation of characters. There is so much involved in developing and animating characters that one chapter is not enough to cover the subject. Therefore, this chapter, along with the next two, will deal specifically with the creation of a character—from a drawing to animation. This chapter will deal with building the character, Chapter 8 will cover texturing and rigging the character, and Chapter 9 will delve into character animation.

It All Starts with a Drawing

Character models are complex and often difficult to complete unless you have some visual clues. A common practice among character artists is to create a character template that they can use as a guide when building a character. The template is similar to a drafting drawing done by architects or product designers. It has at least three, and sometimes more, orthogonal views. They are isometric drawings in that there is no perspective used. Figure 7.1 shows the front view of a character. The character is a young cartoon-style ninja. He is in an open pose, with the legs slightly apart and the arms held out from the body. This is a good pose for animating characters.

Figure 7.2 shows the back view of the character. The back view needs to be an exact duplicate of the proportions of the front view.

When you are creating the back view of a character, a good way to ensure that the proportions and position of the character are exactly correct is to flip the front view and trace it, though changing it from a front to a back view.

Figure 7.1 Having the legs apart and the arms out from the body helps with animation.

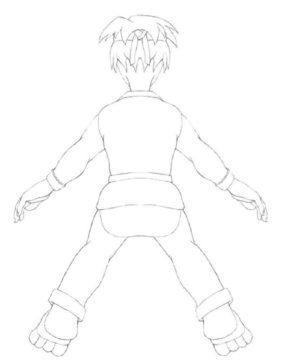

Figure 7.2 The front and back views should have the same proportions.

The side view is shown in Figure 7.3.

Figure 7.3 The side view needs to be proportional to the front and back views.

The side view is a little harder to create because you can't get it from tracing another view, like you can for the back view. It still needs to be exact proportionally. Drawing the side view overlaying the front and back views can help to get things lined up correctly.

On human or other two-legged characters, three views are usually sufficient. Four-legged creatures may need a top view and in some cases a bottom view as well.

Make sure the drawings are centered on the image. If they are drawn on paper, scan them into a 2D paint package and crop them so they are exactly square. You are welcome to scan the drawings from the book to follow along with this project, or you can draw your own character. The original files are on the CD that accompanies the book.

Setting Up the Template

Once the drawings are ready, you can load them into Max and begin using them for building the model. If you're ready, let's get started.

1. Start by creating a single primitive plane that is 180 cm high by 180 cm wide in the Front viewport.
2. Use the three input boxes on the status bar to move the plane to −0.5 cm in the Y axis and set the X and Z axes to 0.0.

3. Clone the plane by holding the Shift key and rotating the existing plane 180 degrees in the Z axis. Move the new plane to 0.5 in the Y axis.

4. Create one more plane and rotate it 90 degrees, as shown in Figure 7.4.

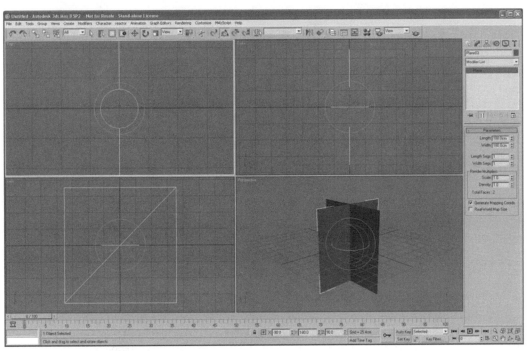

Figure 7.4 Create a third plane.

5. Rename the first three material balls "Front," "Back," and "Side."

6. Set each material to about 30 percent opacity.

7. Load the template drawings (one each) into the first three material balls.

8. Don't forget to toggle the Show Map in Viewport button for each map (on the map level, not the parent level), as shown in Figure 7.5.

9. You may also want to set each material to be 100 percent self-illuminated. This will help keep the template visible from most angles. As an option, you can right-click on the Side view plane and, under the Properties dialog box, toggle the Backface Culling off, and the side plane should be visible from both sides.

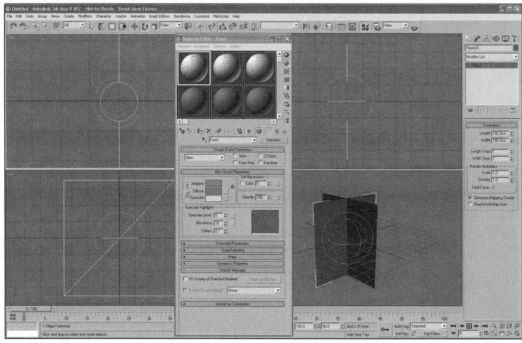

Figure 7.5 Create three materials for the template drawings.

10. Now apply the drawing of the front of the character to the plane facing in the Y axis, the drawing of the back of the character to the polygon facing in the −Y axis, and the drawing of the side of the character to the polygon facing in the X axis, as shown in Figure 7.6. Depending on the setting for your viewport drivers, you may notice that the drawing is displayed in a very low-res, jaggy way. You can adjust this by opening the Preference Settings dialog box under the Customize menu. Find the Viewports tab and click on the Configure Driver button. Set the map lookup sizes to a higher level to see a better result in the viewport. Unfortunately, you will need to save your scene and restart Max to see the results. There is a caveat here: This could slow down your machine once you start adding more textures, so when we get to that stage you may want to adjust these to the default settings (usually 256) if you feel things are running too slowly while you work.

11. You're going to want to group the three planes into one object so you can easily hide or manipulate it. Select all three planes and choose the Group option found under Group on the main menu bar, as shown in Figure 7.7.

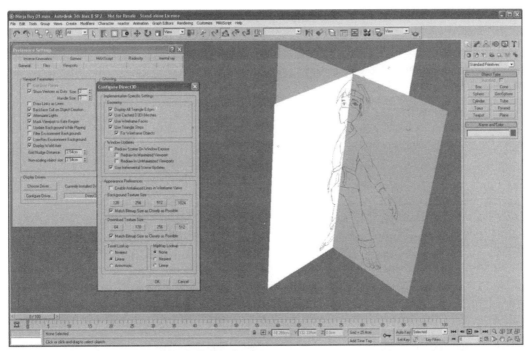

Figure 7.6 Apply the three materials to the three polygons.

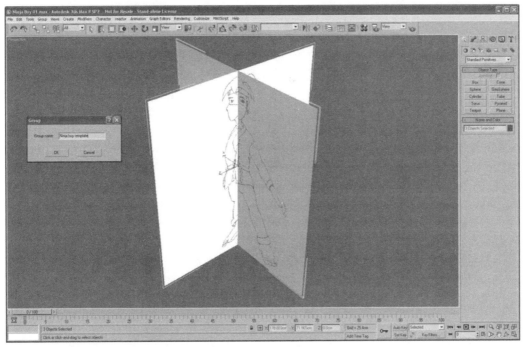

Figure 7.7 Group all three planes into one object.

12. As a last step, set the template to be non-renderable so you can render your model without having to hide the template every time. With the template selected, right-click on it, choose Properties, and uncheck the Renderable box, as shown in Figure 7.8.

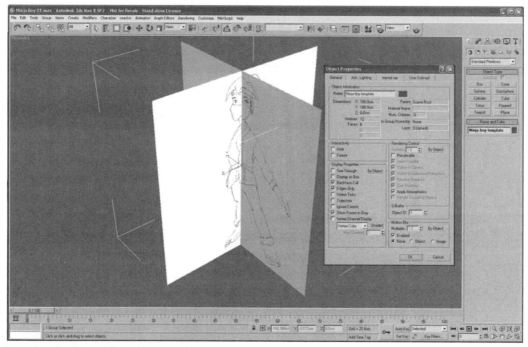

Figure 7.8 Set the template to be non-renderable.

The template is finished and ready to use. Rotate around the model to make sure that everything is lined up as it should be.

Now would be a good time to save the scene. I saved mine as Ninja boy 01, so as I am working, I can call up the Save As dialog box and press the "+" button near the Save button to get Max to automatically increment the number and save a new file. This is a nice way to have multiple files saved so you can jump back a few steps if needed.

Building the Character

There are about as many ways to build characters in 3D as there are 3D artists. No one way is necessarily wrong unless it creates problems in the geometry. In this example, we will use a method called *patch modeling*. The basics of this method are building a spline cage, adding a patch surface to it, and tweaking the surface to achieve the desired look. This is similar to NURBS—where you built a cage with CVs and added the NURBS surface—but quite a bit less complex.

There are a set of two tools (that we will be using) that, when combined, are called Surface tools. The first tool, called Cross Section, helps take a series of splines and turn them into a cage, which we can overlay with a patch surface. The second tool, called Surface, adds the surface to the cage. In an effort to speed workflow, Autodesk (the creators of Max) has added the Cross Section modifier to the Edit Spline modifier and the Surface modifier to the Edit Patch modifier. This helps to cut down the number of modifiers needed, in turn simplifying the patch modeling process. These two modifiers still exist on their own in the modifier list; however, we will be using them as part of the Edit Spline and Edit Patch workflows.

This example has some terms introduced in Chapter 5 that are fairly interchangeable and are used to describe a mathematical curve. Some of these terms are Bezier, Corner, Smooth, Spline, Shape, and Curve.

1. Set your viewport to display the front and left sides. Using the Line tool found under Shapes, create a smooth curve by setting Initial Type and Drag Type to Smooth. In the Front view starting at the top of the eye, click and start the eye shape, as shown in Figure 7.9.

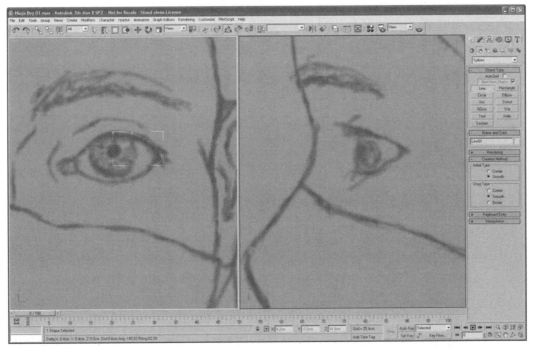

Figure 7.9 Draw a line shape around the upper eyelid.

2. Continue drawing around the edge of the eyelids and around the tear duct, as shown in Figure 7.10.

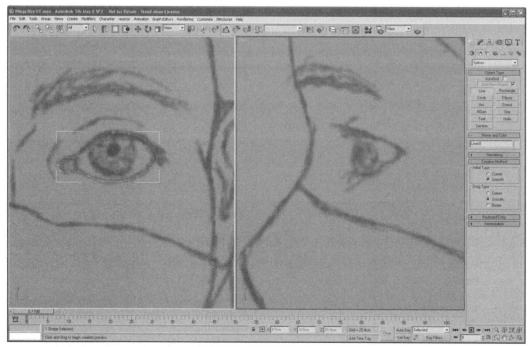

Figure 7.10 Continue to draw in the shape of the eye.

3. Join the shape onto itself by clicking on the first vertices you placed. The finished shape or spline should look like that shown in Figure 7.11.

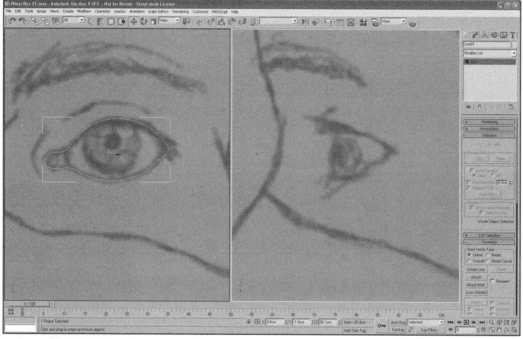

Figure 7.11 Finish drawing the shape around the eye.

4. By default, Max creates new shapes at the origin, so move the shape to the eye, as shown in Figure 7.12.

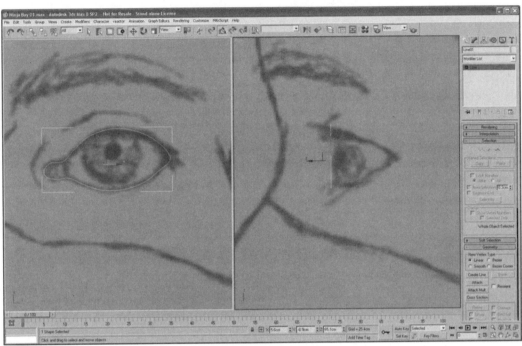

Figure 7.12 Move the shape into place from the Right view.

5. You may want to enter Vertex Sub Object mode and adjust the vertices so the shape of the eyelids matches the drawing.

Note

There are four types of vertices that affect the curve of the splines differently. They are Smooth, Corner, Bezier, and Bezier Corner. Smooth is a simple curve that is not editable and is best used for simple curved surfaces. Corner is a hard line with no curve to it that is useful for creases and hard lines. Bezier and Bezier Corner are editable curves via tangents you can adjust to affect the curve; these are useful in more complex models.

We will be using a mix of curve types to achieve the right look. For example, we will start with Smooth to rough in the shape and change some of the vertex types to Bezier to adjust the curve for more control. In Figure 7.16, I have changed the corner of the eye to a Bezier curve and moved the tangents in to get more of a corner.

To change the type, select one or more vertices and then right-click. Choose the type of curve you need from the resulting menu.

6. The eyelids follow the shape of the eyeball, which is basically a sphere. Round the shape to follow a spherical shape, as shown in Figure 7.13.

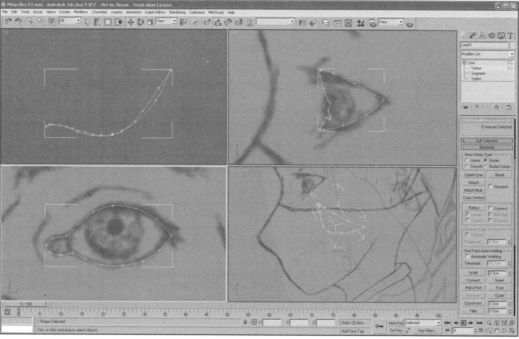

Figure 7.13 Change the spline to follow the shape of an eye.

7. Switch to Spline Sub Object mode and clone the spline by selecting it and scaling it down slightly while holding the Shift key, as shown in Figure 7.14.

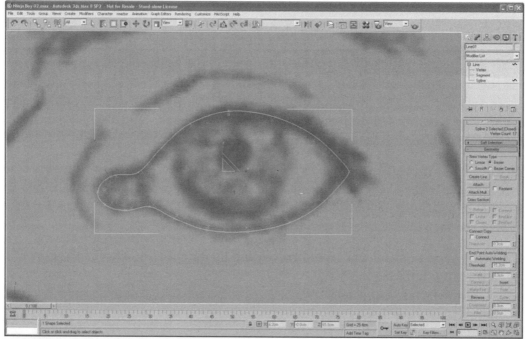

Figure 7.14 Clone the spline.

8. This second spline will be the inside edge of the eyelid. Adjust it to fit the eyelid, as shown in Figure 7.15.

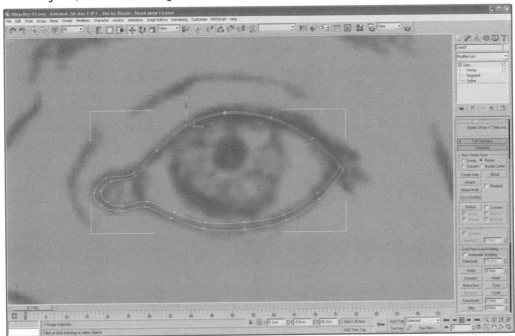

Figure 7.15 Adjust the second spline to fit the inside edge of the eyelids.

9. Clone the original shape and expand it to the area where the eyelid joins the face, as shown in Figure 7.16.

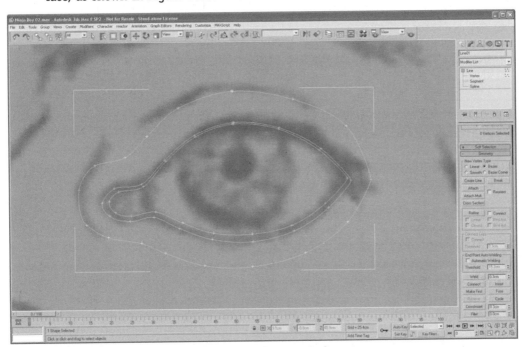

Figure 7.16 Expand the cloned shape to fit where the eyelid meets the face.

10. Adjust the vertices in the Perspective view to match the contours of the face, as shown in Figure 7.17. The shape should recede in the middle and stay close to the same plane as the original shape on either side, as shown.

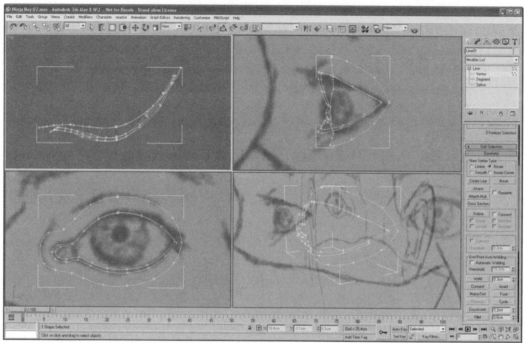

Figure 7.17 Have the shape follow the contour of the eyelids.

11. Let's change the Bezier vertices that we used on the inner eye back to Smooth on this outside spline, as shown in Figure 7.18. The face in this area does not need the sharper angles and the Smooth type will be easier to control.

Note

Now that you are about to move beyond splines and create a polygonal surface, there are a few notes about Surface Tools or patch modeling that you should know.

The Cross Section tool will automatically build a cage for the surface to overlay. It tries to create four-sided sections from the spline sections.

Patches can only be formed from three- or four-sided cages.

The Cross Section–created splines are not connected to the cage and can be moved, deleted, or added to like a normal spline. Just make sure to close a section with three or four sides if you want to build a patch. The Snap tools can help with this.

You will be moving up and down the stack as you build this organic surface, so do not collapse the stack until you are happy with the results and want to convert the final model to a mesh.

When using the Cross Section tool, you must click on the splines in order to build the cage correctly.

When adding to the spline cage, the Cross Section tool does not automatically connect the splines, and you will have hard edges or creases where the new geometry starts. These points must be welded and their types changed to Smooth or Bezier if you want a smooth surface.

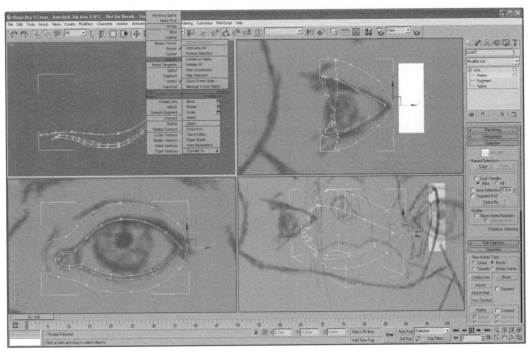

Figure 7.18 Change the Bezier vertices back to Smooth.

12. Now let's start building a surface. Using the Cross Section tool, click on the first spline (nearest the eyeball) and then click on the next one, as shown in Figure 7.19. This will create the start of our spline cage.

13. Continue to use the Cross Section tool and select the next spline, as shown in Figure 7.20.

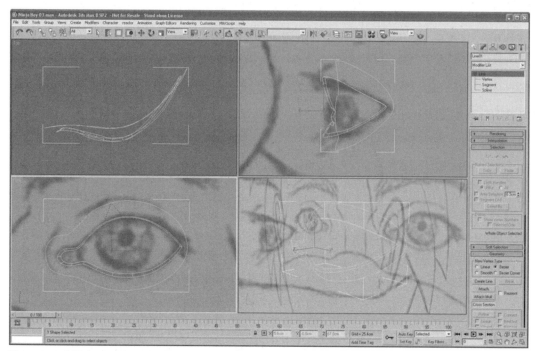

Figure 7.19 Add the cage between the two inner shapes.

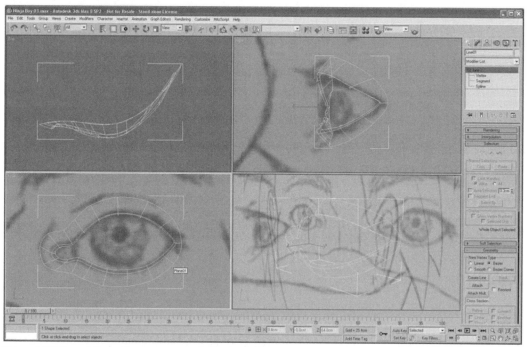

Figure 7.20 The existing splines are now ready for the surface.

14. Notice that no actual geometry has been created. Add the Edit Patch modifier, as shown in Figure 7.21.

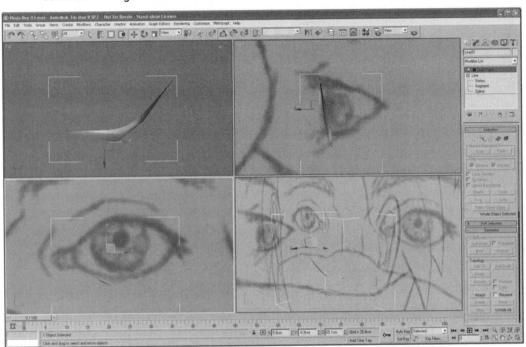

Figure 7.21 The cage overlaid with a surface of patches.

15. Depending on the physical size of your model, you may get some strange results at first. Simply adjust Threshold down to 0, and things should look correct, as shown in Figure 7.22.

16. Jump back down to the Line in the stack and toggle the Show End Results button (see Figure 7.23). Continue to construct the area around the eye by cloning the outer spline by scaling it outward and adjusting the vertices the same way as earlier. Once you have something close, add the cross sections and refine the shape (see Figure 7.23). As pointed out in the previous Note, the new cross sections have a hard edge because they are not really connected. In some cases, this is desirable, but for your model you will want to run around the newly created points, weld the vertices, and change the type to Smooth.

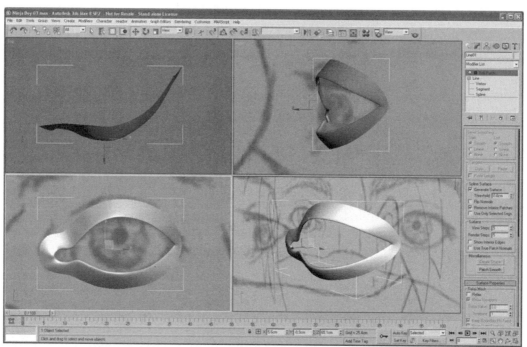

Figure 7.22 Adjust Threshold so the patches show up correctly.

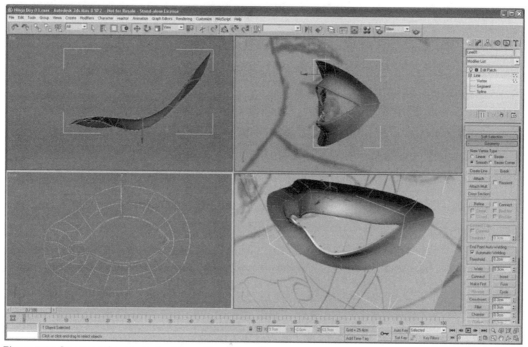

Figure 7.23 Create another band of patches outward from the eye.

17. Select all the vertices as shown and click the Weld button.

18. Right-click on one of the selected vertices and choose Smooth from the resulting dialog box.

19. Repeat the same process again, going yet farther from the eye, following the bridge of the nose, brow, and cheekbone, as shown in Figure 7.24.

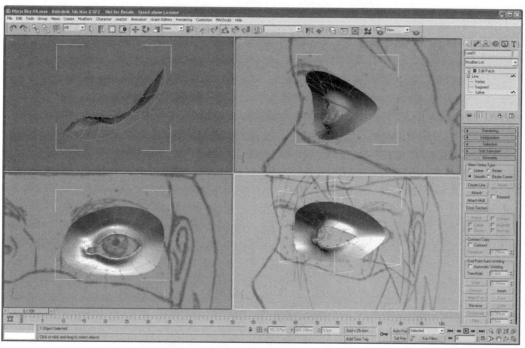

Figure 7.24 Continue to create bands of patches outward from the eye.

20. Create another band of patches in the same manner, going still farther from the eye. Continue this process until you reach the center of the nose and the edge of the mask with a total of two more bands of patches. Now that you are starting to get some shape to the face, adjust individual vertices to refine the shape and remove some of the unwanted bumps or valleys, as shown in Figure 7.25. With only a few exceptions, the character is symmetrical, so there is no need to model both sides. You will model only one side and mirror the model later.

21. Exit Sub Object mode and collapse the stack by right-clicking in a blank area of the stack window and choosing Collapse All, as shown in Figure 7.26.

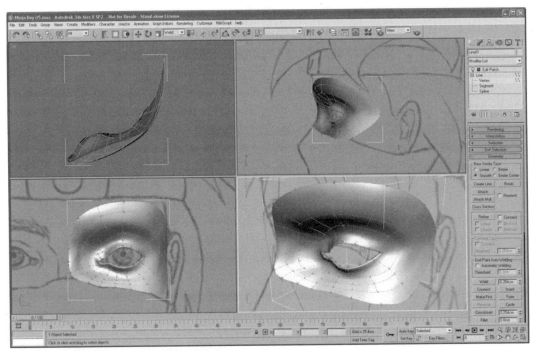

Figure 7.25 Start refining the shape of the face.

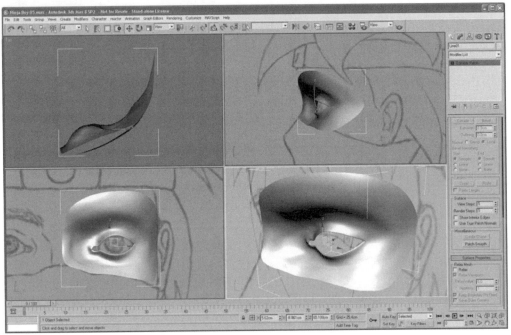

Figure 7.26 Collapse the stack to Editable Patch.

22. Under the Geometry rollout, set View Steps to 1, as shown in Figure 7.27. This setting affects the viewport but also the polygon density when converting to an editable polygon mesh.

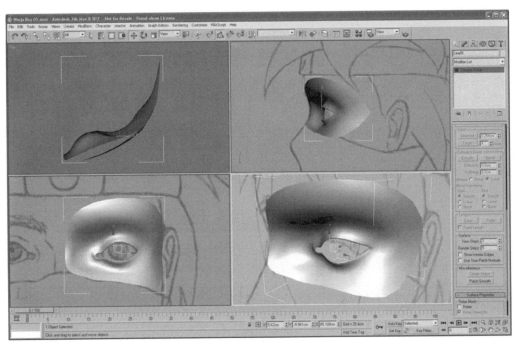

Figure 7.27 Lower the resolution before converting to polygons.

The shapes should only come to the center of the bridge of the nose and no farther.

Polygon Modeling

Rather than using shapes to complete the rest of the face, you will use some polygon modeling techniques, as covered in this section. I have also changed the material color and reduced the default shine for clarity. Collapse the stack one more time, to Editable Poly, for the next series of steps.

1. Select the top edges of the model, and from the Front view, extrude them upward to the headband.

2. You will need additional polygons to fill in the top of the forehead just above the bridge of the nose. Extrude edges and Target Weld vertices to match those shown in Figure 7.28.

3. Follow the same procedure for the nose. Extrude the edges above the nose to the mask as necessary. Extrude extra edges and Target Weld on the bridge of the nose like you did with the forehead.

4. Tweak vertices as necessary to follow the headband above and the mask below, as shown in Figure 7.29.

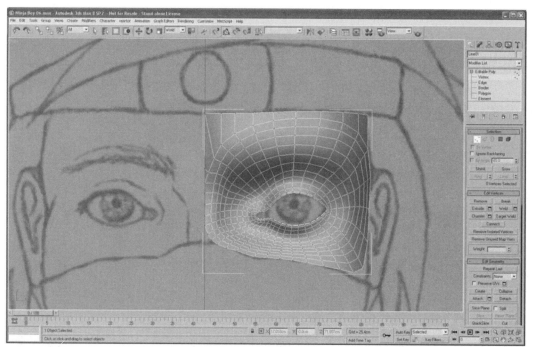

Figure 7.28 Construct the forehead by extruding edges.

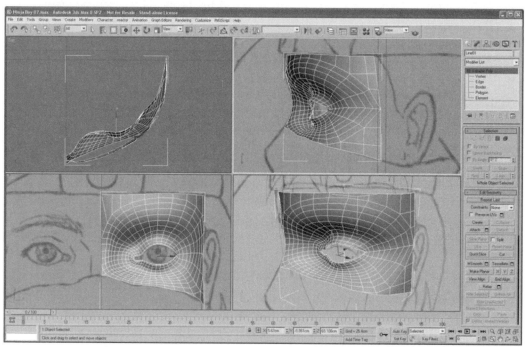

Figure 7.29 Fit the nose, cheek, and forehead to the reference image.

5. Extrude the edges along the side of the model and adjust the extrusion by moving vertices to follow the headband and mask. The new extruded polygons should reach to the edge of the character's hair, as shown in Figure 7.30.

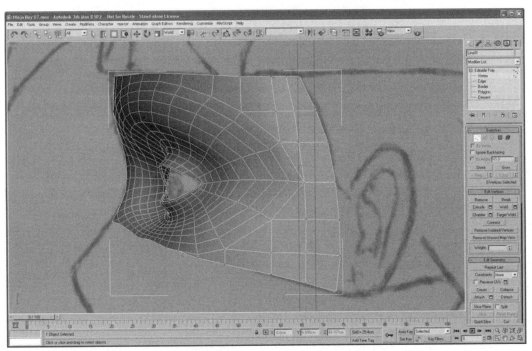

Figure 7.30 Extrude the edge to the character's hair.

6. Again adjust individual vertices to fit the contour of the face.

7. Extrude the edges again and adjust them for the hair and front of the ear, as shown in Figure 7.31. You may want to right-click on the model and select the See Through option found under Properties. This will help in lining up the mesh.

8. Continue to extrude the edge of the model toward the back of the head. Between each extrusion, move vertices to fit the contour of the face and ear.

9. Once past the ear, extrude the edge one more time and adjust the vertices so they fit the back of the skull, as shown in Figure 7.32.

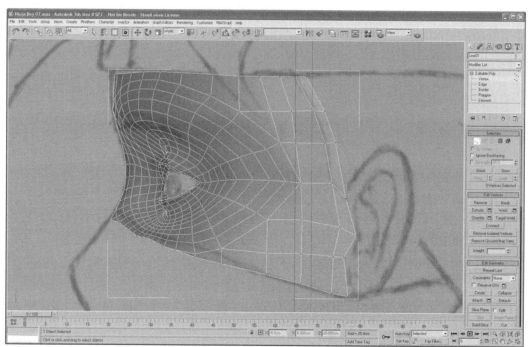

Figure 7.31 Extrude the edges and adjust for the hair.

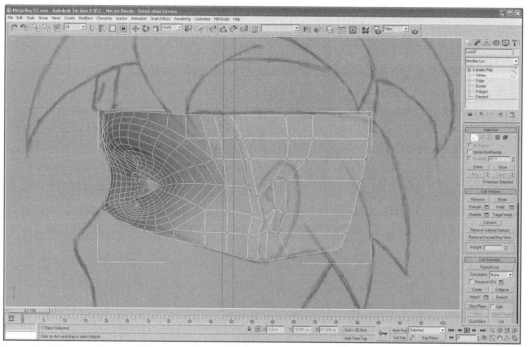

Figure 7.32 Move vertices to fit the back of the skull from the Side view.

10. Right-click on the Viewport label, and then select Back from under Views, as shown in Figure 7.33

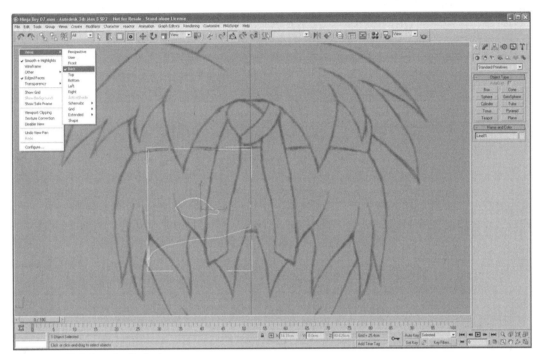

Figure 7.33 Switch to the Back view.

11. Select the vertices at the back of the head and move them to the centerline, as shown in Figure 7.34.

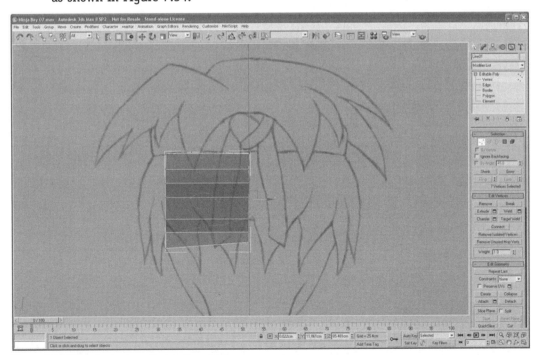

Figure 7.34 Move the back vertices to the center.

12. Now use the Cut tool to divide the polygons, as shown in Figure 7.35.

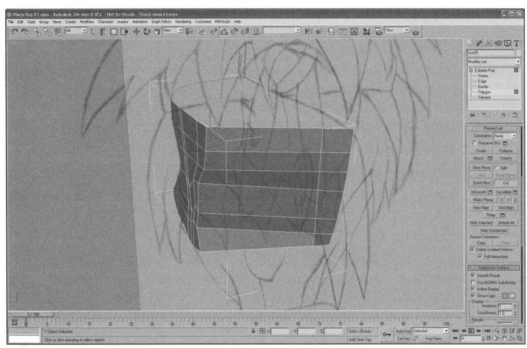

Figure 7.35 Split the polygons on the back of the head.

13. Make two more cuts in the polygons so that there are four columns of polygons, as shown in Figure 7.36.

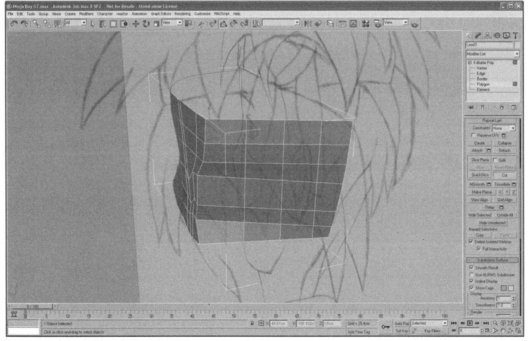

Figure 7.36 Create four columns of polygons.

14. Change the selection mode to Vertex and move the vertices of the newly created polygons to roughly follow the shape of the back of the head, as shown in Figure 7.37.

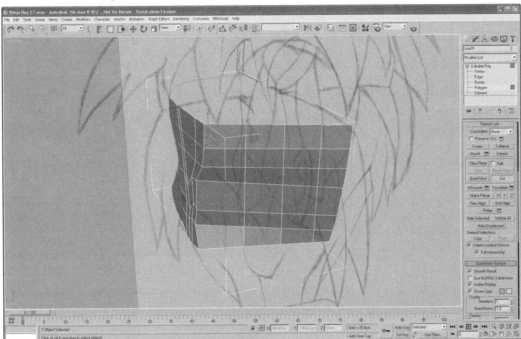

Figure 7.37 Move the vertices to follow the shape of the head.

Move around the model in Perspective view and adjust vertices to get the shape of the head to look right (see Figure 7.38).

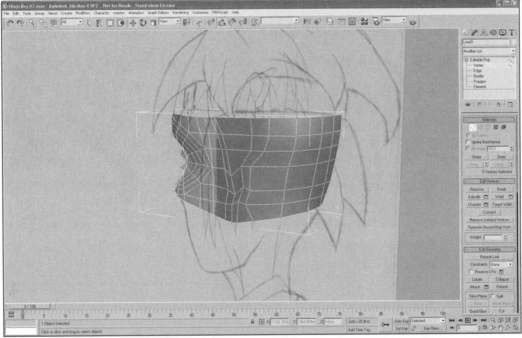

Figure 7.38 View the model from different angles to get the adjustments correct.

Modeling the Ear

Next up for this model will be the ear. The ear is attached to the side of the head just a little more than halfway from the front of the face. Use the Side view drawing to position it correctly.

1. Move vertices and/or use the Cut tool to divide the polygons where the ear attaches to the head, as shown in Figure 7.39.

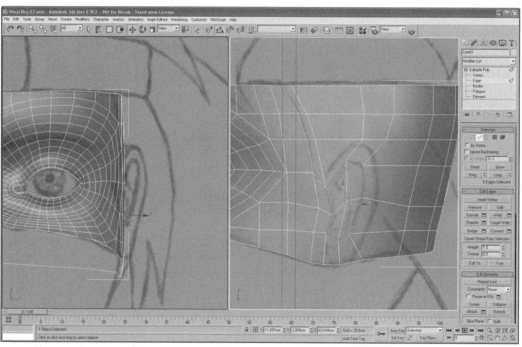

Figure 7.39 Adjust the polygons to outline the base of the ear.

2. Now select the polygon faces of the ear and extrude them outward, as shown in Figure 7.40.

3. The extrusion will need to be adjusted to the shape of the base of the ear, as shown in Figure 7.41.

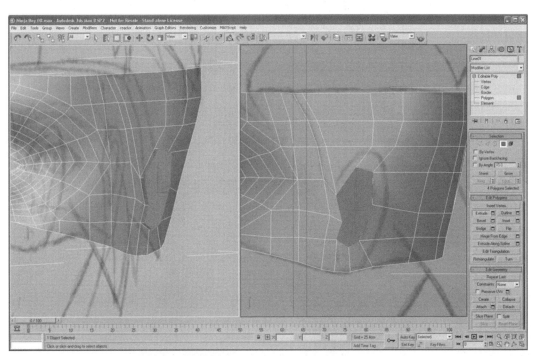

Figure 7.40 Extrude the ear out from the head.

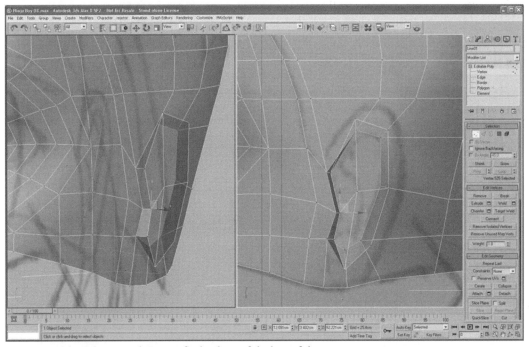

Figure 7.41 Adjust the new polygons to fit the shape of the base of the ear.

4. Extrude the ear polygons again and adjust this second extrusion to again follow the shape of the ear, as shown in Figure 7.42.

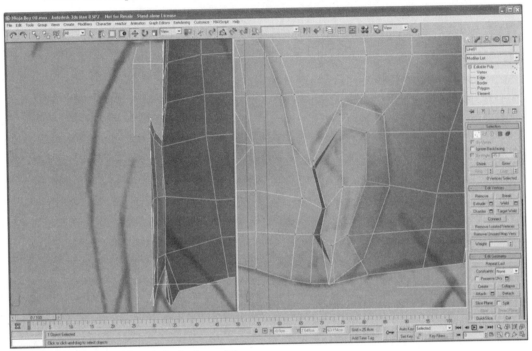

Figure 7.42 Continue to follow the basic shape of the ear.

5. Now extrude once more, to create the basic shape of the ear, as shown in Figure 7.43.

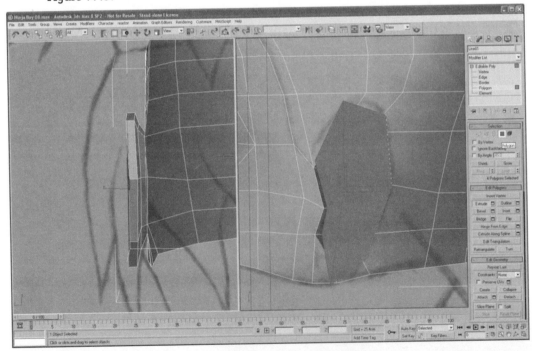

Figure 7.43 Extrude the ear outward.

6. After extruding the ear, go back in and Target Weld some of the vertices of the front of the ear to the skull and pull the outside edge in closer to the head, as shown in Figure 7.44.

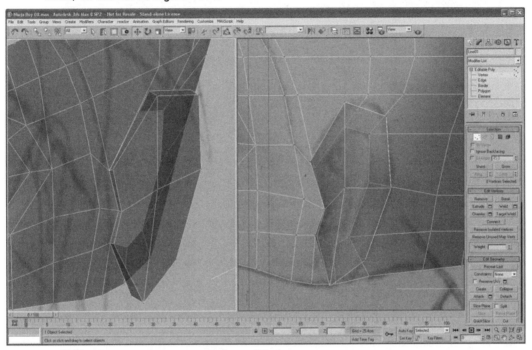

Figure 7.44 Weld and move vertices to start the shape of the inner ear.

7. Extrude the polygon at the top and lobe of the ear to round off those areas. Scale the extrusion and position it as shown in Figure 7.45.

8. Using the Cut tool and moving vertices, adjust the polygons on the inside of the ear to follow the shape of the ear, as shown in Figure 7.46.

9. Select the faces of the inner ear area and extrude them back toward the head, as shown in Figure 7.47.

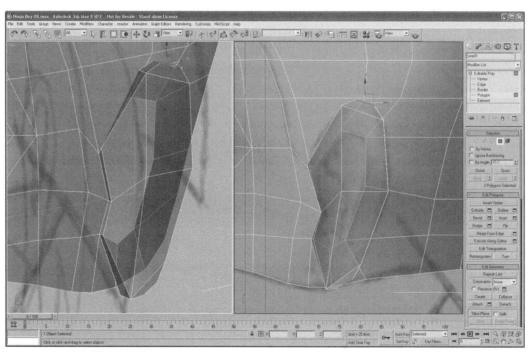

Figure 7.45 Round off the back of the ear.

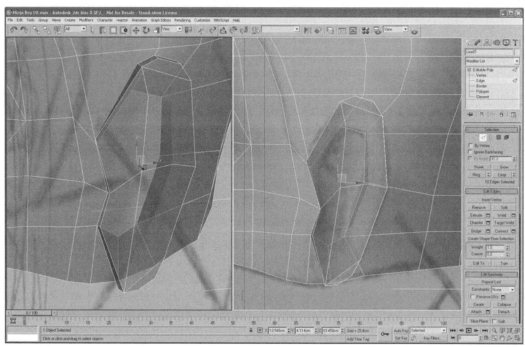

Figure 7.46 Add and adjust polygons for the inner ear.

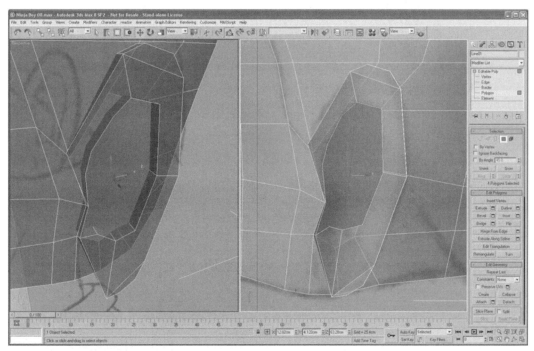

Figure 7.47 Extrude the inner ear area in toward the head.

10. Move and adjust vertices to get the shape of the ear and its inner area, as shown in Figure 7.48.

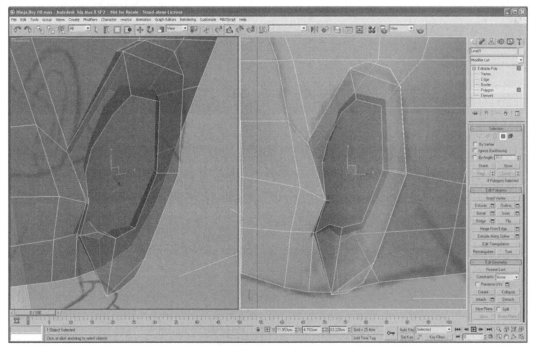

Figure 7.48 Finish modeling the basic shape of the ear.

11. Now select the faces of the ear and use the MSmooth tool twice to smooth the ear, as shown in Figure 7.49.

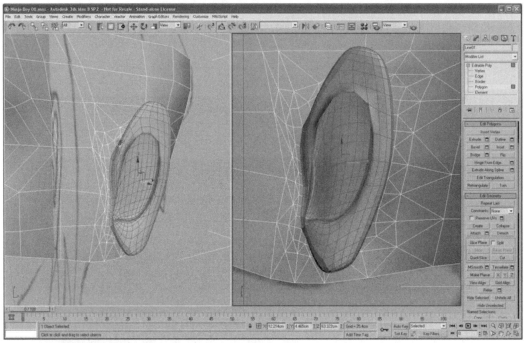

Figure 7.49 Smooth the ear to give it a more natural appearance.

12. Adjust the vertices as needed to make it look more natural, as shown in Figure 7.50.

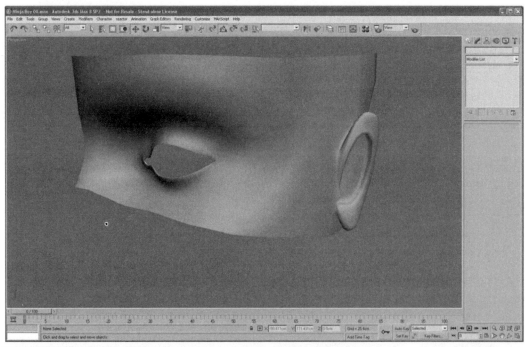

Figure 7.50 Adjust vertices of the ear.

There are certainly better ways to create an ear, but this method works fine for the purposes of this book.

Modeling the Top of the Head

Next will be the top of the head, including the headband. Start with the headband.

1. Select the edges at the top of the model along the headband. Extrude those edges outward and move them up ever so slightly, as shown in Figure 7.51. Adjust the vertices as necessary for an even lip.

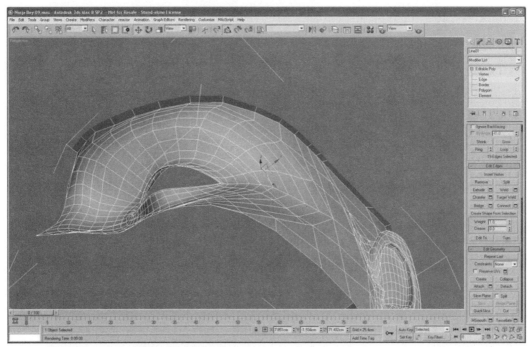

Figure 7.51 Create the lower edge of the headband.

2. Pull the vertices of the headband out in the back to make room for adding hair later, as shown in Figure 7.52.

3. Select the edges again and extrude them upward to form the headband, as shown in Figure 7.53.

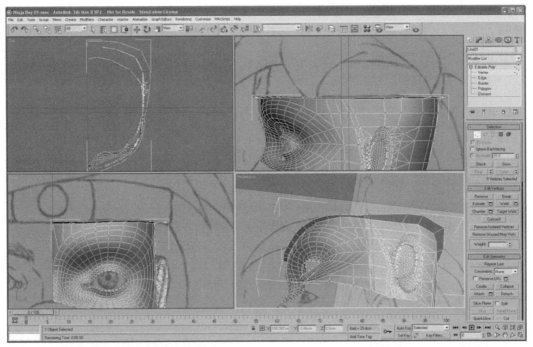

Figure 7.52 Expand the headband in the back.

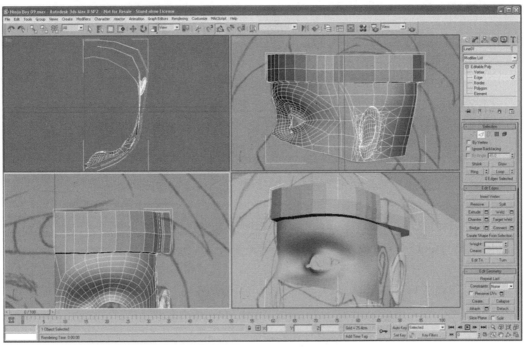

Figure 7.53 Extrude the headband upward.

4. Extrude the headband again using Shift Scale to form its upper lip, as shown in Figure 7.54. Move it up ever so slightly.

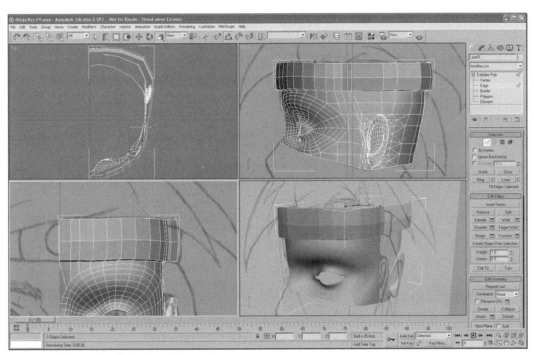

Figure 7.54 Create the upper edge of the headband.

5. Now you need to form the top of the skull, disregarding the hair. Extrude the edges and scale them after each extrusion to create a rounded head, as shown in Figure 7.55.

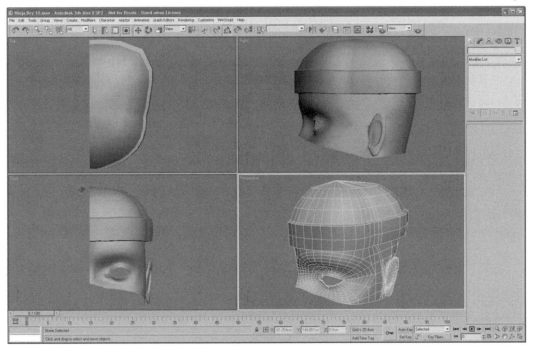

Figure 7.55 Extrude the edges to form the top of the head.

6. At the very top of the head, merge the vertices to a single vertex.

7. Now move to the bottom of the model and extrude the bottom edge outward to form the upper ledge of the mask, as shown in Figure 7.56.

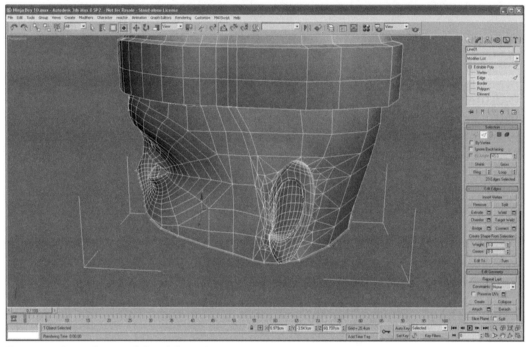

Figure 7.56 Create the upper ledge of the mask.

8. Several vertices will not line up accurately with the centerline. Adjust these vertices by selecting them all and using the Make Planer/X, as shown in Figure 7.57.

Now that you have the top of the head modeled, all you need to do is to continue downward to finish the model. The next section will cover modeling the bottom of the face and the torso using shapes and patches again.

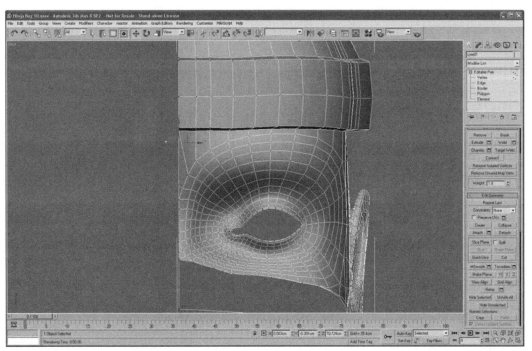

Figure 7.57 Snap vertices to the centerline.

Lofting the Head and Torso

The model is now ready for finishing the face and neck. In this section, you will use shapes and patch surfaces to construct the model. The shapes will allow for greater modeling flexibility than extruding polygons.

1. With the edge selected, choose Create Shape From Selection (see Figure 7.58). This will create a perfect shape that matches the face and will give you a great starting point to create the mask and neck.
2. Exit Sub Object mode and select the newly created shape.
3. Enter Vertex Sub Object mode and delete several of the vertices, as shown in Figure 7.59. You won't need the extra resolution for this example; the patch surface will be more manageable without it.

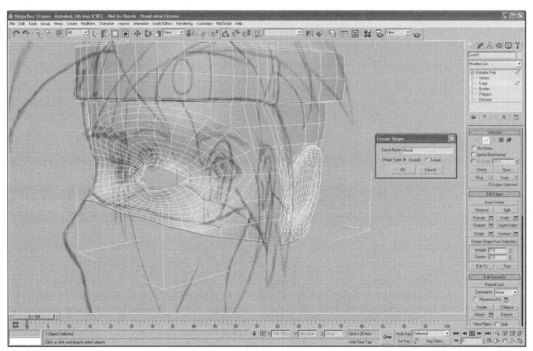

Figure 7.58 Draw a shape along the lower edge.

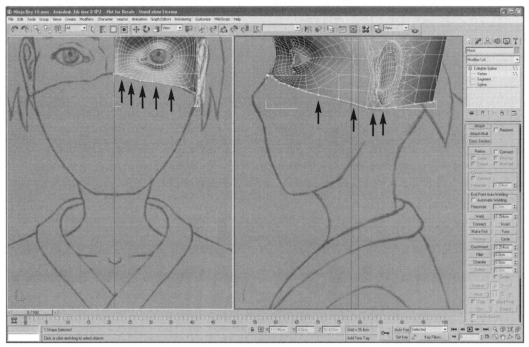

Figure 7.59 Select the shape you will use to create the mask and neck.

4. Select all the vertices in the shape and change their type to Smooth by right-clicking and choosing Smooth.

5. Switch to Spline Sub Object mode and, using the Shift key, clone the shape and adjust it as you move down the mask, as shown in Figure 7.60. You may want to switch from the isometric views (Front/Right) to the Perspective view occasionally so you can check the shape and make adjustments.

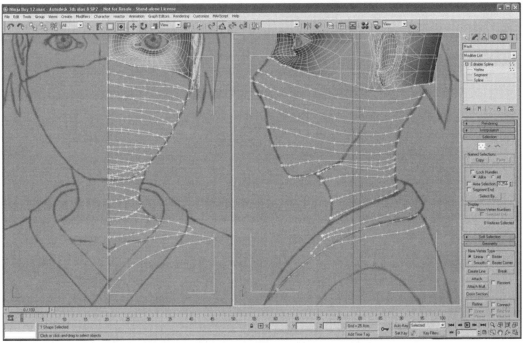

Figure 7.60 Create the shape of the mask and neck by cloning the shapes.

6. Once you have all the cross sections in place, use the Cross Section tool and starting from the top, work your way down the shapes forming the lattice for the mask/neck. Use Figure 7.61 as a guide for your modeling.

7. Once you have the lattice, switch to Vertex Sub Object mode and select all the vertices. Right-click on one of the selected vertices and choose Smooth.

8. Exit Sub Object mode and add the Edit Patch modifier to the stack. Adjust Threshold and Flip Normals so it looks correct. Set View Steps to 1.

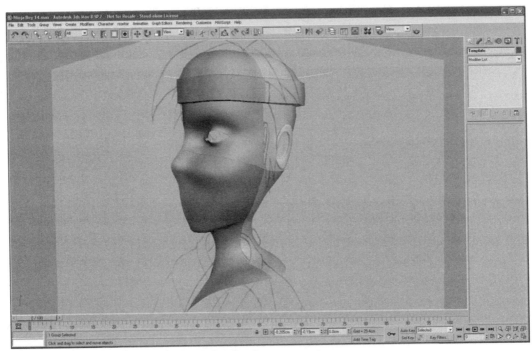

Figure 7.61 The final patch model for the mask and neck.

9. Jump back down the stack and enter Vertex Sub Object mode on the Editable Spline modifier. Toggle the Show End Results on.

10. Using the marquee, select the two vertices that make up each cross section of the lattice and edit them so the mask and neck look correct. It can take some time to get the mask and neck looking good, but keep at it.

11. Collapse the stack twice on the mask so you get to Editable Poly. Using the Attach command, click on the head object so the two models merge into one.

12. The vertices created with the shape will not be exactly the same as those of the upper lip of the mask because you have deleted some and adjusted the mesh resolution. You will need to Target Weld the vertices together to get a closed and complete seam, as shown in Figure 7.62. It may help to select the mask and move it down ever so slightly to open the seam a little bit so you can clearly see the vertices that need to be welded.

13. Adjust any last vertices so your head looks great.

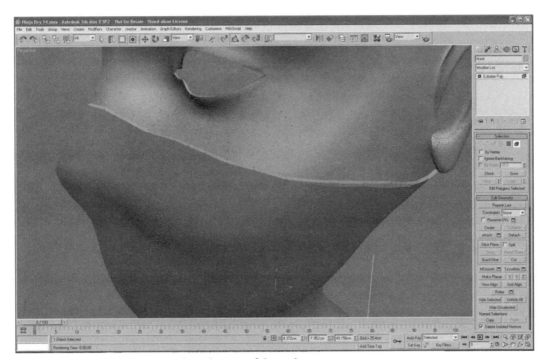

Figure 7.62 Target Weld the vertices along the seam of the mask.

14. Next, you are going to create the character's outfit (gi). Start by selecting an edge from the bottom shape and clicking the Loop button. This should select the entire bottom edge of the neck. Click on the Create Shape From Selection and hit OK on the resulting dialog box.

15. Exit Sub Object mode on the head, select the new shape, enter Vertex Sub Object mode, delete every other vertex, select all the vertices, change their type to Smooth, switch to Spline Sub Object mode, select the spline, clone the spline, move the spline to the top inside of the collar, and adjust vertices so the spline matches the collar in the Front and Side views, as shown in Figure 7.63.

16. Continue to clone and adjust the shapes and build the cross sections of the collar, as shown in Figure 7.64.

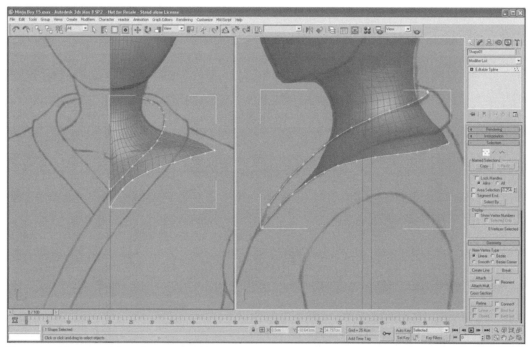

Figure 7.63 The start of the collar cross sections.

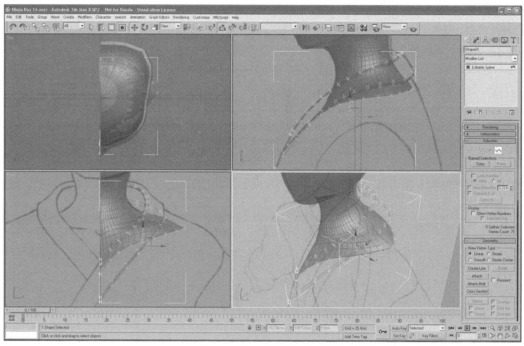

Figure 7.64 Create the collar of the gi.

17. Continue to clone the shape and build outward toward the character's shoulder, as shown in Figure 7.65.

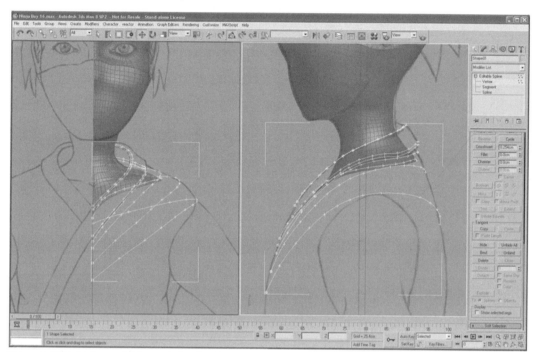

Figure 7.65 Build the model down to the shoulder.

18. Build the torso down to the belt, as shown in Figure 7.66.

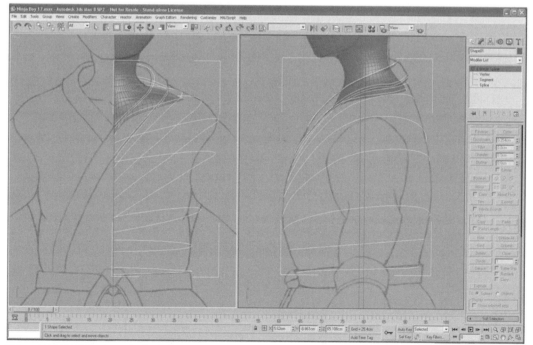

Figure 7.66 Build the torso to the belt.

19. Continue down the character, creating first the belt and then the rest of the gi. Use Figure 7.67 as a guide to how the gi should look when finished. The last shape will be up under the gi. This is where the pants will start.

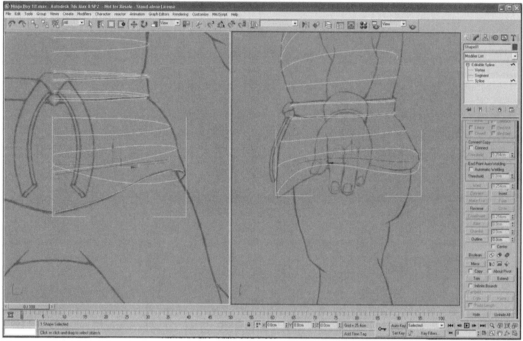

Figure 7.67 Finish building the gi.

20. Continue to build the pelvis and the area where the leg connects. Pull the vertices on the last shape around the top inside of the leg (the crotch area), as shown in Figure 7.68. This is where the leg will later join the body.

21. Using the Cross Section tool, turn the shapes into a lattice for the patch surface.

22. Select all the vertices and set them to Smooth by using the right-click menu.

23. Exit Sub Object mode, add the Edit Patch modifier on the stack, and adjust the Threshold/Normals so the model shows up correctly, as shown in Figure 7.69.

24. Move around your newly created object and adjust any vertices that look out of place. Remember, it's easier to do this by going back down the stack to the Editable Spline modifier and, with Show End Results toggled, adjusting vertices. Don't forget that each vertex is really two stacked on top of each other, so use the marquee to grab and move both vertices at once.

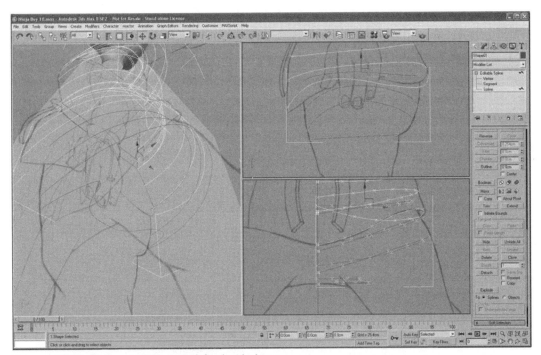

Figure 7.68 The pelvis area of the pants defined with shapes.

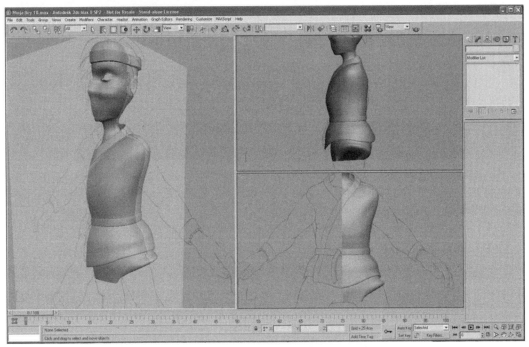

Figure 7.69 The gi patch surface model.

25. Once you're happy with the results, collapse the stack to Editable Patch and set View Steps to 0, as shown in Figure 7.70. It will have some funny shading, but fear not—once you convert it to polygons later, it will shade correctly.

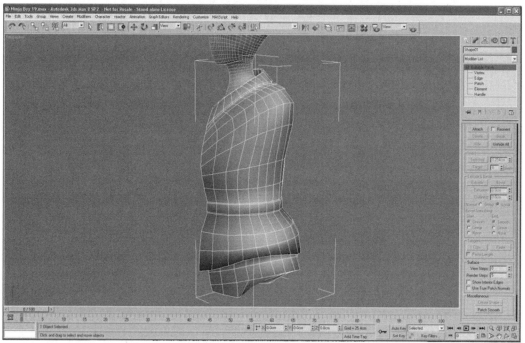

Figure 7.70 Setting the mesh density for later polygon conversion and editing.

The basic shape for the torso is now complete. Later, you will need to make adjustments where the gi overlaps, but that will come after the object is mirrored.

Building the Arms and Legs

For the most part, the arms and legs of the character are cylindrical. You will continue to use patch surfaces to create cylindrical shapes that will later be converted to polygons and attached to the model.

1. Using the Front and Side views, draw a circle shape about the size of the shoulder joint and rotate it into place, as shown in Figure 7.71.

2. With the circle shape selected, collapse the stack to Editable Spline.

3. In Spline Sub Object mode, clone the shapes down the arm as shown and adjust each shape as you go, switching between Vertex and Spline Sub Object modes. These will stay as Bezier curves for more precise editing.

4. Use the Cross Section tool to form the lattice for the patch surface. Add the Edit Patch modifier to the stack and adjust the Threshold/Normals so it shows up correctly, as shown in Figure 7.72. Collapse the stack to Editable Patch.

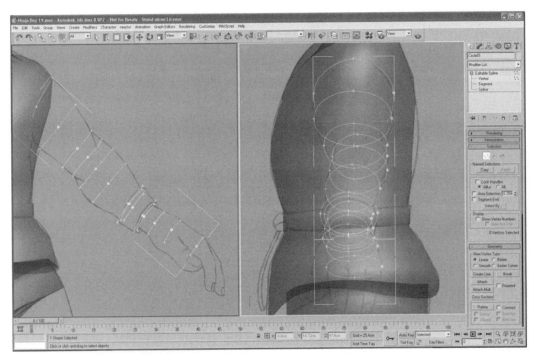

Figure 7.71 Cross sections for the arm.

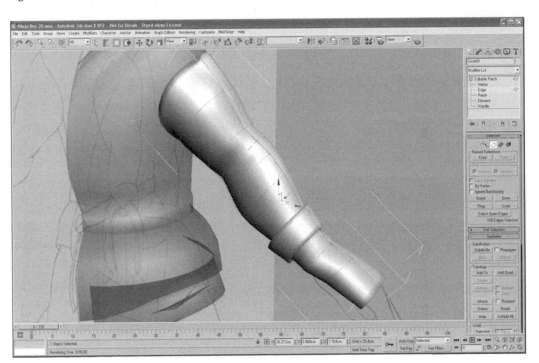

Figure 7.72 The patch surface arm.

5. Move around the arm and adjust vertices so the arm looks correct, as shown in Figure 7.73.

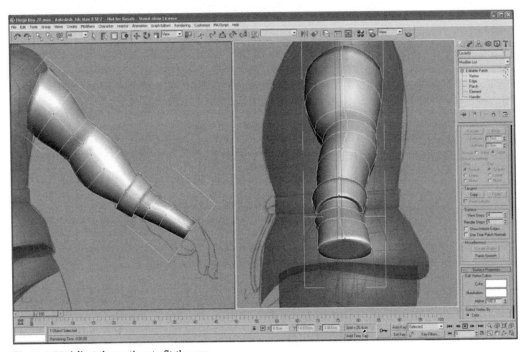

Figure 7.73 Adjust the vertices to fit the arm.

6. Now set View Steps to 1 (see Figure 7.74) so when you convert to polygons, the mesh won't be too dense.

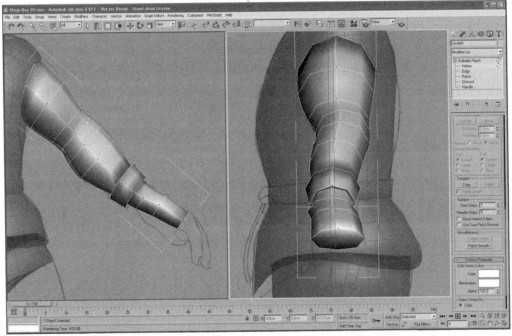

Figure 7.74 Set View Steps for conversion to polygons.

7. Collapse the stack to Editable Poly. The result should look like that shown in Figure 7.75.

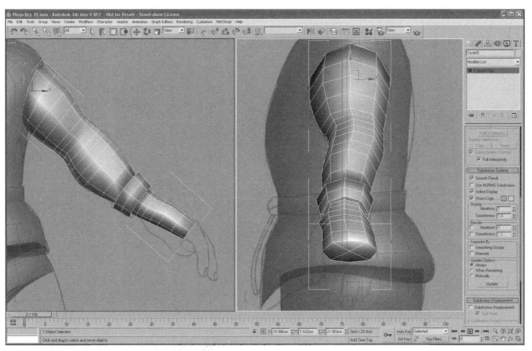

Figure 7.75 Convert the patch surface to polygons.

8. Follow the same process for the leg. Using the Front and Side views, draw a circle shape about the size of the leg joint and rotate it into place, as shown in Figure 7.76.

9. With the circle shape selected, collapse the stack to Editable Spline.

10. Enter Spline Sub Object mode and clone the shape down the arm as shown, adjusting each shape as you go.

11. Use the Cross Section tool to form the lattice for the patch surface. Add the Edit Patch modifier to the stack and adjust the Threshold/Normals so the newly formed patches show up correctly, as shown in Figure 7.77. Collapse the stack to Editable Patch.

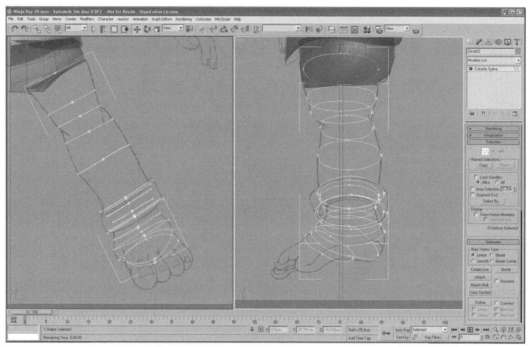

Figure 7.76 Add the leg cross sections.

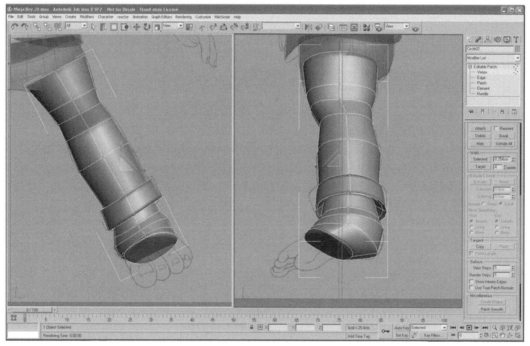

Figure 7.77 Add the patch surface.

12. Move around the leg and adjust vertices so it looks correct, as shown in Figure 7.78.

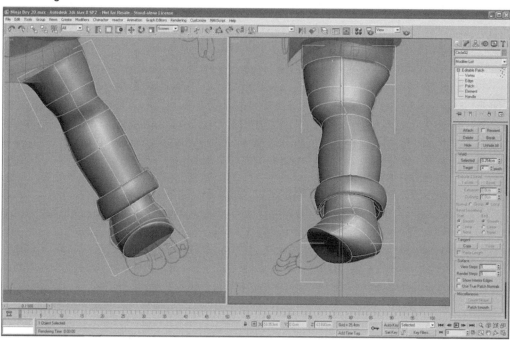

Figure 7.78 Edit the vertices so the leg and heel look good.

13. Now set View Steps to 1 (see Figure 7.79) so when you convert to polygons the mesh won't be too dense.

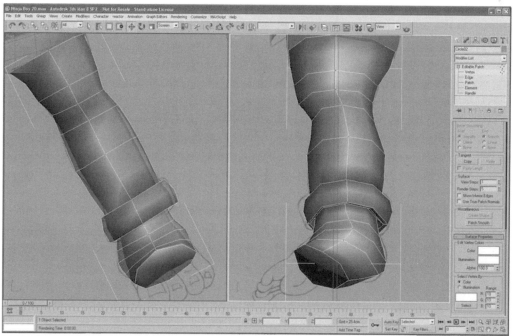

Figure 7.79 Set View Steps to 1.

14. Collapse the stack to Editable Poly. The result should look like that shown in Figure 7.80.

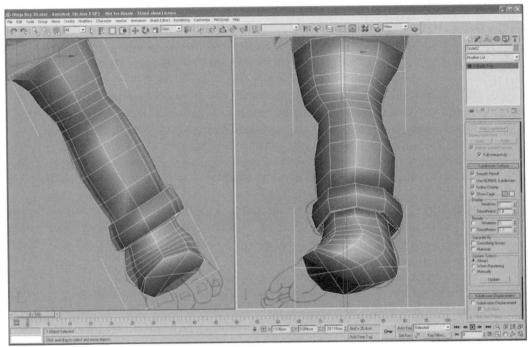

Figure 7.80 The character is now ready for a foot.

15. Zoom out and take a look at your ninja so far (see Figure 7.81).

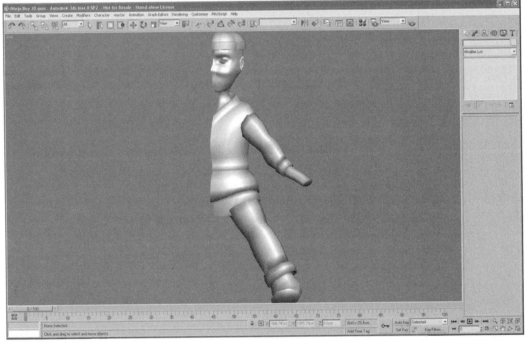

Figure 7.81 Your character so far.

Okay, you are getting close to having a finished character. Hang in there. You only have a few more things to do, like making hands, feet, and a few other items.

Creating the Hands and the Feet

The character is a cartoon character, so we will be using the cartoon standard three-fingered hand (plus thumb) and four-toed foot. Go to the area of the hand first. You will use subdivision modeling to create the thumb and fingers, which will be similar to the monster hand but not nearly as detailed.

1. Toggle the Use NURMS Subdivision box and make sure Iterations is set to 1. Select four polygon faces on the side of the palm and extrude them outward, as shown in Figure 7.82.

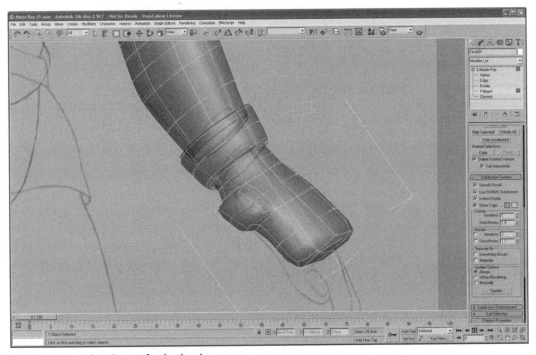

Figure 7.82 Extrude polygons for the thumb.

2. Hide or turn the body to See-Through so you can see the template. Move and/or Target Weld the vertices of the extrusion to fit the contour of the base of the thumb, as shown in Figure 7.83.

3. Extrude the polygon faces of the base of the thumb to form the thumb, similar to what you see in Figure 7.84. Use the Front and Side views to help define its shape. You will need to extrude the faces several times and adjust the vertices after each extrusion.

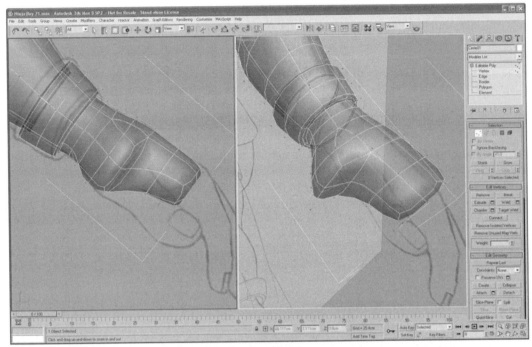

Figure 7.83 Adjust the vertices on the base of the thumb and hand.

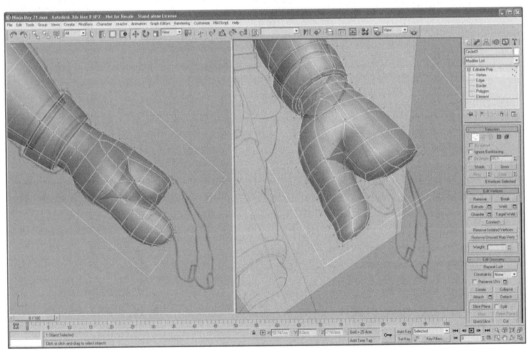

Figure 7.84 Create the thumb by extruding faces from the base.

4. Select the polygons at the base of the fingers, as shown in Figure 7.85. Delete the selected polygons.

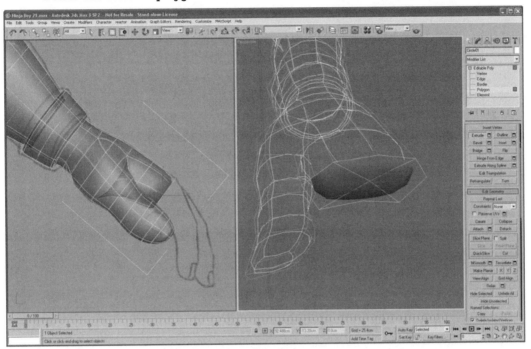

Figure 7.85 Select and delete the polygons at the base of the fingers.

5. Rebuild the polygons using the Create menu in Polygon Sub Object mode. This is best done by creating the polygons in a counterclockwise vertex selection and double-clicking on the final vertex, as shown in Figure 7.86.

6. Once you have the polygons created and selected, use the Tessellate button to get something that looks like what you see in Figure 7.87.

7. Select the area that you are going to extrude for the first finger.

8. Extrude and shape the finger, as shown in Figure 7.88.

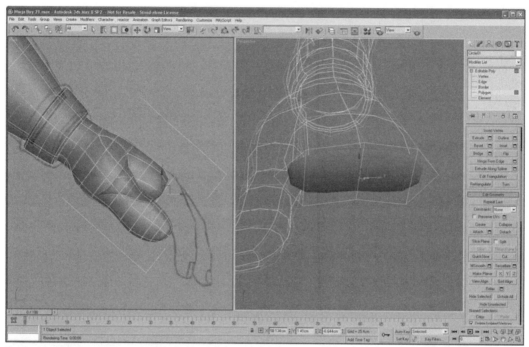

Figure 7.86 Rebuild the base of the fingers.

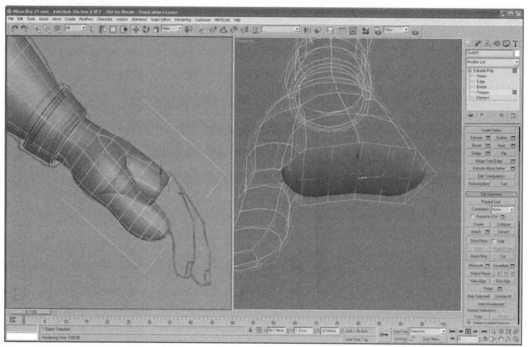

Figure 7.87 Tessellate the selection.

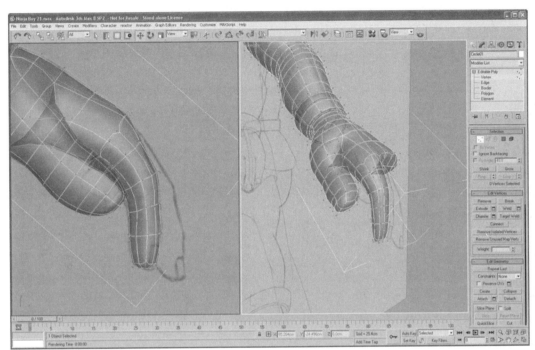

Figure 7.88 Extrude the first finger.

9. Extrude the second finger.

10. Finally, create the third finger in the same way that you did the first and second fingers. Your result should look similar to that shown in Figure 7.89.

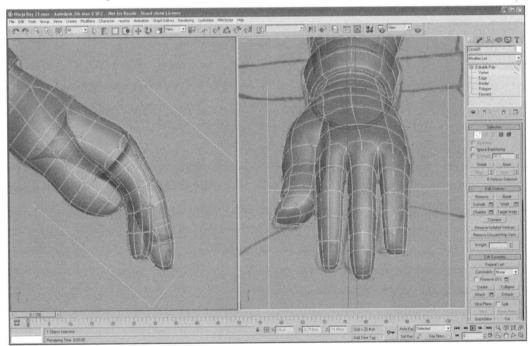

Figure 7.89 Extrude the third finger.

11. Adjust any last vertices for aesthetics before you convert the arm model to its final state (see Figure 7.90).

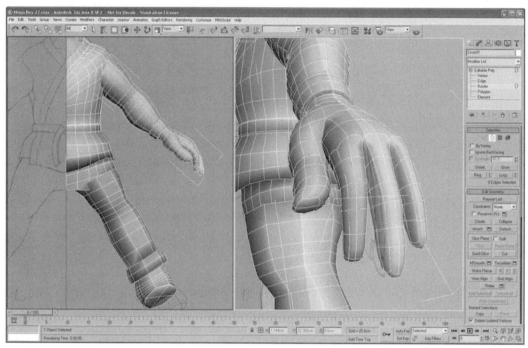

Figure 7.90 Make any last adjustments.

12. Collapse the stack to Editable Poly, as shown in Figure 7.91.

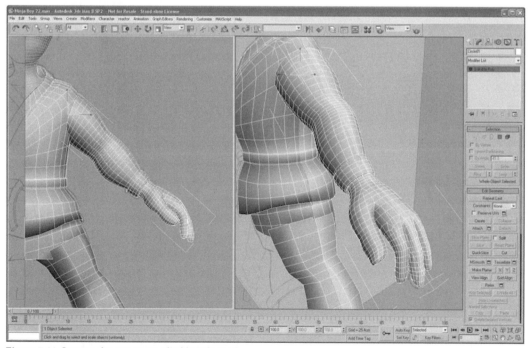

Figure 7.91 Convert the arm to an editable poly mesh.

13. Do the same thing for the foot and toes. Toggle the Use NURMS Subdivision box and set Iterations to 1.

14. Use the Create tool to rebuild the end of the foot, as shown in Figure 7.92. (Rebuild polygons in a counterclockwise order.)

15. Use the Cut tool to make a cut horizontally across the front of the foot, again as shown in Figure 7.92.

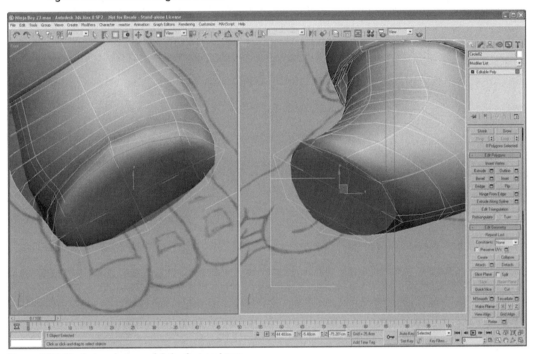

Figure 7.92 The leg ready to model the foot and toes.

16. Now extrude and shape the foot and toes, adjusting the points as you go so the toes will be easy to create when you get there. Figure 7.93 shows the finished foot after the toes are completed. Collapse the stack to Editable Poly when you are happy with the leg and foot.

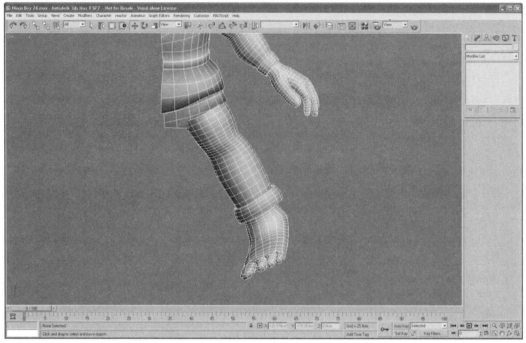

Figure 7.93 Extrude the toes of the foot.

The character is starting to take shape. He is almost to the stage where he can be mirrored to form the other half.

Attaching and Smoothing

Before the character can be mirrored, you will need to attach the legs and the arms to the torso. Also, you should do some smoothing to blend the attached areas.

1. Make sure all geometry is collapsed to Editable Mesh or Poly.
2. Select all of the geometry and combine it into one polygon object. This is done by selecting one of the parts and using the Attach button.
3. Select the torso in Element Sub Object mode and use the Tessellate button so the mesh more closely matches the arm and leg resolution, as shown in Figure 7.94.
4. Where the arm and shoulder join, delete the unneeded faces of the shoulder, as shown in Figure 7.95. You will not be able to Target Weld vertices to a surface. I have hidden most of the arm so I could get to the polygons on the torso.

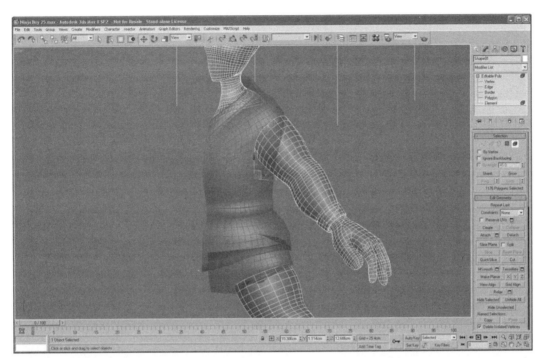

Figure 7.94 Subdivide the torso.

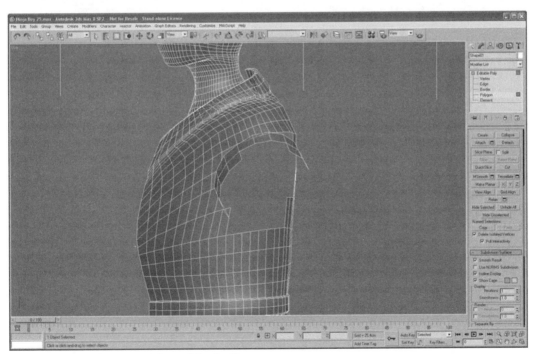

Figure 7.95 Delete the unneeded faces of the shoulder.

5. Target Weld the vertices of the arm to the corresponding vertices of the shoulder. Note that in a few cases where there are more arm vertices than shoulder vertices, you may need to snap two of the arm vertices to one vertex on the shoulder. You may also want to adjust a few vertices on the arm and shoulder for more continuity.

6. Hide most of the leg.

7. Delete the selected polygons where the leg joins the crotch area, as shown in Figure 7.96.

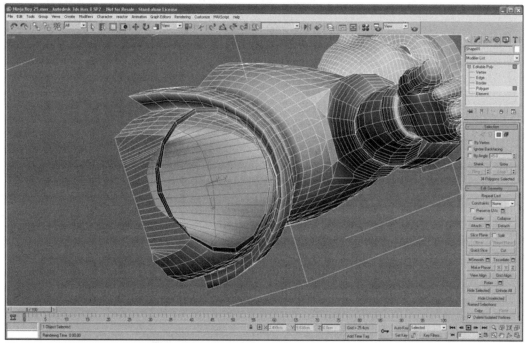

Figure 7.96 Remove some of the polygons in the crotch area to join with the leg.

8. Join the leg to the torso in the same way you did the arm and torso by Target Welding the vertices to the torso and then adjusting the leg and pelvis area.

9. Merge the vertices of the leg and torso, as shown in Figure 7.97.

10. Select all the polygons in the model and click the Clear SG, and then the Auto Smooth button, as shown in Figure 7.98.

11. Go back and select all the areas that you want to have a hard edge, as shown in Figure 7.99.

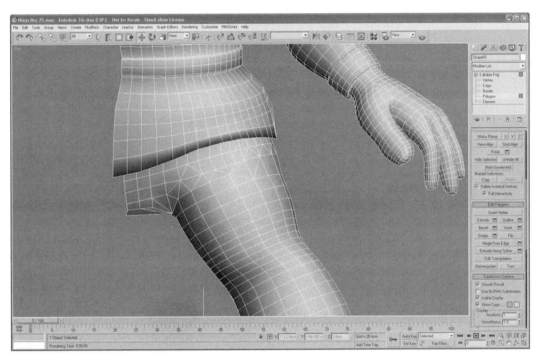

Figure 7.97 Join the torso and leg vertices.

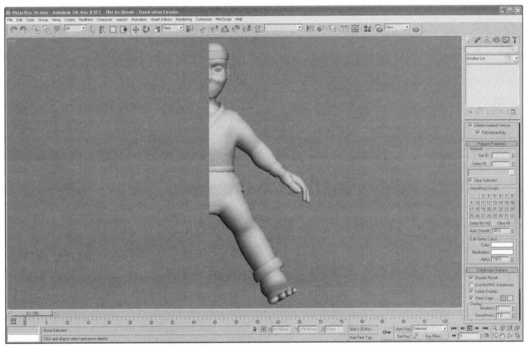

Figure 7.98 Smooth the normals of the model.

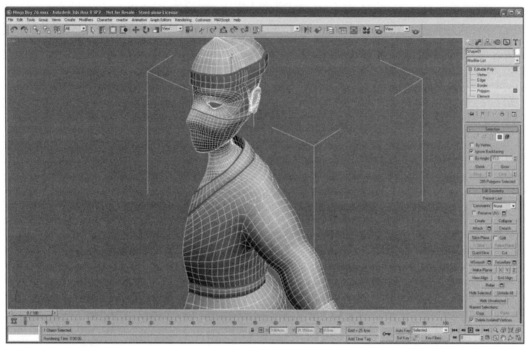

Figure 7.99 Select the hard edges.

> **12.** Uncheck the assigned smoothing group(s) and check an unused group and you will have hard edges.

You now have a finished half of your character model. If this character were completely symmetrical, you would just need to mirror the model and you would be finished. This character, however, has differences between sides, so you will have to build those areas after mirroring.

Mirroring the Model

Before you mirror your model, you should double-check the vertices along the centerline to make sure they are all snapped to that line, as shown in Figure 7.100. Carefully select all the centerline vertices and use the X button (next to the Make Planar button). This will snap all the selected vertices to the X plane.

Exit Sub Object mode and use the Mirror tool. Adjust the offset so the two models meet perfectly in the middle.

You will now need to join the two models by welding the vertices, as shown in Figure 7.101. Make sure the models are aligned precisely; use the Attach button to join them to make one model.

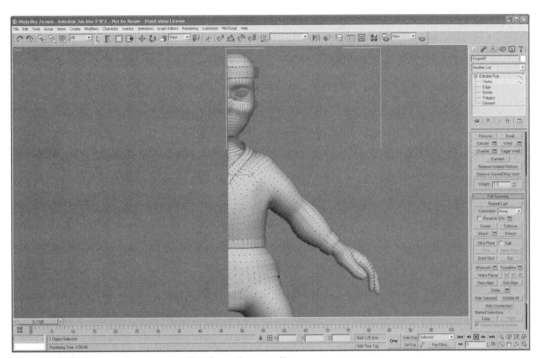

Figure 7.100 Make sure all vertices are directly on the centerline.

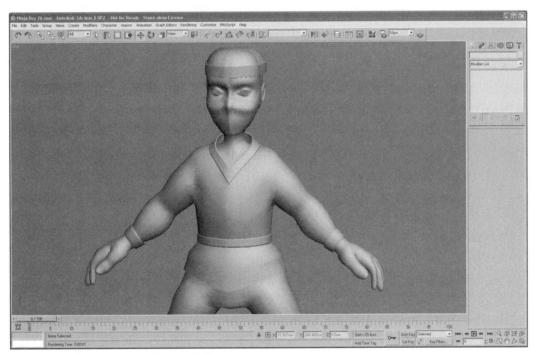

Figure 7.101 Weld the vertices of the two halves.

In Vertex Sub Object mode, select the centerline vertices again and use the Weld button. Make sure the Weld Threshold is small enough so you don't inadvertently weld nearby vertices. If you have seams, then you likely have an unwelded pair of vertices.

Adding Unique Geometry

Several areas of the character—like his hair and the gi—are not symmetrical. Now that you have both sides of the model, you are ready to create this geometry. We will start with the gi.

1. Create a line shape and fit it to the gi, as shown in Figure 7.102.
2. Select an edge on the gi's collar.

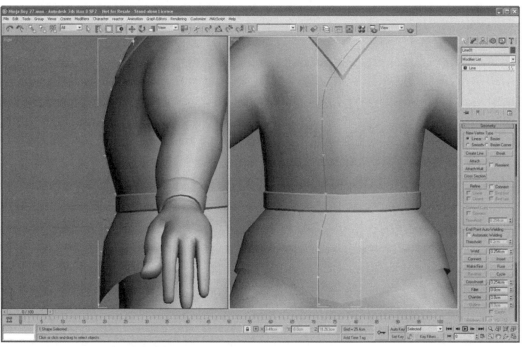

Figure 7.102 Create a path to loft with.

3. Use the Create Shape From Edge button, as shown in Figure 7.103.
4. Select the shape and go to the Hierarchy tab, as shown in Figure 7.104. Select Affect Pivot Only and click on Center to Object.
5. Select the line shape and loft the collar shape, as shown in Figure 7.105. Loft is found under the Create tab, Compound Objects. With the line shape selected, click on Loft, choose Get Shape, and click the collar shape. The initial loft will look odd, but it's easy to adjust.

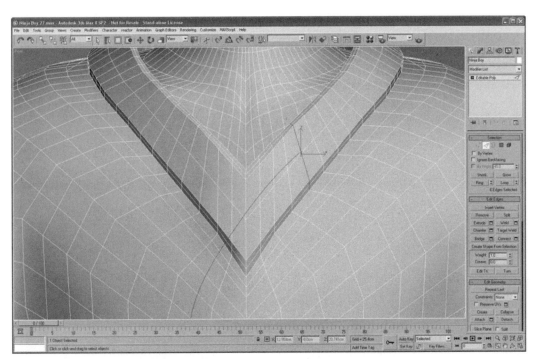

Figure 7.103 Create the shape from the collar.

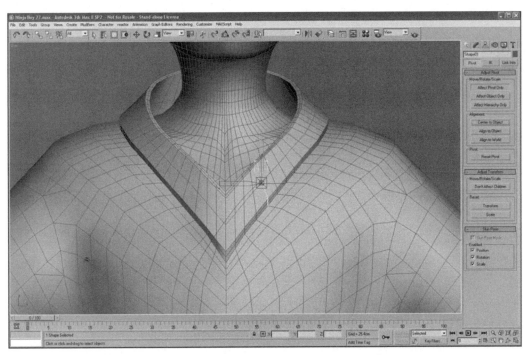

Figure 7.104 Center the pivot.

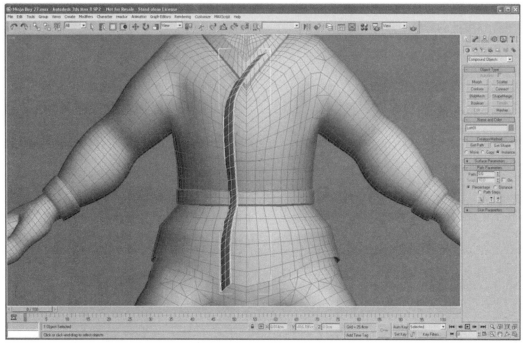

Figure 7.105 Loft the shape to form the edging of the gi.

6. With the loft selected and the Modify tab active, check the Path Steps box
and set Path to 5, as shown in Figure 7.106. Click Get Shape again and click
on the original collar shape you made. This will create another point along
the gi edging that you can edit.

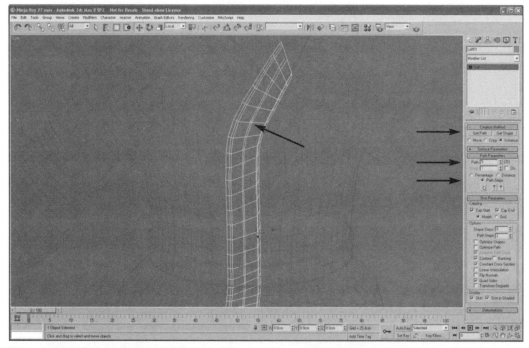

Figure 7.106 Add a second shape to define the edging.

7. It's also a good idea to set Shape Steps to 0 and Path Steps to 2. This will reduce the density a bit.

8. Enter Shape Sub Object mode and rotate each shape (the starting shape and the one you just added) into place, as shown in Figure 7.107. Exit Sub Object mode and select the line you used to create the edging. Enter Vertex Sub Object mode and edit the points so the edging lies against the gi correctly. Work back and forth between the loft shapes and the line to get this looking good.

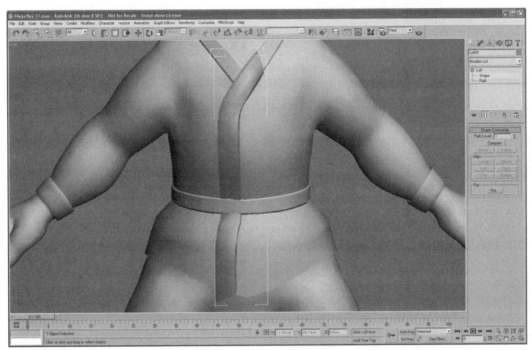

Figure 7.107 Rotate the shapes and adjust the path to fit the gi perfectly.

9. Collapse the stack to Editable Poly and use the Attach tool to combine the main model and the new edging, as shown in Figure 7.108.

10. Adjust the back edge of the edging to follow the gi's geometry, as shown in Figure 7.109.

11. Tweak vertices on the edging and gi to get the final look, as shown in Figure 7.110. Don't forget to square off the bottom on the edging and move the flap on the gi down for the correct look.

12. Create a polygon sphere for the belt knot. Set the number of segments to 8.

13. Place the sphere so it is in the belt, as shown in Figure 7.111.

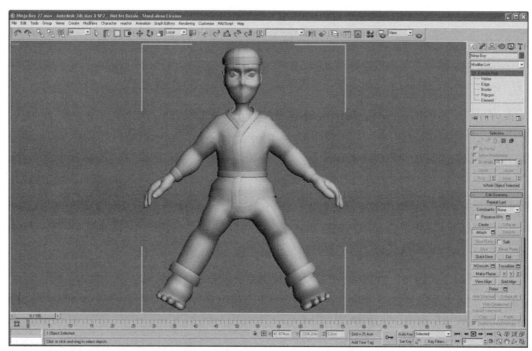

Figure 7.108 Collapse the stack and attach the edging.

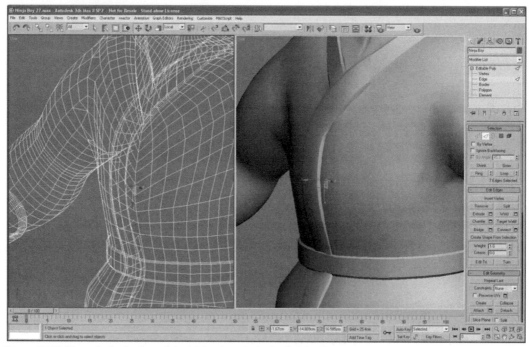

Figure 7.109 Move the back edges of the edging into the body slightly where needed.

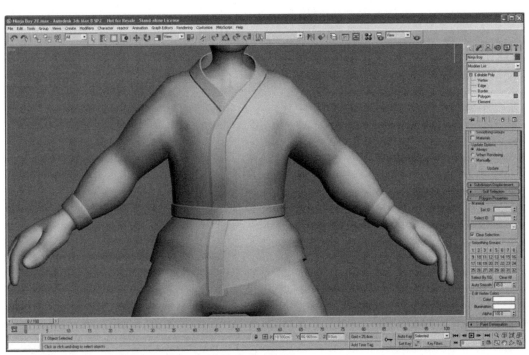

Figure 7.110 Adjust the gi's and edging vertices for a perfect fit.

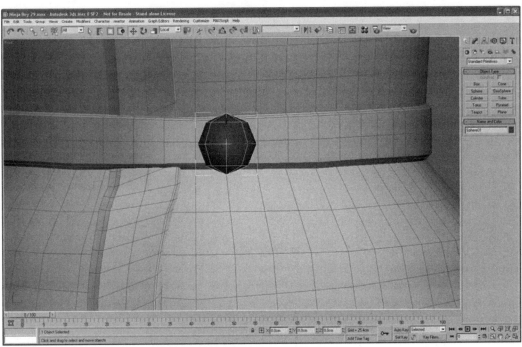

Figure 7.111 Move the sphere to the belt.

14. Extrude and scale the faces of the top of the sphere outward, as shown in Figure 7.112.

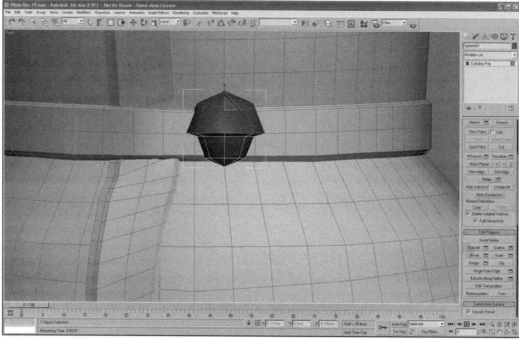

Figure 7.112 Extrude the top of the sphere.

15. Select two faces on the bottom of the sphere and extrude them, as shown in Figure 7.113.

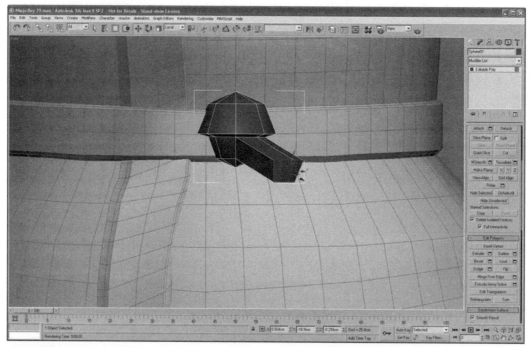

Figure 7.113 Extrude the belt from the knot.

16. Extrude the polygons to form the belt coming out of the knot, as shown in Figure 7.114.

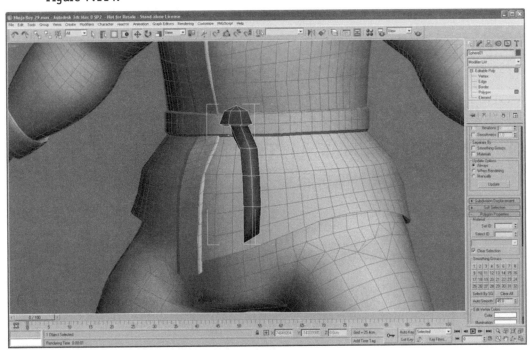

Figure 7.114 Create one side of the belt so it comes out of the knot.

17. Extrude the other side of the belt coming from the knot also, as shown in Figure 7.115.

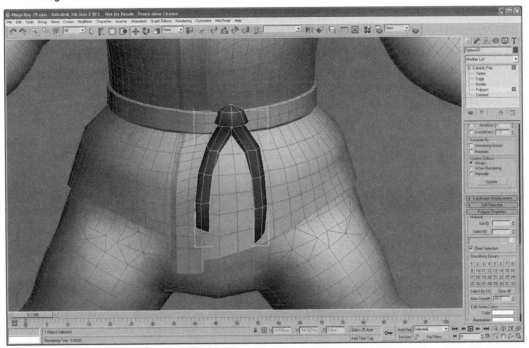

Figure 7.15 Extrude the other side of the belt.

18. Move to the character's eyes. You have not yet created the tear ducts. They need to be in place before you can add the eyeballs. Create the tear ducts by using the Create tool in Polygon Sub Object mode and "drawing" three- or four-sided polygons in a counterclockwise motion, as shown in Figure 7.116.

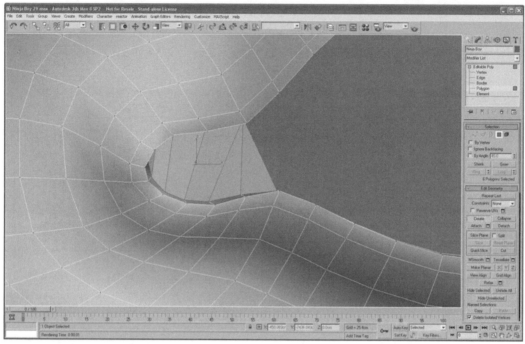

Figure 7.116 Create the tear ducts.

19. Create a polygon sphere about the size of an eye. Set Segments to 24.

20. Place the eyeball in the eye socket, as shown in Figure 7.117. You may need to adjust vertices of the eyelids and the eye size to get the eye to fit properly. Try doing this with Soft Selection. If you have to make big adjustments, you may want to delete half of the head, fit one side, and then remirror the head and reweld it.

21. Create a line and circle shape, as shown in Figure 7.118. These will be used to create the character's lock of hair. The line only needs about five segments or points along it.

22. With the line shape selected, use the Loft tool found under Create, Compound Objects. Click on the circle shape to create the hair. In the Modify tab, set Shape and Path Steps to 3. Using the Scale Deformer, create a line to scale the lock of hair down correctly, as shown in Figure 7.119.

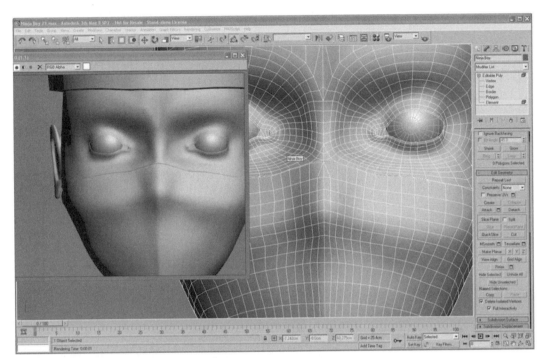

Figure 7.117 Place the eyeball in the eye socket.

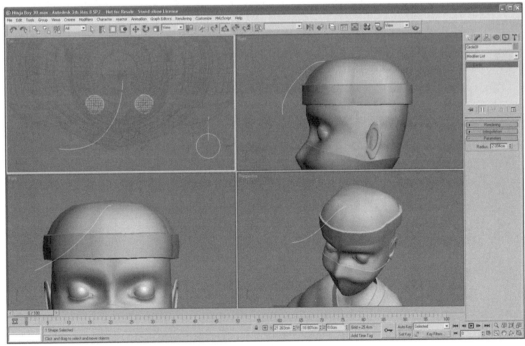

Figure 7.118 The circle and line shapes for lofting.

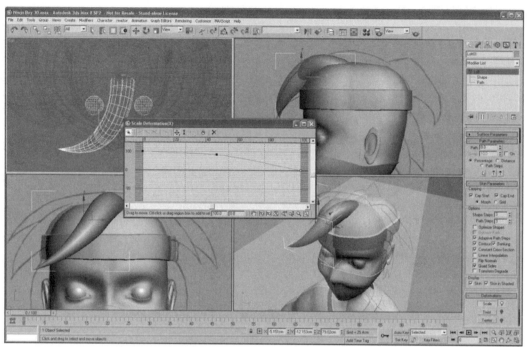

Figure 7.119 Turn the shapes into a lock of hair.

23. This character has wild hair, so clone the loft and randomly place locks of hair around his head and in the back of the head beneath the headband (see Figure 7.120). You can edit each lock on the Sub Object level for size, shape, and scale.

24. Convert the lofts into Editable Polys when you're happy with the hairstyle.

You're done! You have just completed building the geometry for the character. Your finished model should look similar to the model in Figure 7.120.

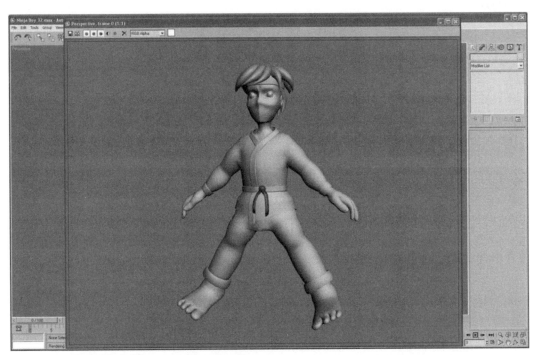

Figure 7.120 The finished character model.

Summary

Well, it was a long process, but I hope you hung in there and created a model. You will need the model for the next chapter, where we will cover texturing and rigging the character.

In this chapter, you created a character using a number of techniques, including the following:

- Patch modeling
- Polygon modeling
- Patches to polygons
- Lofting along splines
- Shapes and curves
- Mirroring polygons

The methods you used for creating the model varied greatly so that you could get some experience using Max's many features for blending patches and polygon-modeling techniques. As mentioned in the beginning of the book, there are many ways to create a character model. Hopefully, you can use what you learned in this chapter to find your own favorite way to create your characters.

Chapter 8

Color and Movement

Building the model is only the beginning of creating a character in a 3D program. In this chapter, you will continue to work on the character model you created in Chapter 7, giving him textures and getting him ready to animate. In the texturing process, you will explore concepts used in texturing human characters. You will also learn about building skeletal systems for the animation of a character and, finally, how to attach a skeletal system to a model.

Adding Color

The process of texturing a human character can often be very complex. The greater the number of UVs, the more intricate the process. Maya has various tools that help to make this job much easier.

One of the most difficult aspects of texturing a human character is dealing with the problem of overlapping UVs. For example, the geometry for the ear will often overlap with the rest of the head. One way to deal with this problem is to go into the UV Texture Editor and move the UVs by hand. This process may be fine for a simple or low-polygon character, but with larger, more complex characters, you may get the feeling that you are unraveling a bowl of spaghetti. An easy way to avoid this problem is to deal with the overlapping before you map your character.

Removing Overlapping UVs

Maya has a nifty little feature where you can transfer UVs from one model to another, as long as both models have exactly the same number of vertices. You will be using this feature to help solve the overlapping UV problem. Make a duplicate of your model and move the duplicate model forward, as shown in Figure 8.1.

Figure 8.1 Create a duplicate model to work on.

The advantage of working on the duplicate model is that you can move the vertices so they are not overlapping before you apply the texture maps, and when you are finished, you can transfer the UVs back to the original model. This gives you the freedom to adjust the vertices for optimum mapping while not destroying the work you went to in creating the model in the first place.

1. Once you have your duplicate, change the selection mode to Vertex and select the vertices of the ear, as shown in Figure 8.2.

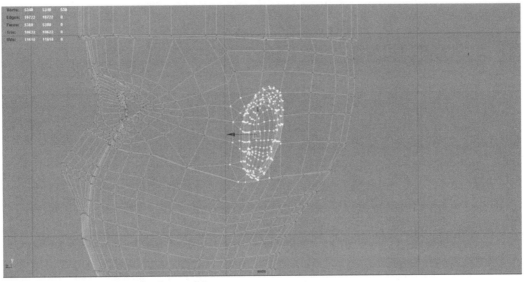

Figure 8.2 Select the vertices of and around the ear.

2. Go to the Polygon Average Vertices Options box in the Mesh menu. You can set Iterations to any number you choose. I like to use the tool in increments of 10 because it allows me to better judge how much averaging is needed. Click the Apply button multiple times until all of the overlapping vertices are gone. The function averages the distance between vertices, spreading them out and removing overlaps. Figure 8.3 shows the ear once the overlapping vertices are removed.

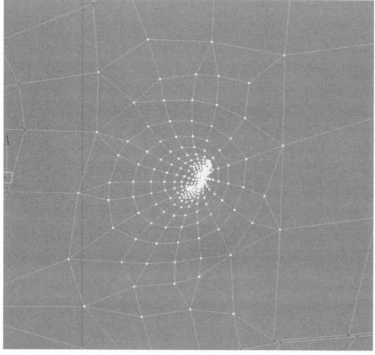

Figure 8.3 Apply the function until all overlapping is removed.

3. When you are finished with the ear, select all of the vertices of the head and neck. Apply the Average Vertices function to them a couple of times to ensure that there are no overlapping vertices.

4. Now the head and neck are ready for mapping. I like to use the Cylindrical Projection mapping tool for heads that are prepared in this way. The tool is located in the Create UVs menu. Figure 8.4 shows the tool in use on the head.

5. Once you have mapped the head and neck, you will need to go into the UV Texture Editor and adjust the UVs a little around the top of the head. Change the left panel to the UV Texture Editor by selecting it from Panel in the Panels menu. Figure 8.5 shows how I have adjusted the UVs.

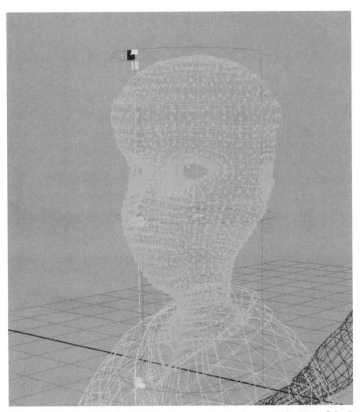

Figure 8.4 Use the Cylindrical Projection mapping tool to map the UVs of the head and neck.

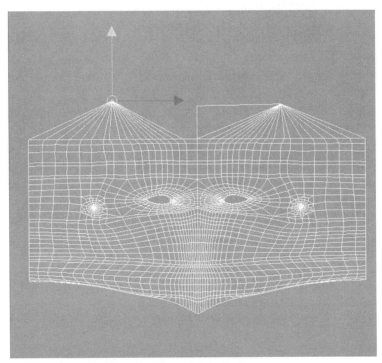

Figure 8.5 Adjust the UVs around the top of the head.

6. Move the UVs of the head off to the side by themselves so they are not on top of the UVs of the rest of the character.

Note

Mapping UVs is mainly a task of organizing them so that you can create textures for the character in a 2D paint program. It helps if the mapping is something that you can recognize when you bring up the templates in a 2D program. By using the cylindrical map for the head, I created a map in which it appears as if the UVs were unwrapped and laid out in a flat plane. I can see how they form a head. This helps me when painting the textures.

Mapping the Hands and Feet

The hands and feet are also complex parts of the body and have the potential for many overlapping UVs. Using a cylindrical mapping technique on the hand will not work very well unless you want to do every finger individually. Instead, I use a planar mapping technique to map the UVs of the hand.

1. Start by selecting the top half of the UVs of the hand and using the Polygon Planar Projection tool found in the Create UVs menu to apply the map, as shown in Figure 8.6. Note that the tool is set to Fit to Best Plane. Because of the organic nature and position of the hand, it is not easily mapped from a cardinal direction.

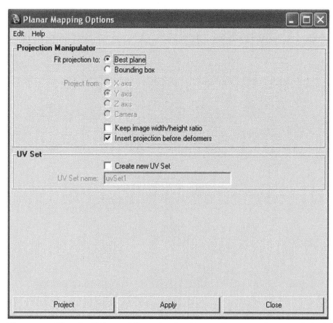

Figure 8.6 Use the Polygon Planar Projection tool to map the top of the hand.

2. Some of the UVs of the hand are overlapping. Move the UVs so they are flattened out with no overlapping areas, as shown in Figure 8.7.

3. Now select all of the UVs for the bottom of the hand. Map and lay out the UVs of the bottom similar to how you did the top of the hand. Take a look at Figure 8.9 to see how I mapped mine.

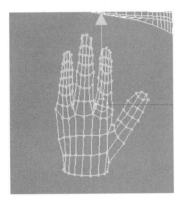

Figure 8.7 Move the UVs to remove any overlapping areas.

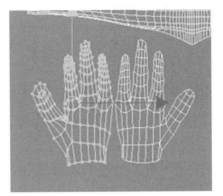

Figure 8.8 Map the bottom of the hand.

4. You will need to repeat the process for the character's other hand. When you are done, your UVs should look similar to what you see in Figure 8.9.

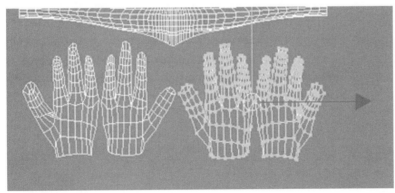

Figure 8.9 Map the UVs of the other hand as well.

Next, you will need to map the UVs of the foot. The foot is a little harder to map because it is not a flat plane like the hand and will have a number of overlapping UVs that will have to be adjusted.

1. First, select the faces of the top of the foot and use the Polygon Planar Projection tool to map the foot, as shown in Figure 8.10.

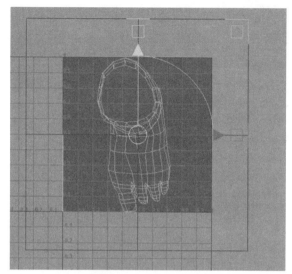

Figure 8.10 Map the UVs of the top of the foot.

2. Move the mapped UVs off to the side and unravel the overlapping UVs, as shown in Figure 8.11.

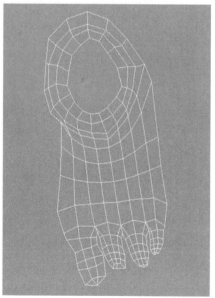

Figure 8.11 Organize the UVs of the upper foot.

Note

When you are unraveling overlapping UVs, it is important to try to maintain the general size and shape of the UVs to match the polygons of the area that you are mapping. This will help you to avoid texture stretching, which can happen when the UVs are distorted.

3. Like the hand, you will also need to map and lay out the bottom of the foot. Remember to look for any overlapping UVs.

4. Place the bottom and top of the foot together off to the side.

5. Go to the other foot and repeat the process to create mapped UVs for that foot as well.

The head, hands, and feet are now mapped and ready to have a texture applied to them. To help organize my work, I will often go ahead and apply a texture to the mapped sections that share the same texture file. This helps me to see the progress I am making with the model. When everything on the model is colored, I know that I have finished the mapping process.

Create a skin-colored texture in a paint program. Although you obviously can't see the color shade in Figure 8.12, you can see that I'm starting with a single-colored texture.

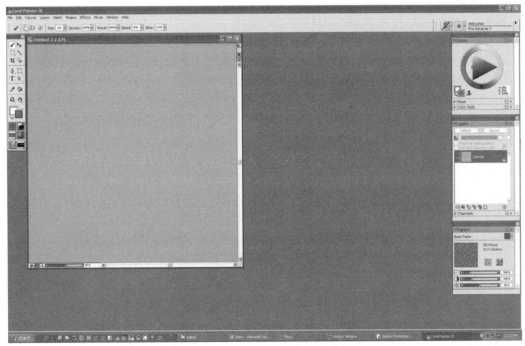

Figure 8.12 Create a skin-colored texture.

While the head will not all be flesh tones, leave it for now with the flesh-colored texture. I will show you how to separate the head's UVs later.

Create a new material in Hypershade for the flesh texture and apply the texture to the mapped UVs, as shown in Figure 8.13. Now you can easily see the areas that are not yet mapped.

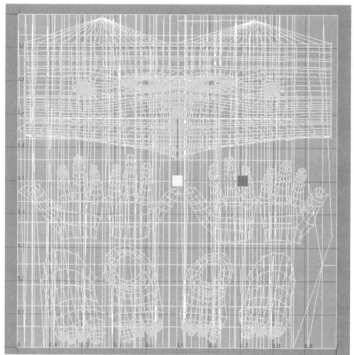

Figure 8.13 Apply the flesh material to the model.

Mapping the Uniform

The next part of the mapping process will be to map the character's uniform. The uniform is made up of several parts: the borders, which will be red; the belt, which will be black; and the rest of the uniform, which will be white. You will map each of these parts of the uniform separately.

It is easier to work on the uniform if it is isolated from the rest of the model using the Isolate Selected option in the Show menu of the Panel menu. An easy way to select all of the unmapped faces is to select the flesh material in Hypershade and then go to Select Objects in Shading Group in the marking menu to select all of the faces that you have already mapped. Make sure the selection mode is Faces, and then while holding down the Shift key, drag a selection box over the entire model. This will reverse the selection; now you should have all of the nonmapped faces selected. You can now use the Isolate Selected option to see only those faces.

Now you are ready to map the uniform, so let's get started.

1. Begin by creating three new materials: red for the borders, black for the belt, and white for the uniform. To give the materials more of a matte look, make them Lambert materials instead of Blinns. If you like, you can add a subtle weave surface to the texture maps.

2. Now it is just a matter of selecting the right faces and applying the materials to those faces. This becomes easier because you isolated the faces of the uniform. Start with the borders and apply the red material to those areas. In Figure 8.14 I show the border areas isolated and mapped with the red material.

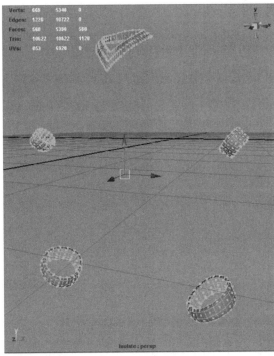

Figure 8.14 Map the border with the red material.

3. Next, you need to organize the UVs of the mapped areas. Start with the cuff on the sleeve and use a cylindrical map, as shown in Figure 8.15.

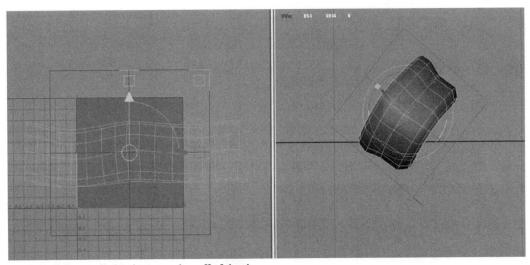

Figure 8.15 Use a cylindrical map on the cuff of the sleeve.

4. Scale the UVs of the mapped cuff and move them to the side.

5. Apply cylindrical maps to the other sleeve cuff and both cuffs on the pants. Scale each one and move them to the side.

6. Use a planar map for the collar, as shown in Figure 8.16.

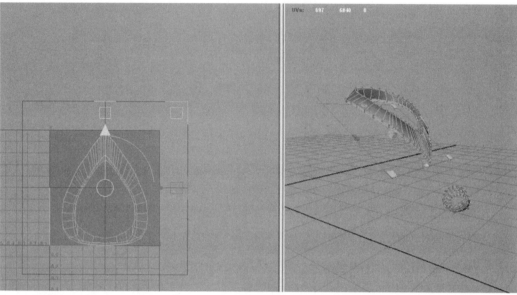

Figure 8.16 Use a planar map on the collar.

7. Scale the collar UVs down and move them to the side with the cuff UVs, as shown in Figure 8.17. Some of the UVs of the collar will be overlapping and will need to be adjusted, as shown in the figure.

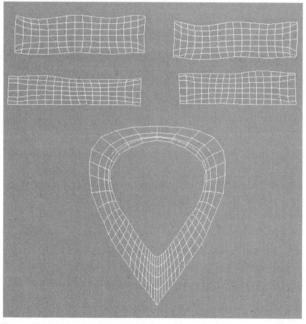

Figure 8.17 Organize the UVs of the uniform boarders.

8. Now isolate the faces of the main part of the uniform and apply the white material to those faces, as shown in Figure 8.18. Instead of individually applying cylindrical to other maps to the uniform, I simply use the Automatic Mapping option, as shown.

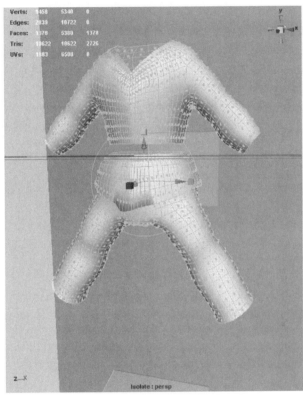

Figure 8.18 Give the uniform a white texture.

9. Mapping the belt is easy. All you need to do is select the faces of the belt and map them using the Cylindrical Mapping option.

You should now have all of the UVs of the proxy model mapped. Examine the model for any faces that you might have missed. They will be gray in color.

Now it is time to apply the mapped UVs of the proxy model to the original model. You will be using the Transfer function in the Mesh menu to transfer the UVs. First, select the proxy model in Object Selection mode and then select the original. With only the UV Sets option checked, as shown in Figure 8.19, click Apply to transfer the UV coordinates from one model to the other.

Figure 8.19 Transfer the UV coordinates from one model to the other.

Once the UVs are transferred, you can hide the proxy model because you will not need it anymore.

Although the UVs are transferred, the materials are not. You will need to apply the materials to the UVs on the original model. This should not be a difficult task if you have them all organized. Figure 8.20 shows the model with the materials applied.

I could have separated the hair, headband, and mask and mapped them with the other elements of the character, but I saved them for the time being to show you how to separate areas using the UV Texture Editor.

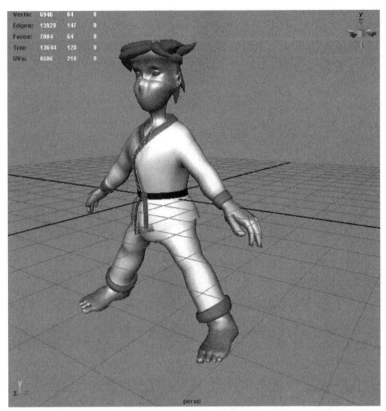

Figure 8.20 Apply the materials to the original model.

Separating UV Sets Using the UV Texture Editor

The UV Editor has a number of great tools for adjusting UVs after they have been mapped. In this section, you will be using some of these tools to separate some of the elements on the character's head.

1. First, start by lining up the UVs at the bottom of the headband in a horizontal line using the Scale tool, as shown in Figure 8.21. Use the Scale tool vertically to cause all of the UVs to line up horizontally.

2. Line up the UVs along the top of the headband horizontally as well.

3. Select the edges that run along the top and bottom of the headband, as shown in Figure 8.22.

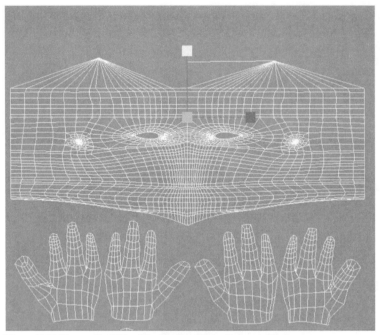

Figure 8.21 Line up the UVs of the headband in a horizontal line.

Note

The reason I had you line up the UVs is to make selecting the edges easier. Change the selection mode to Edges and drag a selection box across the edges of the top of the headband. This will select the edges you want and some that you don't want extending up and down from the top of the headband. You can easily deselect the unwanted edges by holding down the Shift key and dragging a selection box through them.

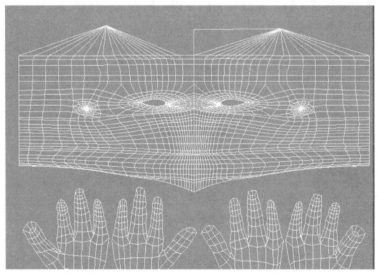

Figure 8.22 Select the edges on the top and bottom of the headband.

4. In the third set of icons at the top of the editor is an icon that has a pair of scissors cutting a checkerboard pattern. This function separates UVs along an edge. Click it to separate the selected edges.

5. Change the selection mode to Faces and select the faces of the head above the headband. This will isolate those faces. You can then change the selection mode back to UVs and drag a selection box over the faces, selecting only the UVs of that area. Move the UVs up to pull them away from the headband. Then do the same thing to pull the UVs of the headband away from the UVs of the forehead.

6. The edge of the mask will not be as easy to select as the headband was because it has too many curves. It would take more time to flatten all of the UVs along a horizontal line than it would to just go in and select the edge by hand. Select all of the edges that run along the top of the mask.

7. Cut the selected edges and then separate the UVs of the mask from the other UVs of the head, as shown in Figure 8.23.

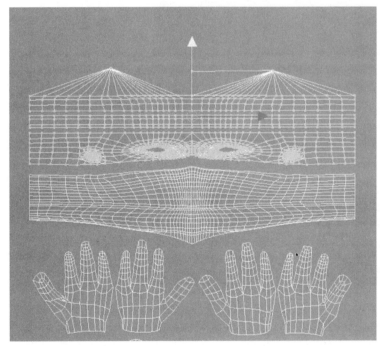

Figure 8.23 Separate the UVs of the mask.

8. You should have four sets of UVs: one each for the flesh tones; red for the boarders; black for the belt, mask, and hair; and white for the uniform. Move the headband to the boarder set and the mask and hair to the belt set. Figure 8.24 shows how I have the UVs set up.

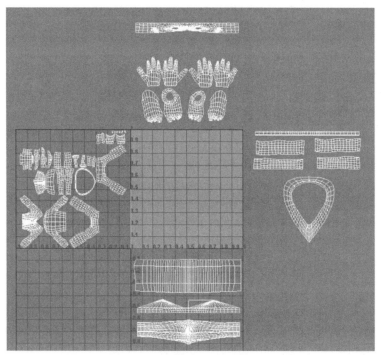

Figure 8.24 Move the UV sets to the right texture groups.

9. You will need to apply the black and red materials to the UVs from the head so they are using the correct materials.

Okay, the main body of the model is now mapped. The only thing left is the separate objects, like the eyes, hair, belt knot, and lapel.

Mapping the Separate Objects

Sometimes it is easier to work with a model if it has a few elements separated into objects. In this section, you will be mapping the remaining parts of the model, completing the mapping process.

Mapping the Hair

Because this is a cartoon character and his hair is basically black, there is no real need to individually map each lock of hair. Instead, just select all of the locks and apply the black material, as shown in Figure 8.25.

Figure 8.25 Apply the black material to the locks of hair.

Mapping the Eyes

For the eyes, create a new material and load an eye texture into it. If you don't have one of your own or you don't want to make one, you can use the eye texture supplied on the CD.

Because the eyes are facing one direction, you can use a Planar Mapping tool to apply the material to them so that the iris of the eye is facing forward, as shown in Figure 8.26.

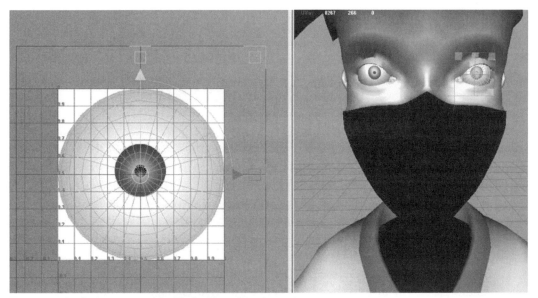

Figure 8.26 Apply the eye material with the Planar Mapping tool.

Notice that the irises look kind of small on the character. To fix this problem, select the UVs of the eyes and scale them down in the UV Texture Editor, as shown in Figure 8.27.

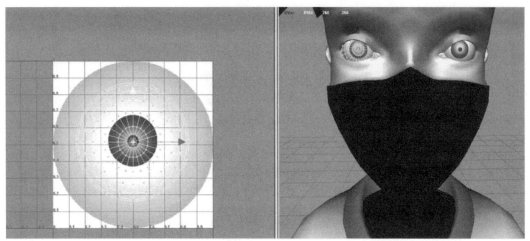

Figure 8.27 Scaling the UVs down in the UV Texture Editor increases the size of the iris.

Mapping the Belt Knot and Lapel

The process of mapping the belt knot and lapel is relatively simple. Apply the red material to the lapel using the Planar Mapping tool and to the belt knot with the Automatic Mapping tool.

You will need to unravel some of the UVs on the lapel or they will be overlapping. This may not be a big deal for this particular model, but it is a good practice for any model you create.

Texture Painting

Our character is a cartoon character and does not require a great deal of texture painting, but to help you understand the process, we will briefly go into how it is done. One of the easiest ways to paint textures in Maya is to use the built-in 3D painting tools, but many artists prefer to work in a 2D program, like Photoshop or Painter. To make the process of texture painting easier for the artist, Maya has a feature that will export a picture—or, as it's called in Maya, a snapshot—of the mapped UVs within the 0 to 1 area of the UV plane. You will be using this feature to help with painting the face of the character.

1. Start by moving your flesh tone UV set into the 0 to 1 area in the UV Texture Editor. This is the area in the center of the grid that changes according to the UVs you have selected.

2. UV Snapshot is the last item in the Polygons menu in the UV Texture Editor. Select it to bring up the tool and take the snapshot, as shown in Figure 8.28.

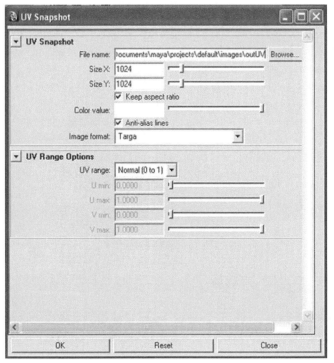

Figure 8.28 Bring up the UV Snapshot tool.

3. I have my size on the tool set to 1024 by 1024 resolution, but you can change that to another size if you like. I also use Targa files as the export option. Use the Browse button to select where you want the image saved. You will have to have the model selected in Object mode to have the tool work. Take a snapshot.

4. In Painter, bring up both the UV snapshot and the flesh texture. Copy the flesh texture and paste it over the UV snapshot. Move the Transparency slider to make the UV snapshot show through, as shown in Figure 8.29.

5. Now you can use the UV snapshot as a guide to paint in some eyelashes around the eye, as shown in Figure 8.30.

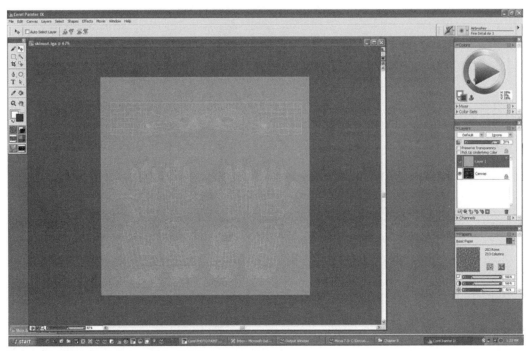

Figure 8.29 Make the flesh tone layer slightly transparent.

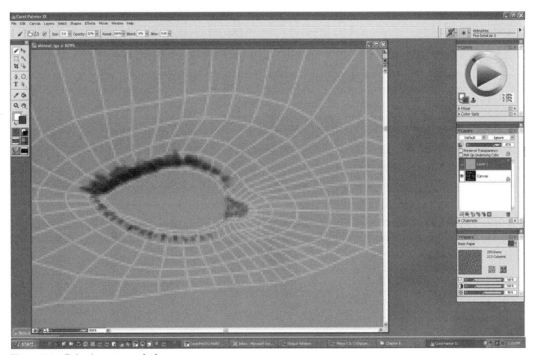

Figure 8.30 Paint in some eyelashes.

6. You can be as detailed as you like when painting textures. In this case, I took a simple approach, just painting in the eyebrows and adding a little color to the cheeks and ears (see Figure 8.31).

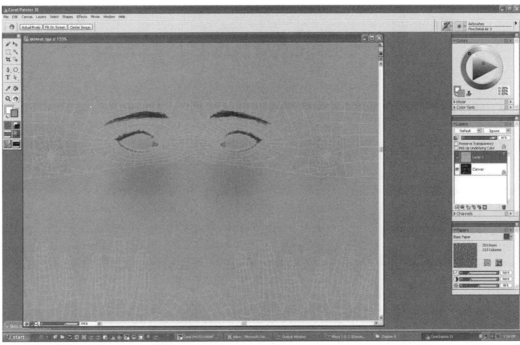

Figure 8.31 Paint other detail into the texture.

7. When you are finished, change the transparency back so the UV snapshot is no longer seen. Drop the layer and save your work. If you want to work on the face more later, it is a good idea to save a version of your work with layers.

Figure 8.32 Replace the old flesh texture with the new one.

8. Now go back to Maya and replace the flesh tone texture with the new painted texture. You can do this in the Attribute Editor the same way you loaded the texture the first time, but instead of loading it, use the option reload. As long as the texture has the same name as the one you used before, the updated texture will be loaded. This is a good way to make incremental changes to your textures and test them in Maya. Figure 8.32 shows the new texture on the model.

If you have followed along with the book, you should have your model completely mapped and ready for animation. In the next section, you will learn how to set up a bone system and attach it to your model.

Character Rigging

The next step in getting your character ready for animation is to give him a skeletal system. Skeletal systems in 3D characters work much like the skeletal systems in our own bodies. Our skeletons give us structure and act as a framework for movement. Skeletal systems in 3D models mimic the human body's system. This is only natural because 3D characters—particularly human characters—are supposed to move like people in real life.

A skeletal system in Maya is made up of joints connected by bones. The model is then attached to the joints. Joints actually influence the individual vertices of the model. Some vertices can be tied completely to one joint, while others may have influence from two or more joints. When multiple joints influence a single vertex, it is called *soft binding.* When a vertex is influenced by just one joint, it is called *hard binding.* Soft binding generally provides better results in lifelike movement.

In the next example, I will show you how to build a skeleton from scratch in Maya. Maya comes with a pre-made skeleton with full body kinematics, but if you were to use that skeletal system now, you would not learn much about Maya's bone system.

Creating a Skeleton

Skeletal systems are easy to create in Maya. All you have to do is place the joints, after which the bones are automatically created to join each joint in a hierarchical chain. Because Maya creates the hierarchy based on the order that you place the joints, it is very important to place the joints in the right order.

1. Change the main menu to the Animation menu set.
2. If the model is not already loaded, load the model into Maya and go to the Side view.

Note

When placing joints in Maya, it is always best to place them from one of the Orthographic views because Maya will automatically place the joints on the centerline so you always know where it is going. If you try to place a joint in the Perspective view, you will often have problems locating the joint.

3. Select the Joint tool from the skeleton menu and place a joint in the lower back. This joint will be the root joint because it is the first joint placed in the model. The root joint is like the parent of all the other joints.

4. Next, click above the root joint along the spinal cord to create a second joint connected to the root joint by a bone. Notice that the bone is shaped like a triangle with the larger end next to the root joint. This indicates that the second joint is a child of the first joint.

5. Continue to place joints along the spinal cord up and into the model's head, as shown in Figure 8.33. Press Enter to finish the joint chain.

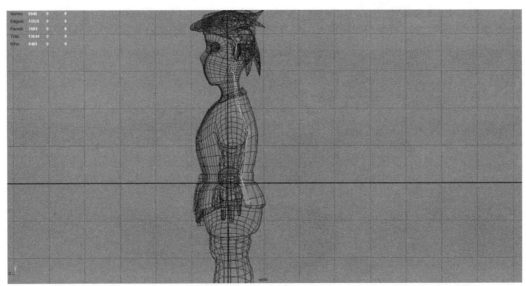

Figure 8.33 Place joints to form the model's spine.

6. Go to the Front view to place the joints of the leg. Place the first joint on the character's left side about where his leg would connect with his pelvis.

7. Place the second joint in the character's left knee, and continue placing joints for the leg. Place the third joint halfway between the knee and the ankle, and then place a joint for the ankle, as shown in Figure 8.34.

Note

There is an extra joint between the knee and ankle to take into account the ability of the human foot to twist from side to side.

8. Now place the bones of the character's left arm. Start with a bone that is just to the character's left of center, then go on to place bones for the shoulder, elbow, twist joint, wrist, and finger, as shown in Figure 8.35.

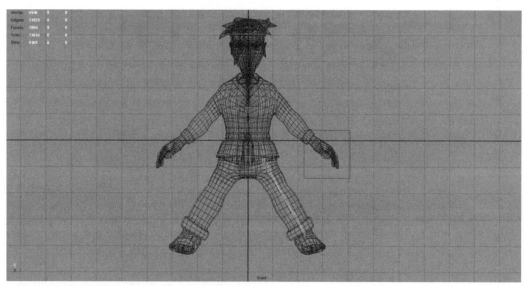

Figure 8.34 Place four joints in the character's left leg.

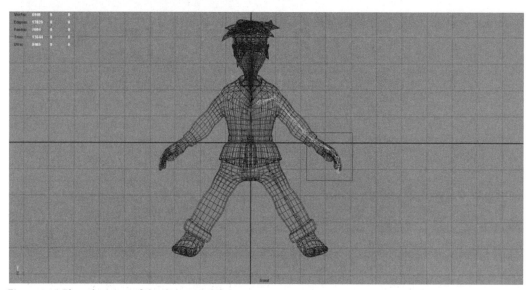

Figure 8.35 Place the joints of the character's left arm.

9. To create the bones for the hand, go to the Perspective view and select the first joint of the finger. This will automatically select that joint and all children of that joint. Duplicate the joint chain by pressing Ctrl+D. Move the joints of the duplicate into place in the model for the index finger.

10. Duplicate the finger joints again and move them over to the third finger. Do the same thing for the thumb.

11. Now move and rotate the finger and thumb joints to fit each appendage. The thumb will have one extra joint. You can go ahead and delete the end joint on the thumb.

12. From the Side view, create two joints for the character's feet, as shown in Figure 8.36. These two joints will appear on the centerline.

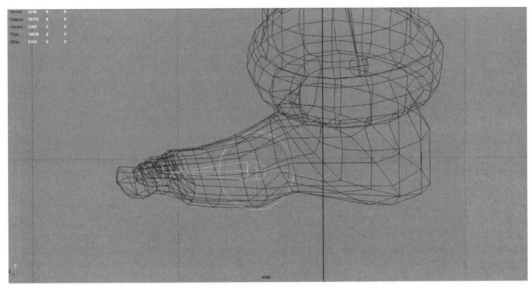

Figure 8.36 Create two joints for the character's left foot.

13. Move the new joints into the foot and connect them with the ankle joint of the left leg. To connect the joints to an existing chain, first select the joint you want to connect, and then select the joint you want to connect to. Press the P key, and a joint forms connecting the two joints, as shown in Figure 8.37.

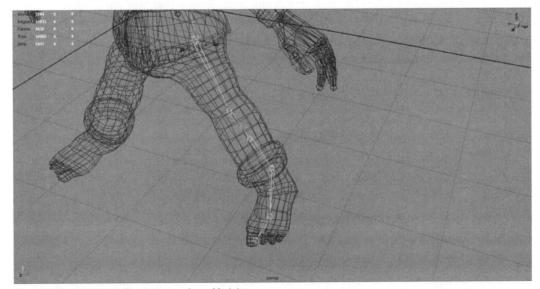

Figure 8.37 Connect the foot joints to the ankle joint.

14. Now that you know how to connect joint chains, connect the leg chain to the pelvis joint and the arm chain to one of the upper spine joints, as shown in Figure 8.38.

Figure 8.38 Connect the leg joints and the arm joints to the character's spine.

15. Rather than creating the joints for the right half of the character, you can simply mirror the joints from one side to the other. The Mirror Joints function is found in the Skeleton menu. It works similar to the Mirror Geometry function you used in creating the model. Select the first joint of the leg chain and mirror it to the character's right side. Notice that the joints are automatically connected to the pelvis joint. Do the same thing for the first arm joint. The skeleton should now look like that shown in Figure 8.39.

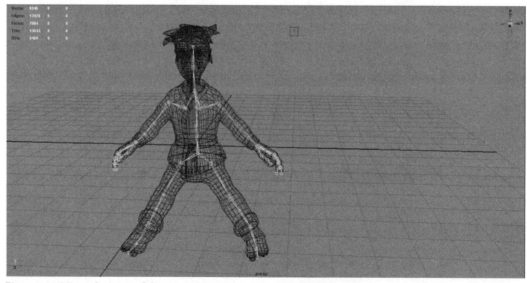

Figure 8.39 Mirror the joints of the arm and leg to the other side of the character.

16. Now you need to create some joints for the eyes. Go to the Side view and create two joints for the eyes. Begin the first joint in the exact center of the eye as seen from the Side view. Place the second joint through the front of the eye. Connect the two joints to the head joint, as shown in Figure 8.40.

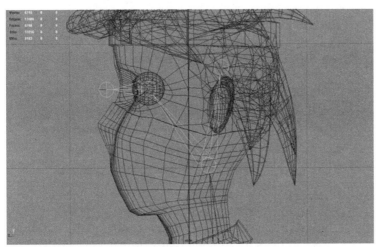

Figure 8.40 Create some joints for the eyes.

17. In the Front view, move the eye joints to the character's left eye so that it fits into the eye socket.

18. Duplicate the eye joints. The first joint set will be used for moving the eye, and the second will be used for moving the eyelid. Rotate the joints for the eyelid to better follow the angle of the lid. The two joints should look like those in Figure 8.41.

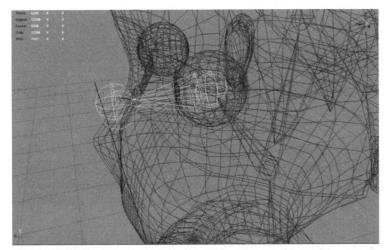

Figure 8.41 Duplicate the eye joints for a second set to control the eyelid.

19. Mirror the eye joints from the character's left side to his right so the character has joints for both eyes.

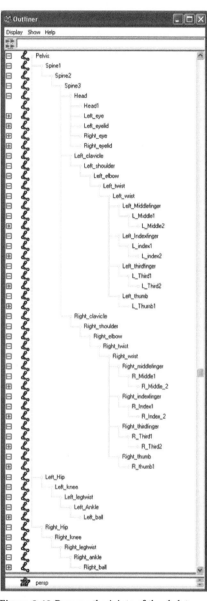

20. You are almost done. The last and final step in creating the joints of the skeleton is to name them so they will be easier to identify during the process of attaching them to vertices in the model. The easiest way to rename the joints is to use the Outliner. The Outliner is in the Window directory. Use the Outliner to select a joint; that joint will then show up in the Channel box, where you can change its name. Figure 8.42 shows how I named the joints of my skeleton.

Now you have a complete skeleton for your model. This skeleton is very basic and simple. For more complex skeletons, it's just a matter of creating more joints for different parts of the body. This skeleton, however, should give you a good start in learning how skeletons work in Maya.

Figure 8.42 Rename the joints of the skeleton.

Applying Skin Weights

Once the skeleton is finished, you are ready to attach it to the model. In Maya the process is called *skinning*. Maya has an automatic skinning process that does most of the work for you. First, select the model. Next, select the root or first joint of the skeleton that you created. It is the one I named *pelvis* in my naming of the joints. Then go to the Smooth Bind Options dialog box found in the Skin menu. Set the Bind To option to Joint Hierarchy, the Max Influences option to 5, and the Dropoff Rate option to 4, as shown in Figure 8.43.

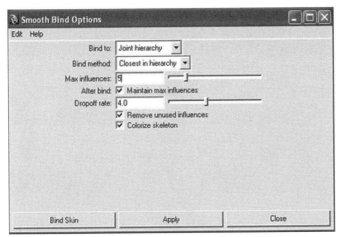

Figure 8.43 Bind the model to the skeleton.

Remember that you will also have to bind the other parts of the model's uniform that are separate objects from the main body. Bind them in the same way as you did the main model.

The character's eyes and hair will need to be bound with a different option than the other model objects. Set the Bind To option to Selected Joints instead of to Joint Hierarchy and the Max Influence to 1 instead of 5. This option binds the model object to one specific joint rather than the whole chain. Bind the hair objects to the head joint one at a time and the eyeballs to their respective eye joints.

Now you are done, right? Wrong! Although Maya does a very good job of distributing the skin weights between the joints, it is at best a general process and does not take into account specific anatomical considerations. For example, try moving the shoulder joint as I did in Figure 8.44. Notice how the shoulder and chest deform. This would make for some very odd-looking animations. You'll need to adjust the skin weights to get them to behave properly during animation. *Skin weighting* is the term used in Maya to describe the ratio of influence that joints have on vertices in the model.

Maya has some great tools for adjusting and tweaking skin weights. One of my favorites is the Paint Skin Weights tool, found in the Edit Smooth Skin submenu of the Skin menu. This tool allows the artist to adjust the skin weighting as if using a paintbrush. Figure 8.45 shows the tool in use on the clavicle.

The Paint Skin Weights tool is one of the Artisan tools in Maya, so it works similarly to the other Artisan tools, like the one you used in Chapter 6 to paint the hair on the claw model.

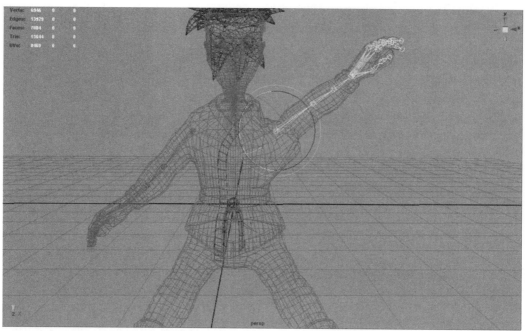

Figure 8.44 The skinning on the shoulder looks odd.

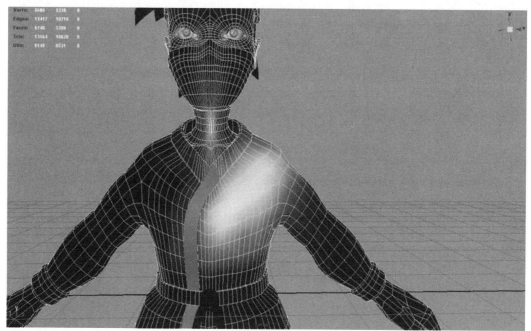

Figure 8.45 The Paint Skin Weights tool in use on the model.

Figure 8.46 shows the shoulder of the character after the skin weighting was adjusted with the Paint Skin Weight tool.

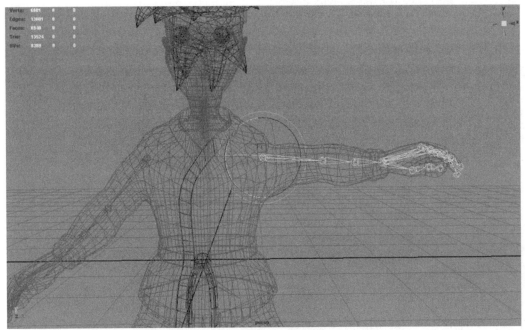

Figure 8.46 The shoulder behaves better after adjusting the skin weights.

Another great tool for adjusting skin weights is the Component Editor, found in the Window menu under General Editors. The Component Editor allows the artist to input specific numbers for the weighting of individual vertices. In Figure 8.47 I am using the Component Editor to adjust the skin weights of the head.

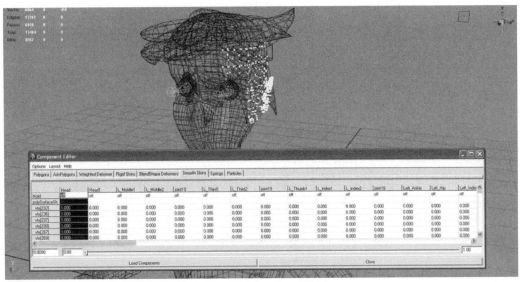

Figure 8.47 The Component Editor can be used to adjust the skin weights.

There are a couple of places that need fine adjustments. One of those is the eyelid. Using the Paint Skin Weights tool, I adjust the skin weights of the eyelid to be mostly connected to the eyelid joint, but I leave some influence for the eyeball so when the character moves his eyes, the eyelid will move just a little like our eyes do. Figure 8.48 shows the weighting of the eyelid.

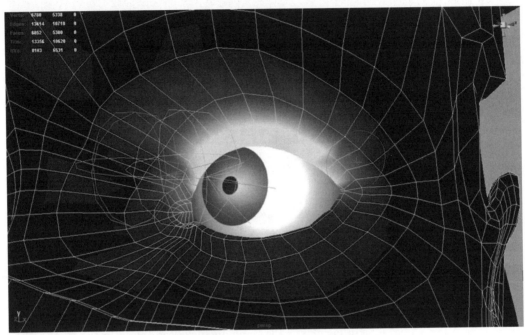

Figure 8.48 The eyelid requires fine adjustments.

Make sure when adjusting the eyelid that you take the time to check how it covers the eye when closed. You don't want the eyeball poking through the eyelid, which can often happen with eyes on 3D models.

Another place that requires some special attention is the hands and fingers. Figure 8.49 shows that part of the thumb is weighted to the hand, causing an odd stretching of the thumb. I used the Paint Skin Weights tool to fix this problem as well.

You only really need to adjust the weighting on half of the model. You can use the Mirror Skin Weights function to duplicate the weighting on the other side as long as your model is symmetrical. Go to Skin, Edit Smooth Skins, Mirror Skin Weights to use this function. Figure 8.50 shows the dialog box for Mirror Skin Weights Options.

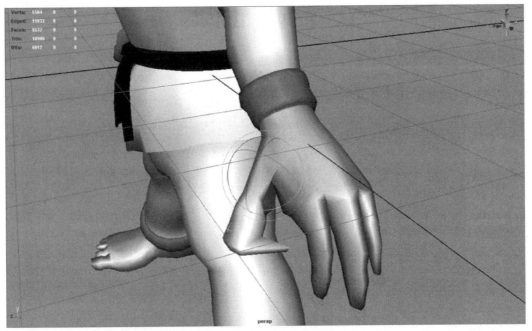

Figure 8.49 The thumb is partially weighted to the hand.

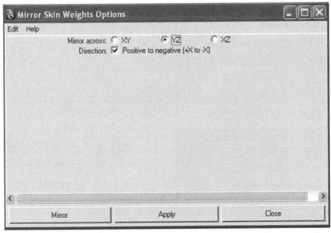

Figure 8.50 Use Mirror Skin Weights options to duplicate the weights from one side to the other.

You also need to remember to adjust the weights of the extra model objects, like the belt shown in Figure 8.51 and the lapel shown in Figure 8.52.

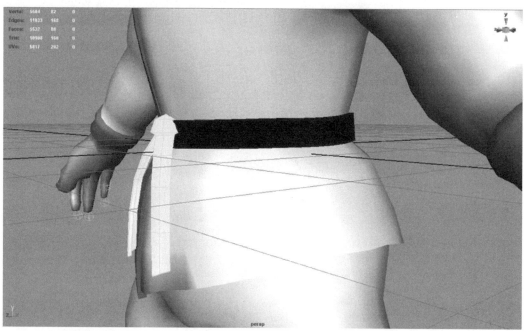

Figure 8.51 Adjust the skin weights of the belt.

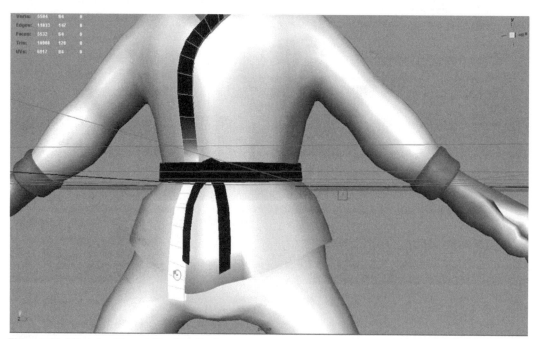

Figure 8.52 Adjust the skin weights of the lapel.

Skin weighting is mostly a matter of trial and error. You need to spend some time getting it just right. Move each joint through the full range of motion for that joint and watch how the model deforms around the joint. That is the best way to judge how the model will look when animating.

Inverse Kinematics

If you wanted to, you could use the model as it is for animating, but you might find some animations difficult to achieve when rotating the joints. If you did animate the model as it is by just rotating joints, you would be using an animation method called *forward kinematics*. This method is valid, and much of the animation you do will be using that method, but Maya has a system of inverse kinematics that makes animating some parts of a character much easier.

In forward kinematics, the motion is created moving down the hierarchy chain. With inverse kinematics, the motion is created moving up the chain. For example, if you animated an arm using forward kinematics, you would start with the shoulder and adjust the movement down to the elbow, the wrist, and so forth. With inverse kinematics, you can move the lower chain elements and the arm would move to the location.

With this model, I will show you how to set up some simple two-joint inverse kinematics.

1. Before you can apply inverse kinematics to a joint chain, you have to define the direction of movement of the joint. You do this by bending the joint slightly in the direction you want it to bend and setting a preferred angle to the joint. In Figure 8.53, I want the joint to rotate around the Y axis, so I bend it a few degrees, as shown in the Channel box.

Figure 8.53 Bend the joint in the direction you want it to bend.

2. Next, I go to the hip joint, which is one joint above the knee joint, and set the preferred angle. The Set Preferred Angle function is found in the Skeleton directory.

3. Once the preferred angle is set, I can now create an IK handle for the joint chain. IK is short for *inverse kinematics*. The IK Handle tool is found in the Skeleton menu. Select the function, and then click first on the joint above (the hip joint) and next on the joint below (the leg twist joint) the knee joint to create the IK handle, as shown in Figure 8.54.

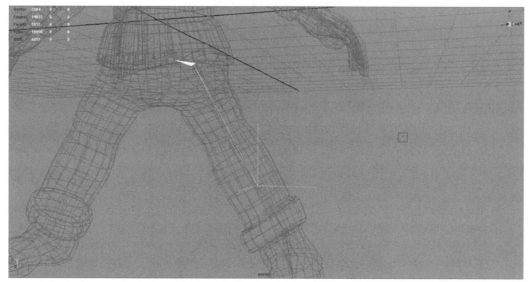

Figure 8.54 Create an IK handle for the leg.

For this character, I created four IK handles, one each for the legs and the arms, as shown in Figure 8.55. The character is now ready for animation, which will be the topic of Chapter 9.

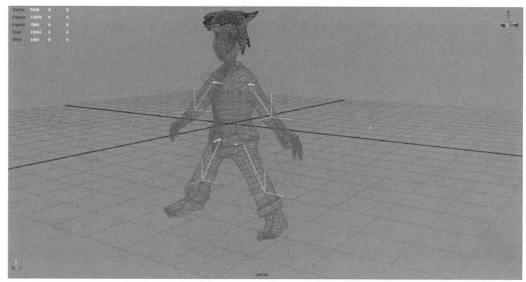

Figure 8.55 Create IK handles for the arms and legs.

Summary

In this chapter, you gave your character model color in the form of textures. You also learned how to prepare the model for animation. Topics covered were as follows:

- UV organization
- Creating UV sets
- Exporting a UV snapshot
- Using a UV snapshot as a guide for texture painting
- Creating a skeletal system for a model
- Skinning a model to a skeleton
- Adjusting skin weights
- Creating IK handles for animation

This chapter only touched on many of the features in Maya for creating textures and rigging a model. While it is not an exhaustive rundown of all the features, it should give you enough information to get started. As with everything in Maya, there are layers of functionality below layers of functionality. Do a little exploring, and you will soon be comfortable with the many features of this great software program.

Chapter 8

Color and Movement

Building the model is only the beginning of creating a character in a 3D program. In this chapter, you will continue to work on the character model you created in Chapter 7, giving him textures and getting him ready to animate. In the texturing process, you will explore concepts used in texturing human characters. You will also learn about building skeletal systems for the animation of a character and, finally, how to attach a skeletal system to a model.

Adding Color

The process of texturing a human character can often be very complex. The greater the number of UVs, the more intricate the process. Max has various good UV tools that help to make this process much easier.

One of the most difficult aspects of texturing a human character is dealing with the problem of overlapping UVs. For example, the geometry for the ear will often overlap with the rest of the head. One way to deal with this problem is to go into the UV Editor and move the UVs by hand. This process may be fine for a simple or low-polygon character, but with larger, more complex characters, you may get the feeling that you are unraveling a bowl of spaghetti. Because your character only needs basic color textures, we will be using a simple method for dealing with the overlap issue.

Removing Overlapping UVs

Rather than duplicating the model as on the Maya side, we will be following similar techniques but using the UVW Unwrap tool for the most part. Load the latest version of your ninja character.

Set the viewport to Perspective and move the ninja character off to the side, as shown in Figure 8.1. Make sure you are not in a Sub Object mode. Add the Unwrap UVW modifier to the stack. For UVs, I would recommend setting the viewport to Shaded, using the F3 key, and the selection mode to Solid Shaded, using the F2 key. This will make it much easier to see what is selected.

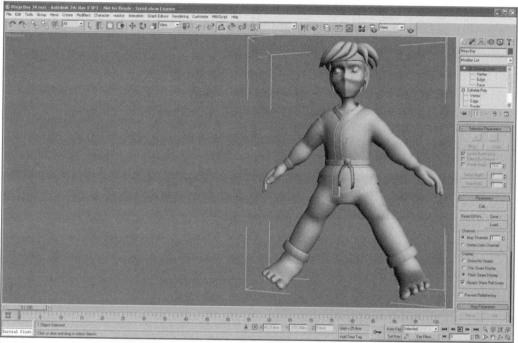

Figure 8.1 Set up the viewport and add the Unwrap UVW modifier.

1. Click on the Edit button to bring up the Edit UVWs window, as shown in Figure 8.2.

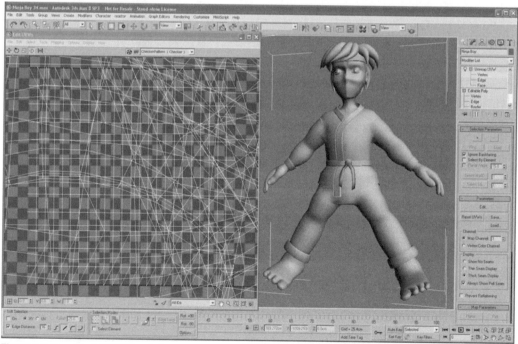

Figure 8.2 Open the Edit UVWs window.

2. Zoom out in the window so you can see the whole character. Select all the vertices or faces and uniformly scale everything down so the character is about one quarter the size of the center box shown in the Edit UVWs window. Move your character near the box but not inside it. You will be breaking him out into pieces and fitting him inside the box as you go. See Figure 8.3 for reference. The view has been zoomed back in after the scale, so you can see the referred to box. (This box is where the map will load by default, so it's an easy way to get things to line up without requiring a lot of work later.) You will also notice a checkered pattern in the editor. This can be displayed on the model so you can see if the UVs are stretching. That will not be very important for this character because he has simple cartoon flat colors, so we will not see any texture stretching.

Figure 8.3 The model ready to be broken apart and final UVs set up.

3. Let's isolate the head and set up some basic UVs so we can deal with the overlapping of the ears and chin. In the Edit UVWs window, select the Face Sub Object mode button and also check the Select Elements box. Select the head by clicking on it (see Figure 8.4). You will notice the head is selected in the viewport as well. You could do the same procedure in the viewport and have it show up in the Edit UVWs window if you prefer, but for this example I will be doing most of the work in the Edit UVWs window.

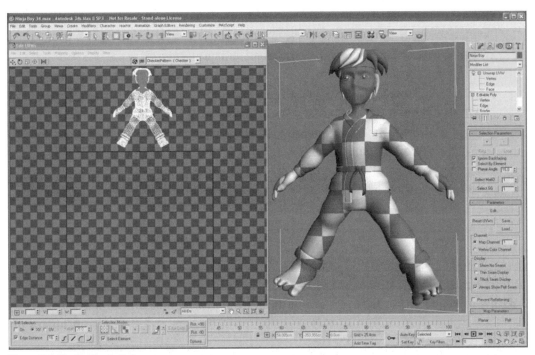

Figure 8.4 The head selected.

4. Scroll down the Command Panel a bit and select the Cylindrical Map Parameter. Click the Align Y and Fit buttons. This will add, align, and size a Gizmo to the selection, and the new UVs will show up in the editor, as shown in Figure 8.5.

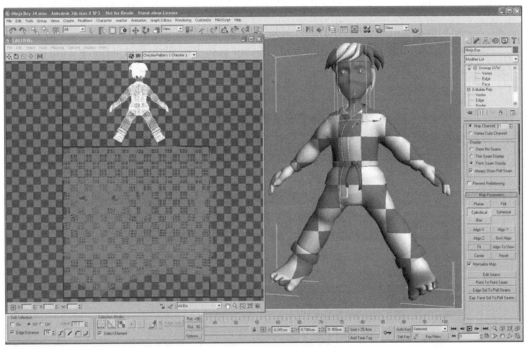

Figure 8.5 Use a cylindrical map projection to map the UVs of the head.

5. Now select the ears and do a relax on them to adjust for the overlapping. Switch to Vertex Sub Object mode (in the editor) and deselect the Select Element box. Select each ear and the surrounding polygons.

6. Select the Relax option under the Tools menu and set the drop-down option to Relax By Centers, Iterations to 300, and Amount to 1.0, and select Keep Boundary Points Fixed. Click Apply, and you should have something that looks like what you see in Figure 8.6.

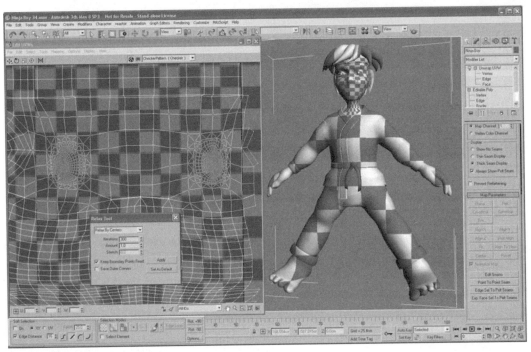

Figure 8.6 Relax the UVs on the ears.

7. Now let's select the head and do a slight relax to adjust for the chin overlapping.

8. Select the Relax option again and set the drop-down option to Relax By Centers, Iterations to 50, and Amount to 1.0, and select Keep Boundary Points Fixed. Click Apply, and you should have something that looks like what you see in Figure 8.7 with the chin exposed.

9. While the head is selected, scale it down some and move it to a corner so you have room for the rest of the UVs.

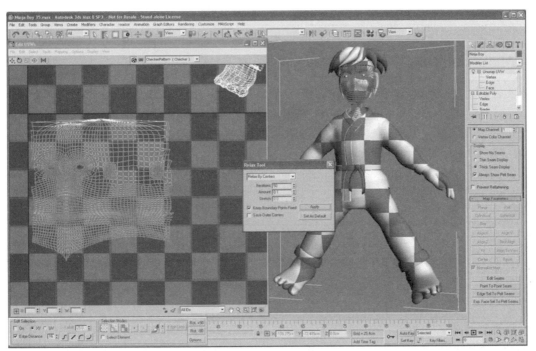

Figure 8.7 Relax the UVs on the head to deal with minor overlapping.

Note

That was the basic process you will be going through to map the rest of the character. Editing the UVs is mainly a job of organizing them so that you can create textures for the character in a 2D paint program. It helps if the mapping is something that you can recognize when you bring up the templates in a 2D program. By using the cylindrical map for the head, you have created a map that appears as if the UVs were unwrapped and laid out in a flat plane. We can see how they form a head. This helps when painting the textures.

Mapping the Hands and Feet

The hands and feet are also complex parts of the body and have the potential for many overlapping UVs. Using a cylindrical mapping technique on the hand will not work very well unless you want to do every finger individually. Instead, I use a planar mapping technique to map the UVs of the hand.

1. For the hands and feet you will be selecting polygons in the Perspective viewport. Switch to Face Sub Object mode in the Unwrap UVW modifier and select the top half of the hand. This time, though, you will be using the planar mapping coordinates to get your initial UVs on the hand. Click on Planar, then click on Best Align. This should get it close, but you may want to rotate it a bit to get it as flat or perpendicular to the selection as possible, as shown in Figure 8.8.

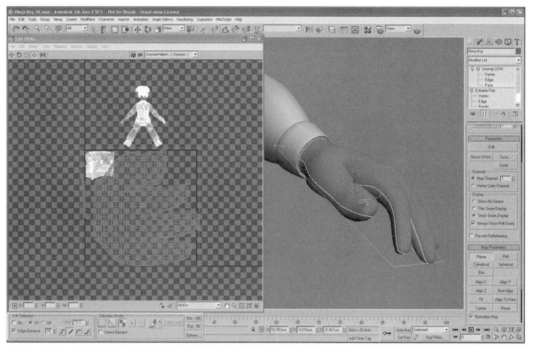

Figure 8.8 Use the Planar Map Parameter to map the top of the hand.

2. Some of the UVs of the hand are overlapping. Rotate and scale the hand UVs so they fit in the map template a bit better. Once that's done, run a slight relax on it to fix the overlap, and then adjust by hand the last few points where the fingers meet the palm, as shown in Figure 8.9.

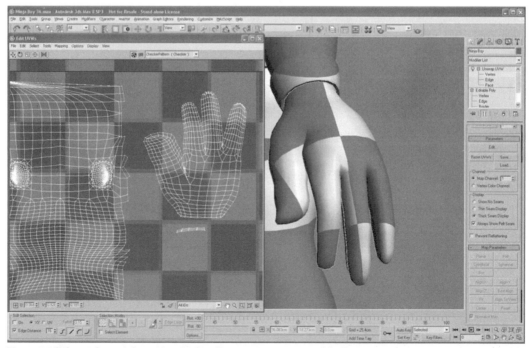

Figure 8.9 Relax and move the vertices in the editor to remove any overlapping areas.

3. Now select and map the UVs for the bottom of the hand similar to how you did the top. There is a quick way to do this step. Select the remaining part of the hand in the UV Editor, and then fine-tune the selection in the Perspective viewport. Take a look at Figure 8.10 to see how the UVs are starting to come together.

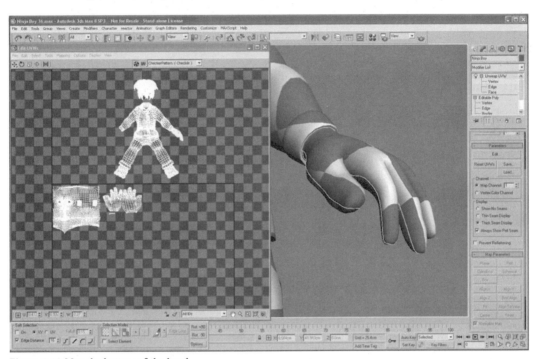

Figure 8.10 Map the bottom of the hand.

4. You will need to repeat the process for the character's other hand. When you are done, your UVs should look similar to what you see in Figure 8.11.

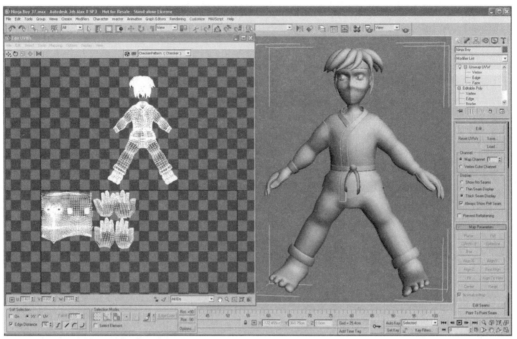

Figure 8.11 Map the UVs of the other hand as well.

Next, you will need to map the UVs of the foot. The foot is a little harder to map because it is not a flat plane like the hand and will have a number of overlapping UVs that will have to be adjusted.

1. First, select the UVs of the top of the foot and use the Polygon Planar Projection tool to map the foot, as shown in Figure 8.12.

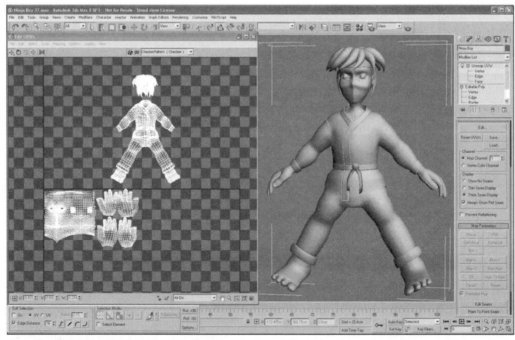

Figure 8.12 Map the UVs of the top of the foot.

2. Scale and position the UVs in the template and relax the whole foot. Select just the heel and relax that a few more times to expose all the faces with no overlapping, as shown in Figure 8.13.

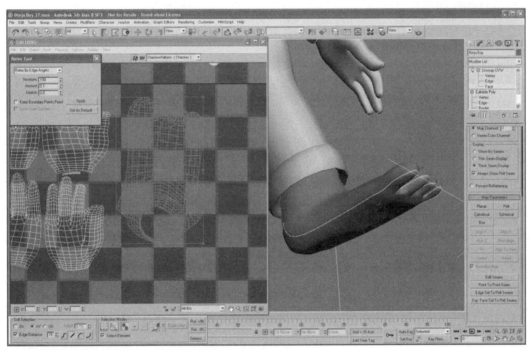

Figure 8.13 Organize the UVs of the upper foot.

Note

When unraveling overlapping UVs, it is important to try to maintain the general size and shape of the UVs to match the polygons of the area you are mapping. This will help to avoid texture stretching, which can happen when the UVs are distorted.

3. Like the hand, you will also need to map and lay out the bottom of the foot.

4. Place the bottom and top of the foot together, as shown in Figure 8.14.

5. Go to the other foot and repeat the process to create mapped UVs for that foot as well. When you are finished, your maps should look similar to those shown in Figure 8.15.

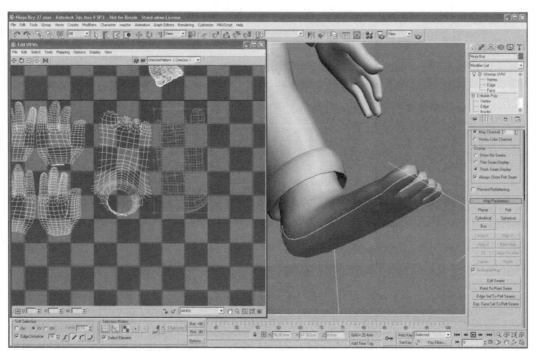

Figure 8.14 One foot mapped.

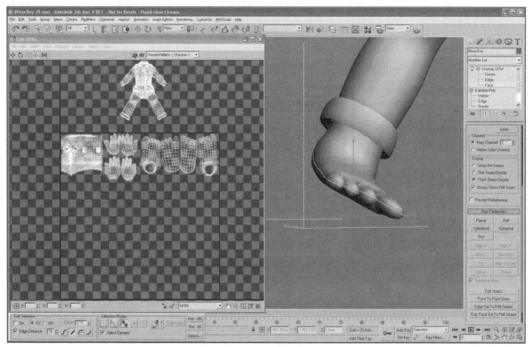

Figure 8.15 Organize the mapped UVs of the character.

The head, hands, and feet are now mapped and ready to have a texture applied to them. To help organize my work, I will often go ahead and apply a texture to the mapped sections that share the same texture file. This helps me to see the progress I am making with the model. When everything on the model is colored, I know that I have finished the mapping process.

Export the template so you can use it to paint on. In the UV Editor under Tools, select the Render UVW Template options and use the Render UV Template with the default options. This will "render" a bitmap, which you can then save and load into a paint program for editing. It will also provide the basic map for your character. Save it with the model by using the small floppy disk icon in the upper-left side of the render.

Load the template into a program like Photoshop and paint some flesh-colored areas where the feet, hands, and head are, which I've done in Figure 8.16, although you obviously can't see the color I've used. Don't spend too much time on this step. You will be saving out a fully mapped template once the uniform is done, and that would be the best time to paint final textures.

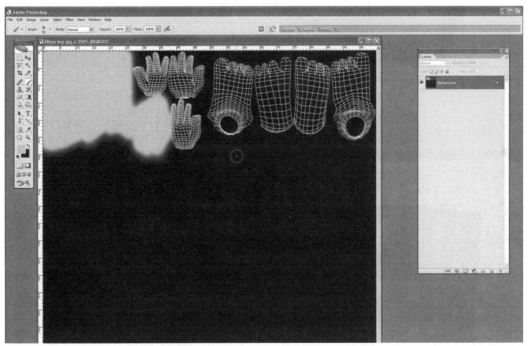

Figure 8.16 Create a skin-colored texture.

While the head will not all be flesh tones, leave it for now with the temporary flesh-colored texture. I will show you how to separate the head's UVs later.

Create a new material ball for the texture and apply the texture to the model, as shown in Figure 8.17. Now you can easily see the areas that are not yet mapped.

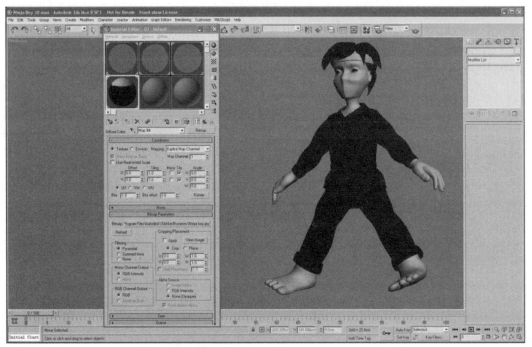

Figure 8.17 Apply the flesh material to the model.

Mapping the Uniform

The next part of the mapping process will be to map the character's uniform. The uniform is made up of several parts: the boarders, which will be red; the belt, which will be black; and the rest of the uniform, which will be white. You will map each of these parts of the uniform separately but using the same texture map.

Collapse the stack in preparation for assigning some material (see Figure 8.18). Don't worry about the UV information. It will be retained with the polygons. All that is needed to work with it again in the future is to add another Unwrap UVW modifier to the stack.

Now you are ready to map the uniform, so let's get started.

1. Enter Polygon Sub Object mode, select the collar and cuffs, and assign them to Material ID 2, as shown in Figure 8.19. Once you have that done, hide the selected faces with the Hide Selected button, and then add the uniform to ID 3, the hair to ID 4, the eyes to ID 5, the belt knot to ID 6, the mask to ID 7, and the headband to ID 8. This should leave everything on separate material IDs.

Figure 8.18 Collapse the stack.

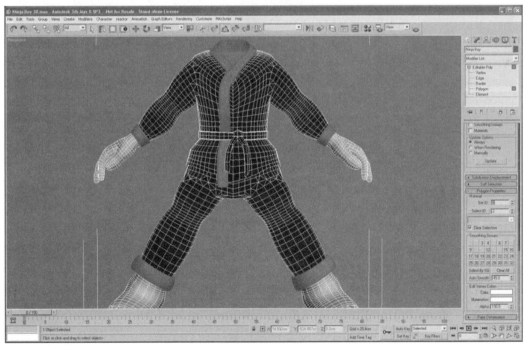

Figure 8.19 Separate the model into easy-to-work-with Material IDs.

2. Now it is just a matter of selecting the right faces and applying the materials to those faces. This becomes easier because you isolated the faces of the model by adding them to separate IDs. Open the Material Editor and pick a new material ball. Click on the Standard button and change it to Multi/Sub-Object, as shown in Figure 8.20. Assign this new material to the model. In slots 1 through 8, add a bitmap to the Diffuse channel and load the template that you saved out in the step preceding Figure 8.16. Don't forget to toggle the Show Map in Viewport button. It will also give you the leeway of tweaking individual parts of the model to get the textures looking just right. And it will save you time in that you will have only one high-res map that you'll need to work with.

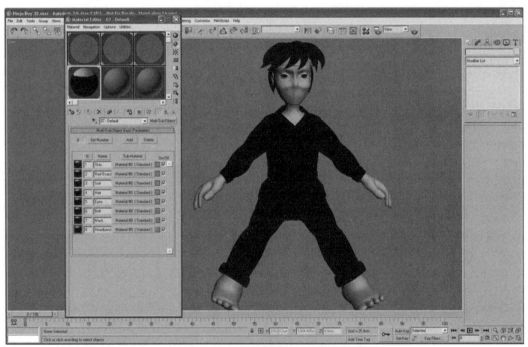

Figure 8.20 The material all set up and ready for the final texture.

3. Next, you need to organize the UVs of the mapped areas. Add the Unwrap UVW modifier to the stack (make sure you are not in Sub Object mode). Start with the cuff on the sleeve and use a cylindrical map, as shown in Figure 8.21. Now that you have Material IDs, you can use the Select MatID button and quickly select parts you want to use. Deselect the parts you don't want by holding down the Alt key.

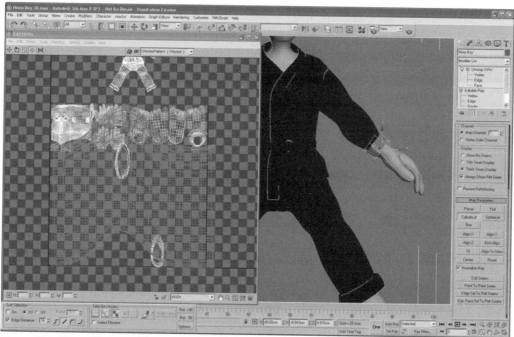

Figure 8.21 Use a cylindrical map on the cuff of the sleeve.

4. Scale the UVs of the mapped cuff and move them into place.
5. Apply cylindrical maps to the other sleeve cuff and both cuffs on the pants. Scale each one and move them into place.
6. Use a planar map for the collar, as shown in Figure 8.22.

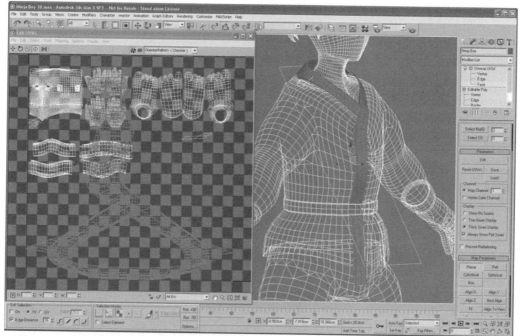

Figure 8.22 Use a planar map on the collar.

7. Scale the collar UVs down and move them to the side with the cuff UVs, as shown in Figure 8.23. Some of the UVs of the collar will be overlapping and will need to be adjusted, as shown in the figure.

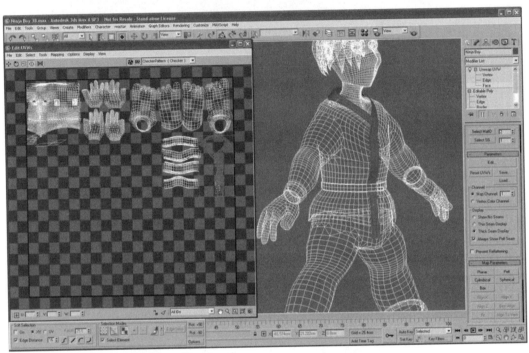

Figure 8.23 Organize the UVs of the uniform boarders.

8. Use planar mapping for the front and back of the uniform, as shown in Figure 8.24.
9. Mapping the belt is easy. All you need to do is select the faces of the belt and map them using the Cylindrical Mapping option, as shown in Figure 8.25.

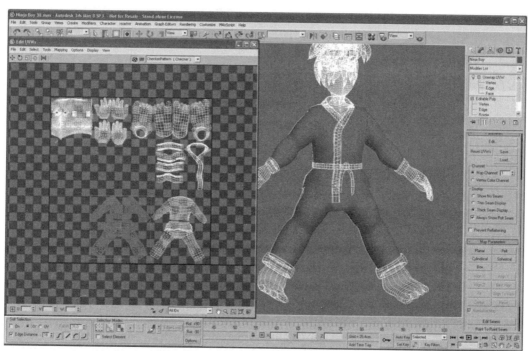

Figure 8.24 Get the uniform UVs in place.

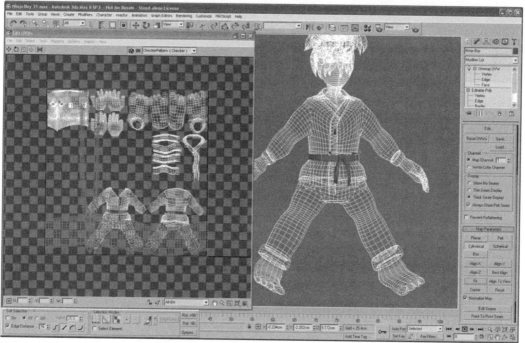

Figure 8.25 Use a cylindrical map on the belt.

You should now have all of the UVs in place and ready to have textures added to them. You can quickly double-check the UVs for stretching and other oddities by using the default checkered pattern, as shown in Figure 8.26. Use the drop-down list toward the top-right of the window and pick the checkered texture. You can also use one of the maps from the list, now that you have the material set up in the Material Editor.

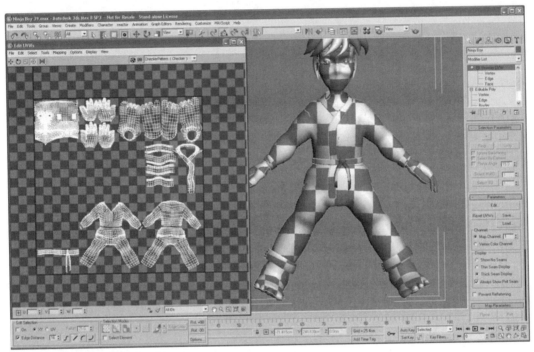

Figure 8.26 The default checkered texture.

Figure 8.27 shows the model with the materials applied. Right now it's just the template we saved out and assigned to each material ID so it looks a little like the wireframe model. Notice that the UVW Editor shows a grid of the texture. While you can have geometry outside the square area, it's good practice to keep your UVs nicely laid out and inside the center square.

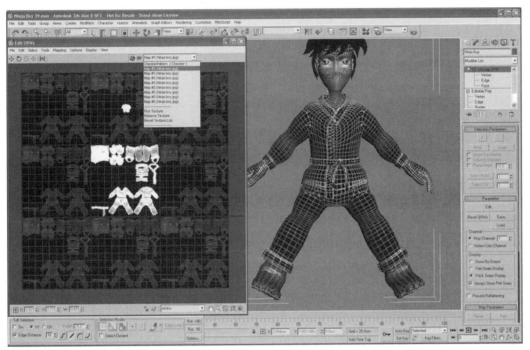

Figure 8.27 Apply the materials to the original model.

I could have separated the hair, headband, and mask and mapped them with the other elements of the character, but I saved them for the time being to show you how to separate areas using the UV Editor.

Separating UV Sets Using the UV Editor

The UV Editor has a number of great tools for adjusting UVs after they have been mapped. In this section, you will be using some of these tools to separate some of the elements on the character's head.

1. First, start by selecting the headband by using the Select MatID button on material ID 8. This will quickly select just the headband, as shown in Figure 8.28.

2. You can easily separate this bit of UVs from the head by using the Detach Edge Verts option under the Tools menu.

3. Move the headband down below the face on the UV layout, as shown in Figure 8.29.

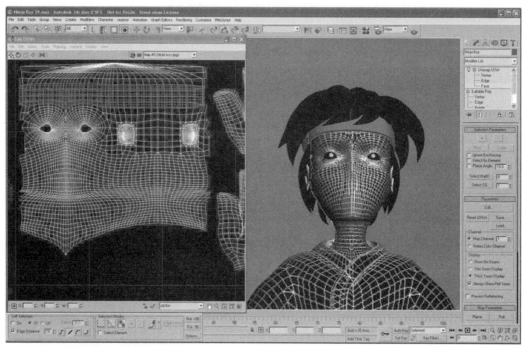

Figure 8.28 Select the headband.

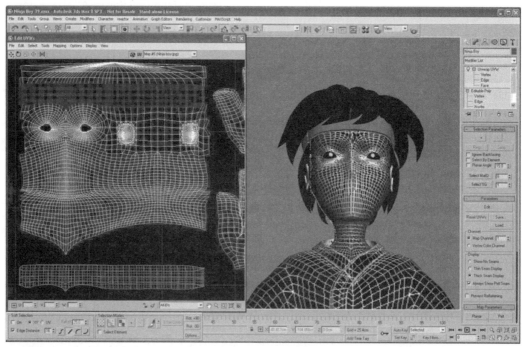

Figure 8.29 Arrange the headband on the UV layout.

4. Next, you'll do the same thing for the mask. Select the mask using Material ID 7, as shown in Figure 8.30.

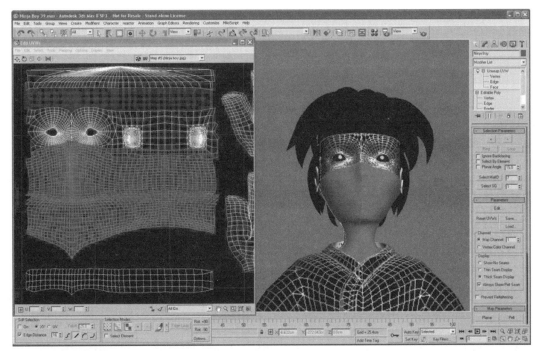

Figure 8.30 Select the mask.

5. Detach the mask and move it down slightly (see Figure 8.31).

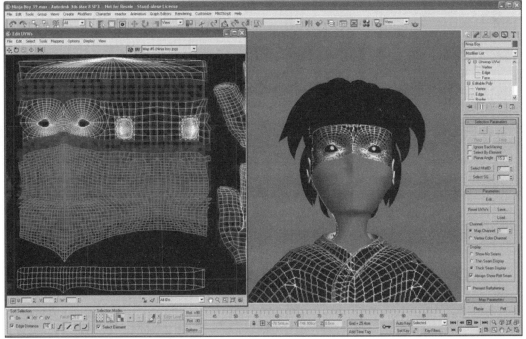

Figure 8.31 Separate the UVs.

Okay, the main body of the model is now mapped. The only thing left is the separate objects, like the eyes and hair.

Mapping the Separate Objects

Sometimes it is easier to work with a model if it has a few elements separated into objects. In this section, you will be mapping the remaining parts of the model, completing the mapping process.

Mapping the Hair

Because this is a cartoon character and his hair is basically black, there is no real need to individually map each lock of hair. Instead, just move the locks down to an empty area of the UV space, as shown in Figure 8.32.

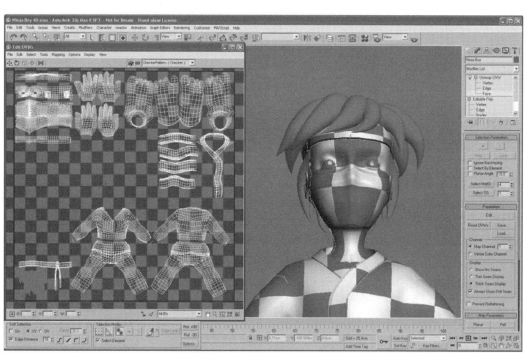

Figure 8.32 Arrange the hair to be on the template.

Mapping the Eyes

For the eyes, create a new material and load an eye texture into it. If you don't have one of your own or you don't want to make one, you can use the eye texture supplied on the CD.

Because the eyes are facing one direction, you can use the planar mapping tool to apply the material to them so that the iris of the eye is facing forward, as shown in Figure 8.33.

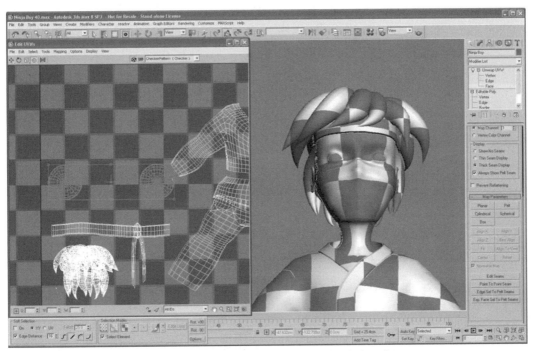

Figure 8.33 Set the eye UVs with the Planar Mapping tool and move and scale into place.

Because the eyes are identical, it makes sense to save some painting work and texture space by laying one eye UV right on top of the other. Just grab one and line it up on the other side, as shown in Figure 8.34.

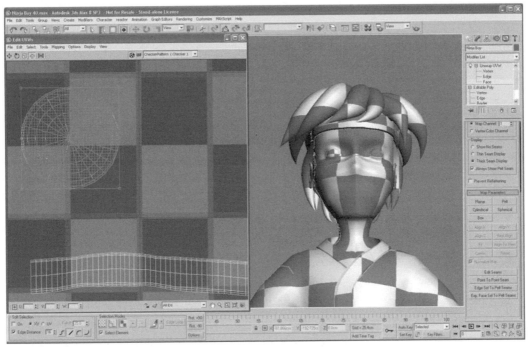

Figure 8.34 Lining up similar UVs to save space.

Now that the character has all his UVs nicely laid out, it seems you have some space free on the UV template. You can take advantage of this space by rearranging some things and scaling up areas where you want more details, like the face, as shown in Figure 8.35. You can also scale down less important areas, like the hair and bottoms of the feet, to make even more space. Some types of 3D work require careful and precise use of this space, but for this character you can just rearrange a few things to make better use of the space.

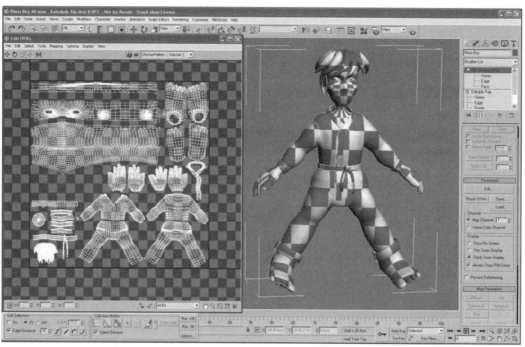

Figure 8.35 The final UV layout, ready for texture painting.

Texture Painting

Our character is a cartoon character and does not require a great deal of texture painting, but to give you a glimpse into this process, we will briefly go into how it is done. One of the easiest ways to paint textures for your model is to use a 2D program, like Photoshop or Painter. To make the process of texture painting easier for the artist, Max has a feature that will export a picture—or, as it's called in Maya, a template—of the mapped UVs. You used this feature on the step preceding Figure 8.16, but now that we have final UVs, let's get into more detail.

1. Save out the final UV template using the Render UVW Template, found under the Tools menu.
2. Load the template into a program like Photoshop (which can have multiple "layers"), as shown in Figure 8.36.

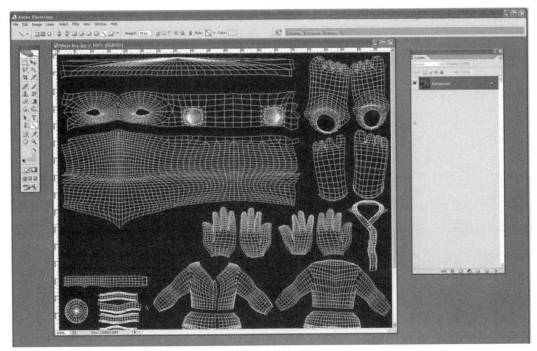

Figure 8.36 Load the texture into a paint program.

3. Make a duplicate layer so that you will have one to "paint" on and one to use as reference. Name the top layer something like "Template" and the bottom layer something like "Texture." When you save this file, you will only save the bottom layer.

4. Move the Opacity slider on the top, or Template, layer to about 10 percent, so it will show the bottom layer (see Figure 8.37). For the most part, this layer can stay hidden while you paint.

5. Now you can use the template as a guide to paint in some eyelashes around the eye, as shown in Figure 8.38. Make sure the Texture layer is selected before painting. Where our character is symmetrical, I only painted one side and copied/flipped the eyes to the other side.

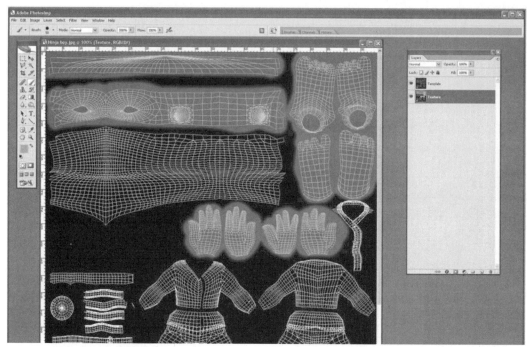

Figure 8.37 The Template layer at 10 percent.

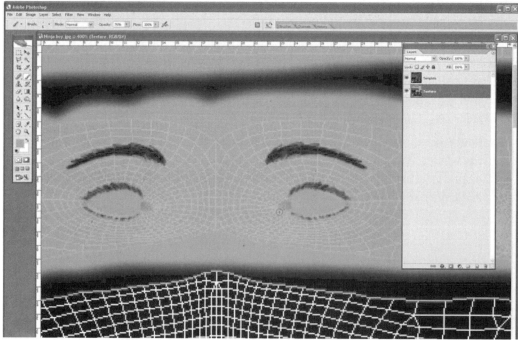

Figure 8.38 Paint in some eyelashes.

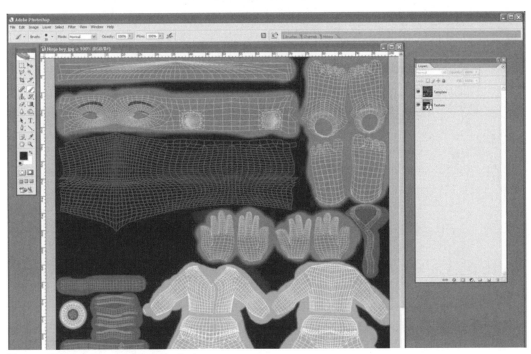

6. You can be as detailed as you like when painting textures. In this case, I took a simple approach, just painting in the eyebrows and adding a little color to the cheeks and ears (see Figure 8.39).

Figure 8.39 Paint other detail into the texture.

7. When you are finished, hide or delete the template and save your work as the same file you set up in the Material Editor. If you want to work on the texture more later, it is a good idea to save a version of your work with layers.

8. Now go back to Max, and you should see the new texture. As long as the texture has the same name as the one you used before and saved over the original, the updated texture will be loaded. This is a good way to make incremental changes to your textures and test them in Max. Figure 8.40 shows the final texture on the model.

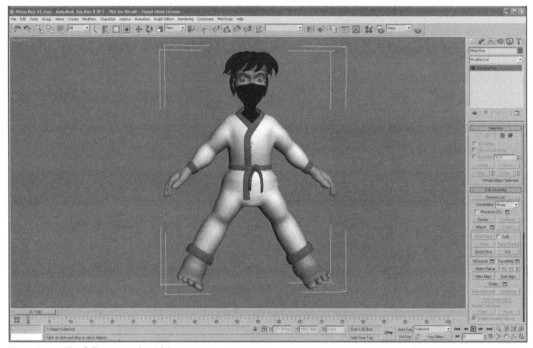

Figure 8.40 The fully textured model.

If you have followed along with the book, you should have your model completely mapped and ready for animation. In the next section, you will learn how to set up a bone system and attach it to your model.

Character Rigging

The next step in getting your character ready for animation is to give him a skeletal system. Skeletal systems in 3D characters work much like the skeletal systems in our own bodies. Our skeletons give us structure and act as a framework for movement. Skeletal systems in 3D models mimic the human body's system. This is only natural because 3D characters—particularly human characters—are supposed to move like people in real life.

A skeletal system in Max is made up of joints connected by bones. The model is then attached to the joints with the Skin modifier. Joints actually influence the individual vertices of the model. Some vertices can be tied completely to one joint, while others may have influence from two or more joints. When multiple joints influence a single vertex, it is called *blending*. When a vertex is influenced by just one joint, it is called *rigid*. Blending generally provides better results in lifelike movement.

In the next example, I will show you how to build a skeleton from scratch in Max. Max comes with a premade skeleton with full body kinematics, but if you were to use that skeletal system now, you would not learn much about Max's bone system.

Creating a Skeleton

Skeletal systems are easy to create in Max. All you have to do is place the joints, after which the bones are automatically created to join each joint in a hierarchical chain.

1. Set up the viewports so you have a Front and Left (or Right) view to work with.
2. It will make things a bit easier for you if you make the model see-through in the Properties menu and freeze the model so it can't be selected.

Note

When placing joints in Max, it is always best to place them from one of the Orthographic views because Max will automatically place the joints on the centerline so you always know where it is going. If you try to place a joint in the Perspective view, you will often have problems locating the joint.

Note

The first time you place bones, they may be huge by default. You can fix this by setting Bone Object Width and Height to something smaller. I used 3.5 cm by 3.5 cm, which gave me a good size to work with.

3. Select the Bone Tools option from the main menu's Character menu. This will bring up a pop-up that makes it much easier to create bones and joints. Click Create Bones and begin the chain at the base of the pelvis to start the spine.
4. Next, click above the root joint along the spinal cord to create a second joint connected to the root joint by a bone. Notice that the bone is shaped like a triangle with the larger end next to the root joint. This indicates that the second joint is a child of the first joint.
5. Continue to place joints along the spinal cord up and into the model's head, as shown in Figure 8.41. Right-click to finish the chain.
6. Go to the Front view to place the joints of the leg. Place the first joint on the character's left side about where his leg would connect with his pelvis.
7. Place the second joint in the character's left knee, and continue placing joints for the leg. Place the third joint halfway between the knee and the ankle, and then place a joint for the ankle, as shown in Figure 8.42.

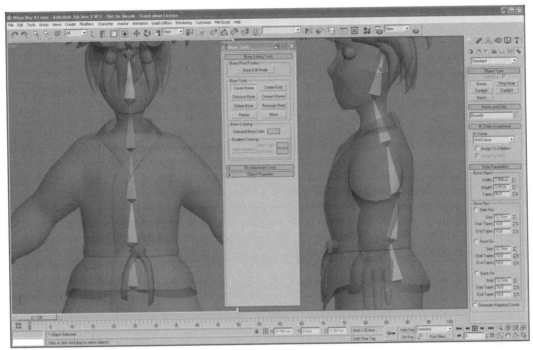

Figure 8.41 Place joints to form the model's spine.

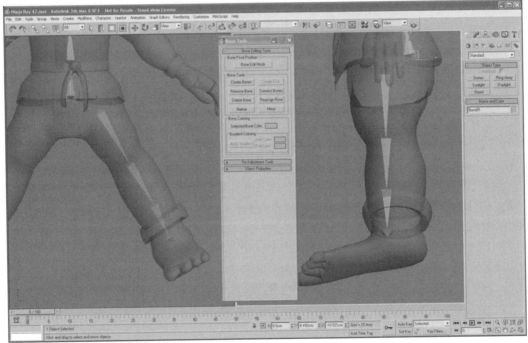

Figure 8.42 Place four joints in the character's left leg.

Note

There is an extra joint between the knee and ankle to take into account the ability of the human foot to twist from side to side.

8. Now place the bones of the character's left arm. Start with a bone that is just to the character's left of center, then go on to place bones for the shoulder, the elbow, a twist joint, the wrist, and finger, as shown in Figure 8.43. I have toggled and sized the side fins for the wrist bone. This will make it easier to attach the fingers visually. I have also colored the arm a dark blue for clarity so that it will be easy to tell the left from the right when animating.

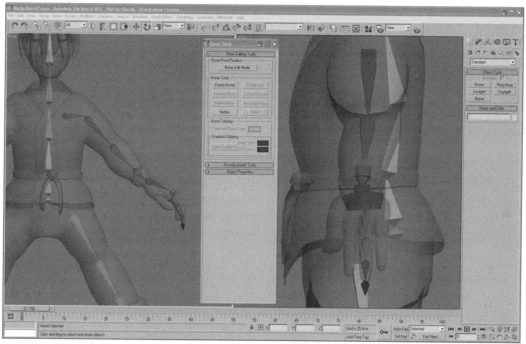

Figure 8.43 Place the joints of the character's left arm.

9. To create the bones for the hand, go to the Perspective view, select all of the finger joints, and move and rotate them while holding the Shift key to clone the joints, as shown in Figure 8.44. You may need to set the pivot to Use Pivot Center to get the Gizmo in the right place. You will also need to use the Select and Link tool to link the new finger bones to the wrist. Toggle the button and click and drag the line from the first finger bone to the wrist bone. Double-check the linking by rotating the wrist bone to make sure all the bones below go with it. After checking, undo the rotate to get the bone back in place.

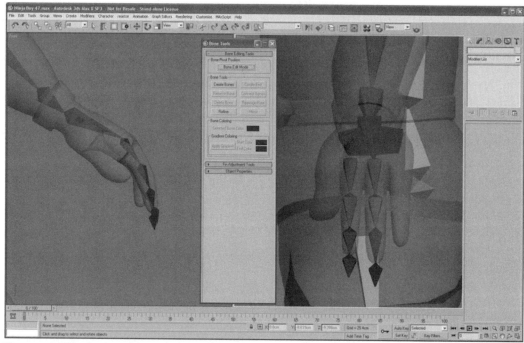

Figure 8.44 Move the finger joints to the index finger.

10. Duplicate the finger again and move it over to the third finger. Do the same thing for the thumb.

11. Turn on the Edit Bone mode, and move and rotate the finger and thumb bones to fit each appendage perfectly. You may need to unlink the fingers to get everything in place. Simply relink them when you are happy with the placement.

12. Now from the Side view, create a bone. This new bone will appear on the centerline, as shown in Figure 8.45.

13. Move the new bone into the foot and connect it with the ankle joint of the left leg. To connect the joints to an existing chain, first select the joint you want to connect, and then using the Connect Bones button, click on the bone you want to connect to, as shown in Figure 8.46. This will create the bone and join the two.

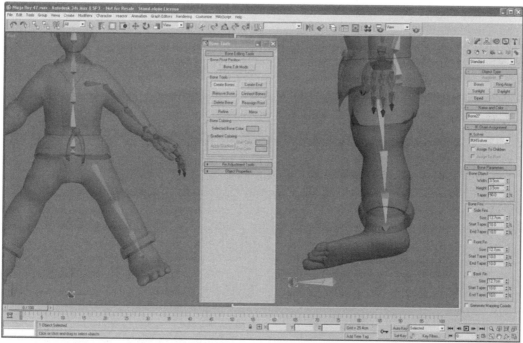

Figure 8.45 Create a bone for the character's left foot.

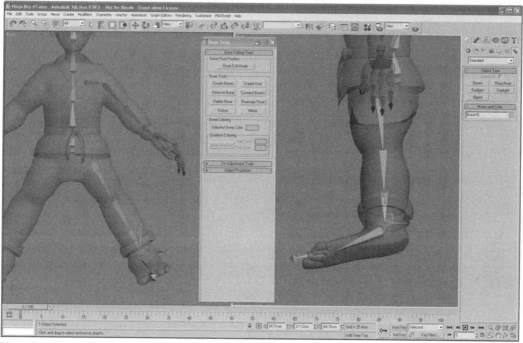

Figure 8.46 Connect the foot joints to the ankle joint.

14. Now that you know how to connect joint chains, connect the leg chain to the pelvis joint and the arm chain to one of the upper spine joints, as shown in Figure 8.47. You may need to select the pelvis bone and click the Refine button to get an extra joint in the pelvis for the connection.

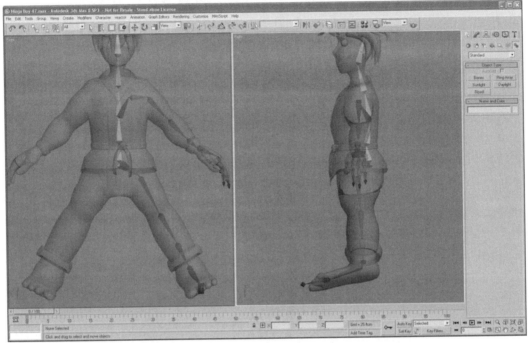

8.47 Connect the leg joints and the arm joints to the character's spine.

15. Rather than creating the joints for the right half of the character, you can simply mirror the joints from one side to the other. Select all of the arm bones and use the Mirror command. Notice that the joints are automatically connected to the pelvis joint. Do the same thing for the first arm joint. The skeleton should now look like that shown in Figure 8.48. I have selected the arm and leg bones and used different colors for the left and right bones so they are easy to identify when animating.

16. Now you need to create a bone for the eyes. Go to the Side view and create a bone for the eye (see Figure 8.49).

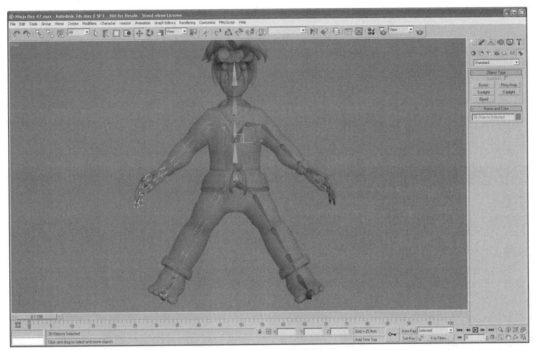

Figure 8.48 Mirror the joints of the arm and leg to the other side of the character.

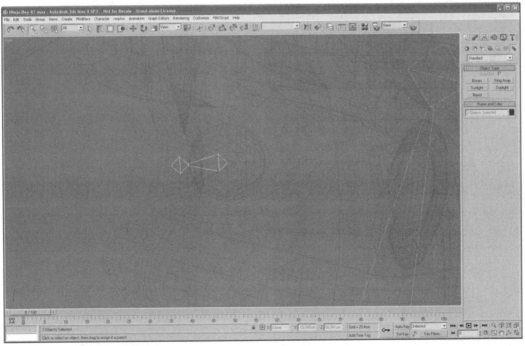

Figure 8.49 Create a bone for the eye.

17. In the Front or Top view, move the eye joint so that it's perfectly centered in the character's left eye, as shown in Figure 8.50. Don't forget to link the joint to the head bone.

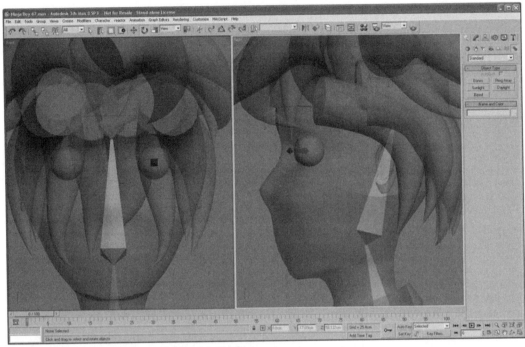

Figure 8.50 Move the eye joints to the character's left eye.

18. Clone the eye bone. You will use the first bone you created for moving the eye and the second for moving the eyelid. Rotate the joints for the eyelid to better follow the angle of the lid. The two joints should look like those in Figure 8.51.

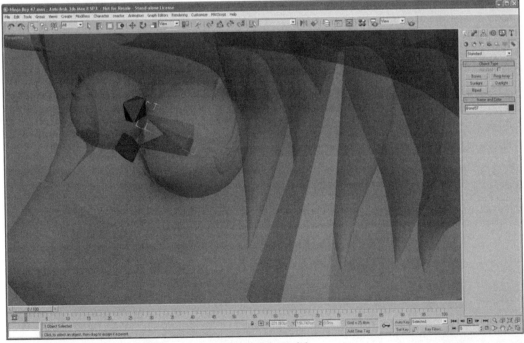

Figure 8.51 Clone the eye joints for a second set to control the eyelid.

19. Mirror the eye joints from the character's left side to his right. The bones for the skeleton should look similar to those in Figure 8.52.

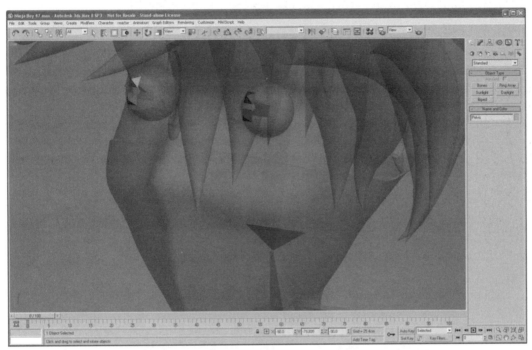

Figure 8.52 Mirror the eye joints to the character's right side.

20. You are almost done. The last and final step in creating the joints of the skeleton is to name them so they will be easier to identify during the process of attaching them to vertices in the model. The easiest way to rename the joints is to use the Schematic view. At its most basic, the Schematic view will show you a nice hierarchical view of your model. Figure 8.53 shows how I have rearranged the hierarchy and renamed the joints of my skeleton.

21. You may need to do a little refining of the bones by adding, removing, moving, or linking to get the same hierarchy as seen in Figure 8.53. Have patience, as this is a complex process and this example has many bones even for a simple model.

22. To make things a little bit simpler, delete all 15 of the ending bones that were created automatically. (The end bones are at the end of each finger, the toes, the eyes and eyelids, and the head.) You can delete them on the model itself or in the Schematic view, if you prefer.

Now you have a complete skeleton for your model. This skeleton is somewhat basic and simple. For more complex skeletons, it's just a matter of creating more joints for different parts of the body. This skeleton, however, should give you a good start in learning how the bones and skinning work in Max.

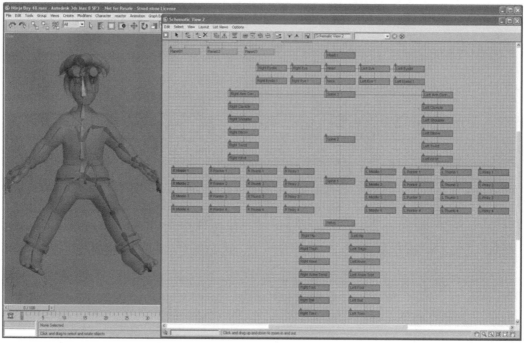

Figure 8.53 Rename the joints of the skeleton.

Applying Skin Weights

Once the skeleton is finished, you are ready to attach it to the model. That process is called *skinning*. Max has an automatic skinning process that does some of the initial work for you. Make sure the model is not frozen or set to See-Through. Select the model and apply the Skin modifier, as shown in Figure 8.54.

Now let's add the bones to the Skin modifier. Max will automatically set up some initial "envelopes," which it will use to deform the model as you move the bones. Click the Add button and highlight all the bones in the list, as shown in Figure 8.54. Then click Select.

At this point, the model has a calculated set of influences for each bone, meaning that Max has assigned each bone some vertices based on distance and nearby bones that it has influence over and can move when it moves. You will want to spend some time tweaking these default settings to get a smooth and convincing effect when you move or rotate any one bone. Let's start with the eyes.

The character's eyes will need to be bound with a different option than the other model objects. You will want to have the eyes be 100 percent influenced by the bone that controls them. Click on the Edit Envelopes button and choose the right or left eye bone. Under Select, check the Vertices and Select Element boxes. Pick a vertex on the eye of the selected bone. Bring up the Weight Tool by clicking on the Wench icon under the Weight Properties. Select the right eye (or left, if you are working on that one) and click the 1 button to assign a 100 percent effect or weight to the selected

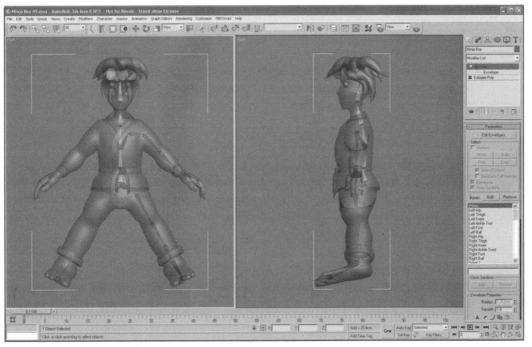

Figure 8.54 All the bones added.

vertices, as shown in Figure 8.55. Now the eye should be a solid red, indicating that it has a 100 percent effect—if you exit Edit Envelopes and move the bone, the eye should follow. Repeat on the other eye.

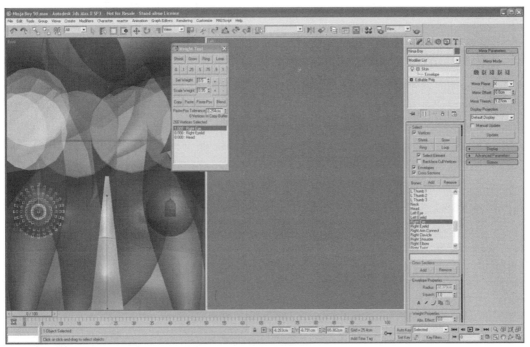

Figure 8.55 Set the eyes to 100 percent influence to the eye bone.

Although Max does a pretty good job of distributing the skin weights between the bones (*skin weighting* is the term used in Max to describe the ratio of influence that joints have on vertices in the model), it is at best a general process and does not take into account specific anatomical considerations. For example, try rotating the shoulder bone as I did in Figure 8.56. Notice how the shoulder and chest deform quite poorly. This would make for some very odd-looking animations. You'll need to adjust the skin weights to get them to behave properly during animation. Undo the rotate and select the model.

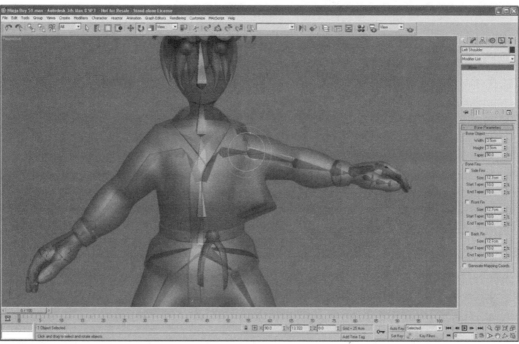

Figure 8.56 The skinning on the shoulder looks quite odd.

To fix this problem, you have to edit the envelopes. This means you will be telling individual vertices how much to be affected by each nearby bone. The basic steps you will go through to get the skin looking great are to adjust the envelopes for a better result, paint some weights where needed to fix problems, and finally, work on individual vertices to fine-tune things. This is the procedure most bones will need to follow to deform the skin correctly.

Something that you may find very helpful is to set up a small animation to test adjustments without having to leave the edit mode. Go to frame 100 and turn on the Auto Key button, move the left arm up a ways, bend the elbow, and bend the fingers in. Do the same for the left leg and foot. Turn off the Auto Key feature and move the Time slider back and forth. The left side of your character should be moving. Now when you make changes, you can see the results quickly or even in real time if you are adjusting things on a frame later in the animation.

Click on the Edit Envelopes button. This lets you work directly with the envelopes that Max has set up. You will notice several dark gray points and two spline "cages" that make up the envelope. Each of these can be moved, and as they are adjusted, the area of effect is updated. This is evident in the color gradient surrounding the selected bone. Colors go from red to blue, with red indicating that the vertices are affected 100 percent and blue indicating the vertices are barely affected. Here, the shoulder bone is selected in Edit Envelopes mode. To edit envelopes, click on one of the dark gray dots. Go ahead and try moving them and adjusting them to get a feel for how they work and affect the mesh. The dots at the end of each bone shown in Figure 8.57 allow you to move the whole envelope.

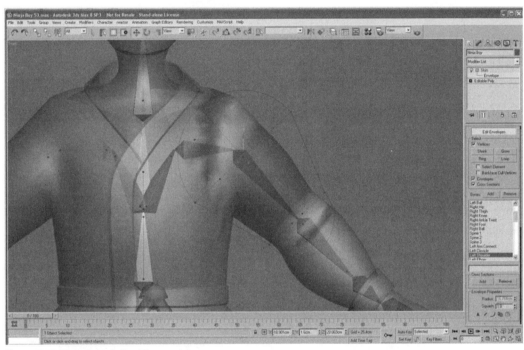

Figure 8.57 The adjusted shoulder envelope.

For the most part, you will not need to adjust the inner spline but will only need to work with the outer one.

One last note. Any one area on the mesh is usually influenced by two or more bones (for example, the armpit area is influenced by the spine, shoulder, and clavicle), so keep this in mind when adjusting envelopes and editing individual areas.

Work your way through the model and get each envelope on the left side and spine adjusted so that the character is starting to deform correctly at the joints. Only worry about whole areas and not minor creasing or folding, which will be addressed in the next step.

Max has some great tools for adjusting and tweaking skin weights. The next tool you will be using is the Paint Weights tool, found in the Command Panel under Weight Properties. This tool allows the artist to adjust the skin weighting as if using a paintbrush of sorts. Figure 8.58 shows the tool in use on the clavicle. Press Shift+Alt and hold the left mouse button to adjust the strength of the painting; press Shift+Ctrl and hold the left mouse button to adjust the size of the paintbrush.

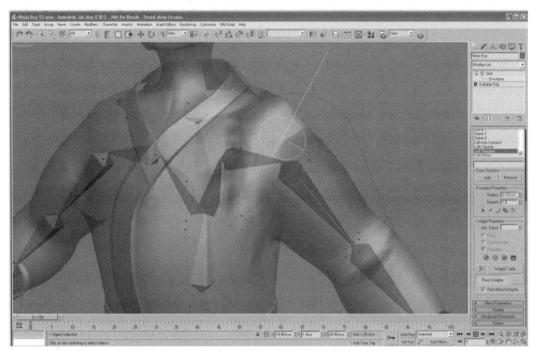

Figure 8.58 The Paint Weights tool in use on the model.

Figure 8.59 shows the shoulder of the character after the skin weighting was adjusted with the envelopes and Paint Weights tool.

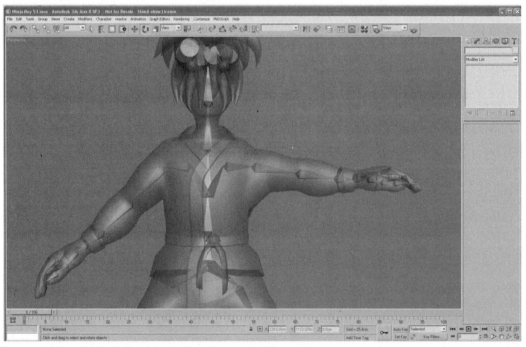

Figure 8.59 The shoulder behaves better after adjusting the skin weights.

Two more tools for editing weights are the Weight Tool and the Weight Table. These two tools allow the artist to input specific numbers for the weighting of individual vertices and even change their assignments from one bone to another. These tasks can be a bit tedious, but the tools are vital to getting everything looking and bending just right. In Figure 8.60, you are going to use the Weight Tool to adjust the skin weights of the thumb.

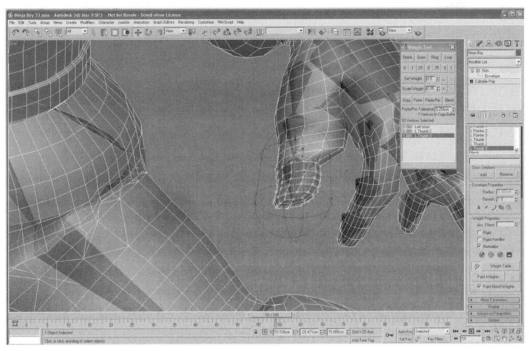

Figure 8.60 The thumb is partially weighted to the hand via the Weight Tool.

To do this, you will need to check the Vertices box under the Select section in the Command Panel. This will allow you to work with individual or groups of vertices.

Figure 8.61 shows that part of the thumb is weighted to the hand, causing an odd stretching of the thumb. Use the Weight Tool to tell the selected vertices to be affected 100 percent by the end of the thumb. This is a good way to adjust the rest of the thumb and fingers.

The Skin Weight Table will allow you even more control over individual vertices. You can change what vertices are assigned to what bone if you are having trouble doing it with the aforementioned tools. You can edit the individual cells with any number from 0 to 1—for example, 0.423. Each vertex must have a total influence of 1, so if you assign bone 1 to 0.500, then bone 2 must also be set to 0.500 so they total 1.

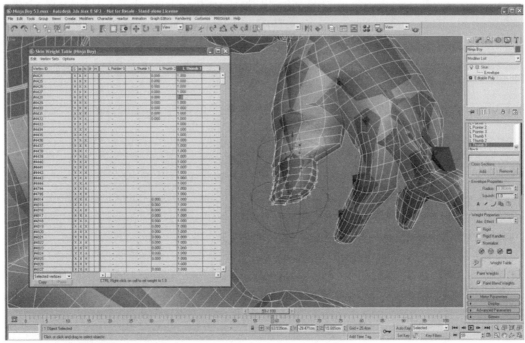

Figure 8.61 The Skin Weight Table can be used to adjust the weights as well.

There are a couple of places that need fine adjustments. One of those is the eyelid. Using the Paint Weights tool, adjust the skin weights of the eyelid to be mostly connected to the eyelid joint, but leave some influence for the eyeball so when the character moves his eyes, the eyelid will move just a little like our eyes do. Figure 8.62 shows the weighting of the eyelid.

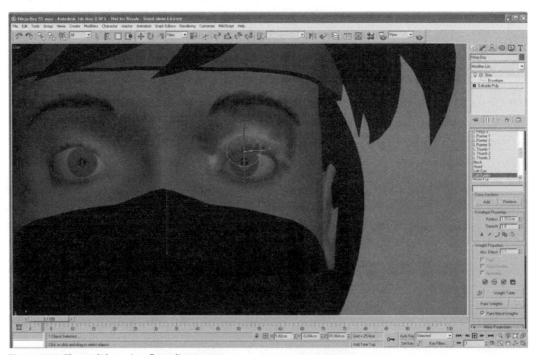

Figure 8.62 The eyelid requires fine adjustments.

Make sure when adjusting the eyelid that you take the time to check how it covers the eye when closed. You don't want the eyeball poking through the eyelid, which can often happen with eyes on 3D models.

You only really need to adjust the weighting on half of the model. You can use the Mirror Skin Weights function to duplicate the weighting on the other side as long as your model is symmetrical. Turn on Mirror mode and adjust the offset until one side is green and the other side is blue. It won't be perfect because parts of the model are not symmetrical. Once you have it about right, use the appropriate Paste button. Figure 8.63 shows the model ready to mirror. Once you are done, check your model and fix any last issues.

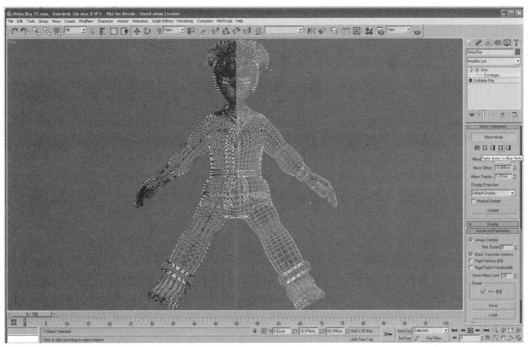

Figure 8.63 Use Mirror mode to duplicate the weights from one side to the other.

You also need to remember to adjust the weights of the extra model objects, like the belt (shown in Figure 8.64).

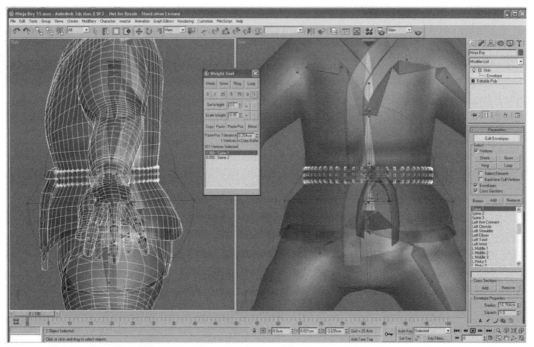

Figure 8.64 Adjust the skin weights of the belt.

Skin weighting is mostly a matter of trial and error. You will need to spend some time getting it just right. Move each joint through the full range of motion for that joint and watch how the model deforms around the joint. That is the best way to judge how the model will look when animating.

Inverse Kinematics

If you wanted to, you could use the model as it is for animating, but you might find some animations difficult to achieve when rotating each of the joints one my one. If you did animate the model as it is by just rotating joints, you would be using an animation method called forward kinematics. This method is valid, and much of the animation you do will be using that method, but Max has a system of inverse kinematics (IK) that makes animating some parts of a character much easier.

In forward kinematics, the motion is created moving down the hierarchy chain from the root. With inverse kinematics, the motion is created moving up the chain. For example, if you animated an arm using forward kinematics, you would start with the shoulder and adjust the movement down to the elbow, the wrist, and so forth. With inverse kinematics, you can move the lower chain elements and the arm would move to the location affecting the joints upstream from the kinematics handle.

Let's set up some inverse kinematics.

1. Start off by hiding the model so just the bones are visible. This will help in selecting bones and assigning IK. For arms and legs, it's best to use the HI Solver, which is found on the main menu under Animation, IK Solvers (see Figure 8.65).

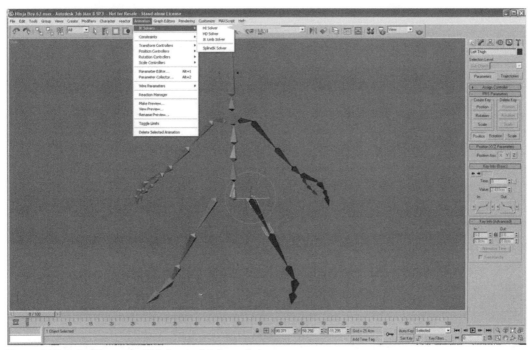

Figure 8.65 Assign the proper IK Solver to this bone chain.

2. With the thigh bone selected, choose the HI Solver and drag the line down to the ankle twist bone. This will create the IK chain needed for the leg and allow you to move the leg via the ankle. This will also create a white crosshair at the ankle, as shown in Figure 8.66. Select the white crosshair and try moving it around. This should control the leg. Undo any changes for now.

3. Now that you have the IK Solver in place, you need to set the preferred angle. Do this by moving the IK target or crosshairs up slightly and pressing the Set As Pref Angles button.

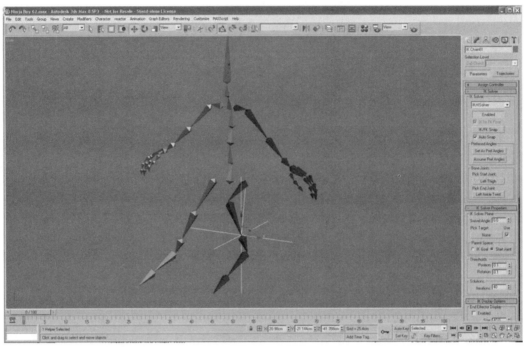

Figure 8.66 The leg with IK.

For this character, I created four IK handles, one each for the legs and the arms, as shown in Figure 8.67. The character is now ready for animation, which will be the topic of Chapter 9.

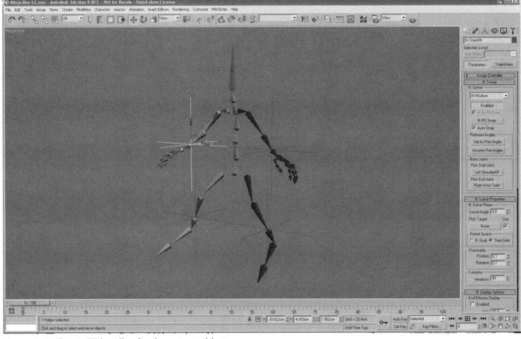

Figure 8.67 Create IK handles for the arms and legs.

Summary

In this chapter, you gave your character model color in the form of textures. You also learned how to prepare the model for animation. Topics covered were as follows:

- UV organization
- Creating UV sets
- Exporting a UV template
- Using a UV template as a guide for texture painting
- Creating a skeletal system for a model
- Skinning a model to a skeleton
- Adjusting skin weights
- Creating IK handles for animation

This chapter only touched on many of the features in Max for creating textures and rigging a model. While it is not an exhaustive rundown of all the features, it should give you enough information to get started. As with everything in Max, there are layers of functionality below layers of functionality. Do a little exploring and you will soon be comfortable with the many features of this great software program.

Chapter 9

Motion Control

While there are a few similarities, 3D animation is different in many ways from 2D animation. In 2D animation, each frame of animation is a different picture. In 3D animation, characters and objects are moved in the 3D world, and their motion is stored in a motion file that becomes part of the Maya file. Motion files can contain data on almost every attribute of a 3D model, including translation, rotation, size, color, and many others. The animation possibilities are almost endless.

With your model rigged, you are now ready to learn how to make him move. Maya has a long history as an animation tool. This is possibly one of its greatest attributes because of how easy it is to animate complex characters using Maya. In this chapter, you will be learning how to use some of Maya's powerful animation features to apply motion to your character. You will be learning about the following:

- Maya's animation controls
- Moving objects
- Path animation
- Setting up the rigging hierarchy for animation
- Creating a simple character animation

Maya's Animation Controls

Animation in Maya is controlled primarily with the use of the animation controls at the bottom of the screen. Figure 9.1 highlights these controls. The numbers correspond to the following list, which indicates what each control does.

1. **Current Frame.** This control indicates the current animation frame that is shown in the view screen.
2. **Time Line.** This control shows in a visual sequence the available frames in an animation. The Current Frame indicator slides along the Time Line.
3. **Current Frame Number.** This control enables the user to change the current frame by typing in a new number.

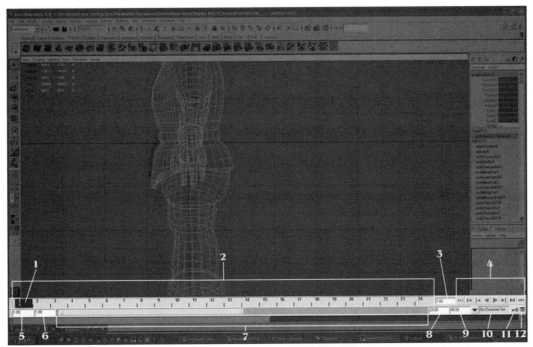

Figure 9.1 Maya's animation controls are located near the bottom of the interface.

4. **Playback Controls.** These controls, which are similar to the controls on a DVD player, are used for viewing animations or navigating through an animation.

5. **Start Time.** This control indicates the beginning frame of an animation. Note that the start time does not need to be 1; it can be any number.

6. **Playback Start Time.** This control indicates the start time of a playback sequence.

7. **Range Slider.** This control shows the playback range of an animation within the total number of frames.

8. **Playback End Time.** This control indicates the last frame of the playback range.

9. **End Time.** This control indicates the last frame of the animation.

10. **Current Character.** This control shows what the current character is.

11. **Auto Keyframe.** This control indicates whether the Automatic Keyframe feature is turned on or off.

12. **Animation Preference Button.** This button brings up a window that lets you change the frame rate, time lines, and other playback options.

Take some time to familiarize yourself with the controls.

Moving Objects

Object animation is the simplest form of 3D animation. All it requires is to set key frames in the locations that you want the object to move to. When the animation is played back, the object will travel to each location. Let's try it out with a simple ball animation.

1. In the Y axis, create a polygon sphere that has a radius of 3. Set Axis Divisions to 16 and Height Divisions to 8, as shown.

2. Next, build a single polygon for the ground that is 32 units square.

3. Move the ball up 3 units so it is setting on the ground.

4. Create a new material using the default checkerboard texture, as shown in Figure 9.2.

5. Apply the new material to the ball.

Figure 9.2 Choose Checker from the Create Render Node dialog box.

Figure 9.3 Give the ground a fractal texture.

6. Create another new material, but this time use the Fractal texture and apply it to the polygon plane, as shown in Figure 9.3.

7. Use the Polygon Planar Projection tool to scale the fractal texture, as shown in Figure 9.4.

8. Go to the Front view and move the ball up in the Y axis to 24 and over in the X axis to −20, as shown in Figure 9.5.

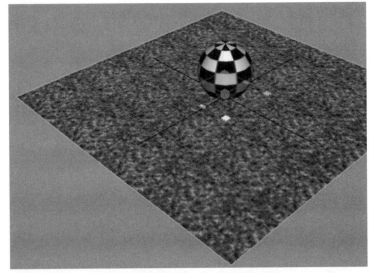

Figure 9.4 Scale down the fractal texture on the polygon plane.

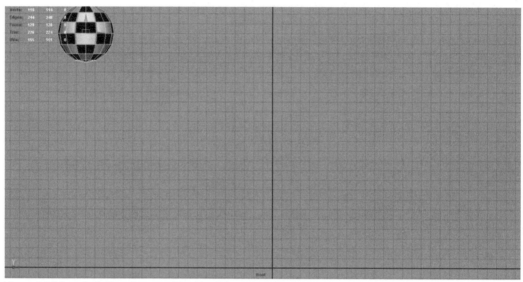

Figure 9.5 Move the ball to the upper-left side of the screen.

9. If you haven't already done so, change the main menu set to Animation.

10. There are several ways to set key frames in Maya. If you go to the Animate menu, you will notice that the first item in the menu is Set Key. You should also notice that there is a hot key associated with the function. To set a key frame, all you need to do is press the S key. Set a key frame for frame 0.

Note

Setting a key frame is kind of like taking a picture of the current scene. Maya remembers the positions of all the selected elements in the scene. Items that are not selected when setting a key frame will not have a key associated with them. You can only set keys for selected items. This will become very important later when you start working on more complex character animation.

11. Another easy way to set key frames is to use the Auto Key Frame function. You can toggle this function off and on by clicking the Auto Key Frame Toggle on the lower-right corner of the screen. When it is on, the toggle turns red. Turn it on now.

12. Move the Current Frame indicator to frame 9.

13. Move the ball to −1 in the X axis and 3 in the Y axis.

14. Move the Current Frame indicator to frame 10. Notice that there is a red marker on frame 9. These red markers indicate that there is a key frame on that frame.

15. Move the ball to 0 in the X axis and 2.5 in the Y axis. Use the Scale tool to squash the ball so it looks like it is hitting the ground, as shown in Figure 9.6. You will need to enlarge the ball a little so it looks like it is the same size or it will appear to shrink.

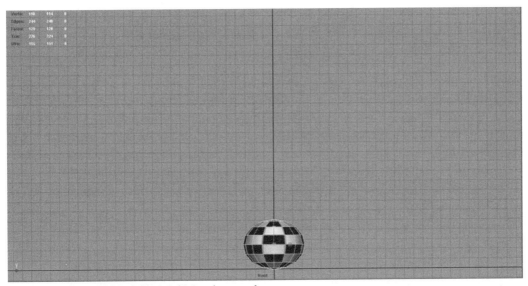

Figure 9.6 Make the ball look like it is hitting the ground.

16. Move the Current Frame indicator to frame 18.

17. Move the ball to 20 in the X axis and 20 in the Y axis.

18. Go to the Perspective view and click the Play button on the Playback controls, as shown in Figure 9.7. The ball should look like it is bouncing off the ground.

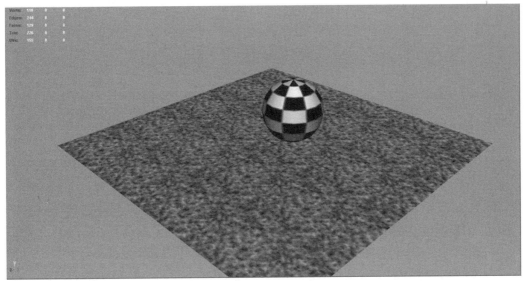

Figure 9.7 View your animation.

That wasn't too hard, was it? Now that you know how to move things around and record key frames, you can do some experimenting with a variety of shapes.

Chapter 9
Maya

Path Animation

Another way to move objects in Maya is to have them follow a path. Path animation attaches an object to a curve. Path animation is especially useful when animating objects that need to travel along a specific path—for example, a car on a road or an airplane coming in for a landing.

To show you how to set up a path animation in Maya, we will use the bouncing ball animation from the last section.

1. Create a NURBS circle with a sweep of 360 degrees and a radius of 50. This will be the path.

2. Select the polygon plane, and then with the Shift key held down, select the circle.

3. Go to Animate, Motion Paths, Attach To Motion Path to bring up the Attach to Motion Path Options box. Set the animation time (Time Range) to Time Slider. To have the plane follow the path, check Follow. Front Axis should be X and Up Axis should be Y. Attach the plane to the path, as shown in Figure 9.8.

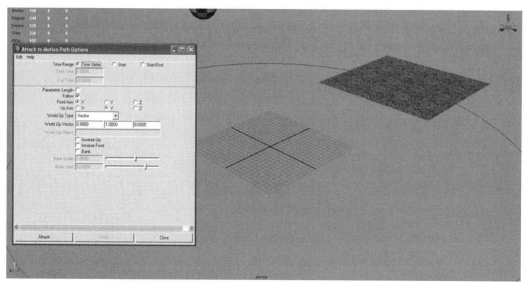

Figure 9.8 Attach the plane to the path.

4. Select the circle and move it to −50 in the Z axis, as shown in Figure 9.9.

5. Click the Play button and watch what happens. The ball should hit the ground just as the ground comes underneath it, as shown in Figure 9.10.

This example is a very simple application of the path animation in Maya. Try a few experiments with the features associated with paths until you become comfortable with them.

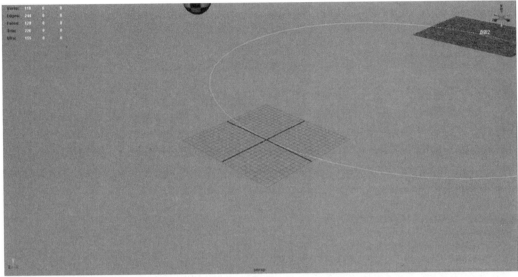

Figure 9.9 Move the circle so the plane will match up with the ball when it hits the ground.

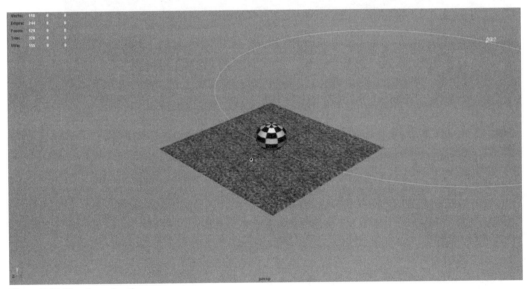

Figure 9.10 Play the animation.

Rigging Hierarchy

In Chapter 8, we covered rigging a character model with bones. In the rest of this chapter, you will be learning how to animate your character. But before we get started, you need to make one adjustment to the bone system you created in Chapter 8 to help with animating the character.

One of the basic problems for animators is keeping the character's feet on the ground during animation. The problem results from the fact that most bone systems have the pelvis as the root bone. This means that if the animator moves the pelvis up or down, the bones in the legs follow, punching them through the ground or having them hover just above the ground. A simple though not quite perfect way to help with this problem is to separate the IK handles from the rest of the bone hierarchy.

Go to Hypergraph and find the bone hierarchy. You will notice that there is a tree system for all of the joints. You will also notice that the four IK handles are off to the side of the tree structure. You want them to be part of the tree structure, just not tied to the pelvis joint. To do this, you need to create a root that is above the pelvis. Select the pelvis joint and press Ctrl+G to create a new group just above the pelvis and name it IKgroup, as shown in Figure 9.11.

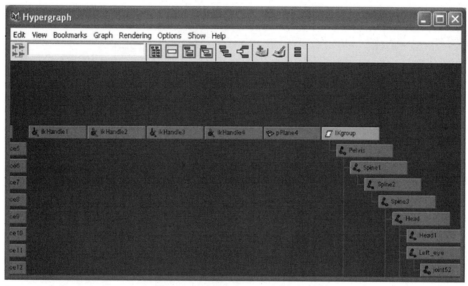

Figure 9.11 Create a new node just above the pelvis joint.

This new group is not a joint, but it is a new node that you can select and manipulate as if it were a joint. Part of the flexibility of Maya is its node-based architecture. This is just one example of using nodes to adjust things so they will work the way you want them to.

Select the four IK handles, then select the IKgroup and press the P key to make the IKgroup the parent of the IK handles. The result should look like Figure 9.12.

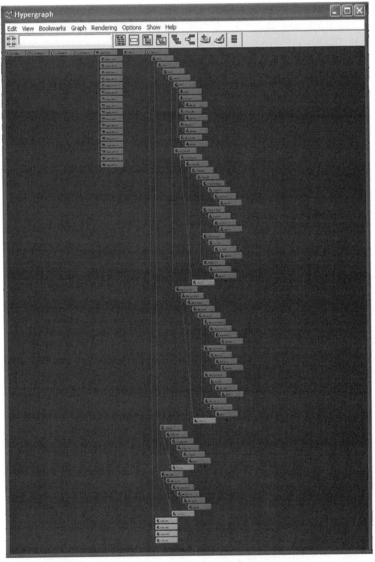

Figure 9.12 Make the IK handles the children of the IKgroup.

Now you can move the pelvis and other joints in the bone hierarchy without the IK handles moving.

Simple Character Animation

You are ready to begin animating your character. Press the Auto Key button so it is turned on. This will help you by automatically setting keys to the attributes that you animate. Maya treats every aspect of each part of a bone hierarchy as a separate element that can be keyed.

When Auto Key is on, it will set keys for any aspect of a bone that changes and ignore those that don't change. It is very important that you remember this when animating. There are times that you will want a key set even if that part of the bone didn't move. For example, if you are having a character turn his head at a particular time in your animation, you may want to have a key set for the rotation of the head just before it is time for him to turn his head. If you didn't set a key there and just used Auto Key, the head would start moving at the last set key rather than when you wanted it to turn. A good rule is to set keys for any element that you want to move at the beginning and end of each movement.

Now let's get started animating.

1. First, you need to take your character out of the spread eagle pose that you used for modeling. You can do this by clicking and dragging the IK handles closer in to the character's body, as shown in Figure 9.13. The IK handles are easy to find. They have three lines radiating out from them at right angles. All you need to do is click on one of these lines to select the IK handle.

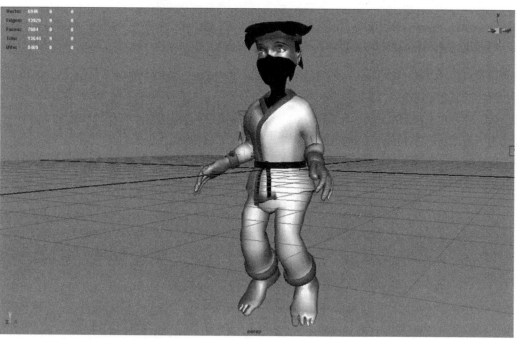

Figure 9.13 Move the arms and legs in.

2. Now pull the IK handles for the arms and legs down a little to have the character look like he is standing in a relaxed position, as shown in Figure 9.14.

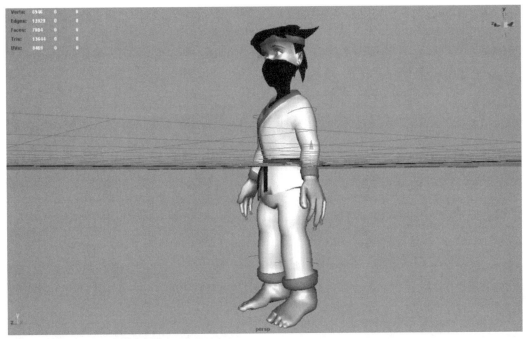

Figure 9.14 Move the character to a standing position.

3. The hands will most likely look as if the character is holding them out. Press the 4 key to go to Wireframe mode so you can see the joints. Select the wrist joint and use the Rotate tool to rotate the hand in, as shown in Figure 9.15.

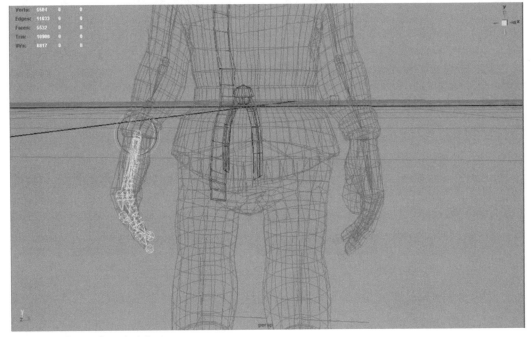

Figure 9.15 Rotate the wrist joint in.

4. Now that you have your character in a standing position, you need to establish a floor for him to stand on. Create a polygon plane that has a width and height of 8.

5. Move the floor plane down near the bottom of the character's feet, as shown in Figure 9.16.

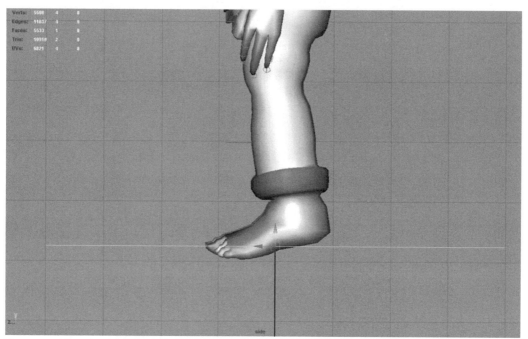

Figure 9.16 Move the plane down to the character's feet.

6. Apply a texture to the floor. You can use any texture that you like. I applied a tatami mat texture, as shown in Figure 9.17.

7. From the Side view, rotate the ankle joints of the feet up so they are not poking through the floor (see Figure 9.18).

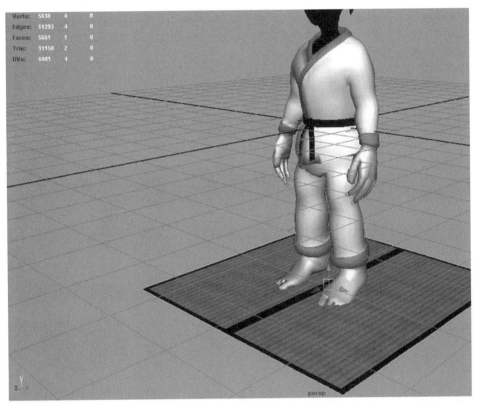

Figure 9.17 Apply a texture to the floor.

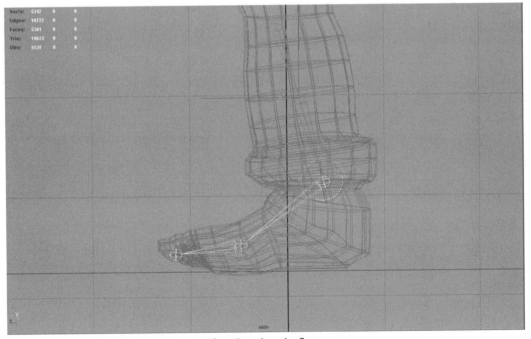

Figure 9.18 Rotate the ankle joint to have the feet planted on the floor.

8. Now go to the Front view and rotate the ankles so the feet are flat to the ground, as shown in Figure 9.19.

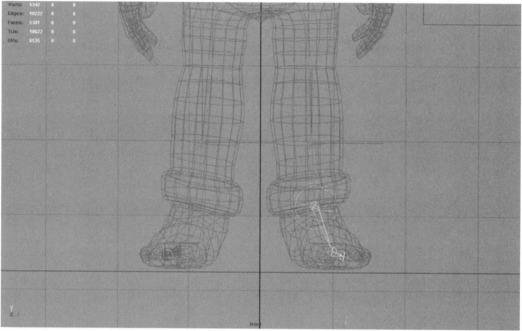

Figure 9.19 Rotate the ankles from the front.

9. You will probably need to move the floor up or down to match the feet, as shown in Figure 9.20.

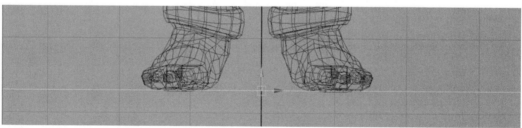

Figure 9.20 Fine-tune the floor so it matches the feet.

10. The character should now look similar to that shown in Figure 9.21. Make any adjustments necessary to make your character look like he is in a relaxed standing position.

Figure 9.21 Put the character into a relaxed standing pose.

11. If it is not already there, move the Current Frame indicator to frame 0 and change the animation range and animation length to 24 and 48, respectively.

12. In the Quick Select Layout area, click on the layout that has three windows, including Hypergraph and the Graph Editor. Make sure that the Hypergraph window is not minimized at the bottom of the work area (if it is minimized, it will not come up as it should in the layout).

13. In Hypergraph, select all of the nodes in the bone tree.

14. By selecting all of the nodes in the bone tree, you can set a key for all of the joints at once. Set the key. This will be the beginning frame of a bow animation.

15. Move the Current Frame indicator to frame 8 for the next key frame.

16. From the Side view, rotate the pelvis joint to cause the character to lean forward, as if he is bowing.

17. Continue up the spine to the neck, rotating the joints for the bow, as shown in Figure 9.22.

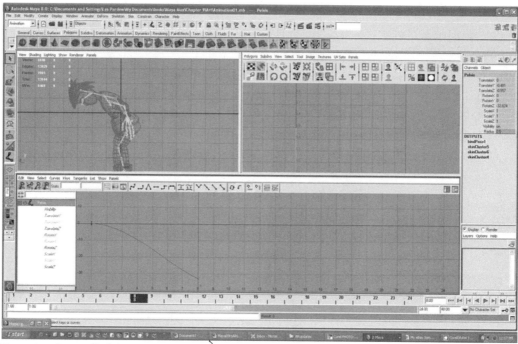

Figure 9.22 Rotate all of the joints along the spine.

18. Move the IK handles for the legs forward to bring the feet back up through the floor, as shown in Figure 9.23.

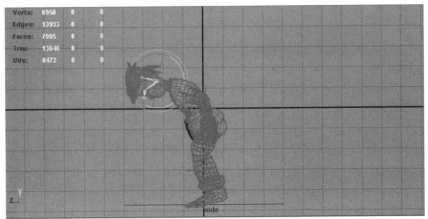

Figure 9.23 Move the feet of the character toward his front.

19. Select all of the nodes in the bone tree and set a key at frame 8. Although Auto Key has already set keys for the joints that have moved, by setting a key here, I ensure that the character will be in this exact position on this frame.

20. With all of the nodes still selected, move the Current Frame indicator back to frame 1 and right-click on it to bring up the Animation menu. Select Copy from the menu to copy the keys set in frame 1.

21. Move the Current Frame indicator to frame 16 and, using the Animation menu again, paste the keys into frame 16.

22. If you look at the Graph Editor, you will notice a network of lines appearing as you set key frames. These lines represent the motion paths of the character and can be adjusted to fine-tune animation. You can use many of the same commands for moving about a screen in the Graph Editor that you use for other editors in Maya. Zoom in to frame 16.

23. You will notice that many of the motion paths have a bump to them just before they approach frame 16. These bumps cause the character to move just beyond the key frame and back again, which isn't bad if that is how you want him to animate. However, to show you how to adjust the animation, we will change the motion curves so they go just to the key position and no farther. With the Move tool selected from the Toolbox, click one of the motion paths. A manipulator will appear at the key frame. Click on one of the arms of the manipulator to select it. Now use the center mouse button to rotate the line, as shown in Figure 9.24.

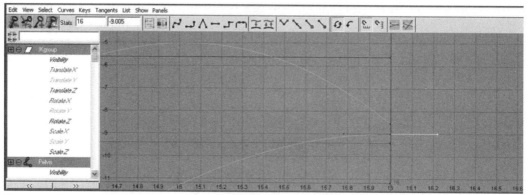

Figure 9.24 Rotate the motion path to remove the extra jog in it.

24. Now go along frame 16 and flatten all of the jogs in the motion paths.

25. You will notice that the motion paths that start at frame 1 are straight. Movement either up or down represents motion in the Graph Editor, while time is represented by movement from left to right. By rotating the keys to start flat (similar to how you changed them at frame 16), you can cause your animation to start slower and pick up speed as it goes. Called *easing in*, this will make your animation look more natural. Rotate the motion paths at frame 1 so they are more horizontal at the start, as shown in Figure 9.25.

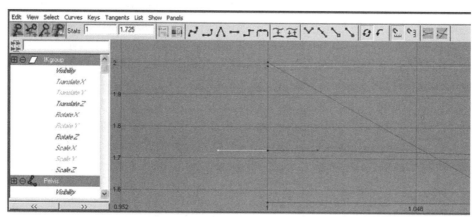

Figure 9.25 Flatten the motion paths at frame 1.

26. Slide the Current Frame indicator along the Time Line to see how your bow animation looks.

You now have an animation for your character. Although it is only a simple bow, I hope that you can see how you can create other animations in Maya by using the tools described.

As you can see, animating in Maya is a simple process once you understand how the tools work. Of course, there is a lot more to animating than we covered here, but this should get you started. Work on a few other animations and be creative. If you want to learn more about animating characters Maya, you can try my other book, *Game Character Animation All in One* (Thomson Course Technology PTR, 2006).

Summary

In this chapter, you worked on learning how to animate objects and characters in Maya. Topics covered were as follows:

- Maya's animation controls
- Moving objects
- Path animation
- Setting up the rigging hierarchy for animation
- Creating a simple character animation
- Using the Graph Editor to adjust the animation

This chapter only touched on some of Maya's animation features. A lot of aspects of animating in Maya were not included, and other features can be found in Trax Editor, which we did not cover. This book is just not long enough to deal with all of the many aspects of Maya. If you want to learn more about animation in Maya, refer to the Maya user manuals for further information.

We are limited in how much we can put into this book, so we can't cover every aspect of both of these great programs. Hopefully, we have given you enough of a foundation that you can now pick up the rest by experimenting and using the online help features. Good luck in your work.

Chapter 9

Motion Control

While there are a few similarities, 3D animation is different in many ways from 2D animation. In 2D animation, each frame of animation is a different picture. In 3D animation, characters and objects are moved in the 3D world, and their motion is stored as part of the Max file. Max files can contain data on almost every attribute of a 3D model, including translation, rotation, size, color, and many others. The animation possibilities are almost endless.

With your model rigged, you are now ready to learn how to make him move. Max has a long history as an animation tool. This is possibly one of its greatest attributes because of how easy it is to animate complex characters using Max. In this chapter, you will be learning how to use some of Max's animation features to apply motion to your character. You will be learning about the following:

- Max's animation controls
- Moving objects
- Path animation
- Setting up the rigging hierarchy for animation
- Creating a simple character animation

Max's Animation Controls

Animation in Max is controlled primarily with the use of the animation controls at the bottom of the screen. Figure 9.1 highlights these controls. The numbers correspond to the following list, which indicates what each control does.

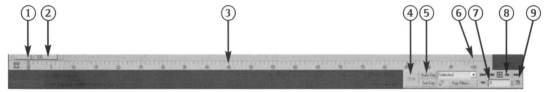

Figure 9.1 Max's animation controls are located near the bottom of the interface.

1. **Current Frame.** This marker indicates the current animation frame that is shown in the view screen.
2. **Time Slider.** Use this slider to move or scrub through the animation.
3. **Track Bar.** This control shows in a visual sequence the available frames in an animation. The Current Frame indicator is a light-blue marker that slides along the bar. Red markers indicate set key frames on the selected item.
4. **Set Key Button.** Click this control to set a key when the Set Key button (to the right; see #5) is active.
5. **Auto Key & Set Key.** Indicates whether the Automatic Keyframe feature is turned on or off.
6. **Last Frame Indicator.** This control points to the end frame of the animation.
7. **Current Frame Number.** Typing a new number in this box can change the current frame.
8. **Playback Controls.** These controls, which are similar to the controls on a DVD player, are used for viewing animations or navigating through an animation.
9. **Animation Preference Button.** This button brings up a window that lets you change the frame rate, time lines, and other playback options.

Take some time to familiarize yourself with the controls.

Moving Objects

Object animation is the simplest form of 3D animation. All it requires is to set key frames in the locations that you want the object to move to. When the animation is played back, the object will travel to each location. Let's try it out with a simple ball animation.

1. Create a sphere in the Perspective viewport, as shown in Figure 9.2.
2. Next, create a plane for the ground that is about the size of the grid, as shown in Figure 9.3.
3. Move the ball up so that it is sitting on the ground.
4. Create a new material using the default checkerboard texture, as shown in Figure 9.4.

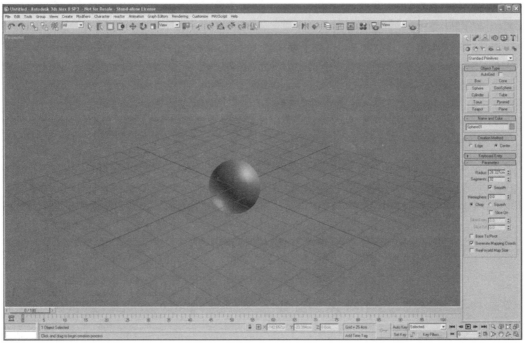

Figure 9.2 Create a sphere.

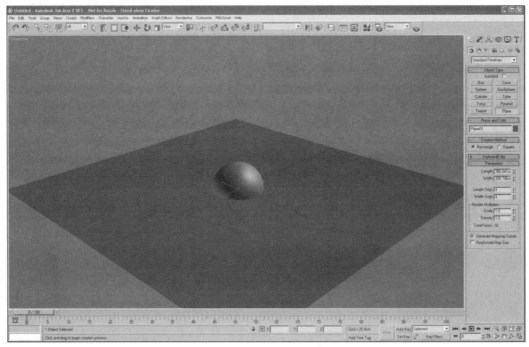

Figure 9.3 Create a plane for the ground.

5. Apply the new material to the ball.

6. Create another new material, but this time use the Swirl texture and apply it to the polygon plane, as shown in Figure 9.5.

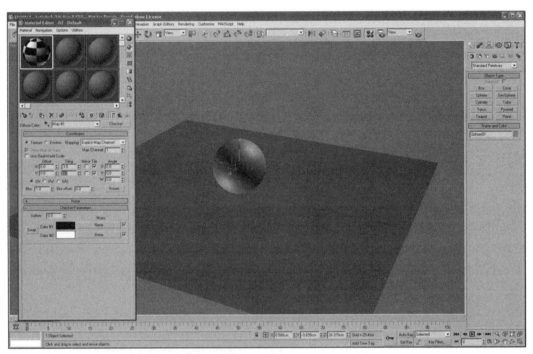

Figure 9.4 The checkered material assigned to the material ball.

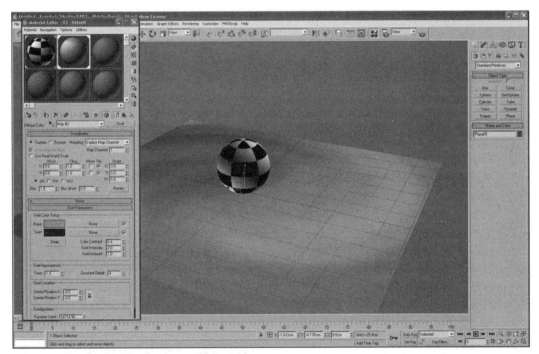

Figure 9.5 Give the ground a fun texture, like a swirl.

7. Adjust some of the settings for the texture to get a look you like (see Figure 9.6).

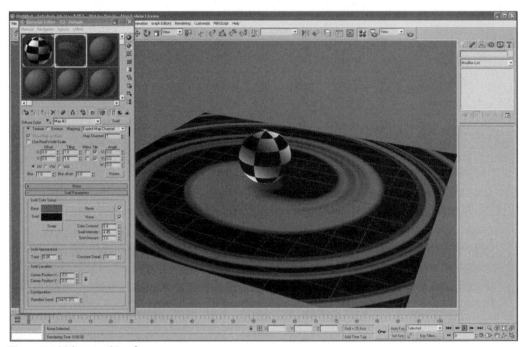

Figure 9.6 Make something fun.

8. Go to the Left viewport and move the ball up and to the left, as shown in Figure 9.7.

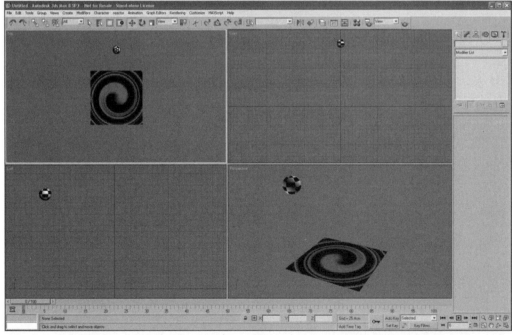

Figure 9.7 Move the ball to the upper-left side of the screen.

9. If you haven't already done so, toggle Set Key on the bottom of the screen, as shown in Figure 9.8. Notice that the slider bar and active viewport outline have changed to red. This indicates that you are in Animation mode.

10. Set the first key frame for the sphere. Make sure the sphere is selected and press the K key or click the interface button with the key symbol on it to set a key frame. Notice the dark blue key that has appeared on the current frame in the time line.

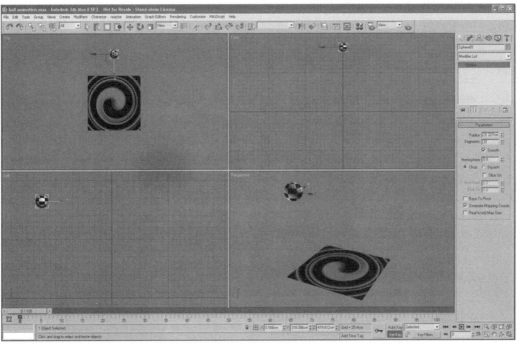

Figure 9.8 Set a key frame.

Note

Setting a key frame is kind of like taking a picture of the current scene. Max records the positions, rotations, scales, and other changed information of the selected elements in the scene when you set a key. Items that are not selected when setting a key frame will not have any key frame data associated with them. You can only set keys for selected items. This will become very important later when you start working on more complex animation.

11. Another easy way to set key frames is to use the Auto Key function. You can toggle this function off and on by clicking the Auto Key button on the lower-right area of the screen. When it is on, the toggle turns red. Turn it on now.

12. Move the Current Frame indicator to frame 20. Notice that no key frame was set even though you are in Auto Key mode.

13. In the Left viewport, move the ball back to the plane where the bottom of the ball is just sitting on the plane. You also need to set a scale key so the ball will stay scaled to 100 percent until it hits the plane. Go to the Motion tab on the Command Panel and click the Scale button under Create Key.

14. Move the Current Frame indicator to frame 22. Notice that there is a key frame marker on frame 20 now that we have made a change.

15. Nonuniformly scale the ball in the Y axis slightly and move it down in the Y axis (so it's touching the ground) so it looks like the ball is compressing as it hits the ground, as shown in Figure 9.9. For a better idea and to better see what's happening, you may want to toggle the trajectory for the ball. Under the Motion tab on the Command Panel, click the Trajectories button. Now it's easy to see exactly what the ball will do at any frame. Small ticks on the line are frames and large ticks are set key frames, as shown in Figure 9.9.

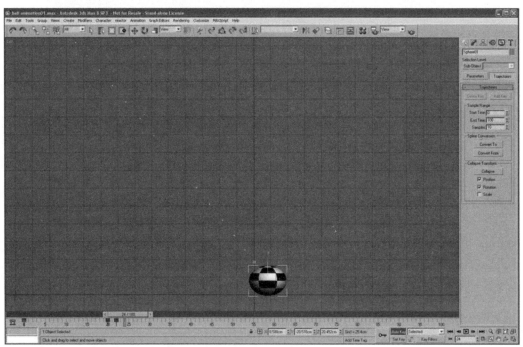

Figure 9.9 Make the ball look like it is hitting the ground.

16. Move the Current Frame indicator to frame 30.

17. In the Left viewport, move the ball up and to the right a bit and set a scale key frame so the ball is back to 100 in the Y axis.

18. Go to the Perspective view and click the Play button on the Playback controls, as shown in Figure 9.10. The ball should look like it is bouncing off the ground.

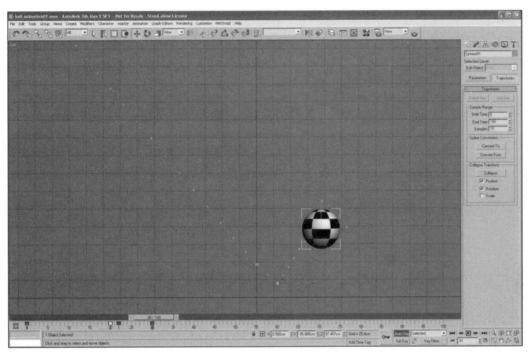

Figure 9.10 View your animation.

That wasn't too hard, was it? Now that you know how to move things around and record key frames, you can do some experimenting with a variety of shapes.

Path Animation

Another way to move objects in Max is to have them follow a path. Path animation attaches an object to a curve. Path animation is especially useful when animating objects that need to travel along a specific path—for example, a car on a road or an airplane coming in for a landing.

To show you how to set up a path animation in Max, we will use the bouncing ball animation from the last section.

1. Make sure you turn off the Auto Key feature and create a circle shape, as shown in Figure 9.11. This will be the path.
2. To assign a path constraint, select the plane and choose Path Constraint under Animation, Position Controller, Path Constraint on the main menu.
3. Select the circle shape that you just created and the plane will jump to the start of the path or spline, as shown in Figure 9.12.

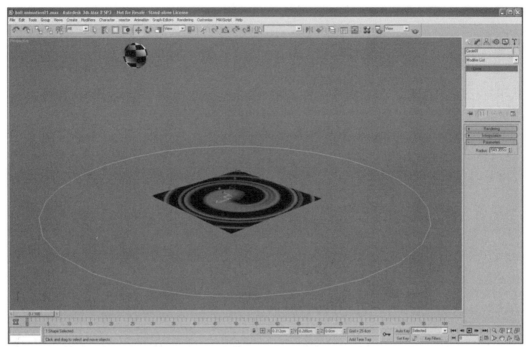

Figure 9.11 Create a spline (circle shape) for the path.

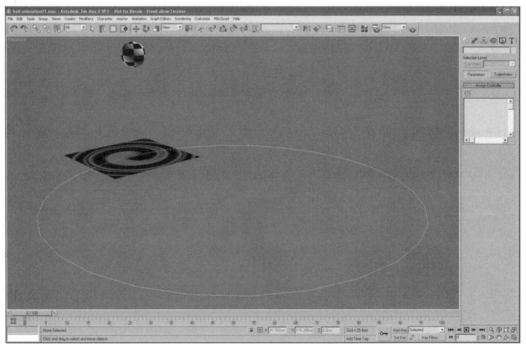

Figure 9.12 Attach the plane to the path.

4. Go to frame 22 in your animation and move the circle shape so the sphere lines up with the center of the plane, as shown in Figure 9.13.

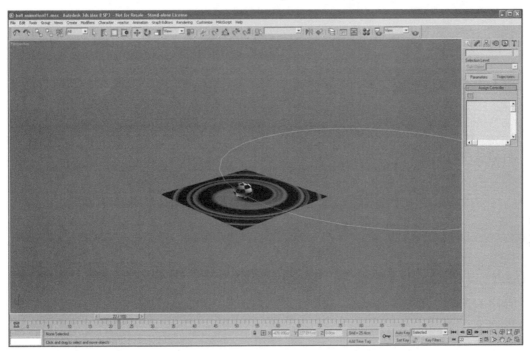

Figure 9.13 Move the circle so the plane will match up with the ball when it hits the ground.

5. Click the Play button and watch what happens. The ball should hit the ground just as the ground comes underneath it.

6. Open the Time Configuration dialog box and set the end frame to 30, as shown in Figure 9.14.

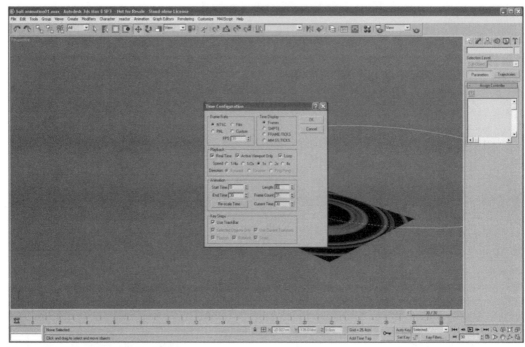

Figure 9.14 Adjust the animation length.

7. Play the animation.

This example is a very simple application of the path animation in Max. Try a few experiments with the features associated with paths until you become comfortable with them.

Rigging Hierarchy

In Chapter 8, we covered rigging a character model with bones. In the rest of this chapter, you will be learning how to animate your character. But before we get started, you need to make one adjustment to the bone system you created in Chapter 8 to help with animating the character.

One of the basic problems for animators is keeping the character's feet on the ground during animation. The problem results from the fact that most bone systems have the pelvis as the root bone. This means that if the animator moves the pelvis up or down, the bones in the legs follow, punching them through the ground or having them hover just above the ground. A simple though not quite perfect way to help with this problem is to add the IK handles to the bone hierarchy in the right spot.

Add a Dummy object to the scene near the pelvis, as shown in Figure 9.15.

This new object is not a joint, but it is a helper node that you can select and manipulate as if it were a joint.

Using the Select and Link tool, link the pelvis and IK handles to the Dummy object. The result should look like Figure 9.15.

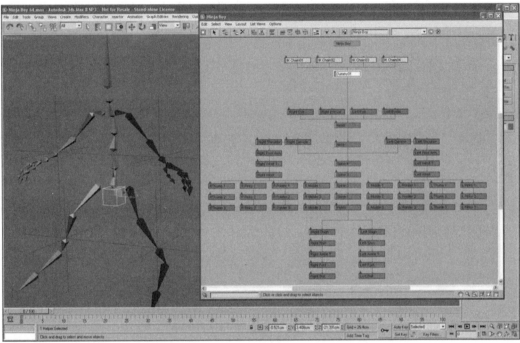

Figure 9.15 Make the IK handles the children of the Dummy object.

Now you can move the pelvis and other joints in the bone hierarchy without the IK handles moving.

Simple Character Animation

You are ready to begin animating your character. Press the Auto Key button so it is turned on. This will help you by automatically setting keys to the attributes that you animate. Max treats every aspect of each part of a bone hierarchy as a separate element that can be keyed.

When Auto Key is on, it will set keys for any aspect of a bone that changes and ignore those that don't change. It is very important that you remember this when animating. There are times that you will want a key set even if that part of the bone didn't move. For example, if you are having a character turn his head at a particular time in your animation, you may want to have a key set for the rotation of the head just before it is time for him to turn his head. If you didn't set a key there and just used Auto Key, the head would start moving at the last set key rather than when you wanted it to turn. A good rule is to set keys for any element that you want to move at the beginning and end of each movement.

Now let's get started animating.

1. First, you need to take your character out of the spread eagle pose that you used for modeling. You can do this by clicking and dragging the IK handles closer in to the character's body, as shown in Figure 9.16. The IK handles are easy to find. They have lines radiating out from them at right angles. All you need to do is click on one of these lines to select the IK handle.

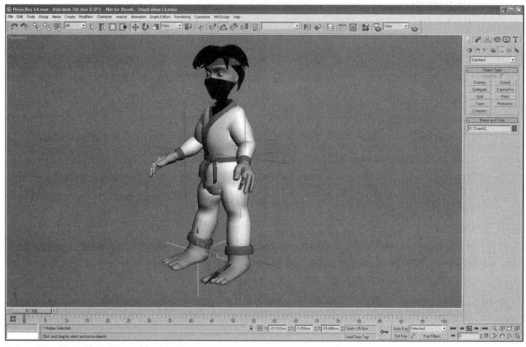

Figure 9.16 Move the arms and legs in.

2. Now pull the IK handles for the arms and legs down a little to have the character look like he is standing in a relaxed position, as shown in Figure 9.17. To make things easier for selecting bones and handles, you may want to freeze and set your character model to See-Through. This way it's impossible to select the mesh and not a bone. Both options are found by selecting the mesh and right-clicking.

3. The hands will most likely look as if the character is holding them out. Press the 4 key to go to Wireframe mode so you can see the joints. Select the wrist joint and use the Rotate tool to rotate the hand in, as shown in Figure 9.18.

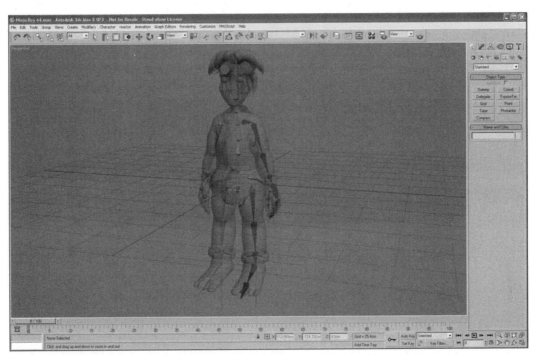

Figure 9.17 Move the character to a standing position.

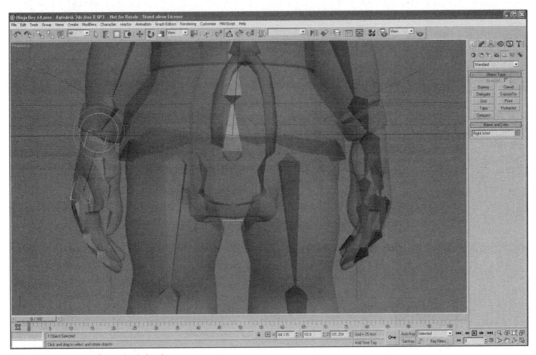

Figure 9.18 Rotate the wrist joint in.

4. Now that you have your character in a standing position, you need to establish a floor for him to stand on. Create a polygon plane that has a width and length similar to the one shown in Figure 9.19.

Figure 9.19 Create a polygon plane for a floor.

5. Select the Dummy object and move the character up so his toes and feet are resting on the plane, as shown in Figure 9.20.

6. Apply a texture to the floor (see Figure 9.21). You can use any texture that you like. I applied a wood floor texture from the Max maps directory. I also gave the plane some depth and applied a slight reflection.

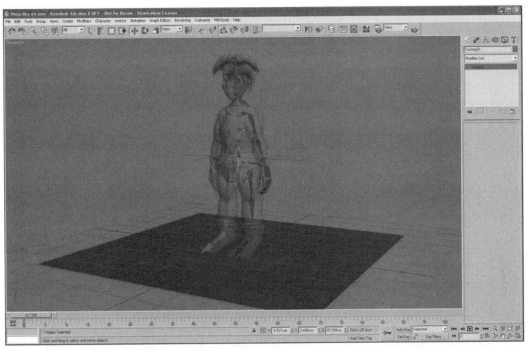

Figure 9.20 Move the character up.

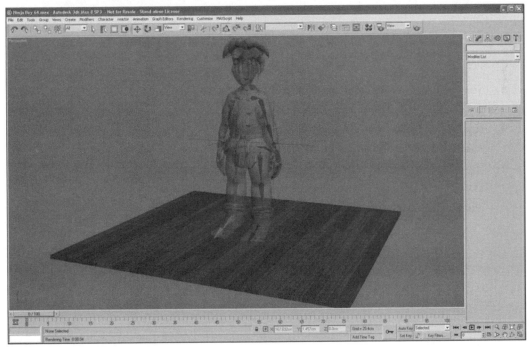

Figure 9.21 Apply a texture to the floor.

7. From the Side view, rotate the ankle joints of the feet up so they are not poking through the floor (see Figure 9.22). Don't worry about getting the feet to touch the ground; we will take care of that in a few steps.

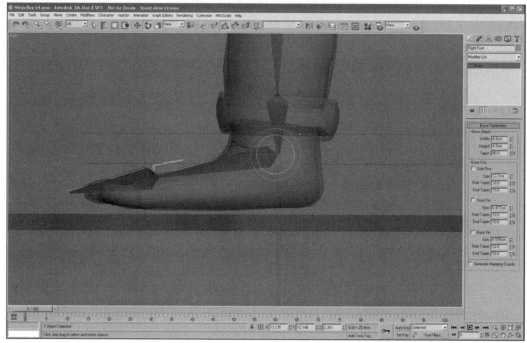

Figure 9.22 Rotate the feet up to match the floor.

8. Now go to the Front view and rotate the ankles so the feet are flat to the ground, as shown in Figure 9.23.
9. You will probably need to move the character (via the Dummy) up or down to match the floor, as shown in Figure 9.24.
10. The character should now look similar to that shown in Figure 9.25. Make any adjustments necessary to make your character look like he is in a relaxed standing position.

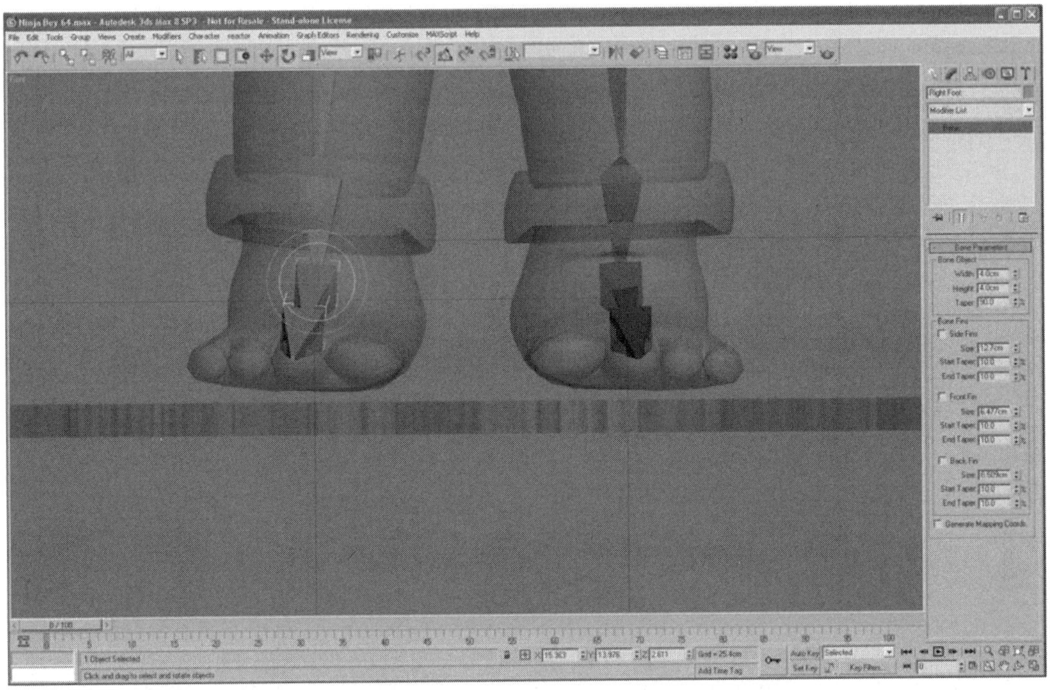

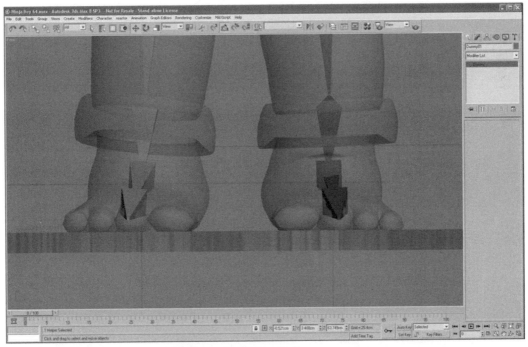

Figure 9.23 Rotate the ankles from the front.

Figure 9.24 Fine-tune the character's position so he matches the floor.

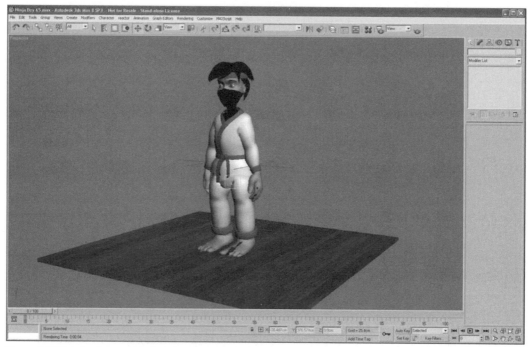

Figure 9.25 Put the character into a relaxed standing pose.

11. Remember the animation controls from the beginning of the chapter? They are highlighted in Figure 9.26. Set your animation length to 24 using the Time Configuration dialog box. Make sure your Current Frame indicator is set to 0.

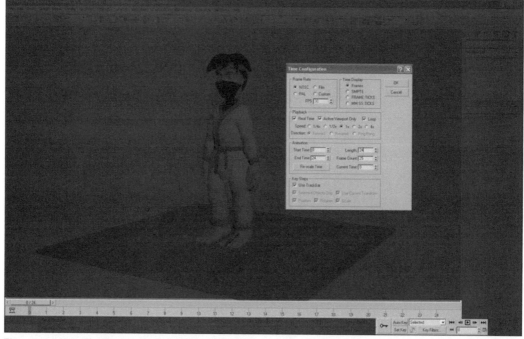

Figure 9.26 Move the Current Frame indicator to frame 0.

12. Using the Set Key and Key icon, set a key for all the bones in the default standing pose. Select the model and the floor, and using the freeze selection, freeze the models so they cannot be selected.

13. Select all the bones by drawing a marquee around them.

14. Toggle the Set Key button and click on the large Key button, as shown in Figure 9.27. This will set a key frame for all the selected bones and be the beginning frame of a bow animation.

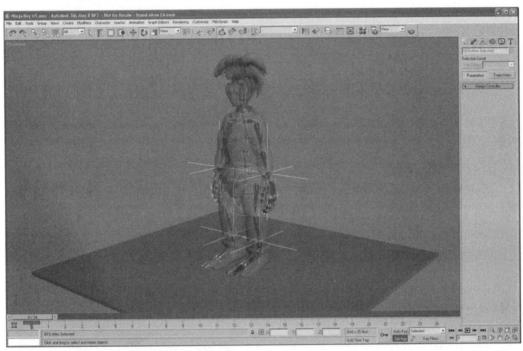

Figure 9.27 Set a key at frame 1 for all of the joints.

15. Move the Current Frame indicator to frame 8 for the next key frame and toggle the Auto Key on.

16. From the Side view, rotate the pelvis joint to cause the character to lean forward as if he is bowing (see Figure 9.28).

17. Continue up the spine to the neck, rotating the joints for the bow, as shown in Figure 9.29.

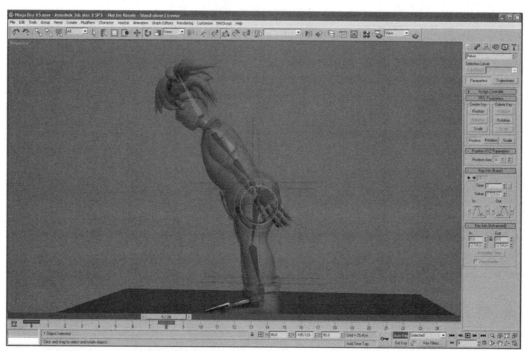

Figure 9.28 Rotate the pelvis to begin the character's bow.

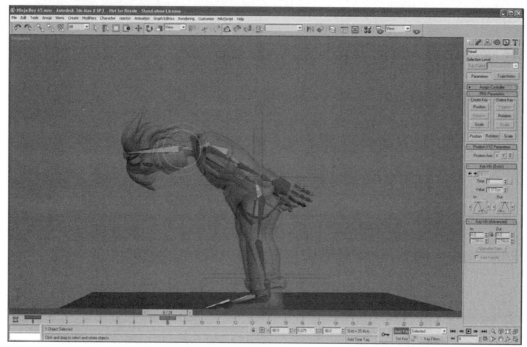

Figure 9.29 Rotate all of the joints along the spine.

18. Move the IK handles for the legs and arms forward to bring the feet back up through the floor, as shown in Figure 9.30. Rotate the hands and fingers so the character looks natural.

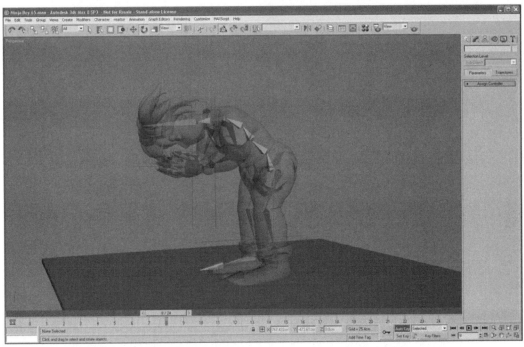

Figure 9.30 Adjust the feet and hands of the character.

19. Select all of the nodes in the bone tree and set a key, as shown in Figure 9.31. Although Auto Key has already set keys for the joints that have moved, by setting a key here at frame 8, I ensure that the character will be in this exact position on this frame.

20. With all of the nodes still selected, move the Current Frame indicator back to frame 1 and click on the key to select it, as shown in Figure 9.32. Hold the Shift key and drag a clone of those keys to frame 16.

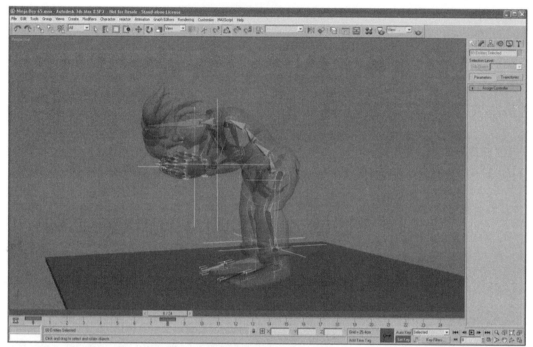

Figure 9.31 Set a key at frame 8 for all of the nodes in the bone tree.

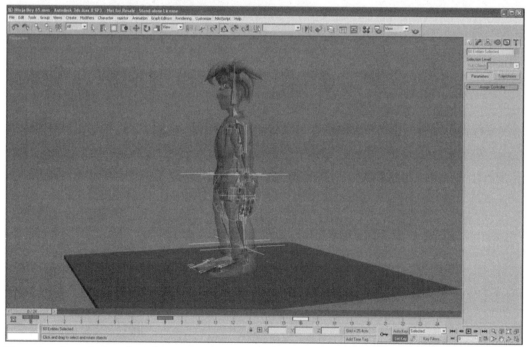

Figure 9.32 Paste the keys from frame 1 to frame 16.

21. Move the slider back and forth. You should see the ninja boy bow and return to the standing position.

22. You can fix any rotation of the feet due to the movement in the pelvis by rotating the ankle twist bone in frame 8. Take note of the foot rotation in frame 0, and with the Auto Key on, move to frame 8 and rotate the ankle twist bone, as shown in Figure 9.33.

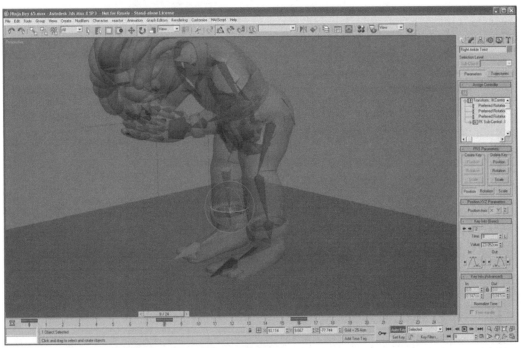

Figure 9.33 Adjust any odd rotations on the feet.

23. You can also use the Track View Editor to adjust any key frames on a more detailed and finer level.

24. Adjust any keys or motion that is not as expected or add some motion by adjusting keys or curves in the Track View Editor, as shown in Figure 9.34.

25. Slide the Current Frame indicator along the Time Line to see how your bow animation looks (see Figure 9.35).

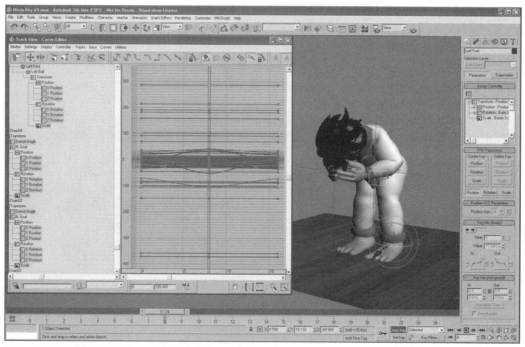

Figure 9.34 Flatten the motion paths at frame 1.

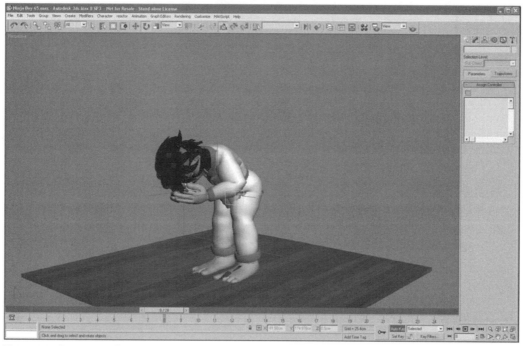

Figure 9.35 Inspect your bow animation.

You now have an animation for your character. Although it is only a simple bow, I hope that you can see how you can create other animations in Max by using the tools described.

Summary

In this chapter, you worked on learning how to animate objects and characters in Max. Topics covered were as follows:

- Max's animation controls
- Moving objects
- Path animation
- Creating a simple character animation

This chapter only touched on some of Max's animation features. There are many other features that we have not covered, and a lot of other aspects of animating in Max that were not included. This book is just not long enough to deal with all of the many aspects of Max. If you want to learn more about animation in Max, refer to the online Max user manuals for further information.

Index

Numerics

A

License Agreement/Notice of Limited Warranty

By opening the sealed disc container in this book, you agree to the following terms and conditions. If, upon reading the following license agreement and notice of limited warranty, you cannot agree to the terms and conditions set forth, return the unused book with unopened disc to the place where you purchased it for a refund.

License:
The enclosed software is copyrighted by the copyright holder(s) indicated on the software disc. You are licensed to copy the software onto a single computer for use by a single user and to a backup disc. You may not reproduce, make copies, or distribute copies or rent or lease the software in whole or in part, except with written permission of the copyright holder(s). You may transfer the enclosed disc only together with this license, and only if you destroy all other copies of the software and the transferee agrees to the terms of the license. You may not decompile, reverse assemble, or reverse engineer the software.

Notice of Limited Warranty:
The enclosed disc is warranted by Thomson Course Technology PTR to be free of physical defects in materials and workmanship for a period of sixty (60) days from end user's purchase of the book/disc combination. During the sixty-day term of the limited warranty, Thomson Course Technology PTR will provide a replacement disc upon the return of a defective disc.

Limited Liability:
THE SOLE REMEDY FOR BREACH OF THIS LIMITED WARRANTY SHALL CONSIST ENTIRELY OF REPLACEMENT OF THE DEFECTIVE DISC. IN NO EVENT SHALL THOMSON COURSE TECHNOLOGY PTR OR THE AUTHOR BE LIABLE FOR ANY OTHER DAMAGES, INCLUDING LOSS OR CORRUPTION OF DATA, CHANGES IN THE FUNCTIONAL CHARACTERISTICS OF THE HARDWARE OR OPERATING SYSTEM, DELETERIOUS INTERACTION WITH OTHER SOFTWARE, OR ANY OTHER SPECIAL, INCIDENTAL, OR CONSEQUENTIAL DAMAGES THAT MAY ARISE, EVEN IF THOMSON COURSE TECHNOLOGY PTR AND/OR THE AUTHOR HAS PREVIOUSLY BEEN NOTIFIED THAT THE POSSIBILITY OF SUCH DAMAGES EXISTS.

Disclaimer of Warranties:
THOMSON COURSE TECHNOLOGY PTR AND THE AUTHOR SPECIFICALLY DISCLAIM ANY AND ALL OTHER WARRANTIES, EITHER EXPRESS OR IMPLIED, INCLUDING WARRANTIES OF MERCHANTABILITY, SUITABILITY TO A PARTICULAR TASK OR PURPOSE, OR FREEDOM FROM ERRORS. SOME STATES DO NOT ALLOW FOR EXCLUSION OF IMPLIED WARRANTIES OR LIMITATION OF INCIDENTAL OR CONSEQUENTIAL DAMAGES, SO THESE LIMITATIONS MIGHT NOT APPLY TO YOU.

Other:
This Agreement is governed by the laws of the State of Massachusetts without regard to choice of law principles. The United Convention of Contracts for the International Sale of Goods is specifically disclaimed. This Agreement constitutes the entire agreement between you and Thomson Course Technology PTR regarding use of the software.